The Database Book

MARY E. S. LOOMIS

THE DATABASE BOOK

Macmillan Publishing Company

New York

Collier Macmillan Publishers

London

Macmillan Publishing Company
866 Third Avenue, New York, New York 10022

Collier Macmillan Canada, Inc.

Library of Congress Cataloging in Publication Data.

Loomis, Mary E. S.
  The database book.

  Includes bibliographies and index.
  1. Data base management.   2. System design.   I. Title.
II. Title: Data base book.
QA76.9.D3L68 1987   005.7   86-19256
ISBN 0-02-371760-2

 2 3 4 5 6 7 8   Year: 7 8 9 0 1 2 3 4 5

ISBN 0-02-371760-2

To Tim, Allison, and Ellie

PREFACE

This book is a practical text about database design and data management. The emphasis is on design and the focus is on techniques for developing data resources. The book is not mathematical or theoretical, but is rigorous and concise. It conveys the database principles that are important for developing computer science and information systems skills to support both applied and research work.

The Database Book discusses the major techniques for logical data modeling and approaches to physical database structuring. It covers the fundamentals of database protection and emphasizes the role of data dictionary/directory support in data administration. The promise, problems, and peculiarities of distributed database systems are introduced throughout the book. Major commercially available database management systems are surveyed throughout the text, but the material does not go into the details of particular packages. The emphasis is on database design, rather than design of database management systems.

These principles provide a foundation upon which the reader can build as this rapidly moving field evolves. The prospective reader who is interested in learning how to use a particular database management system or how to code a special algorithm found deep in a database management system's kernel should look elsewhere.

The book has three major parts: Part I consists of seven chapters that discuss the principles of logical database design; Part II has four chapters that discuss physical database design principles; the two chapters of Part III discuss the principles of database administration and protection.

The reader equipped with at least one programming language and experience in systems analysis and design will have all the prerequisites needed to learn a great deal from the book. A course in data structures (covering linked lists, trees, and so forth) is helpful background for a thorough understanding of Part II, on physical database design.

The first chapters introduce database design methodologies and emphasize databases as the integrators of systems. Shared databases can pull together many applications, be they traditional Management Information Systems applications (accounting, payroll, personnel, and so forth) or engineering applications (design, analysis, rule checking, and the like) or manufacturing applications (process planning, MRP, shop floor control, and others) or combinations of these.

Chapter 3 introduces a semantic data modeling technique, which is independent of particular database management systems or implementation approaches. The technique used is a hybrid of entity-relationship, relational, and generalization modeling. This technique is representative of the several good ones currently available.

Chapters 4 through 7 introduce the popular logical data models supported by commercial database management systems—the relational, network, and hierarchic systems. Techniques for designing databases using the foundation of semantic data modeling are emphasized.

Chapter 9 starts Part II with a review of fundamental data structuring concepts. Chapters 10 through 12 discuss implementation techniques for relational, network, and hierarchic database systems. Database machines and distributed database implementations are discussed, as are the more conventional physical database implementation techniques.

The last part of the book focuses on database protection and management. Chapter 13 discusses data management through data dictionary systems, with emphasis on the potential of these systems to support both database design and transaction processing. Chapter 14 covers the principles of shared access control, backup and recovery, security protection, and transaction management.

The book closes with observations regarding trends in database management. It considers both the business and engineering applications areas, as well as trends in fundamental database technology.

Each chapter closes with a list of important terms. The glossary at the back of the book defines every term that appears in the end-of-chapter lists. One of the objectives of the text is to give the reader a good understanding of the common terminology of database design and management.

Each chapter also has a set of review exercises. The great majority of these exercises are thought-provoking questions, rather than ''echo'' questions. Many of them ask the reader to determine how the principles introduced in the text are applied in the reader's world.

This book is a result of combining many years of refinement of database courses for both academic and industrial audiences with broad experience in applying database technology in the real world. I hope that it proves interesting and useful.

ACKNOWLEDGMENT

I wish to acknowledge Dan Appleton and Dave Judson, for their foresight regarding the importance of semantic data modeling in developing integrated systems. The Air Force's IDEF1 technique and Robert G. Brown's logical database design techniques are the parents of the semantic data modeling technique used here.

The book has benefited substantially from the reviewers' thoughtful comments and by conversations and feedback from many colleagues, notably Bob Brown, Mark Lipp, and Dale Rollins. Thanks also to the countless students of the University of Arizona Department of Management Information Systems, who persevered through my database courses and contributed to my understanding of the importance of fundamentals.

Special thoughts go to Sally Elliott, who got me started on this project; to my husband Tim, who continually encouraged me to finish it; and to Allison and Eleanor, who helped make it take forever.

M.E.S.L.

CONTENTS

3   Logical Data Modeling   **37**

11 Physical Design of Network Databases   302

12 Physical Design of Hierarchical Databases

338

III DATABASE ADMINISTRATION AND PROTECTION

363

13 Data Dictionary/Directory Systems

365

14 Data Protection 384

Introduction:
The Database Approach

This book is about databases—their design, implementation, administration, and protection. It will help you answer questions about database management. What are databases, and what do they mean to an organization? How can data resources be organized so that they effectively and efficiently provide information to decision makers? How can data resources be protected so that they can continue to be valuable throughout their lifetimes? What hardware and software support is needed for database management?

This book explains the principles of database management, which will help you continue to build your expertise in this rapidly evolving field and will prepare you to function effectively in today's information-based world.

This first chapter will acquaint you with the database approach to information resource management and will introduce you to the functions of database management in information systems. In the following chapters you will learn about the techniques used to design databases and the alternatives to database implementation. We shall look at the commercially available database management systems (called DBMSs) and discuss the selection of good database software and hardware and the administration and protection of databases. Finally, we shall consider both centralized and distributed computer environments.

Basic Concepts

The database approach recognizes that data are assets to be managed along with the other, more familiar resources of an enterprise, including its personnel, inventories, and capital.

Organizations spend tremendous sums of money collecting and manipulating data and trying to extract the information needed to make decisions. One of the objectives of the database approach is the preservation of that investment in data resources, by protecting and managing that investment by managing data rather than just the applications that access the data.

Managing data implies both managing the facts represented by strings of bits on magnetic storage media and managing the meanings of those facts. Meanings are managed by organizing those meanings into logical structures of entities.

Meanings

An entity is data about a specific object, either real (i.e., physical—an object that can be picked up and handled) or abstract. An entity has properties; it is something about which something is known. An example of an entity is the employee Adam Brown, some of whose properties are

> Employee name = Adam Brown
> Employee number = 12751
> Social security number = 123456789
> Height = 6′ 2″
> Birth date = May 25, 1946
> Birth location = Whittier, CA
> Hire date = June 1, 1980
> Job title = Instructor
> Department = Training and Education

A collection of entities with similar properties is called an *entity type* or, sometimes, an *entity class*. For example, Adam Brown, Janice Smith, and Ellen Kolb all are employee entities; they all have the properties of employee name, employee number, social security number, height, birth date, birth location, hire date, job title, and department. They all, therefore, are members of the employee entity type.

Managing data is managing entities, entity types, and their relationships. In fact, we focus on managing entity types rather than the individual occurrences of entities. An entity type represents *meaning,* whereas an entity instance represents *facts*.

For the remainder of this book, the term *entity* will be used rather than entity type, and *entity instance* will be used to refer to an individual occurrence of an entity.

The properties of an entity will be called its *attributes*. Other sources sometimes call attributes *data elements* or *data items* or *fields*. Data are facts plus meanings, and facts are attribute values. One can know the meaning of a fact by knowing to which attribute and entity the fact applies.

In addition to being named, an entity must have one or more attributes whose values uniquely identify an entity instance. These distinguishing attributes are called the entity's *primary key*. A social security number or employee number could be the primary key of the employee entity introduced earlier.

Databases

Data from a collection of entities can be aggregated and summarized in various ways to produce information (Fig. 1.1). Information is data placed in context, which may be supplied by a situation or other data. Who decides what information is valuable to a business? That burden generally rests with the decision maker. In fact, one decision maker may try several possible sets of information before deciding which is really useful. To complicate matters further, useful information today is frequently different from useful information tomorrow.

Pertinent information can be retained as part of a person's memory and become part of that person's knowledge. To augment our mentally stored knowledge bases, we also collect data and store it in automated form. Such a collection is called a *database*. It can be shared by many users and is protected and managed to retain its value and quality over time. A database represents not just data about entities but also data about relationships among entities.

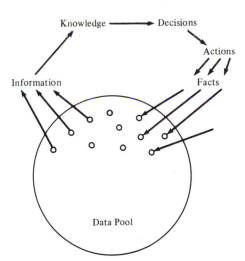

FIGURE 1.1. Data as an integral part of the decision-making process.

Physical and Logical Databases

There are two forms of databases:

- Physical databases, which are representations on storage media of entities, attributes, and their relationships.
- Logical databases, which represent entities, attributes, and relationships independently of how the data and relationships are actually represented and stored in a physical database.

The design of logical databases is the topic of Part I, and the design of physical databases is the subject of Part II.

Data Management

Data management includes all the activities that ensure that high-quality data are available to produce needed information and knowledge. The objective of data management is to keep data assets resilient, flexible, and adaptable. Data management responsibilities include

- The representation, storage, and organization of data so that they can be selectively and efficiently accessed.
- The manipulation and presentation of data so that they can effectively support the user environment.
- The protection of data so that they can retain their value.

A database management system (DBMS) is a tool for implementing effective data management. This book's emphasis is on the design of databases (managed by DBMSs) rather than the design of DBMS software and hardware. Designers of DBMSs are concerned with issues like interprocess communication, staging of data among storage media of various speeds and capacities, buffer management, code generation and optimization, and language parsing and compilation. By contrast, designers of databases are concerned with issues like representing data meanings in various forms of data structures and effectively using DBMS services.

The Database Approach

The database approach recognizes that data are absolutely necessary to organizations' decision-making cycles (see Fig. 1.1.). Who decides what data will be made available to decision makers? In many organizations, data-processing personnel and programmers decide which data will be given to whom. But do programmers always know the decision makers' information needs? Unfortunately, data-processing departments too often respond to information requests from users by saying either that the information is ''not available'' or that it will take three months to extract, even though the user may need the information this afternoon. Effective data resource management is thus driven by user needs, not just by data-processing hardware and software capabilities.

This may at first suggest that the data-processing group is not important. On the contrary, the data-processing group is very important, but it cannot just promote its own existence. It must support and respond to users' information requirements.

The database approach emphasizes managing data rather than applications. The data-oriented approach can help ensure that programs really do what they were intended to do. It relieves programmers of many of the responsibilities of defining and protecting data. A data orientation can also make the efforts of the data-processing group more effective in the eyes of the user community.

TRADITIONAL ENVIRONMENTS

Traditional (or applications-oriented) environments focus on procedure. Data flows from one program to another; indeed, the lifetime of applications-oriented data largely depends on a program's duration.

Each program manages its own files: a *file* is a collection of data managed and accessed as a unit. It need not be shareable. Relationships among different kinds of data and across files are estabished by application-program logic and are not an inherent part of the files themselves.

The data required to process one program are often also needed for another program; yet the two programs typically do not expect the data in the same format. The result is the same data in many files, as each file is essentially "owned" by a different program (Fig. 1.2). This redundancy causes difficulties in data *consistency* and *correlation*.

Consistency Problems

It is difficult to keep several consistently up-to-date copies of anything. For example, assume that you have three calendars. One you keep by your desk;

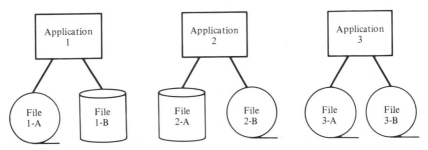

FIGURE 1.2. File-oriented approach.

one is hanging on your kitchen wall; and one is in your briefcase. What is the probability of all of them containing the same appointment record? This same inconsistency also plagues environments in which data are duplicated across files.

The applications-oriented method implies that the various data files are formatted and organized to suit the needs of particular programs (or programmers). Traditional files, organized by sequential, relative, or indexed-sequential techniques, support only limited types of access. Developing another program to use the same data commonly means creating another file, and then there are two copies to try to keep consistent.

Correlation Problems

Different applications and programs use different schemes to encode data; consequently, trying to correlate data across files can be time-consuming and frustrating. For example, there may be five (or even more) sets of codes used to identify academic departments in a university: a four-digit code, a five-digit code, a four-character code, a five-character code, and a code of two characters followed by three digits. There may be no obvious means of translating the coding schemes, as each may have been correct at some time but may be inconsistent with one another. In one such situation, one code had sixty entries; another had sixty-three; and another had fifty-eight. Only a woman in the basement of the administration building knew the key to translation; and fortunately she was willing to help.

The inherent inflexibility of the traditional application-oriented approach is the reason that sometimes information is "not available," even though the users know that they already are getting the data in another form.

The ability to correlate information across traditional applications boundaries and to provide information for all levels of decision making, from operational through tactical through strategic, is increasingly important. Data must be available to an enterprise's daily operations, as well as for medium- and long-range planning. Management at all levels is becoming more aware of the potential power of information systems, and the database approach can fulfill users' information needs.

DATABASE ENVIRONMENTS

In database environments, the focus is on data, not on procedure. The data resource is separate from the programs that happen to access it today, existing to meet users' information needs both today and tomorrow. It is not the data-processing function but, rather, the users who "own" the data.

The data resource is physically implemented so that it can be shared by several users. It thus is not necessary to make several copies of data for different types

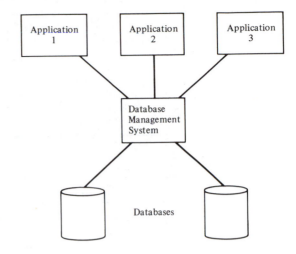

FIGURE 1.3. Database-oriented approach.

of access, as the data are integrated instead of serving only certain programs (Fig. 1.3).

Database Management Systems

To receive a satisfactory return on the large and growing investment in its data assets, an organization must ensure that the data resource is well defined and documented, well organized and controlled, shareable, and relevant to the decisions that need to be made. A database management system (DBMS) is software (and sometimes hardware) specially designed to protect and manage databases.

A DBMS can

- define data and their relationships.
- document data definitions and structures.
- represent, organize, and store data for selective and efficient access.
- interface congenially with users of the data resource.
- protect the data resource so that it is secure, reliable, consistent, and correct.
- separate logical and physical concerns so that changing the database's physical implementation does not require users to change their views of the data.
- provide for data sharing, giving several users concurrent access to the data resource.

The relationship of DBMS software to other systems and applications software is shown in Fig. 1.4. A DBMS generally relies on the host operating system to provide access to the physical databases. Programs are written to interact with databases through the DBMS, not directly. Rather than using conventional pro-

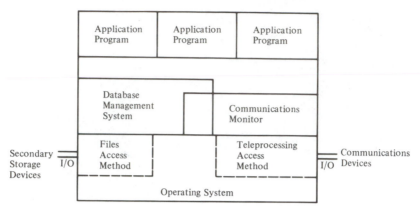

FIGURE 1.4.   Software relationships.

gramming language facilities, for example, the READ and WRITE verbs of COBOL, to access the database, a programmer uses language facilities provided by the DBMS.

End users sometimes can interact with the data resource through natural-language facilities. These capabilities let the user express requests in human language, for example, "Who bought the most widgets today?" rather than in data-processing terms.

The database environment is more than using a collection of software called a DBMS. A DBMS should not be viewed as just a fancy file-access method, as that would ignore its potential benefits. Rather, a DBMS should be viewed as a tool to protect data assets, to improve data quality, and to respond more quickly to changing information needs.

Database Development

Development in the database environment focuses first on the design of the logical database, then on implementation of the logical database as a physical database, and finally on the programs supported by that database. By contrast, in the traditional applications-oriented environment, the data are given secondary consideration. Because of its orientation, the database environment is more capable of accommodating new solutions, new data, and new types of access.

Implications

There are several long-range implications of establishing a database environment and properly managing data. The data-processing function should be able to respond more quickly and effectively to changing information needs. Data quality, accessibility, and relevance should improve, and both users and data-processing personnel can become more productive.

The short-range implication of deciding to implement a database environment is primarily the commitment of adequate resources to start the effort correctly. Time and money are required to train programmers, analysts, and users in database concepts and in the functions of the particular DBMS(s) chosen for the organization. Computing facilities must be acquired or committed to the database support; and the software for database management must be procured and maintained. Finally, organizational structure and job responsibilities may need to be adapted to the data-oriented philosophy.

OBJECTIVES OF THE DATABASE APPROACH

Adopting a data-oriented approach to managing a company's data resources has several objectives:

- Protecting the value of data assets.
- Making the data resource responsive to changing information needs.
- Enabling the data-processing organization to support better the company's business plans and goals.
- Reducing the costs of improving performance.

Protecting the Value of Data Assets

One objective of adopting a data-oriented approach is protecting the value of the data by providing controls for data integrity, security, and reliability. DBMSs offer some of these controls in software and hardware with built-in audit, recovery, and security protection capabilities.

Making the Data Resource Responsive

Another objective of the database approach is enabling the data-processing function to be more responsive to new information requirements caused by changing company needs. Some DBMSs include flexible data-structuring techniques that can accommodate change. They provide standard interface languages for accessing databases, thus freeing programmers from needing to know the details of physical data storage and structuring.

The database approach uses logical data-modeling techniques that allow data resources to be defined independently of their physical implementations. The database approach emphasizes the management of data meanings rather than facts.

Supporting Business Plans and Goals

The third objective of the database approach is to enable the data-processing organization to support better the company's systems of management and decision making. Data-planning and data resource management must be aligned with the organization's business plans and goals. The joint planning of data processing, work-place automation, and telecommunications facilities can enhance the organization's overall productivity. Effective logical database design methodologies use organization business objectives as constraints and guidelines for planning information systems.

Reducing Costs of Improving Performance

The fourth objective of a database environment is to reduce the costs associated with improving performance and keeping up with the evolution of computing technologies. Vendors are continually offering better storage media; a DBMS can provide the logical-to-physical independence necessary to shield users' views and application-program code from the details of physical storage devices. Storage media can also be upgraded without significantly changing the data resource or the code that accesses it.

A DBMS that offers data independence ensures that all applications can continue to run (though perhaps with poorer performance) if the stored data are reorganized to provide better performance for some applications. Data independence insulates users' views and application code from changes in representation, formatting, and location of stored data.

BENEFITS OF THE DATABASE APPROACH

The database approach can

- improve data control.
- increase data accessibility.
- improve data quality.
- improve data shareability.
- improve data resiliency.
- improve data security.
- improve performance.

Data Control

Improved data control offers more consistency in data descriptions, facilitates standardization of data-naming conventions, and reduces the programming effort required to change data implementations.

Data Accessibility

Data accessibility is a user's ability to extract needed information from the data resource. Data accessibility is enhanced by user-friendly interface languages and well-designed input and output screens. Good accessibility is being able to relate data in different ways to produce information and being able to represent that information in various forms. Good accessibility also makes data easier to manipulate and enables cost-effective, general-purpose queries for the user.

Data Quality

Data quality is measured by the database's completeness and consistency. Does it contain data relevant to the user's decision-making needs? Does it contain all of the required interrelationships among types of data, and does it satisfy all of the specified constraints?

Data Shareability

Data shareability is needed to keep common data truly common. Without shareability, data proliferate, and their quality becomes uncontrollable. Without shareability, data are private and personal, with no control over their quality. Data shareability refers not just to database contents but also to the logic that accesses and manages data. Reduced data duplication streamlines data access, facilitates the programming required for updating data, and reduces the possibility of inconsistent data. Less redundancy in the data management effort also improves the productivity of the data-processing personnel.

Data Resiliency

Data recoverability is needed to keep the data resource resilient in the wake of errors. Errors should be detected and corrected or, better, should be prevented from occurring in the first place. Part of the difficulty in providing a resilient data resource is making the data available to users while it is recovering from errors.

Data Security

Data security prevents unauthorized access to data. Not all environments require the same, elaborate security schemes, but nearly all organizations' data assets must have some degree of access protection. Some databases (e.g., the Dow Jones reports) are open to public retrieve-only access, others (e.g., Internal

Revenue Service) records require strict authentication for retrieval. Many databases have more stringent restrictions on changes to database contents than on accesses that only read the database's contents.

Performance

Performance of the data resource refers to its efficiency and effectiveness. *Efficiency* measures the utilization of physical computer resources, and *effectiveness* measures how well the data system meets users' information needs. The characteristics are closely related. For example, a user may be dissatisfied with the system if its response time is measured in hours rather than seconds. Response time is generally considered to be an efficiency measure, but it certainly also affects effectiveness.

COSTS OF THE DATABASE APPROACH

The costs of establishing and operating a database environment include

- DBMS technology costs.
- database operation costs.
- data and logic conversion costs.
- planning costs.
- risk costs.

DBMS Technology Costs

DBMS software is expensive, its cost varying according to the size of its host computer. For example, a DBMS that will run on a large mainframe can easily cost $40,000 and usually costs more than $100,000. Few people will spend that kind of money on software for a personal computer! A DBMS for a micro can be as cheap as $150 but more commonly ranges from $600 to $1,500. The functionality of a DBMS targeted for a micro is generally a subset of the functionality of a DBMS for a mainframe.

DBMS technology costs include software, hardware, and personnel. The effective use of DBMS software capabilities, especially in large mainframe environments, may require a substantial investment in acquisition and/or training of programmers, systems analysts, and data administrators. These costs seem to be declining as DBMSs become more familiar to data-processing personnel and other types of users, but they still are significant.

Operation Costs

The costs of operating a database environment include hardware costs for CPU resources, storage media, and communications, as well as software costs to maintain the DBMS and programs that access the databases. Using a DBMS commonly requires more hardware and software overhead than does using a conventional file organization, not just during system implementation, but also on a continuing basis. Many organizations devote a mainframe to the storage and access of their database systems.

Conversion Costs

Conversion from an applications-oriented environment to a database environment implies that (1) the data must be drawn out of conventional file systems and fed to a DBMS and that (2) the applications logic must be changed to work with the DBMS facilities. Most organizations simply cannot afford to convert all of their files and programs at once.

A reasonable solution for the massive conversion problem is to let applications-oriented systems live through their useful life spans (generally seven to ten years) and to convert each when it nears the end of its life. This approach requires careful planning, as data elements and relationships not identified during the early cycles of implementation may result in expensive database restructuring activity later.

Planning Costs

In order to ensure the longevity of databases and the continuing effectiveness of data-processing-related expenditures, data resource planning should address

- controls and methods for transferring to a data-driven environment.
- identification and prioritization of implementation projects.
- computer system hardware and software technology needs, acquisition, and control.

Controls and methods include standards and procedures, systems development methodologies, data-modeling techniques, data administration roles and responsibilities, and methods to select from hardware and software technologies to respond effectively and efficiently to users' information needs.

Risk Costs

There are also risk costs associated with a database environment. A poorly designed database environment can hurt much of the user community, but a poorly designed file in a process-oriented environment, especially one for an application that executes in batch mode, may affect users less. Unless properly designed, structured, and maintained, a database environment may not respond to users' needs and will be more expensive than it is worth. And the inappropriate application of DBMS capabilities can hurt performance over a long period.

POSITIVE AND NEGATIVE INDICATIONS

The database environment especially benefits an organization with

- a need for interactive inquiry and update capability.
- an expected growth in data volumes.
- an expected expansion in the range of decision making to be supported by information systems.
- a commitment to the importance of data resource management.

Not all data-processing organizations are ready to use a DBMS effectively to implement a database environment. Some of the indications that the traditional applications-oriented approach is still satisfactory for an organization include

- relatively small data volumes with little expected growth in volumes.
- little or no redundancy in the applications' data requirements.
- a relatively fixed data-processing environment, with extensive batch processing and little desire for interactive access.

WHAT CAN A DBMS NOT DO?

Just installing a DBMS does not guarantee that an organization's data-handling woes will end or that data integrity, shareability, accessibility, resiliency, security, and performance will be achieved. What it does mean is that the organization has a promising tool to control the data resource.

Software Interfaces

Some DBMSs are sold as basic systems to which the buyer can add options, and other DBMSs are sold as "complete" packages. In either case, the DBMS must interface with the other software in the environment. For example, many DBMSs do not have a built-in data communications monitor but, rather, interface with a monitor. Some DBMSs have only rudimentary built-in data description facilities, which may require separate data dictionary systems (see Chapter 13). Many DBMSs do not have built-in screen management capabilities, and the user data-processing organization must either acquire or write software "screen painters." These software interfacing tasks are important.

Many organizations are drawn to the DBMS packages that provide a full complement of capabilities. Several of the major DBMS vendors (especially Cullinet Software, Inc.) now also offer applications software that interfaces well with their DBMS packages. Many customers find this compatibility comforting and attractive, though it is also costly!

Getting Started

An organization that acquires a DBMS may not know how to use it. Some DBMS vendors provide consulting services to help the customer start the first database, but rarely do they help establish a solid database environment. The organization thus needs to apply systems development methodologies that take advantage of DBMS support.

Other Problems

A database environment needs to be nurtured by humans to survive. The DBMS is just one tool that makes the nurturing job more likely to be successful, but it cannot find the causes of poor-quality data, cannot reconcile data ownership issues, cannot decide who needs what information, cannot determine how the databases should be designed, cannot decide which database evolution strategy will have the greatest payback for the business, cannot decide on appropriate policies and procedures for data administration, and cannot convert an applications-oriented environment to a data-oriented one; rather, the DBMS is just part of successful data management.

Tools and Methods

The available tools and methodologies that enable the DBMS to be used more effectively are

- data dictionary systems.
- performance monitors.
- application and transaction development tools.
- utilities for validating database storage structures.
- query and report writer features.
- database design methodologies.

Some of these may be provided by the DBMS vendor; others must be written internally or otherwise acquired.

HOW DO THE PEOPLE FIT IN?

As with many technologies, the key to the success of a DBMS lies with the people who work daily with the technology. Data-processing personnel and users share the responsibility for a database environment's effectiveness.

Users

Users must help define the data requirements and help design the logical databases to support their information systems. If they sit back and "let DP do it," they will get whatever DP feeds them, which may not be the most appropriate solution for their needs. Without input and influence from the users, DP can only try to "read the mind" of the organization.

Data Administrators

One user function necessary in an effective database environment is that of the data administrator. The data administrator (DA) ensures that the enterprise's databases continue to offer effective service to their users. His or her primary responsibilities are to control and manage the data resource, establish data-naming standards, build and maintain a data dictionary system, resolve incompatibilities and communication problems among user groups, set development priorities, plan and implement training for users, develop user documentation materials, and design logical databases. This requires a person who can be a liaison between the DP and the user communities.

Analysts

One data-processing role is filled by the systems analyst, who is responsible for both the database design and the applications program design. The database systems analyst requires skills in

- use of the data dictionary.
- the logical database design methodology.
- basic logical database design tasks, including recognition and cataloging of entities and attributes and identification of relationships among entities. ·
- database tools, including database design aids, query/report writer capabilities, application development aids, and programmer interfaces.
- communication with users and the data administrator.

  Conversion to a database environment not only broadens the scope of responsibility of applications analysts; it also may modify an analyst's approach to developing systems. Increasingly successful are prototype-based database development methods, in which a database is designed rather quickly and then tuned over time to meet effectiveness and efficiency requirements.

Programmers

Programmers in the database environment are responsible for generating code that accesses the user databases. The main differences between a programmer's job in the database environment and in a conventional applications-oriented environment are the following:

- Traditional coding responsibilities for describing attributes and their physical characteristics are eliminated for data residing in the database. This can result in as much as a 30 to 50 percent reduction in application coding time, depending on how much effort is expended in writing file descriptions.
- Traditional coding languages, for example, COBOL, are generally augmented with commands to access databases, requiring that the programmer gain new skills.
- Certain DBMSs provide a programmer–user language, which can preclude the need for coding in traditional languages, like COBOL. These programmer–user languages are distinct from any available end-user language facility.
- The programmer yields to the users more or less responsibility for generating ''code.'' Users can write their own database accesses using available congenial, nonprogrammer languages.

Programmers can also become more productive because the DBMS assumes responsibility for providing recovery and security controls over data, eliminating that coding from the programmer's duties. Rather than coding data definitions and routines for backup and recovery and security protection, the programmer may use the DBMS to do this.

Programmer (and analyst) training is required not only on the particular DBMSs to be used but also on the advantages and disadvantages of the database environment in general. This conceptual training should be conducted before a DBMS vendor's on-site, detailed training. Vendor-supplied training should include hands-on use of the DBMS.

An additional, sometimes traumatic, impact on programmers is the users' greater independence, because of their new ability to access databases by themselves, using end-user interfaces.

Database Administrators

The database administrator (DBA) is responsible for the physical database design. (The logical database design is the responsibility of the data administrator.) The similarity in titles has led some organizations to refer to DAs as Information Resource Administrators. The DBA manages and controls physical database design, evaluates database performance, reorganizes the database as needed to maintain satisfactory performance, and evaluates new DBMS features.

In many organizations, the data administrator and the database administrator are the same person.

CLOSING COMMENTS

The main objective of the database environment is to provide a consistent, accurate, accessible, secure, controlled, and extensible pool of data to serve the information needs of a growing community of users. The initial investment in

DBMS software, logical and physical database design efforts, and skilled personnel will have its payoffs and justifications, but they may not be evident immediately. The real benefits of the database environment are improved data quality and availability and reduced costs for continually supporting users' data needs and for adding new data and types of data usage to the environment.

TERMS

accessibility	entity
application program	file
attribute	information
data	integrity
data administrator (DA)	logical database
database	methodology
database administrator (DBA)	performance
database management system (DBMS)	physical database
	primary key
data communications monitor	query
data dictionary system	recoverability
data element	report writer
data independence	security
data integrity	shareability
data management	transaction

REVIEW EXERCISES

1. Define each of the terms in the preceding list.
2. Why is it important to distinguish between data and information?
3. Why is it important to distinguish between logical and physical databases?
4. What are the difficulties of maintaining data consistency when there are many copies of data?
5. How do the applications-oriented approach and the database approach differ?
6. What are a DBMS's responsibilities?
7. What are the objectives of the data-oriented approach?
8. Explain the benefits of the database approach.
9. What are the costs of establishing and operating a database environment?
10. Describe the conversion from a traditional applications-oriented environment to a database environment.
11. Contrast an organization that is ready for the database approach with one that should receive satisfactory support from an applications-oriented solution.

12. Find out who in your organization is responsible for data resource management. (If you are a student, investigate the college administrative data-processing department or a company in your community.) What is his or her job title? Job description? To what job title does he or she report?

13. Find out who in your organization is responsible for data administration. What is his or her job title? Job description? To what job title does he or she report?

14. Talk to the data administrator in your organization. Find out what his or her career path has been and what the most interesting aspects of the job seem to be. Find out whether there are any uninteresting parts of the job.

15. Attend a local meeting of the Association for Computing Machinery (ACM), the Data Processing Management Association (DPMA), or the IEEE Computer Society. Become an active member of such a professional organization.

REFERENCES

Durrel, W. *Data Administration*. New York: McGraw-Hill, 1985.

Kahn, B. K. Some realities of data administration. *Communications of the ACM*, 26 (October 1983): 794–799.

Weldon, J-L. *Data Base Administration*. New York: Plenum Press, 1981.

LOGICAL DATABASE DESIGN

Part I consists of seven chapters that discuss the principles of logical database design. Chapter 2 introduces the database design and implementation process, considering the lifecycles of data and database projects and the framework of much of the rest of the book. The other chapters of Part I address logical data-modeling techniques and their application in environments that use commercial DBMSs.

The success of a database environment is determined largely by how well the databases are logically structured, apart from the physical structuring and implementation of databases on computer storage media. Part II covers physical database implementation and access.

This book emphasizes the separation of logical and physical aspects of database environments, so as to be able to develop data resources that can meet new business challenges and opportunities. The distinction between what is logical and what is physical will become clearer when each is described.

The Database Design Process

This chapter introduces basic concepts of database design; a data lifecycle, which is distinct from the traditional systems development lifecycle; and a framework known as the *three-schema approach*, which leads to a data-driven lifecycle of implementation projects that differs from the lifecycles of projects in applications-oriented environments.

LIFECYCLES

The word *lifecycle* is commonly used in systems analysis and data processing for a sequence of stages in the evolution of software. Lifecycle concepts are used to explain systems development, to organize systems projects, to standardize documentation, and to communicate systems progress.

People disagree about what the stages of the systems lifecycle should be. Some use as many as seventeen stages to describe a system's development; others use as few as three stages. Many proposals fall somewhere in between.

The following stages describe the typical perception of the systems development process (see Fig. 2.1):

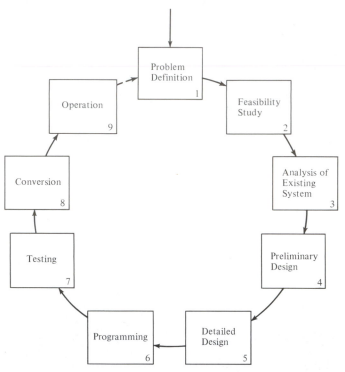

FIGURE 2.1. Conventional systems-development lifecycle.

- Problem definition: recognizing that a new system is needed, identifying goals and objectives, and drawing up cost targets and delivery constraints.
- Feasibility study: deciding on the magnitude of development effort, surveying resource availability, estimating preliminary costs and schedules, and assessing costs versus benefits.
- Analysis of existing system: reviewing existing system documentation, software, and procedures and identifying deficiencies and shortcomings of existing systems.
- Preliminary design: identifying major subsystems, their functions, and subsystem interfaces, describing basic files and system flow diagrams, and analyzing host-computing and communications environments and basic input and output forms.
- Detailed design: identifying coding modules and developing detailed algorithms, procedures, controls, file and report layouts, and input forms.
- Programming: writing code to implement the modules identified in the detailed design stage, and testing the units.
- Testing: developing system integration test data, testing the system, evaluating the system's performance, and obtaining acceptance of the system.
- Conversion: transferring the system to production status; converting files to new formats, conducting parallel operations, and performing cutover.

• Operation: managing the system, collecting problem reports, providing operational data and reports, and projecting work loads.

Documentation, training, and project management parallel these lifecycle stages.

This is a traditional view of systems development, which bases systems development on precise statements of functional requirements and then proceeds through preliminary design and detailed design until the finished system is delivered to its users. It presumes that systems are born, live, and then eventually get sick and die, whereupon they are replaced by younger, ''improved'' generations of code. The lifecycle of large-scale systems applications code is about ten years.

Data, as well as systems, have lifecycles. When data are born, they are personal, as they are owned by the person who created them, and are completely in that person's control. If personal data prove to be useful, there is pressure to make them known to more and more people, and so personal data become shared data.

Data never die. Historic data may be archived, but they never disappear. They are not replaced by new data, although they may be relegated to different roles (e.g., archived) when newer data are acquired. New application systems are not created to replace old data but to improve the ways of processing and managing data.

As data are shared, their quality must be better controlled. As data mature, the need for control increases. And as people come to rely on data, it becomes more and more important that data be protected, accessible, and of high quality.

Recognizing a data lifecycle leads to understanding that data have lives distinct from those of the systems built to access and manipulate them, that shared data are corporate resources that should be managed, and that personal and shared data should be managed differently.

THE NEED FOR A DATA-DRIVEN SYSTEMS DEVELOPMENT METHODOLOGY

If databases are implemented using the traditional applications orientation discussed in Chapter 1, then database projects will follow the traditional lifecycle. Again, this lifecycle assumes that databases will die, and it prepares them from the start for their eventual disposal.

An alternative is to let the data resource evolve, without constraining it to today's boundaries of applications and organizations. Indeed, some companies move people in order to improve communication within the organization and its employees' understanding of its business. Natural application boundaries tend to shift more slowly than do organizational boundaries, but they nevertheless do change.

One way of implementing an effective data-oriented environment is to adopt a framework that (1) explains the types of data relationships pertinent to database environments, (2) stresses the independence of the user-oriented and implementation aspects of data management, and (3) is independent of any particular vendor's DBMS data-modeling approach. One such framework is the *three-schema approach,* which was proposed in the mid-1970s and then published in 1977 in a report from a committee of the American National Standards Institute, "The ANSI/X3/SPARC DBMS Framework: Report of the Study Group on Database Management Systems."

A dictionary definition of schema is "a diagram, plan, or scheme." In a data management context, the word *schema* means a data structure that is formalized according to a set of rules. A schema is a model, usually depicted by a diagram and sometimes accompanied by a language description.

The three-schema approach has three types of schemas, each with a specific purpose. In addition, alternative approaches can be mapped onto the three-schema approach, which will be done in later chapters.

THE THREE-SCHEMA APPROACH

The three-schema approach is based on the assumptions that

- computers and users need to be able to view the same data in different ways.
- different users need to be able to view the same data in different ways.
- it is desirable for users and computers to be able to change the ways that they view data.
- it is undesirable for the computer to dictate or constrain the ways that users view data.

Thus it is necessary to be able to offer different views of a data resource.

Separation of User Views and Implementation Views

Users need to be able to work with representations of data that are independent of the ways that the data are actually stored and managed on computer facilities. Users view data as high-level entities, like staff members, tools, vehicles, products, orders, and customers. Meanwhile, computer facilities (including access methods, operating systems, and DBMSs) need to be able to work with physical representations. They view data in terms of records and files, with index structures, B-trees, linked lists, pointers, addresses, pages, and the like.

These requirements lead us to conclude, first, that there are two different types of data views, user views and implementation views. User views are models of the real world; they communicate with users. Implementation views, on the other hand, are computer oriented.

Using the three-schema approach terminology, *external schemas* are user views of data as seen by one or more applications, and *internal schemas* are implementation views of databases.

Schemas contain metadata, that is, data about data. For a simple example, CUSTOMER-NAME and CHARACTER(17) are metadata describing the data value CHRISTOPHER ROBIN. Metadata give meanings; data values give facts; and meanings and facts together make data.

Interschema Mappings

The objective of data management is to allow users to access computerized data. Thus, there must be *mappings*, or *transformations*, between user views and implementation views. These mappings would be simple if there were only one external schema and one internal schema. But there are multitudes of external schemas and commonly many (sometimes hundreds or thousands) of internal schemas in an enterprise.

Each external schema can be mapped directly to the underlying databases (Fig. 2.2). This solution suffers, however, when either type of schema is changed. For instance, if a physical database is restructured on a disk to provide more

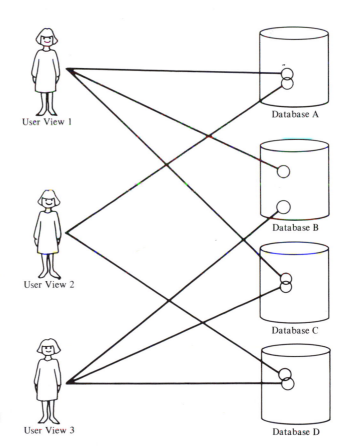

User View 1

User View 2

User View 3

Database A

Database B

Database C

Database D

FIGURE 2.2. Direct mapping of user views and implementation views.

efficient performance, then the mapping to each of the external schemas that references that database can be affected. If an external schema is revised to present the data in a somewhat different way, then the mapping to each of the referenced databases may be affected. Use of the direct external-to-internal schema mapping prevents independence between application and implementation. Physical computer factors thus constrain the ways that users view their data.

To enable several users to share a data resource that may be implemented on many physical databases, the three-schema approach inserts a neutral, integrated view of the data resource between the external schemas and the internal schemas. In three-schema approach terms, this view is called a *conceptual schema,* an *enterprise view,* or a *community view.*

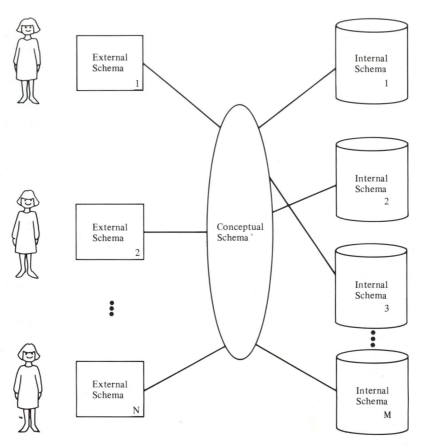

FIGURE 2.3. The three-schema architecture: one conceptual schema that provides for integration and independence of many external and internal schemas.

Conceptual Schema

A conceptual schema is extensible, consistent, accessible, and shareable and enables the data resource to evolve as needs change and mature. Figure 2.3 illustrates the relationships among the three types of schemas. The schemas and the mappings among them enable both data independence and the support of several views. An internal schema can be changed to improve efficiency and take advantage of new technical developments without altering the conceptual schema or external schemas. External schemas can be changed to reflect modifications in an application view or the use of data without affecting the conceptual schema or internal schemas.

The conceptual schema represents knowledge of shareable data. There may be access controls and security restrictions on these common data, but they are not restricted to being known by only one user. The conceptual schema does not describe personal data but, rather, data controlled by the enterprise.

The scope of the conceptual schema expands through time. The data-driven approach to database projects, which is discussed in the next section, continually expands the conceptual schema to include knowledge of more shared data. A data-driven database project does not redefine the data resource, nor does it create another stand-alone database. Instead, each project must determine how the data within its scope relate to what is already known by the conceptual schema. The result is an integrated data resource whose scope is expanded gradually. An organization's data resources cannot be integrated all at once; the job must be done piecemeal, and the conceptual schema is the integrator.

A DATA-DRIVEN PROJECT LIFECYCLE

The primary objective of the data-driven project lifecycle[1] presented here is to implement databases and end-user software on an integrated conceptual schema. It is not the only possible data-driven project lifecycle, but it is one that has been tested and shown to be successful in a variety of environments.

This data-driven project lifecycle is not the same as the conventional systems-development lifecycle introduced at the beginning of this chapter. Rather, the conventional approach builds separate databases and files, whereas the data-driven approach builds integrated databases. The conventional approach relies on complete and correct statements of requirements before offering anything concrete to the user. But the data-driven approach promotes prototyping to help discover requirements, and users are active and essential contributors to this prototyping process.

Prototypes provide relatively low-cost opportunities to determine what the target system's function should be, as they allow experimentation before a design has been finally realized.

---

[1]This project lifecycle is based on the Prototype Development Methodology PDM℠, a methodware product of the D. Appleton Company, Inc.

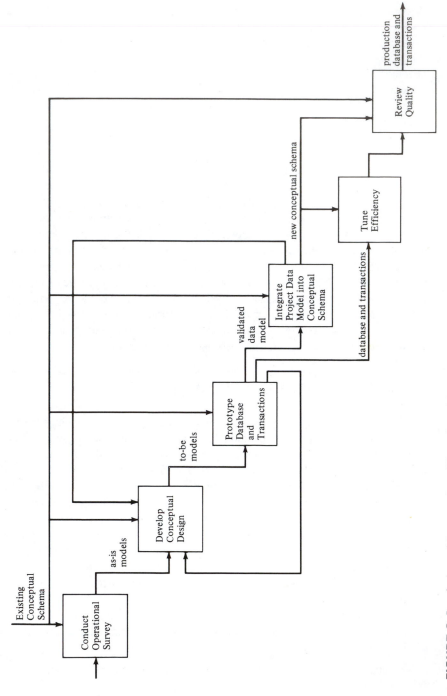

FIGURE 2.4. A data-driven project lifecycle, with prototyping.

The Stages

The stages of a data-driven project lifecycle (Fig. 2.4) are

- Survey: to establish the scope and schedule for the project, collect and analyze information about the data within the scope of the project, develop high-level logical data models of the scope of the project, and identify improvement opportunities.
- Design: to develop detailed logical data models of the new environment, plan the prototyping process, and draw up draft specifications of database transactions.
- Prototype: to design the physical database structure for the initial database prototype, load the prototype, use the prototype to refine and validate user views and define required transactions, address effectiveness concerns, develop transactions, and transfer the prototype to working status.
- Integration: to integrate the prototyped logical data models with the conceptual schema, and adjust interschema mappings.
- Tuning: to refine physical database structures and optimize the software.
- Review: to monitor the quality of project outputs and transfer the prototype from working status to production status.

This approach to design relies heavily on building data models that represent the data resources from various perspectives. The emphasis in the survey, design, prototype, and integration stages is on logical data models, which represent data meanings.

Database Prototyping

Note the feedback loops in the lifecycle of Fig. 2.4. The feedback loops from the prototype stage enable modification of the user views and this project's contribution to the conceptual schema, before moving the database into production status. Users are heavily involved in the prototype stage, being given prototype databases and the opportunity to discover their information and transaction needs, before there is a complete statement of requirements. Contrast this with the conventional systems development lifecycle, which waits until all the requirements are known before designing anything.

Using this project lifecycle, prototypes can be constructed and put into service rapidly, sometimes in a matter of days. The lifecycle also works with larger-scale prototyping, in which it may take months to move from initiating a project to having a working database.

A prototype database's physical structure may be modified so that it will fulfil more efficiently the production performance needs. Its logical data model, however, is not thrown away but is integrated into the conceptual schema and mapped to the physical structure, that is, to the production version's internal schema. Prototyping in this context is not ''throw-away'' or ''quick and dirty'' prototyping.

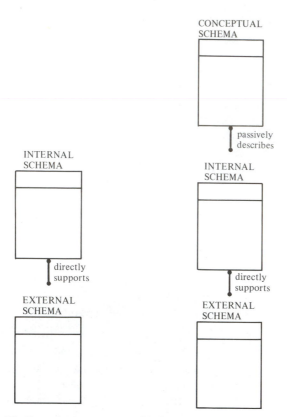

CONCEPTUAL
SCHEMA

passively
describes

INTERNAL
SCHEMA

directly
supports

EXTERNAL
SCHEMA

INTERNAL
SCHEMA

directly
supports

EXTERNAL
SCHEMA

(a) The "legacy": direct
coupling of external and
internal schemas

(b) Step 1: Superimpose data-description
control in the conceptual schema via a
passive data dictionary

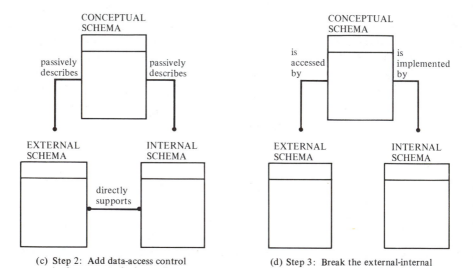

CONCEPTUAL
SCHEMA

passively
describes

passively
describes

EXTERNAL
SCHEMA

INTERNAL
SCHEMA

directly
supports

(c) Step 2: Add data-access control
in the conceptual schema via a
passive data dictionary.

CONCEPTUAL
SCHEMA

is
accessed
by

is
implemented
by

EXTERNAL
SCHEMA

INTERNAL
SCHEMA

(d) Step 3: Break the external-internal
linkage with conceptual-schema control
via an active data dictionary.

FIGURE 2.5. Steps to conceptual-schema control.

Project Teams

The data-driven approach to database development requires project teams composed of both data-processing personnel and end users. Rather than submitting their requests for systems to the data-processing department and then waiting to see what is eventually rolled out the door, users help determine the data relationships and transactions. They are involved with the system as it develops, not just after it has been developed, when they have to live with it.

INTEGRATION AND THE CONCEPTUAL SCHEMA

One of the most important characteristics of this development lifecycle is that each project does not re-create its own, separate database. Rather, each project must examine how the data within its scope relates to the data in the existing conceptual schema. The conceptual schema evolves as additional data-driven projects come to life and extend it.

Each project may create its own, physically separate prototype database, but the integration of those databases is tracked. Sometimes a project will be initiated, and then it will be discovered that the data required to support it are already available and described in the conceptual schema. A new external schema then may be developed and mapped to the conceptual schema, which is mapped to one or more internal schemas.

There is no implication that one huge physical database is created to support all production information needs, because according to the three-schema approach, the conceptual schema can be mapped to many internal schemas, each of which represents a physical database. Those physical databases may reside on several computers and may be geographically distributed throughout an enterprise. The conceptual schema integrates these distributed components.

Thus the conceptual schema integrates the applications-oriented views represented by the external schemas, or from another perspective, it integrates the implementation-oriented views represented by the internal schemas.

Passive Versus Active Conceptual Schema

Data are not integrated until the tight bond between the internal schemas and the external schemas is broken. The conceptual schema, rather than the application programs, must control the access to and manipulation of the data resources.

Breaking the link between the internal and the external schemas is not simple. There are two intermediate steps that superimpose, first, a passive conceptual schema and, then, a full three-schema view on top of the direct internal-external linkage. The legacy of most database applications environments is shown in Fig. 2.5(a). Internal and external schemas are joined through application-program code. There is no enterprise view of the data resource.

The "big-dot" notation used in Fig. 2.5 shows the type of relationships possible among the entities in the boxes. A big dot means "many." Figure 2.5(a) says that an internal schema can directly support many external schemas, and an external schema can be directly supported by many internal schemas.

In the first step (Fig. 2.5[b]), the conceptual schema is introduced, and the internal and external schemas continue to be directly linked. One conceptual schema describes all of the data available in all the internal schemas, in an integrated, neutral, passive view of the data resources. Any control that the conceptual schema has over the data resources completely depends on the data resources' policies, procedures, and administration. The conceptual schema resides in a data dictionary (see Chapter 13) and is described as a logical data model (see Chapter 3).

The second step (Fig. 2.5[c]) provides another bridge to integration. The external schemas are mapped to the conceptual schema, and the data dictionary can be used to determine who accesses which data.

The third step (Fig. 2.5[d]) provides an active conceptual schema. When an active conceptual schema is in place, data management software performs the operations needed to take a user's request from external- to conceptual- to internal-schema form. Application programs are aware only of external schemas. A particular transaction or application program can access data in several databases, without concern for where the data actually are stored. The database may be distributed to various computers of a network. Interschema transforms are not done in application program code but by data management software that provides active conceptual schema control. The logic then can be shared by many applications and users.

Although data management software to perform interschema transforms in distributed database environments does not yet exist in production form, prototypes have been constructed by various research projects. The efforts spent in building passive conceptual schemas today should pay off in both the short and the long run, in improved information systems planning and implementation.

PLANNING FOR A DATABASE ENVIRONMENT

The probability of implementing a successful database environment can be enhanced by following these guidelines:

- Recognize that a DBMS represents a tool for managing the data resource, not just a fancy file-access method.
- Gain adequate management commitment of resources.
- Keep the scope of each implementation project reasonable and doable. Results should be available in six months.
- Plan the development process and establish review points.
- Phase in implementation (and conceptual schema evolution) in attainable increments with a conservative staging plan.

- Shift responsibilities to the experts, and be sure that users define their require-ments and validate the system's capabilities.
- Train a technical staff in database technology early and continuously.
- Establish a data administration function.
- When appropriate, use prototyping to define requirements.
- Ask for, and accept, help from the vendor.
- Be wary of entanglements, including overdependence on the DBMS vendor.

Planning for the database environment means understanding the data-oriented approach to data management. A database should be designed for generality, flexibility, and extensibility. After the database has been designed, the appli-cations-oriented programs and transactions that depend on that database can be specified. More important to the project's long-term success than the program-ming is the neutrality and quality of the logical database design. Planning for the database environment also means recognizing that the DBMS is a support tool for that environment, not the objective.

TERMS

ANSI/X3/SPARC
conceptual schema
data-driven
enterprise view
external schema
internal schema
lifecycle

logical view
mapping
metadata
physical view
prototype
schema

REVIEW EXERCISES

1. Define each of the terms in the preceding list.
2. What is the main difference between the applications-oriented project lifecycle and the data-driven project lifecycle introduced in this chapter?
3. What are each of the schemas of the three-schema approach? Who is the intended "audience" of each type of schema?
4. What is the effect of changing a physical database's structure in a two-schema environment? In a three-schema environment?
5. What are the stages of a conventional systems development lifecycle? With how many different versions of this conventional lifecycle are you acquainted?
6. Why should personal data and shared data be managed differently?
7. Why should users be involved in projects that implement database systems?
8. What lifecycle concepts are in use in your organization? (If you are a student, investigate the college administrative data-processing department or a company in your community.)

9.   How are database-implementation projects organized and managed in your organization?

10. How long does it usually take to implement a database in your organization?

11. How is project documentation organized in your organization?

12. What methodology does your organization use to design and implement databases?

13. Read the ANSI/X3/SPARC report on the three-schema approach. Determine the status of the movement to standardize DBMS architectures based on that approach.

REFERENCES

Appleton, D. S. Data-driven prototyping, *Datamation,* November 1983, pp. 259–268.
Prototype Development Methodology for the 80's—PDM80. Release 4.0. D. Appleton Company, Inc., 1984.
Tsichritzis, D., and A. Klug, eds. The ANSI/X3/SPARC DBMS framework report of the study group on database management systems. *Info Systems* 3 (1978).

Reports of research projects implementing database management capabilities in distributed, heterogeneous computer environments:

Integrated Computer-aided Manufacturing (ICAM) Integrated Center Manufacturing Control—Materials Management System Interim Reports on the Integrated Information Support System (IISS) Test Bed. ITR6201150001ff. Materials Laboratory, Air Force Wright Aeronautical Laboratories, U.S. Air Force Systems Command, Wright-Patterson Air Force Base, Ohio 45433.
Mitchell, M. J., and E. J. Barkmeyer. Data distribution in the NBS automated manufacturing research facility, unpublished report. Washington, D.C.: Center for Manufacturing Engineering, National Bureau of Standards, 1984.
Smith, J. M., et al. *Multibase—Integrating Heterogeneous Distributed Database Systems.* Technical Report on Basic Architecture, November 1980. Computer Corporation of America, 575 Technology Square, Cambridge, Mass. 02139.

CHAPTER 3

Logical Data Modeling

One of the most powerful techniques for establishing and maintaining control over data resources is logical data modeling. There are many logical data-modeling techniques in use today, and the references at the end of the chapter list some of the most common ones. To illustrate the properties of enterprise data that a logical data model should capture, one graphical technique will be described here, which should also explain many of the other logical data-modeling approaches. Logical data models can be represented by either diagrams or language statements. We have elected to use diagrams here.

INTRODUCTION

Modeling is an important technique for defining requirements and analyzing alternative designs. A model depicts features of particular interest, while suppressing relatively unimportant details. Various modeling techniques focus on different types of features of a system—for example, on data, process, or dynamics.

Logical Data Models

A *logical data model* is a rigorous representation of the meaning of data within some scope of interest. A logical data model is sometimes called a *semantic data model,* because the model's emphasis is on data meanings (i.e., semantics).

A logical data model typically represents entities, attributes, and relationships. As stated in Chapter 1, an *entity* is something that exists in the real world, a concept, person, place, thing, or event about which we want to keep facts. An *attribute* is a property or characteristic of an entity, and a *relationship* is a logical association between entities.

A logical data model is typically represented using a graphical technique. For example, boxes may represent entities, and arcs between the boxes may represent relationships between entities. The symbols on the ends of the arcs represent the number of the entities' occurrences that can be related to one another. Figure 2.5 shows four simple logical data models.

Physical Data Models

Physical data models represent the implementation of data structures and are concerned with the optimization of resources such as memory space and access times. Their elements generally include physical records, files, addresses, and pointers. Physical data modeling is discussed in Chapter 9.

Activity Models

Logical and physical data models can be contrasted with *activity models* (sometimes called *function models* or *process models*), which represent processes (rather than data) and their relationships. These models typically are represented using a graphical notation where boxes (or circles) represent activities and arcs between the boxes (or circles) represent flows among activities. A flow may contain data, documents, materials, and the like. Figure 2.4 shows an activity model.

An activity model focuses on processes more than on flows among processes. Data models, on the other hand, focus on the meanings of data entities, attributes, and relationships. Data-modeling techniques usually do not represent the activities that use the data.

Unless otherwise indicated, we shall use the term *data model* to refer to a logical data model rather than a physical data model, which is consistent with the terminology generally used in the database field.

USING LOGICAL DATA MODELS

Data models have two principal purposes, to facilitate communications about data and to aid in the discovery of data semantics.

Communicating Data Meanings

Because they are rigorous representations, data models can be used to convey to another person one person's understanding of data semantics. As long as both parties are familiar with the notation used in the model, the communication will be understood. Increasingly, companies are standardizing the way that they model data, by selecting a particular approach to data modeling and using it throughout their systems and database development efforts.

Discovering Data Semantics

Building a data model requires answering questions about entities and relationships. In doing so, the modelers discover the organization's data semantics, which exist whether or not they happen to be recorded in a formal data model. Entities and their relationships are fundamental to all organizations; however, data semantics may remain undiscovered (and perhaps poorly understood) until the organization successfully documents them.

A data model makes it easier to discover data semantics. Without a way to represent entities and relationships, it is easy to say, "Oh yes, we all agree that this is how products and salespeople are related," without really knowing what is being agreed to, and it may not be as simple as "salespeople represent products." For example, some salespeople may represent only certain products; some types of products may be represented by only certain salespeople; the salespeople responsible for a product sale may change during the sale; and so forth.

APPLYING LOGICAL DATA MODELING

By facilitating communications and the discovery of data semantics, data modeling is useful for

- increasing an organization's understanding of its data and operations.
- documenting data resources.
- assessing off-the-shelf software packages.
- planning information systems.
- designing information systems.
- integrating data resources.
- designing and implementing physical databases.

Understanding Data

When developing data models, both data-processing personnel and users who are expert in the subject area are needed. A data model constructed by data-processing people alone and built to portray data about products is likely to be different from one constructed by representatives from engineering, manufacturing, and sales. In fact, the data model constructed by data-processing people alone is likely to be incorrect and/or inaccurate. Thus the users are crucial to the successful development of data models.

Documenting Data

As a communications vehicle, a data model is often a good way to document explanations of data. If the modeling technique is capable and clear, then its models may be considerably more valuable as documentation than natural-language (e.g., English) statements would be.

Evaluating Software

As off-the-shelf software packages become more popular, companies increasingly ask, "Will this software fit comfortably into our environment?" The answer depends on the software's processing and the ensuing data model. For example, a payroll package that assumes that an employee is paid from only one project account will not fit well in a company whose employees are paid from multiple accounts. If the payroll package were documented with a logical data model and if the candidate buyer were familiar with the company's data model, then the buyer could better predict whether or not a particular payroll package was the appropriate selection.

Planning Information Systems

As facilitators of communications and discovery, data models are powerful tools for planning information systems and databases. Data models are used in IBM's BSP (Business Systems Planning), James Martin's Strategic Planning Methodology, and DACOM's RAP (Requirements Analysis and Planning) to identify an enterprise's main data subject areas.

As part of the planning process, high-level entities are then mapped against organizational units (who is responsible for what data?), activities (what functions do what to the data?), and existing files and systems (where are the data currently stored and managed?). Information systems planning should include identification of implementation projects and descriptions of the scope of data to be implemented by each project.

Designing Information Systems

An implementation project can add to a high-level data-planning model details about attributes, volumes, and frequencies of access for data within its scope.

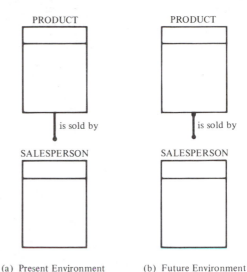

FIGURE 3.1. Present and future models.

(a) Present Environment (b) Future Environment

The resulting detailed model can be transformed to a physical database design. Data modeling can be used effectively to document the pertinent existing data environment and to help design the future data environment. Data modeling used to capture the present environment is a process of discovery, and data modeling used to design the future environment requires invention.

For example, Fig. 3.1 illustrates simple present and future models. Without explaining the diagramming technique at this point, the figure contrasts a discovered environment in which a salesperson sells just one type of product (e.g., typewriters) and a future environment in which a salesperson's responsibilities have been expanded to include several types of products (e.g., typewriters, word processors, terminals, and office computers).

In general, a data model of the future is not pure invention but shares a great deal with its root model of the present. Figure 3.2 contrasts an existing environment, in which undergraduate students cannot enroll in graduate courses, and a future environment, in which graduate courses have been opened to undergraduates.

Integrating Data Resources

Data models can also help integrate the data resource and are used to represent conceptual schemas, as shown in Chapter 2. If the models produced by implementation projects use a consistent, clear syntax, then those models together can give an overall view of how their data fit together, and inconsistencies and redundancies can be identified and resolved.

The evolving integrated data model of an enterprise is its conceptual schema.

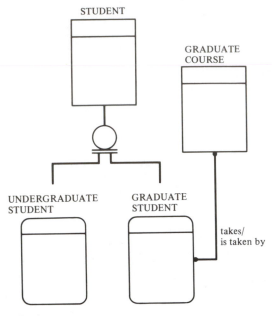

(a) Present Environment

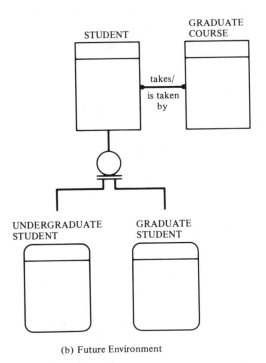

(b) Future Environment

FIGURE 3.2. Present and future models.

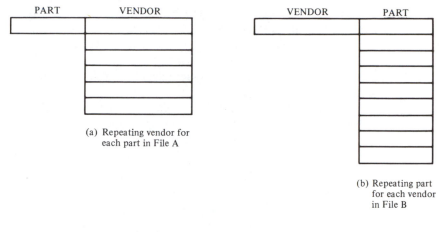

(a) Repeating vendor for
each part in File A

(b) Repeating part
for each vendor
in File B

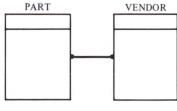

(c) Logical data model

FIGURE 3.3. Many-to-many relationship.

This neutral view of data can be mapped to the various physical database structures (internal schemas) as they are implemented and to the user views (external
schemas) as they are identified.

It can be difficult to integrate data resources without using data models.
Physical structures, for example, do not present a complete picture. Physical
database structures, like conventional file structures, are designed to meet the
performance objectives of particular applications, rather than to mirror logical
structures.

For example, in Fig. 3.3, the PART record in File A contains a repeating
group for the vendors who supply that part. The applications that use File A
access the vendor data for particular parts. Each part has many associated vendors.

By contrast, the VENDOR record in File B is in a record structure that says
each vendor offers many parts. The applications that use File B access part data
for particular vendors. Each vendor has many associated parts.

The combination of these two views indicates that there is a many-to-many
relationship between the parts and the vendors, as shown by the data model in
Fig. 3.3(c). Each box in the figure represents an entity and the arc represents a

relationship between the entities. The big dots at the ends of the arc indicate that the relationship is "many-to-many." This structure means that a particular part may be supplied by many vendors and that any vendor may supply many parts. Neither physical file structure shows the "big picture," but the superimposed logical data model shows the integration of the two data-view orientations.

Detecting the true logical structure of data from physical structures becomes even harder when interrecord relationships are buried in applications code. For example, if parts in the PART file are related to vendors on the VENDOR file through a table hard-coded into an applications program, then the discovery of the logical relationship between the parts and the vendors depends on deciphering that table.

A sound approach to database design is first to build the data model and then to use it as a foundation for the physical database design and implementation. Users must contribute to the data modeling, even though they need not be involved in the physical database design.

It can also be useful to build a data model for an area already supported by physical databases and files. This data model can then be mapped to the physical structures: the physical structures are used for scoping; the data model is used for documentation of data semantics; and the mapping is used to document where data are stored. The data model can show how the data in different physical databases and files are related.

Supporting Physical Database Design

A data model gives the physical database designer information about what data should be included in the database, what the types of relationships are that structure the database, and how this database relates to other databases. Building the data model first emphasizes introducing the correct data into the databases. Physical database design techniques are then used to ensure efficient access to that data.

Keeping the Technique Consistent

Organizations that use data modeling have benefited from consistently using a particular modeling technique for information systems planning, project planning, and database implementation. Conversely, when many modeling techniques are used for these various phases of systems development, there can be problems in translating the meaning of the model built with one technique into a model represented in another technique.

CHARACTERISTICS OF LOGICAL
DATA-MODELING TECHNIQUES

A data-modeling technique should

- produce graphical diagrams.
- provide an explicit representation of semantics.
- be at an appropriate level of detail.
- be DBMS independent.
- have automated support.
- be easy to learn and use.

Graphical Diagrams

Most of the data-modeling techniques in use today offer both a modeling language (with well-defined syntax, keywords, and so on) and graphical diagrams of models. Pictures help convey both the big picture and the details of data semantics. Most of the techniques use boxes or circles to represent entities and arcs or lines to represent relationships.

Some techniques use different shapes for different kinds of entities; for example, rectangles and puffy boxes (rectangles with rounded corners) may be used in the same model to distinguish between identifier-independent entities and entities that depend on other entities for their identification. Some techniques use different line conventions for different kinds of relationships, for example, single lines for groupings and double lines for "is a kind of" relationships. Other techniques use a special symbol, like a circle, to show attributes.

Explicit Representation of Semantics

There is a range of personal preference as to what graphics best represent data semantics. Some people prefer a lot of different symbols, each of which has an explicit meaning, whereas others prefer just a few symbols, which makes the model diagrams appear to be simpler and less cluttered. The ideal data-modeling technique produces model diagrams that clearly represent data meanings. The diagrams should be uncluttered, but one symbol should not have several different meanings.

Appropriate Level of Detail

A modeling technique should provide detail at the appropriate level for the model's use. Data models for high-level (companywide or divisionwide) information-systems planning should carry less detail than should models for physical database design.

The most flexible data-modeling techniques support several levels of detail. For example, they can be used to construct models that show only high-level entities and relationships, as well as models that show all entities, detailed attributes, and refined relationships.

DBMS Independence

A data-modeling technique should be independent of any particular DBMS and should be able to represent models that can be supported by a variety of DBMSs. Many of the current data-modeling techniques are DBMS independent.

Sometimes the data-modeling techniques used with particular DBMSs are considered general-purpose data-modeling techniques, such as the hierarchic model, the network model, and the relational model. The major problem with any of these three techniques is that each has limitations in the data semantics that it can represent. These limitations are outgrowths of the underlying DBMS capabilities.

Automated Support

The ideal data-modeling technique has automated support to draw diagrams, find inconsistencies and redundancies in models, combine models from many sources, report on model components and characteristics, and so on. Having automated support generally means providing both a language for specifying models and graphics-based user interfaces. The data-modeling techniques in use today increasingly are automated.

Easy to Learn and Use

The ideal data-modeling technique is easy to learn and use. Highly labor- and paper-intensive modeling techniques often are avoided after their initial attraction disappears, and so more extensive automation will undoubtedly lead to a more widespread use of data modeling.

BASIC DATA-MODELING CONCEPTS

The basic concepts of data modeling, introduced in Chapter 1, are the concepts of entities, entity instances (sometimes called occurrences), and attributes:

- An entity instance describes a specific object, either real or abstract.
- It is useful to distinguish between entity instances and entities: entities are classes of objects that all have the same properties.
- The properties of an entity are called attributes.
- An entity has a name, which is a noun or noun phrase.
- An entity has one or more attributes whose values uniquely identify, or distinguish, one entity instance from another.

ENTITIES

The entity is the basic concept of data modeling, and it can be a class of real or abstract objects. For example, the following are names of entities that represent "real" objects:

EMPLOYEE	DEPARTMENT
TEACHER	STUDENT
BUILDING	ROOM
CUSTOMER	PRODUCT
PART	VENDOR

whereas the following are names of entities that represent "abstract" objects:

DEGREE_PROGRAM	SALARY_HISTORY
INVESTMENT	WORK_EXPERIENCE
INSURANCE_COVERAGE	COLOR_OPTION
PURCHASE	SALE
COURSE_OFFERING	EMPLOYMENT

Each of the abstract objects has a real meaning but is not a physical object.

Data-modeling techniques do not distinguish between real and abstract entities but represent them in the same way. In our example, the Data Modeling Technique,[1] an entity is always represented by a rectangular box. The entity's name is recorded above the box, and the entity may be assigned a reference tag number, which appears after the name, separated from it by a slash (Fig. 3.4[a]).

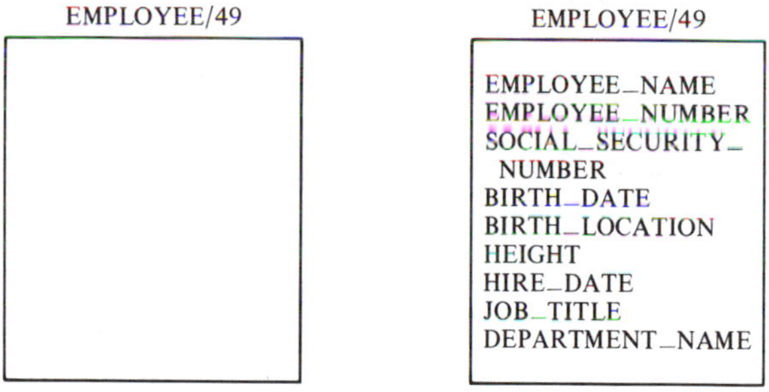

EMPLOYEE/49

EMPLOYEE/49

EMPLOYEE_NAME
EMPLOYEE_NUMBER
SOCIAL_SECURITY_
   NUMBER
BIRTH_DATE
BIRTH_LOCATION
HEIGHT
HIRE_DATE
JOB_TITLE
DEPARTMENT_NAME

FIGURE 3.4. Entities and attributes.

(a) Entity: basic representation

(b) Entity with attributes: basic representation

[1]The Data Modeling Technique (DMT) of D. Appleton Company, Inc. (DACOM) Data Resource Techniques and Tools product is used as our example of a logical data-modeling technique. DMT builds on the concepts of the Logical Database Design Technique developed by Robert G. Brown of the Database Design Group, Inc. (DBDG). Automated support for DMT became available in 1984 through a product named Janus, developed by DACOM and DBDG in conjunction with the Bank of America. DMT syntax and semantics are in the public domain as the U.S. Air Force's IDEFIX.

From a data management viewpoint, it is important to be able to distinguish between individual occurrences of things and classes of things that have the same properties. Individual entity instances are not represented in a data model; classes of entities are. The EMPLOYEE entity provides a template for the meanings of the facts associated with each real employee instance.

ATTRIBUTES

An entity's properties are called its *attributes*. Each entity instance has a value for each of its attributes, which are represented in a model diagram by a list of their names in the entity's box (Fig. 3.4[b]).

Data-modeling techniques assume that two attributes with the same name are the same attribute. Thus, if LOCATION appears as an attribute in both the EMPLOYEE entity and the DEPARTMENT entity, the data-modeling software may flag the attribute as being redundant or inconsistently used, or it may even delete one of the attribute's appearances.

If the two appearances are not meant to be the same attribute, then more precise attribute names should be used. For example, use "BIRTH_LOCATION" in the employee entity and "DEPARTMENT_LOCATION" in the DEPART-MENT entity.

Our discussion later of foreign-key attributes will show that sometimes in a model an attribute may appear in more than one entity. In these cases, the multiple appearances have a definite meaning and indicate a relationship among the entities.

Nulls

It is important to know whether an attribute can have a null value. Although much work has been done in defining types of null values, it is sufficient for our purposes here to understand that a *null* value is an "unknown" or "in-applicable" value. A null-valued attribute does not have a known value at a point in time but still exists conceptually in the data model.

In our data-modeling technique, an attribute that may have a null value is annotated with (0). For example, if an employee may or may not have a value for the attribute SECOND_HOME_PHONE_#, then that attribute would be listed as

SECOND_HOME_PHONE_#(0)

Domains

The values of an attribute are drawn from a *domain,* which determines the valid set of values for one or more attributes. Several attributes may have the same domain. For example, the attributes BIRTH_DATE, HIRE_DATE, MEET-

ING_DATE, and TERMINATION_DATE all are drawn from the DATE domain, and the attributes PURCHASE_PRICE and LIST_PRICE both are drawn from the MONEY domain. A domain shows an attribute's range of values.

A domain may have several alternative representations of its values. For example, values in the MONEY domain can be represented by dollars, pesos, marks, or whatever; values in the LENGTH domain can be represented by feet, miles, centimeters, rods, and the like; and values in the DATE domain can be represented as Gregorian dates (month-day-year), Julian dates (year-day), manufacturing dates (day), and so on. There should be a way to convert values from one representation of a domain to another representation of that same domain.

Domains can also be composed of domains. For example, the DATE domain is made up of three subdomains, MONTH, DAY, and YEAR. And in turn, the MONTH domain has several alternative representations: 1 through 12, "Jan" through "Dec," "January" through "December," and others.

A fully developed data model includes the domains for each of the model's attributes. A data model used to guide physical database design must be driven down to this level. Domains (1) determine the allowable operations on an attribute, (2) determine which attributes can be compared with one another or used in combination with one another, (3) determine the allowable set of values for an attribute, and (4) can be used to help determine the sizes and formats of the corresponding physical database fields.

CANDIDATE KEYS

Instances of an entity are distinguished from one another by the values of their candidate keys. A candidate key is simply a set of attributes whose values uniquely identify the instances of an entity. There may be more than one candidate key for an entity. For example, the candidate keys of the EMPLOYEE entity may be the attribute EMPLOYEE_NUMBER, or SOCIAL_SECURITY_NUMBER, or, collectively, an EMPLOYEE_NAME, BIRTH_DATE, BIRTH_LOCATION, and MOTHERS_MAIDEN_NAME. Any of these three candidate keys uniquely identifies EMPLOYEE entity instances. Two different instances of an entity cannot have the same candidate key value, because then the candidate key would not be a unique identifier.

The term *key* is a shortened form of *candidate key* and is commonly used instead. But we shall avoid using *key* because of its many connotations in various contexts.

Note that a candidate key need not be a single attribute. Our third EMPLOYEE entity candidate key contains four attributes, whose values *together* are the unique identifier. EMPLOYEE_NAME alone is not enough to be a candidate key; EMPLOYEE_NAME, BIRTH_DATE, and BIRTH_LOCATION together are not enough to be a candidate key (e.g., Joe Smith on March 15, 1963, in New York City); rather, all four attributes are required. A key made of more than one attribute is called a *compound key*.

A part of a candidate key cannot also be a candidate key. For example, if a candidate key has three attributes, then all three are necessary for uniqueness. No two will suffice.

What is and is not suitable for a candidate key depends on the scope of the data of interest. For example, if the database included employees from a coalition of companies, then perhaps EMPLOYEE_NUMBER would not be sufficient to be a candidate key. EMPLOYEE_NUMBER and COMPANY_NAME together might be required to form the unique identifier. Similarly, in some situations, EMPLOYEE_NAME and BIRTH_DATE together may be a satisfactory candidate key, and BIRTH_LOCATION and MOTHERS_MAIDEN_NAME may not be required. The identification of candidate keys, then, depends on the data being modeled.

Primary Keys and Alternate Keys

One of an entity's candidate keys is selected to be its primary key. In the EMPLOYEE entity example, either the EMPLOYEE_NUMBER or the SOCIAL_SECURITY_NUMBER would probably be chosen as the *primary key*. The other candidate keys are then called *alternate keys*.

In our example, the Data Modeling Technique, the keys are listed in the same way as are the other attributes in the entity's box. The primary key appears above the line, and the alternate keys appear below the line, appended by an AK notation. Figure 3.5 shows the EMPLOYEE entity, with the SOCIAL_SECURITY_NUMBER designated as the primary key. The EMPLOYEE_NUMBER is an alternate key, and, collectively, EMPLOYEE_NAME, BIRTH_DATE, BIRTH_LOCATION is another alternate key.

Because there can be many alternate keys, the Data Modeling Technique distinguishes them by assigning each a number. Figure 3.5 shows two alternate

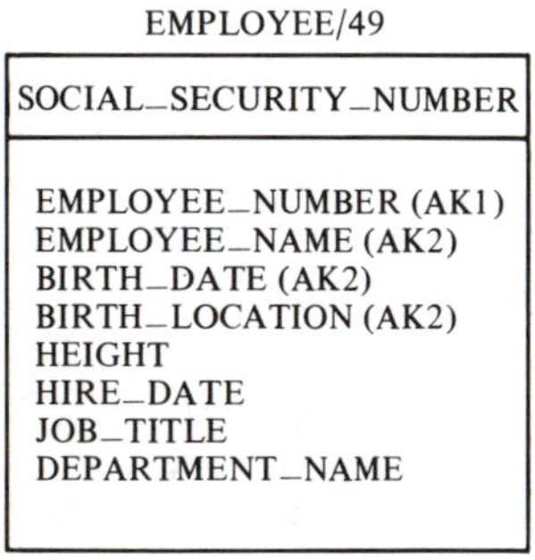

EMPLOYEE/49

```
┌─────────────────────────────┐
│ SOCIAL_SECURITY_NUMBER      │
├─────────────────────────────┤
│ EMPLOYEE_NUMBER (AK1)       │
│ EMPLOYEE_NAME (AK2)         │
│ BIRTH_DATE (AK2)            │
│ BIRTH_LOCATION (AK2)        │
│ HEIGHT                      │
│ HIRE_DATE                   │
│ JOB_TITLE                   │
│ DEPARTMENT_NAME             │
│                             │
└─────────────────────────────┘
```

FIGURE 3.5. Entity with primary key, two alternate keys, and four nonkey attributes.

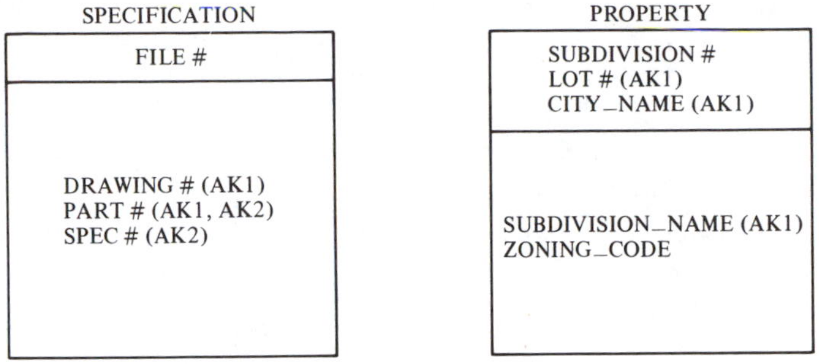

SPECIFICATION

FILE #
DRAWING # (AK1) PART # (AK1, AK2) SPEC # (AK2)

(a) Overlapping alternate keys

PROPERTY

SUBDIVISION # LOT # (AK1) CITY_NAME (AK1)
SUBDIVISION_NAME (AK1) ZONING_CODE

(b) Overlapping primary and alternate key

FIGURE 3.6. Examples of overlapping alternate and primary keys.

keys, denoted AK1 and AK2, respectively. Figure 3.6(a) shows an entity with overlapping alternate keys, and the SPECIFICATION entity's primary key here is FILE#. One alternate key is DRAWING#, PART#, and the other alternate key is PART#, SPEC#. Figure 3.6(b) shows that an alternate key may overlap with the primary key. A PROPERTY can be identified by its primary key SUBDIVISION#, LOT#, CITY_NAME or by an alternate key SUBDIVISION_NAME, LOT#, CITY_NAME.

Two or more entities may have the same attributes for their primary keys. For example, GRADUATE_STUDENT and UNDERGRADUATE_STUDENT are different entities because they have different attributes. They may, however, have the same primary key, the MATRIC_NUMBER. Similarly, HOURLY_EMPLOYEE and SALARIED_EMPLOYEE are different entities but have the same primary key, the SOCIAL_SECURITY_NUMBER.

The basic concepts of candidate keys in a data model are, then, the following:

- Instances of an entity are distinguished from one another by their candidate-key values.
- A candidate key is a set of one or more attributes whose values together uniquely identify the instances of an entity.
- No part of a candidate key can also be a candidate key itself.
- If two instances of an entity have the same candidate-key value, then they are the same instance.
- There may be more than one candidate key for an entity.
- One of the candidate keys is selected as the primary key.
- The other candidate keys are known as alternate keys.
- Each entity instance must have one, and only one, primary-key value.
- A primary-key attribute can never have a null value.
- Multiple entities may have the same primary key.

DEPARTMENT

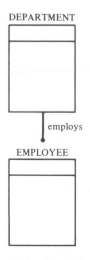

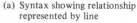

employs

EMPLOYEE

(a) Syntax showing relationship
   represented by line

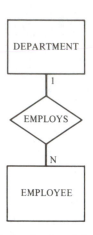

(b) Syntax showing relationship
   represented by diamond

FIGURE 3.7.   Relationship syntax.

RELATIONSHIPS

Relationships in a data model are associations among entities and are commonly represented by lines between the entity boxes (Fig. 3.7[a]), though some data-modeling techniques use a special symbol, such as a diamond, to represent relationships (Fig. 3.7[b]).

There are two types of relationships, connection and category. A *connection relationship* associates different entities, for example, DEPARTMENT and EMPLOYEE. A *category relationship* associates similar entities, for example, STUDENT, GRADUATE_STUDENT, and UNDERGRADUATE_STUDENT. Categories can be thought of as "is a kind of" relationships, with the following example English interpretations:

• Graduate student is a kind of student.
• Undergraduate student is a kind of student.
• A student may be either a graduate student or an undergraduate student.

Connections, on the other hand, do not represent subtype relationships. Their English interpretations typically use action verbs:

• Department employs employee.
• Employee is employed by department.
• Student takes course.
• Course is taken by student.

In the data-modeling literature, connection relationships are typically called *aggregation* relationships, and category relationships are typically called *generalization* relationships.

CONNECTION RELATIONSHIPS

A connection relationship:

- has a verb name.
- has *cardinality,* which indicates how many instances of one of the entities are related to how many instances of the other entity.

In addition, a connection relationship between entities A and B:

- may have *existence dependency,* which means that instances of entity B cannot exist unless an instance of entity A also exists.
- may have *identifier dependency,* which means that the primary key of entity B includes the primary key of entity A. Identifier dependency implies existence dependency.

A connection relationship with existence dependency must adhere to the referential integrity rule:

> Instances of entity B cannot exist unless an instance of entity A also exists, *and* the values of particular attributes of entity B are matched by the value of the primary key in entity A.

In the Data Modeling Technique, a connection relationship is depicted graphically by a "big-dot line."

Figure 3.7(a) shows a connection relationship. The line terminates with a big dot at one end and no symbol at the other end. The line can be read as "One instance of the DEPARTMENT entity is connected by the EMPLOYS relationship to many instances of the EMPLOYEE entity." But more usually, it would be read as "Each department employs many employees." Note that the correct interpretation of the relationship is that each employee is related to only one department.

Figure 3.8 shows a connection line with a big dot at each end. This relationship can be read as "Many instances of the DEPARTMENT entity are connected by the EMPLOYS relationship to many instances of the EMPLOYEE entity." But more usually, it would be read as "Each department employs many employees, and each employee may be employed by many departments," or "There is a many-to-many relationship between departments and employees." These all are equivalent interpretations of this diagram.

There is a major difference between one-to-many connection relationships (e.g., Fig. 3.7[a]) and many-to-many connection relationships (e.g., Fig. 3.8): they do not have the same meaning. The one correctly representing the relationship between departments and employees is determined by the business rules of the real world being modeled.

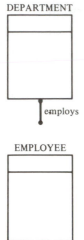

FIGURE 3.8. Many-to-many connection relationship.

Cardinality

A data-modeling technique that uses lines to represent relationships in a model diagram typically uses a symbol at the end of a line to represent relationship cardinality. The *cardinality* of any given connection between entities A and B usually is one of the following:

- One instance of A is related to many instances of B.
- One instance of A is related to at least one instance of B.
- One instance of A is related to exactly n instances of B.
- One instance of A is related to between n and m instances of B.

FIGURE 3.9. Connection relationship with positive (P) cardinality.

For example, we saw in Fig. 3.7(a) that a line terminating without a symbol at an entity box means "one instance of this entity." The big-dot termination symbol means "many instances of this entity." More precisely, the big dot means "0, 1, or more."

The cardinality of a connection relationship can be specified more precisely by annotating the big dot. For example, Fig. 3.9 shows that a graduate student must have on file at least one letter of recommendation. The big dot is accompanied by a *p*, indicating positive.

In some connection relationships, an instance of one of the entities is related to a certain number of instances of the other entity, and the Data Modeling Technique annotates the big dot with that number. For example, Fig. 3.10 shows a connection line terminating with a big dot and 12, and it can be read as "One instance of the DEPARTMENT entity is related by the HAS relationship to twelve instances of the MONTHLY_BUDGET entity." But more usually, it would be read as "Each department has twelve monthly budgets." Note again that each monthly budget is for just one department.

In some connection relationships, an instance of one of the entities can be related to a range of numbers of instances of the other entity, and the Data Modeling Technique annotates the big dot with that range of numbers. For example, Fig. 3.11 shows a connection line terminating with a big dot and 28–31. This example can be read as, "Each month has between twenty-eight and thirty-one days."

Occasionally a cardinality range is zero-to-one. The Data Modeling Technique denotes this special case by annotating the big dot with a *z*, as shown in Fig. 3.12, which can be read as "Each manager has either one secretary or no secretaries." Note that the correct interpretation of the model is that a secretary works for no more than one manager. (If this is not true, then the model does not represent reality.)

FIGURE 3.10. Connection relationship with exact (*n* = 12) cardinality.

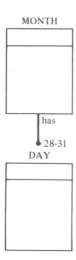

FIGURE 3.11. Connection relationship with range (28–31) cardinality.

Other conventions used to represent cardinality ranges are shown in Figs. 3.13(a) and 3.13(b). The first can be read as "Each class section enrolls a maximum of forty-five students, and each student can be enrolled in a maximum of seven class sections." The second can be read as "Each professor teaches at least two class sections, and each class section is taught by only one professor."

Note that a model with cardinality more explicitly represents data semantics than does a model without cardinality and that cardinality is a form of constraint that can be used to check and maintain data quality. The cardinality of a relationship is an assertion about entity instances. This assertion can be applied when the database is updated, to determine whether or not the update violates the stated rules of data semantics.

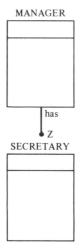

FIGURE 3.12. Connection relationship with zero-or-one (Z) cardinality.

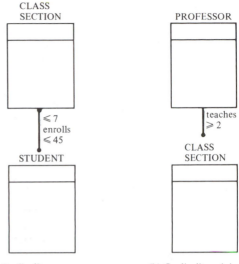

FIGURE 3.13. Examples of cardinalities.

(a) Cardinality range on many-to-many connection relationship

(b) Cardinality minimum on one-to-many connection relationship

For example, consider the assertions made by the relationship cardinalities in Figs. 3.13 and 3.9. An update that would add a forty-sixth student to a class section should be rejected; an update that would add an eighth class section to a student's enrollment should be rejected; an update that would change a professor's responsibilities below the level of teaching two class sections should be rejected; an update that would delete a graduate student's one and only letter of recommendation should be rejected; and, finally, an attempt to add a graduate student with no letters of recommendation should be rejected.

Similarly, consider the assertions made by the relationship cardinalities in Fig. 3.7(a). An update that would cause an employee to be employed by more than one department should be rejected, as the EMPLOYEE–DEPARTMENT relationship is one-to-many, not many-to-many.

Resolving Many-to-Many Relationships

Many-to-many relationships are resolved (divided) into component one-to-many relationships when a data model is refined to show more detail. The resolution of these relationships is shown in Fig. 3.14, which splits the many-to-many relationship between the CLASS_SECTION and STUDENT entities of Fig. 3.13(a) into two one-to-many relationships that have the same base entity. An instance of this base ENROLLMENT entity represents the enrollment of one student in one class section. Each class section has many of these enrollments, up to a maximum of forty-five. And each student has many of these enrollments, up to a maximum of seven.

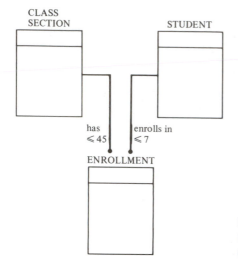

FIGURE 3.14. Resolution of the many-to-many relationship of Fig. 3.13(a), into two one-to-many connections.

Another example of resolving a many-to-many relationship is given in Fig. 3.15. Here the many-to-many connection between the COUNSELOR and CLASS entities is split into two one-to-many relationships that share a base entity called TEACHING_ASSISTANT. An instance of this base entity represents a counselor's staffing of a particular class with a teaching assistant.

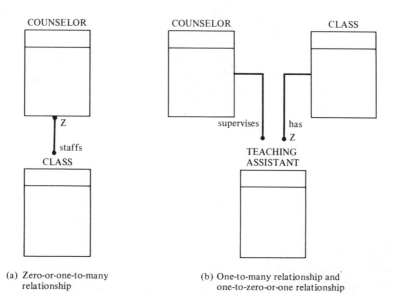

(a) Zero-or-one-to-many
    relationship

(b) One-to-many relationship and
    one-to-zero-or-one relationship

FIGURE 3.15.   Resolution of zero-or-one-to-many relationship.

The entity at the "one" end of a one-to-many relationship is commonly called the relationship's *parent entity*, and the entity at the "many" end of a relationship is commonly called the relationship's *child entity*.

Foreign-Key Attributes

After many-to-many connection relationships have been resolved, foreign-key attributes can be identified. An attribute of one entity that is in the primary key of another entity is called a *foreign-key attribute*. The sharing of that attribute indicates a relationship between the entities. The rule is:

> When two entities are associated (linked) by a connection relationship, the primary-key attributes of the parent entity migrate into the child entity, there becoming foreign-key attributes.

Note that no migration occurs with a many-to-many connection relationship, because no distinction can be made between the parent and the child entity.

For example, in Fig. 3.13(b), the primary-key attribute of PROFESSOR, FACULTY_ID, migrates into the CLASS_SECTION entity, there becoming a foreign-key attribute. In Fig. 3.9, the primary-key attribute of GRADUATE_STUDENT, MATRIC#, migrates into the LETTER_OF_RECOMMENDATION entity, there becoming a foreign-key attribute. Keys cannot, however, migrate across the many-to-many relationship of Fig. 3.13(a).

One of the tests of a foreign-key attribute's validity is

> An entity instance should have only one value of any of its foreign-key attributes.

This indicates in which direction the key migrates in a relationship. For example, if the primary key of CLASS_SECTION—COURSE#, SECTION#—were to migrate into PROFESSOR, there becoming a foreign-key attribute, this test would not be satisfied. Each professor teaches at least two class sections, and therefore each PROFESSOR entity instance must have at least two values of COURSE#, SECTION#.

The rule then is

> The primary key always migrates from the entity at the "one instance side" of a connection relationship to the entity at the "many instances side" of the relationship, there becoming a foreign key.

Rolenames

When there is more than one relationship between a pair of entities, the foreign-key attributes are assigned rolenames. Rolenames permit the distinction among multiple appearances of a foreign-key attribute name in an entity. Because the

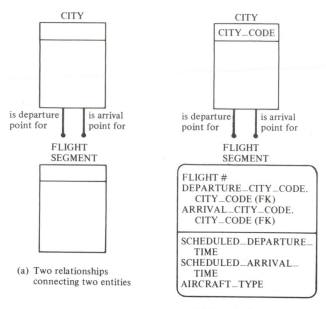

(a) Two relationships
    connecting two entities

(b) Use of rolenames
    for CITY_CODE as
    foreign-key attribute   **FIGURE 3.16.** Rolenames.

appearances migrated in through different relationships, they have different meanings.

For example, Fig. 3.16(a) models the relationships found in an airline schedulé. Each city can be the departure city for many flight segments, and the arrival city for many other flight segments. Each flight segment has just one departure city and one arrival city. The model shows two entities, CITY and FLIGHT_SEGMENT. The primary key of CITY migrates into FLIGHT_SEGMENT twice—once through the relationship IS_DEPARTURE_POINT_FOR and once through the relationship IS_ARRIVAL_POINT_FOR.

In order the distinguish between the two appearances of the foreign-key attribute CITY_CODE in the FLIGHT_SEGMENT entity, one appearance is given the rolename DEPARTURE_CITY_CODE, and the other is given the rolename ARRIVAL_CITY_CODE. Without rolenames, CITY_CODE would initially appear twice in FLIGHT_SEGMENT. One occurrence would be eliminated by the ''same name, same meaning'' rule, but one of the relationships would be lost in the process.

Figure 3.16(b) shows more completely the rolenames assumed by the CITY_CODE attribute in the FLIGHT_SEGMENT entity. The Data Modeling Technique uses the convention of ''dotting'' a rolename, for example, DEPARTURE_CITY_CODE. CITY_CODE, to show also its source name.

Existence Dependency

A connection relationship may have *existence dependency*. That is, if there is an existence dependency between two entities, A and B, then the rule is

Each instance of entity B must have a corresponding instance of entity A.

Entity B is then said to be existence dependent on entity A. Note that entity A must be the parent of entity B in the connection relationship and that an existence dependency occurs when the foreign key for the relationship cannot be null.

If there is an existence dependency in Fig. 3.13(b) associated with the TEACHES relationship, then a CLASS_SECTION entity instance cannot exist without being associated with a PROFESSOR entity instance. Each CLASS_SECTION entity instance must have a nonnull FACULTY# for its professor. If there is an existence dependency associated with the HAS_ON_FILE relationship of Fig. 3.9, then a LETTER_OF_RECOMMENDATION instance cannot exist without being associated with a GRADUATE_STUDENT instance. Each LETTER_OF_RECOMMENDATION instance must have a nonnull MATRIC# for its associated graduate student.

Many-to-many connection relationships do not exhibit existence dependency. For example, there is no existence dependency associated with the ENROLLS relationship of Fig. 3.13(a). A class section will exist regardless of the existence of students enrolled in it (at least until it is canceled), and a student will exist regardless of whether he or she is currently enrolled in any class sections. Note, however, that there are existence dependencies in the resolution of this many-to-many relationship in Fig. 3.14. An ENROLLMENT instance cannot exist without being associated with a CLASS_SECTION instance and with a STUDENT instance.

Another example of a connection relationship without existence dependency is shown in Fig. 3.15(a). This model can be read as "A counselor may staff many classes, but a class can be staffed by no more than one counselor; some classes may not be staffed by any counselor." Thus the class will exist regardless of whether it has been staffed by a counselor, and a counselor will continue to exist regardless of whether he or she has staffed a class.

This relationship can be resolved into two relationships that do have existence dependency, as shown in Fig. 3.15(b). Here the TEACHING_ASSISTANT entity is existence dependent on both the COUNSELOR and the CLASS entities. A person cannot be a teaching assistant unless he or she is assigned to a class by a counselor. Note that the process of resolution used here is the same as that used in obtaining Fig. 3.14 from Fig. 3.13(a).

Many-to-many relationships and zero-or-one-to-many connection relationships are sometimes known as *nonspecific relationships* because they bury existence dependencies. These relationships are made specific by resolving a nonspecific relationship into two specific relationships, making a many-to-many connection into two one-to-many connections. A zero-or-one-to-many connection becomes a one-to-many relationship and a one-to-zero-or-one relationship.

Call the parent entity of a relationship E1 and the child entity E2. The primary key of E1 is the set A of attributes, which are also a foreign key in E2. If the attributes A in E2 cannot be null, then E2 is existence dependent on E1. If an instance of E2 exists, it must be associated with an instance of E1. On the other hand, if one or more attributes of A in E2 can be null, then E2 is not existence dependent on E1. An instance of E2 can exist without being associated with an instance of E1.

Identifier Dependency

A connection relationship may have identifier dependency. If there is a relationship between entities A and B, then entity B is said to be identifier dependent on entity A if, and only if,

> the primary key of A appearing as a foreign-key attribute in B is completely contained in the primary key of B.

Entity A's migrated key thus is an essential part of the identifier of entity B.

In the Data Modeling Technique, the distinction between relationships that have identifier dependency and those that do not is shown by whether the relationship arc is a solid or dashed line. For example, the model from Fig. 3.14 with key attributes is shown in Fig. 3.17. Both relationships are identifying relationships, and the primary keys both appear in the child entity's primary key.

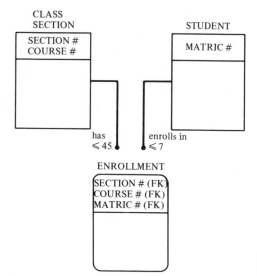

FIGURE 3.17. Logical data model with two identifying connection relationships.

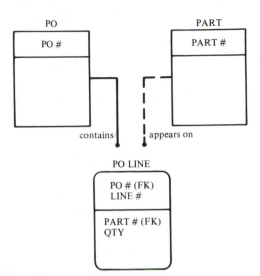

FIGURE 3.18. Logical data model with one identifying and one nonidentifying relationship.

In Fig. 3.18, one of the relationships has identifier dependency and one does not. The primary key of P_O_LINE includes the primary key of P_O but does not include the primary key of PART.

The Data Modeling Technique has an option that suppresses the printing of foreign-key attributes on diagrams. When this option is used, there must be a distinction other than the placement of attributes to indicate identifier dependency. Here the distinction is made by using either solid or dashed arcs.

An entity that is not identifier dependent on any other entity is graphed with a square-cornered box, and an entity that is identifier dependent on at least one other entity is graphed with a round-cornered box. Non-identifier-dependent entities can stand alone, but identifier-dependent entities are always found with other entities. Note that identifier dependency always implies existence dependency.

Referential Integrity

Referential integrity is a constraint that must hold for connection relationships with existence (or identifier) dependency. Referential integrity is the assertion that if entity B is existence dependent on entity A, then

> the value of the foreign-key attribute(s) in an instance of entity B must equal the value of the primary key of the associated instance of entity A.

For example, if employee is existence dependent on department in Fig. 3.7, then referential integrity asserts that

for every instance of the EMPLOYEE entity the value of the foreign-key attribute DEPARTMENT# must match the value of the primary key DE- PARTMENT# in the associated DEPARTMENT entity instance.

Similarly, for the relationships in Fig. 3.15(b), if teaching assistant is exist- ence dependent on counselor and on class, then referential integrity asserts that

for every instance of the TEACHING_ASSISTANT entity, the value of the foreign-key attribute COUNSELOR_ID must match the value of the primary key in the associated COUNSELOR entity instance, and

for every instance of the TEACHING_ASSISTANT entity, the value of the foreign-key attribute CLASS# must match the value of the primary key in the associated CLASS entity instance.

The representation of referential integrity constraints in a data model is im- portant because (1) a model that expresses referential integrity constraints more explicitly represents data semantics than a model that does not and (2) referential integrity can be used to check and maintain data quality.

Referential integrity is an assertion about entity instances. This assertion can be applied when the database is updated to determine whether the update violates the stated semantic rules. For example, an update of the database modeled in Fig. 3.7 should be rejected if it attempts to add an EMPLOYEE instance with a DEPARTMENT# that does not already exist as the primary key of a DE- PARTMENT instance. Any update that relates an EMPLOYEE instance to a DEPARTMENT instance with a nonmatching DEPARTMENT# should also be rejected. An update should be rejected if it attempts to delete a DEPARTMENT instance for which EMPLOYEE instances would continue to exist. The EM- PLOYEE instances cannot exist without being associated with that DEPART- MENT instance. Note that changing their DEPARTMENT# values would be a valid way to associate them with other DEPARTMENT instances.

For the database modeled in Fig. 3.15(b), all of the following updates should be rejected:

- Add a TEACHING_ASSISTANT instance for which either the CLASS# or COUNSELOR_ID does not match the key of an existing CLASS or COUN- SELOR instance.
- Relate a TEACHING_ASSISTANT instance to either a CLASS or a COUN- SELOR instance without a match on CLASS# or COUNSELOR_ID, respec- tively.
- Delete a CLASS instance for which there is a TEACHING_ASSISTANT instance that would continue to exist.
- Delete a COUNSELOR instance for which there are TEACHING_ ASSISTANT instances that would continue to exist.

CATEGORY RELATIONSHIPS

Connection relationships associate different kinds of entities, whereas category relationships associate similar entities.

A *category relationship* has the following characteristics:

- Is named MUST_BE_A or CAN_BE_A.
- Relates a generic entity to a subtype entity.
- Has cardinality of one-to-zero-or-one.
- Has a subtype discriminator.
- The attributes of the generic entity are inherited implicitly by the subtype entity.
- Has existence dependency.
- Must conform to the referential integrity constraint.
- May have identifier dependency.

The Data Modeling Technique uses an open circle to represent a category relationship. Figure 3.19(a) models a situation in which there are two types of employees, hourly and salaried. Each employee must be either an hourly employee or a salaried employee but cannot be both. The attributes of the generic entity EMPLOYEE are also applicable to the subtype entities HOURLY_EMPLOYEE and the subtype SALARIED_EMPLOYEE.

Figure 3.19(b) models another situation in which there are three types of employees, student, faculty member, and staff. An employee can be a student or a faculty member or staff or none of these.

In the real world, an instance of the STUDENT entity represents exactly the same object as the EMPLOYEE entity instance with which it is associated in this relationship. By contrast, a connection relationship always associates instances that represent different real-world objects. For example, a FLIGHT_SEGMENT instance in Fig. 3.16 represents a real-world object different from those represented by the CITY instances to which it is related.

Subtype Discriminator

A diagram of a category relationship shows the generic entity on top, with a circle containing an attribute of the generic entity whose value determines in which subtype a particular dependent entity instance resides. This attribute is called the *subtype discriminator*. In Fig. 3.19(a), the subtype discriminator is the attribute COMPENSATION_TYPE, whose value determines whether a particular employee is hourly or salaried. In Fig. 3.19(b), the subtype discriminator is the attribute STATUS, whose value determines whether a particular employee is student, staff, or faculty. Note that the subtype discriminator is an attribute of the generic entity, not of the relationship itself.

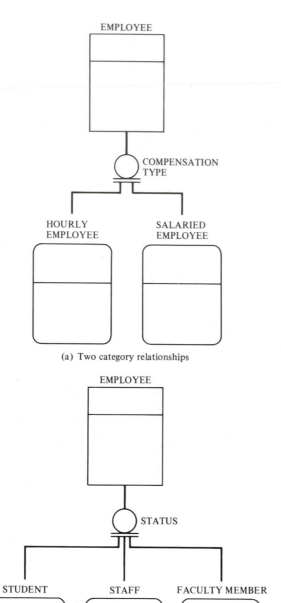

EMPLOYEE

○ COMPENSATION
  TYPE

HOURLY
EMPLOYEE

SALARIED
EMPLOYEE

(a) Two category relationships

EMPLOYEE

○ STATUS

STUDENT   STAFF   FACULTY MEMBER

(b) Three category relationships

FIGURE 3.19. Examples of category relationships.

A set of category relationships with the same subtype discriminator is called a *class of categories*. Figure 3.19(a) has two category relationships, both in one class; Fig. 3.19(b) has three category relationships, all in one class. Each category circle on a Data Model diagram represents a class of category relationships.

An entity may have more than one subtype discriminator, as shown in Fig. 3.20. Here there are two subclassifications of buildings: a BUILDING instance's USAGE_TYPE indicates whether it is for residential, office, retail or other purposes; its CONSTRUCTION_TYPE indicates whether it is custom built, prefabricated, or other. A given BUILDING instance can have values for both USAGE_TYPE and CONSTRUCTION_TYPE, for example, a custom-built office building or a prefabricated residential building. Merging the models of Figs. 3.19(a) and 3.19(b) also yields an entity with more than one subtype discriminator.

Mutual Exclusivity

A subtype discriminator can have only one value for any instance of the generic entity. Thus an instance of the generic entity may be related to only one subtype

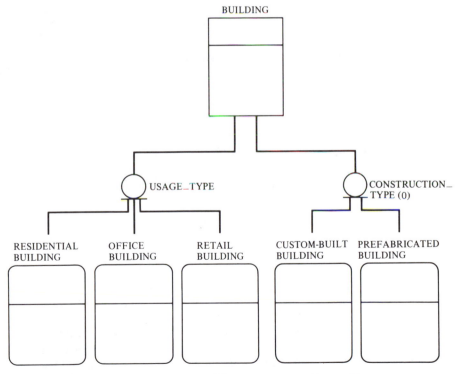

FIGURE 3.20. Example of entity with two category hierarchies.

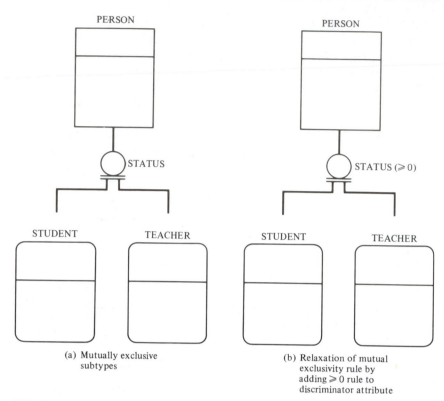

FIGURE 3.21. Examples of category hierarchies.

instance in a class of categories. According to Fig. 3.20, a building cannot be both an office building and a residential building, nor can it be both custom built and prefabricated. If these rules are not true, then the model does not correctly reflect reality. This model does not depict a building that is partly residential, partly office space, and partly retail stores.

Similarly, the model of Fig. 3.21(a) says that a person can be either a student or a teacher and cannot depict a situation in which a person can be both a student and a teacher. Figure 3.21(b) models this situation by adding a rule to the discriminator attribute, indicating that PERSON instance can have more than one value for STATUS. This convention for relaxing the mutual exclusivity constraint is rarely used.

Mutual exclusivity can be used to check and maintain data quality. Thus an update of the database modeled in Fig. 3.20 should be rejected if it attempts to make a building both an office building and a residential building.

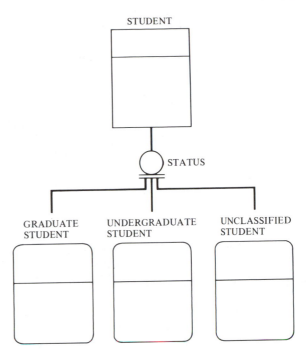

FIGURE 3.22. Examples of category relationships with total set of subtypes. Every value of this discriminator attribute has a matching subtype entity.

Totality

A class of categories is said to be *total* if every valid value of the subtype discriminator has a corresponding subtype entity. The Data Modeling Technique represents a total class of categories by drawing a double line rather than a single line below the category relationship circle. For example, Fig. 3.22 shows a complete set of student subtypes. The domain of values for the subtype discriminator and the subtype entities shown in the model together determine whether a class of categories is total.

Existence Dependency

Existence dependency always holds in a category relationship. For an instance of a subtype to exist, it must have an associated instance of the generic entity. An office building cannot exist without being a building; an hourly employee cannot exist without being an employee.

If a subtype discriminator is allowed to have a null value and/or the set of values is larger than the number of subtypes (i.e., the class of categories is not total), then the existence of an instance of the generic entity does not necessarily imply the existence of a corresponding subtype entity. For example, a null value in CONSTRUCTION_TYPE in Fig. 3.20 would indicate that a given BUILD-ING instance is neither custom built nor prefabricated. Its construction type could be unknown or unavailable.

Referential Integrity

A category relationship must always conform to the referential integrity constraint. Primary keys migrate to become foreign-key attributes in category relationships in the same way that they do in connection relationships. A subtype entity instance must be associated with the generic entity instance whose primary-key value matches the subtype's foreign-key attribute value.

Identifier Dependency

A category relationship may or may not have identifier dependency. For example, Fig. 3.23 shows a situation in which identifier dependency does not hold. The generic entity is INVESTMENT, with a primary key of DATE, SOURCE, and TYPE. The subtype entities are STOCK, BOND, REAL_ESTATE, and CD. Although each of these subtypes inherits the generic entity's primary key (as well as implicitly all the rest of its attributes), the foreign-key attribute is not part of the subtypes' primary keys.

This example shows that a subtype entity may itself be a generic entity. The REAL_ESTATE entity has two subtype entities, COMMERCIAL_PROPERTY and RESIDENTIAL_PROPERTY. Just as attributes are inherited implicitly from INVESTMENT by REAL_ESTATE, so also are attributes inherited implicitly from REAL_ESTATE by its subtypes.

If all category relationships were required to have identifier dependency, then it would be possible only to model category hierarchies, not category networks. All the examples shown so far have been hierarchies.

OTHER AVAILABLE DATA-MODELING TECHNIQUES

Many data-modeling techniques have been proposed in the technical database literature, though only a few are used in companies and organizations. In this section we shall describe the best-known techniques.

The Network Model

The network model was developed by the CODASYL (Conference on Data Systems Languages) DBTG (Data Base Task Group) in the late 1960s and the

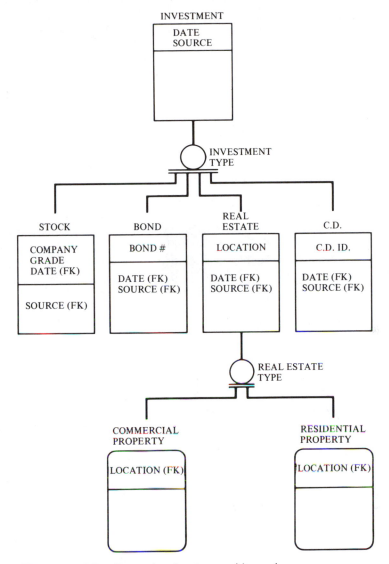

FIGURE 3.23. Example of category hierarchy.

1970s and by Cincom Systems, Inc. with its commercial database management system TOTAL. The network model attempts to raise data management concern above the level of physical file structures to a consideration of logical structures. Today it is not generally considered to be a semantic data-modeling technique, because it is closely tied to the capabilities of particular DBMSs and has limited semantic expression capability.

The network model deals with *record types, data items,* and *set types,* which are roughly analogous to entities, attributes, and relationships. Until the late

1970s, however, there was considerable mixing of logical and physical database parameters within a single network model. The network model will be covered in greater detail in Chapters 6 and 11.

The Relational Model

The *relational model* was introduced by E. F. Codd of IBM in the early 1970s, and it offers a simple, yet mathematically rigorous approach to data modeling. It deals with data in terms of tables, and relationships across tables are formed through the sharing of attributes, usually through foreign-key attributes.

The relational model has received the attention of many database researchers over the years and is currently in vogue in commercial DBMSs. But despite its widespread use, the relational model today is not generally considered to be a logical data-modeling technique, primarily because of its limited semantic expression capability. The relational model will be covered in greater detail in Chapters 4, 5, and 10.

The Entity-Set Model

One of the early logical data-modeling techniques was the *entity-set model,* introduced in 1973 by researchers at IBM. This model recognizes entities as collections of *entity name–value pairs.* There is no concept of attributes; everything (e.g., name, age, department number) is an entity. Relationships are binary; that is, any given relationship can associate only two entities. An outgrowth of this modeling technique is the Information Analysis (IA) product from Control Data Corporation. All relationships are binary.

The Entity-Relationship Model

The *entity-relationship model* was introduced in 1975 by Peter Chen as an alternative to the relational, network, and entity-set models. It depicts entities, relationships, and attributes. Relationships are *n*-ary; that is, any given relationship can associate one, two, or more entities, and a model can show existence dependency among entities.

The Smiths' Abstraction Model

The primary contribution of the *Smiths' abstraction model,* published in 1977, is the distinction between *aggregation* and *generalization relationships,* which we call *connection* and *category relationships.* The model introduces the convention of entities' having noun names and includes a graphical notation for aggregation and generalization networks.

The Semantic Data Model

The *semantic data model,* published in 1978, introduces another level of explicitness in the representation of logical data–modeling constructs, recognizing three types of entities (which it called *classes*): *concrete objects* (physical), *abstractions* (generalizations), and *aggregates* (homogenous collections). The model also introduces the concept of *events,* which are actions in which objects participate, and identifies three types of attributes.

IDEF1

IDEF1 (ICAM [Integrated Computer-Aided Manufacturing] Definition Method—1) was developed in the late 1970s under the auspices of the U.S. Air Force. It is a practical hybrid of the entity-relationship model and the relational model and has companion methods for modeling activities (IDEF0) and system dynamics (IDEF2).

A later generation of IDEF1 is called the *IDEF1-Extended (IDEF1X).* IDEF1-Extended is derived from the Data Modeling Technique, which has its roots partially in IDEF1.

The Functional Data Model

The functional data model and its modeling language, DAPLEX, published in 1981, provide a rigorous framework for modeling data as entities. It expresses relationships among entities as functions that can be nested, for example, Rank(Instructor(Course)). Like the early entity-set model, it has no concept of attribute, rather, the properties of an entity result from applying functions to the entity. DAPLEX can be used to describe data models, to define constraints in a data model, and to pose requests against data models.

Data Designer

Data Designer is a commercial product licensed by Knowledgeware, Inc., formerly Database Design, Inc. (DDI). It is an automated design tool and combines user-view data models. The data-modeling technique is based on a bubble-charting technique developed by James Martin, in which ovals represent entities and arcs represent relationships. Data Designer generates normalized data models (see Chapter 5), based on input regarding dependencies among attributes.

Design Manager

Design Manager is a commercial product licensed by MSP, Ltd. that works in conjunction with MSP's data dictionary product, Data Manager, for the storage and analysis of data models. It provides automated support for describing data models and transforming them into database designs.

CLOSING COMMENTS

The success of commercial data-modeling techniques attests to the growing recognition of the importance of data modeling in communicating and discovering data semantics. Data modeling is used routinely to

- increase organizations' understanding of their data and their operations.
- document data resources.
- assess off-the-shelf software packages.
- plan information systems.
- design information systems.
- integrate data resources.
- design and implement physical databases.

Logical data modeling is an essential part of the database project lifecycle and is used to document existing environments and to plan future data resources. Data modeling is also used to develop project data models and to integrate those models into an evolving conceptual schema, which is a special-purpose logical data model. The results of data modeling can then be transformed into physical database designs.

TERMS

activity model	function model
aggregation relationship	generalization relationship
alternate key	generic entity
assertion	hierarchic model
attribute	identifier dependency
candidate key	key
category relationship	logical data model
class of categories	network model
compound key	physical data model
connection relationship	primary key
entity	process model
existence dependency	referential integrity
foreign-key attribute	relational model

relationship   semantics
rolename   subtype discriminator
semantic data model

REVIEW EXERCISES

1. Define each of the terms in the preceding list.

2. Select a business of interest to you, for example, banking, real estate, trucking, or education. List twenty-five to thirty objects of interest in that business, and determine whether each is an entity, attribute, or relationship.

3. Using the diagramming syntax introduced in this chapter, draw a data model from the entities and relationships you found in answering Exercise 2.

4. Identify the relationship cardinalities and designate the keys for the entities in the model you developed in answering Exercise 3.

5. Resolve the many-to-many relationships in the model you developed in answering Exercise 4.

6. Identify the foreign-key attributes in the model you developed in answering Exercise 5.

7. Add nonkey attributes to the model you developed in answering Exercise 6.

8. Identify occurrences of each of the following in your model:
    a. connection relationships.
    b. category relationships.
    c. existence dependencies.
    d. identifier dependencies.

9. Give an example of a situation in which an alternate key could have a null value.

10. Under what circumstances does the sharing of an attribute by multiple entities indicate a connection relationship? A category relationship?

11. What is the difference between existence dependency and referential integrity? Does one imply the other?

12. What is the difference between a category relationship in which the subtype discriminator can have a null value and one in which it cannot?

13. Model a three-level category hierarchy. Explain the inheritance of attributes from the generic entity to the subtype entities. (Hint: Zoo animals make a good example.)

14. What is the difference between a category hierarchy and a category network? Give an example of a modeling situation that requires a category network.

15. Build a data model that represents the following:
    • All students are either graduate students or undergraduate students.
    • All employees are either faculty or staff.
    • Some staff employees are students.

16. Build a data model that represents the following:
    • All parts are either purchased or manufactured.
    • All products are either custom made or stock.
    • All products are made of one or more parts.
    • A product can be used in making other products.

17. Build a data model that represents the following:
    • A record type can contain many fields.
    • A file can contain many record types.
    • A database can contain many files.
    • A DBMS can manage many databases.
    • A database can be managed by only one DBMS.
    • A file can be part of only one database.
    • A record type can appear in many files.
    • A field can appear in many records.

18. Find out whether a logical data–modeling technique is used in your organization. If you are a student, investigate the college administrative data-processing department or a company in your community. Which one(s) are used? How are they used?

19. Compare two or more of the available data-modeling techniques.

20. Compare two or more of the automated data-modeling techniques.

21. Database researchers have extensively investigated the problem of null values. Write a report that distinguishes among the various types of nulls and includes a proposal for how these types of nulls could be represented in a data-modeling technique.

22. Compare the principles of data modeling introduced here with the principles of semantic networks from the artificial intelligence field.

23. Compare the principles of data modeling introduced here with the principles of frames from the artificial intelligence field.

REFERENCES

Brodie, M. The application of data types to database semantic integrity, *Information Systems* 5 (1980):287–296.

Brown, R. G. *ADAM—General Information Manual*. Mountain View, Calif.: The Database Design Group, 1983.

———. *Logical Database Design Techniques*. Mountain View, Calif.: The Database Design Group, 1982.

Chen, P. P-S. The entity-relationship model—Toward a unified view of data, *ACM Trans. on Database Systems* 1 (March 1976):9–36.

CODASYL. *Data Base Task Group Report*. New York: ACM, 1971.

CODASYL, *Data Description Language Committee Journal of Development 1978*. Ottawa: Material Data Management Branch, Canadian Federal Government, 1978.

CODASYL. *Data Description Language Journal of Development, June 1973. National Bureau of Standards Handbook 113*. Washington, D.C.: U.S. Government Printing Office, January 1974.

Codd, E. F. Extending the database relational model to capture more meaning, *ACM Trans. on Database Systems* 4 (December 1979):397–434.

———. A relational model of data for large, shared data banks,'' *Communications ACM* 13 (June 1970):377–387.

D. Appleton Company, Inc. *Data Modeling Technique Reference Manual, PCFS-DMT-3.0*. Manhattan Beach, Calif.: 1985.

Database Design Inc. *Data Designer User Guide*. Ann Arbor, Mich.: Database Design, Inc., 1981.

Hammer, M., and D. McLeod. The semantic data model: A modelling mechanism for data base applications, *Proc. ACM SIGMOD Int'l. Conf. on Management of Data*. Austin, Tex., May 31–June 2, 1978, pp. 26–36.

Martin, J. *Computer Data Base Organization*. Englewood Cliffs, N.J.: Prentice-Hall, 1977.

Roussopoulos, N., and J. Mylopoulos. Using semantic networks for data base management, *Proc. 1975 Conf. on Very Large Databases*. Framingham, Mass., September 22–24, 1975, pp. 144–172.

Senko, M. E., E. B. Altman, M. M. Astrahan, and P. L. Fehder. Data structures and accessing in data-base systems, *IBM Systems Journal* 12 (1973):30–93.

Shipman, D. W. The functional data model and the data language DAPLEX, *ACM Trans. on Database Systems* 6 (March 1981):140–173.

Smith, J. M., and D. C. P. Smith. Database abstractions: Aggregation, *Communications ACM* 20 (June 1977):405–413.

———. Database abstractions: Aggregation and generalization, *ACM Trans. on Database Systems* 2 (June 1977):105–133.

CHAPTER 4

Mapping to the Relational Model

This chapter shows how logical data modeling can be used to design relational databases. The relational model was proposed by E. F. Codd, who initially published it in 1970. His ideas were based on set theory and relational calculus, and through the 1970s and 1980s, the relational approach received the attention of many database researchers. *Relational database* is an important buzzword in today's commercial data management marketplace. Many organizations are implementing relational databases for their decision support systems, and some are converting their production databases to support by relational database management systems.

OBJECTIVES

The original objectives of the relational model were simplicity, data independence, and the rigorous treatment of derivability, redundancy, and consistency.

Simplicity

The basic relational model is simpler than are other data-modeling techniques, as it views data as if they were formatted into tables. A table's columns represent the table's properties, and a table's rows represent the values of those properties. Connections between tables are formed by columns with the same name or comparable values.

Humans find it quite natural to view data in tables: general ledgers, tax rates, class lists, grade records, and telephone listings are just a few examples of commonplace tables.

Data Independence

The relational model provides more data independence than do the other data-modeling approaches that are tied directly to commercial DBMS support (see Chapters 6 and 7). The relational model insulates application programs from growth in the data resource and changes in data representation, as users of a relational database need not know anything about that database's physical characteristics. Logical and physical database considerations are separate. The relational model addresses only logical concerns, whereas the physical characteristics of a relational database are "left to the implementor." Viewing data logically as tables does not imply that they are physically stored as tables.

Rigor

The relational model has a firm mathematical foundation, which allows issues to be addressed that can be elusive in the less theoretical models. Such questions include, "What data are derivable from other data?" "Is there redundancy in these data?" and "Are there inconsistencies in these data?"

RELATIONAL STRUCTURE

The structural components of the relational model are *relations, attributes, domains, tuples, keys,* and *representation*. Formally, a relational database has been defined as

> a finite collection of time-varying relations defined according to a finite collection of domains. A relation on *n* domain sets D1, D2, . . . , D*n* (not necessarily distinct), is a set of elements of the form (d1, d2, . . . , d*n*). Each d*j* is a value from a domain D*j*.

Relations

A *relation* is a named table with columns and rows. An example of a relation named TEACHER is shown in Fig. 4.1. The *degree* of a relation is its number of columns. The relation in Fig. 4.1 has eight columns; thus its degree is 8. It

TEACHER

TEACHER NAME	FACULTY #	RANK	DEPARTMENT NAME	COLLEGE NAME	PHONE	BIRTH DATE	HIRE DATE
Wiley	62186	Assist.	MIS	BPA	12346	7-11-48	8-15-78
Ganguly	13462	Full	GEOLOGY	GEOSCI	14946	10-1-46	8-15-77
Loomis	54216	Full	GEOLOGY	GEOSCI	14648	5-25-46	8-15-76
Brown	12345	Full	MIS	BPA	12613	10-3-50	8-15-82
Smith	71246	Lect	ACCTG	BPA	19126	12-1-56	9-1-83
Boronov	42136	Lect	COMP SCI	ENGR	16216	3-15-52	8-16-82
Lee	32143	Assoc.	COMP SCI	ENGR	15266	7-1-40	6-15-69
Hall	51362	Assoc.	ACCTG	BPA	12614	7-8-56	8-15-76
Little	42137	Lect	GEOLOGY	GEOSCI	14222	3-6-58	8-15-84
Hill	31192	Assist.	MIS	BPA	12346	12-2-58	8-15-84
Brown	52163	Assist.	COMP SCI	ENGR	12111	3-2-51	8-15-82
North	12916	Lect	GEOLOGY	GEOSCI	12513	6-9-54	8-15-84
North	12917	Assoc.	MIS	BPA	12877	10-3-52	8-15-84

FIGURE 4.1.   Example of relation instance table.

might also be called an *8-ary relation,* although the *n-ary* terminology is more often used to distinguish binary relations (where $n = 2$) from other relations (where $n > 2$).

Attributes

Each column or *attribute* (see definition in Chapter 3) of a relation has a name. The attributes of the TEACHER relation in Fig. 4.1 are TEACHER_NAME, FACULTY#, RANK, DEPARTMENT_NAME, COLLEGE_NAME, PHONE, BIRTH_DATE, and HIRE_DATE. The attributes in a relation can appear in any order, and the relation will convey the same meaning. For example, switching the order of FACULTY# and BIRTH_DATE in the TEACHER relation does not change its meaning.

Domains

An attribute's values are taken from a *domain,* using the same terminology as in Chapter 3. There are eight domain sets represented in the TEACHER relation; however, two attributes take their values from the same domain. BIRTH_DATE and HIRE_DATE both are drawn from the DATE domain.

Tuples

The elements of a relation are the rows, or *tuples,* in the table, each row containing *n* values, one for each attribute. When a relation represents an entity, each row represents an entity instance.

Rows, or tuples, can appear in any order, and the table will convey the same meaning. Note that order independence is not found in all data models. For example, the CODASYL network model (introduced in Chapter 6) allows a collection of related entity instances (there called *records*) to be designated as either FIFO (first-in, first-out) or LIFO (last-in, first-out), so that their order will convey a meaning.

Keys

Every relation has a set of candidate keys, one of which is selected as the primary key. Candidate key, primary key, and alternate key all have the same definitions in the relational model as were used in Chapter 3.

Representation

A common convention for representing a relation is to give its name, followed by its attribute names, with its primary key underscored. For example, the relation shown in Fig. 4.1 is

TEACHER (TEACHER_NAME, FACULTY#, RANK,
        DEPARTMENT_NAME, COLLEGE_NAME, PHONE,
        BIRTH_DATE, HIRE_DATE)

The table in Fig. 4.1 is formally called an *instance table* and shows example rows of the TEACHER relation. A relation's structure is sometimes called its *intension,* or *schema.* By contrast, an instance table for a relation reflects the relation's rows at some point in time. The attribute values in those rows are called the relation's *extension,* which changes as the population of the database changes. Conversely, a relation's intension is fixed, unless the relation's meaning is changed to include different attributes. Intension conveys meaning, whereas extension conveys facts.

It is not possible just to look at an instance table and determine whether the primary key of the relation has been designated correctly. If there are duplicate values for the selected key, then clearly an error has been made. The absence of duplicate values, however, does not imply that the key is correct but shows only that the key is sufficient for this set of rows. Unless all possible valid instances (i.e., rows) have been shown, it is not possible to determine whether the key might have duplicate values. As in other aspects of logical data modeling, it is necessary to know the characteristics of the real world being modeled in order to identify the candidate keys.

RELATIONAL ASSERTIONS

There are two assertions in the relational model that protect the integrity of a set of relations. An *assertion* is merely a constraint or qualification or restriction that applies to a model. The first assertion concerns primary-key values, and the second, foreign-key attribute values.

Primary-Key Assertion

The primary-key assertion is

No component of a primary-key value may be null.

In Chapter 3, an entity's primary key was defined as a unique identifier for instances of that entity, and the same terminology is used in the relational model. So, if a primary key had a null value, then its tuple (i.e., entity instance) would not have a unique identifier. Similarly, parts of a compound primary-key value cannot be null, because then unique identification would not be possible.

In the TEACHER relation (Fig. 4.1), FACULTY# is the primary key, and so each TEACHER tuple's FACULTY# must have a nonnull value.

Foreign-Key Attribute Assertion

The foreign-key attribute assertion again uses the terminology introduced in Chapter 3, with the term *home relation* referring to the relation from which the foreign-key attribute migrated. The foreign-key attribute assertion is

A foreign-key attribute's value must be either null or equal to the primary-key value of some tuple in its home relation.

When this assertion is tightened to exclude null foreign-key attribute values, it becomes the referential integrity constraint, which was introduced in Chapter 3.

Assume that in the TEACHER example, DEPARTMENT_NAME, COL-LEGE_NAME is a compound foreign-key attribute, relating the TEACHER relation to a UNIVERSITY_UNIT relation:

UNIVERSITY_UNIT (<u>COLLEGE_NAME</u>, <u>DEPARTMENT_NAME</u>, DEAN_FACULTY#, DATE_ESTABLISHED)

According to the foreign-key attribute assertion, either each TEACHER tuple must have a null value for COLLEGE_NAME, DEPARTMENT_NAME, or there must be a tuple in UNIVERSITY_UNIT with that value for its primary key. If the referential integrity constraint holds, then the null-value option is not allowed.

RELATIONAL OPERATORS

Any relational data manager should provide data manipulation capabilities that are at least as powerful as the relational model's operators are. The relational operators' operands are always relations, and the result of applying a relational operator is always a relation. There are several different notations for the relational operators, one of which we shall use here.

The three basic relational operators are PROJECT, SELECT, and JOIN. Many languages provide higher-level commands, using the basic relational operators as primitives.

Project

The PROJECT operator extracts attributes from a relation, forming a new relation:

$$R2 := PROJECT (R1) (A1, A2, \ldots, An);$$

The source relation is R1, and the resulting relation R2 contains the n attributes A1, A2, through An, which are projected (i.e., extracted) from R1. Any duplicate tuples that may result in the projected relation are removed and do not appear in R2.

For example,

TEACHING_UNIT := PROJECT (TEACHER)
(DEPARTMENT_NAME, COLLEGE_NAME);

creates a new relation named TEACHING_UNIT with two attributes, DEPARTMENT_NAME and COLLEGE_NAME. These columns are extracted from the TEACHER relation, and the new relation represents those departments and colleges that have teachers. Each row of the TEACHING_UNIT relation is distinct; any duplicate DEPARTMENT_NAME, COLLEGE_NAME tuples are removed during the projection. Figure 4.2 shows the instance table for the TEACHING_UNIT relation.

A variation of this PROJECT operator allows the attributes in the result relation to be renamed.

Select

The SELECT operator, or the RESTRICT operator, extracts rows from a relation, selecting those that meet some criterion and forming a new relation:

$$R2 := SELECT (R1) (condition);$$

TEACHING_UNIT

DEPARTMENT NAME	COLLEGE NAME
ACCTG	BPA
MIS	BPA
GEOLOGY	GEOSCI
COMP SCI	ENGR

FIGURE 4.2. Instance table after applying PROJECT (TEACHER) (DEPARTMENT_NAME, COLLEGE_NAME) to instance table of Fig. 4.1.

The source relation is R1, and the resulting relation R2 contains the same attributes as does R1. Only the rows of R1 that meet the stated condition are used, and any duplicate rows that may result are removed as part of the selection and do not appear in R2.

For example,

$$\text{TENURED\_TEACHER} := \text{SELECT (TEACHER)}$$
$$(\text{RANK} = \text{'Full' OR 'Assoc.'});$$

creates a new relation named TENURED_TEACHER with the same eight attributes that TEACHER has, but with a subset of TEACHER's rows. These rows are extracted from the TEACHER relation, and the new relation represents those teachers whose rank is either 'Full' or 'Assoc.' Each row of the TENURED_TEACHER relation is distinct; any duplicate tuples are removed during the selection. Figure 4.3 shows the instance table for TENURED_TEACHER.

The following example shows a SELECT followed by a PROJECT:

$$\text{TEMPORARY} := \text{SELECT (TEACHER) (DEPARTMENT\_NAME} =$$
$$\text{'MIS');}$$
$$\text{MIS\_TEACHER\_NAMES} := \text{PROJECT (TEMPORARY)}$$
$$\text{(TEACHER\_NAME);}$$

This creates a relation named MIS_TEACHER_NAMES, which contains the names of the teachers in the MIS department.

Join

The JOIN operator extracts rows from two relations, matching the two by some criterion and forming a new relation with those rows.

$$\text{R3} := \text{JOIN (R1) (condition) (R2);}$$

The source relations are R1 and R2, and the resulting relation R3 contains the combined attributes of R1 and R2. Rows from R1 and R2 are matched according

TENURED_TEACHERS

TEACHER NAME	FACULTY #	RANK	DEPARTMENT NAME	COLLEGE NAME	PHONE	BIRTH DATE	HIRE DATE
Ganguly	13462	Full	GEOLOGY	GEOSCI	14946	10-1-46	8-15-77
Loomis	54216	Full	GEOLOGY	GEOSCI	14648	5-25-46	8-15-76
Brown	12345	Full	MIS	BPA	12613	10-3-50	8-15-82
Lee	32143	Assoc.	COMP SCI	ENGR	15266	7-1-40	6-15-69
Hall	51362	Assoc.	ACCTG	BPA	12614	7-8-56	8-15-75
North	12917	Assoc.	MIS	BPA	12877	10-3-52	8-15-84

FIGURE 4.3. Instance table after applying RESTRICT (TEACHER) (RANK = "Full" OR "Assoc.") to instance table of Fig. 4.1.

to the stated condition; any duplicate rows that may result are removed as part of the join and do not appear in R3.

For example, we shall use as sources the following relations:

STUDENT (STUDENT_NAME, AGE, DEGREE_EXPECTED,
     MATRIC#)
TEACHER (TEACHER_NAME, FACULTY#, RANK,
     DEPARTMENT_NAME, COLLEGE_NAME, PHONE,
     BIRTH_DATE, HIRE_DATE)
UNIVERSITY_UNIT (COLLEGE_NAME, DEPARTMENT_NAME,
     DEAN_FACULTY#, DATE_ESTABLISHED)

The operation

STUDENT_TEACHER := JOIN (STUDENT) (STUDENT_NAME =
                         TEACHER_NAME) (TEACHER);

creates a new relation named STUDENT_TEACHER with twelve attributes (four from STUDENT and eight from TEACHER). Each row of STUDENT_TEACHER is the result of combining a row from STUDENT and a row from TEACHER, which have matching values of STUDENT_NAME and TEACHER_NAME. The new relation represents those students who are also teachers. Instance tables for STUDENT and STUDENT_TEACHER are given in Fig. 4.4. See Fig. 4.1 for the instance table for the TEACHER relation.

As another example,

TEMP1 := JOIN (TEACHER) (FACULTY# = DEAN_FACULTY#)
                                    (UNIVERSITY_UNIT);
TEMP2 := SELECT (TEMP1)(HIRE_DATE > 70/01/01);
DEAN_INFO := PROJECT (TEMP2)(TEACHER_NAME, RANK);

first uses a JOIN to match tuples from TEACHER and UNIVERSITY_UNIT on equal FACULTY# and DEAN_FACULTY# values, then SELECTs from the resulting tuples those with a HIRE_DATE after the first day of 1970, and finally PROJECTs the TEACHER_NAME and RANK attributes. The resulting DEAN_INFO relation has two attributes, with a row for each dean hired after January 1, 1970.

The STUDENT_TEACHER and DEAN_INFO examples illustrate EQUI-JOINS, which are JOINS whose conditions are equal comparisons.

The general JOIN is sometimes called a THETA-JOIN, where theta is $<$, $>$, $<=$, or $>=$, according to the operator in the condition. The general form of the JOIN is

R3 := JOIN (R1) (A1 operator1 T1, A2 operator2 T2,
          . . . , Aj operator$j$ Tj) (R2);
where the A1, A2, . . . , Aj are attributes of R1,
     and the T1, T2, . . . , Tj are attributes of R2.

STUDENT

STUDENT NAME	AGE	DEGREE EXPECTED	MATRIC #
Ellen	25	BA	213461
Jones	28	MA	201136
Smith	29	PHD	141632
Crane	42	PHD	112463
Bell	36	MS	311426
Wayne	30	MA	201336
Sanders	22	BA	321621
Hanes	26	BA	124918
Haley	26	BS	139176
North	28	PHD	412132

STUDENT_TEACHER

STUDENT NAME	AGE	DEGREE EXPECTED	MATRIC #	TEACHER NAME	FACULTY #	RANK	DEPARTMENT NAME	COLLEGE NAME	PHONE	BIRTH DATE	HIRE DATE
Smith	29	PHD	141632	Smith	71246	Lect	ACCTG	BPA	19126	12-1-56	9-1-83
North	28	PHD	412132	North	12916	Lect	GEOLOGY	GEOSCI	12513	6-9-54	8-15-84
North	28	PHD	412132	North	12917	Assoc.	MIS	BPA	12877	10-3-52	8-15-84

FIGURE 4.4 Instance tables: STUDENT_TEACHER results from applying JOIN (STUDENT) (STUDENT_NAME = TEACHER_NAME) (TEACHER) to instance tables of STUDENT and TEACHER from Fig. 4.1. Note that more than one row may result when a join is performed on columns that are not keys.

For example,

TEMP1 := JOIN (TEACHER)(BIRTH_DATE <
                    DATE_ESTABLISHED)
                    (UNIVERSITY_UNIT);
YOUNG_UNIT := PROJECT (TEMP1)(COLLEGE_NAME,
                    DEPARTMENT_NAME);

uses a LESS-THAN JOIN to find all the university units that are younger than some teacher. Figure 4.5 shows the instance table for the UNIVERSITY_UNIT and YOUNG_UNIT relations.

To find the university units that have at least one teacher who is older than the unit:

TEMP1 := JOIN (TEACHER)(BIRTH_DATE <
                    DATE_ESTABLISHED,
                    DEPARTMENT_NAME =
                    DEPARTMENT_NAME,
                    COLLEGE_NAME = COLLEGE_NAME)
                    (UNIVERSITY_UNIT);
RESULT := PROJECT (TEMP1) (COLLEGE_NAME,
                    DEPARTMENT_NAME);

JOINing on DATEs compares the ages of teachers and university-units, but JOINing on DEPARTMENT_NAME, COLLEGE_NAME qualifies only those teachers who work in that university-unit. Figure 4.6 shows the instance table for the RESULT relation.

UNIVERSITY_UNIT

COLLEGE NAME	DEPARTMENT NAME	DEAN FACULTY #	DATE ESTABLISHED
BPA	ACCTG	12345	1960
BPA	MIS	12345	1975
GEOSCI	GEOLOGY	61928	1930
GRAD	ADMIN	01926	1922
GRAD	COMP CTR	63142	1972
ENGR	COMP SCI	32143	1970

FIGURE 4.5. Instance tables: YOUNG_UNIT after applying JOIN (TEACHER) (BIRTH_DATE ⟨ DATE_ ESTABLISHED) (UNIVER- SITY_UNIT) and PRO- JECT to UNIVERSITY_ UNIT and TEACHER from Fig. 4.1.

YOUNG_UNIT

COLLEGE NAME	DEPARTMENT NAME
BPA	ACCTG
BPA	MIS
GRAD	COMP CTR
ENGR	COMP SCI

RESULT

COLLEGE NAME	DEPARTMENT NAME
BPA	MIS
BPA	ACCTG
ENGR	COMP SCI

FIGURE 4.6. Instance table after applying JOIN (TEACHER) (BIRTH_DATE ⟨ DATE_ESTABLISHED, DEPARTMENT _NAME = DEPARTMENT_NAME, COLLEGE_NAME = COLLEGE_NAME) (UNIVERSITY_UNIT) to UNIVERSITY_ UNIT from Fig. 4.5 and TEACHER from Fig. 4.1.

Natural Join

A special case of the JOIN operation is called the NATURAL JOIN, which matches its operand relations on equal values of attributes with matching names. The NATURAL JOIN is used to combine relations for which the primary-key attributes of one appear as foreign-key attributes in the other.

Although there can be an arbitrary number of matching columns, usually there are only one or two. No condition need be given, because it is implicitly A1 = T1, where A1 and T1 are matching attribute names. The matching columns appear only once in the resulting relation.

The NATURAL JOIN of relations R1 and R2 is typically denoted as simply R1 |X| R2. For example,

MORE_TEACHER_INFO := TEACHER |X| UNIVERSITY_UNIT;

creates a relation named MORE_TEACHER_INFO, which appends the DEAN_FACULTY# and DATE_ESTABLISHED from UNIVERSITY_UNIT to each TEACHER tuple. The match across the two relations is made on equal DEPARTMENT_NAME, COLLEGE_NAME values, as those are the attributes that the relations share. The resulting relation has ten attributes; COLLEGE_NAME and DEPARTMENT_NAME appear only once. Figure 4.7 shows the instance table for MORE_TEACHER_INFO.

Set Operators

The set operators of UNION, INTERSECT, and DIFFERENCE can also be applied to relations, though one must be sure that the operand relations really are comparable. For example, the UNION of the UNIVERSITY_UNIT and STUDENT relations may not make much sense.

Tuple Update Operators

Other operators update tuples in relations and permit the insertion of new tuples into existing relations, the deletion of tuples from existing relations, and the

MORE_TEACHER_INFO

TEACHER NAME	FACULTY #	RANK	DEPARTMENT NAME	COLLEGE NAME	PHONE	BIRTH DATE	HIRE DATE	DEAN FACULTY #	DATE ESTABLISHED
Wiley	62186	Assist.	MIS	BPA	12346	7-11-48	8-15-78	12345	1975
Ganguly	13462	Full	GEOLOGY	GEOSCI	14946	10-1-46	8-15-77	61928	1930
Loomis	54216	Full	GEOLOGY	GEOSCI	14648	5-25-46	8-15-76	61928	1930
Brown	12345	Full	MIS	BPA	12613	10-3-50	8-15-82	12345	1975
Smith	71246	Lect	ACCTG	BPA	19126	12-1-56	9-1-83	12345	1960
Boronov	42136	Lect	COMP SCI	ENGR	16216	3-15-52	8-16-82	32143	1970
Lee	32143	Assoc.	COMP SCI	ENGR	15266	7-1-40	6-15-69	32143	1970
Hall	51362	Assoc.	ACCTG	BPA	12614	7-8-56	8-15-76	12345	1960
Little	42137	Lect	GEOLOGY	GEOSCI	14222	3-6-58	8-15-84	61928	1930
Hill	31192	Assist.	MIS	BPA	12346	12-2-58	8-15-84	12345	1975
Brown	52163	Assist.	COMP SCI	ENGR	12111	3-2-51	8-15-82	32143	1970
North	12916	Lect	GEOLOGY	GEOSCI	12513	6-9-54	8-15-84	61928	1930
North	12917	Assoc.	MIS	BPA	12877	10-3-52	8-15-84	12345	1975

FIGURE 4.7. Instance table after applying TEACHER|×|UNIVERSITY_UNIT to TEACHER of Fig. 4.1 and UNIVERSITY_UNIT of Fig. 4.5.

modification of tuples in existing relations. None changes the relation's intension (or schema).

SCHEMA DEFINITION

The language used to describe the structure of a database to a database management system is sometimes called the *data definition language (DDL)*, or the *schema definition language*. The schema definition language for a relational database must be able to create, modify, and delete descriptions of relations and their attributes.

There are several schema definition languages for relational databases, but here we shall use the part of the SQL (pronounced see-quel) relational data language that is oriented toward schema definition. SQL also enables the insertion, modification, and deletion of tuples of relations and provides a data control facility that

- enables users to authorize other users to access data.
- specifies assertions about data integrity.
- specifies transactions to be triggered by various events.

SQL is the basis for many of the commercial relational data languages and of the relational database language being developed by the ANSI/X3H2 committee, which proposes standards for computer systems languages.

In order to define a new relation, the user must specify the table name, its attribute names, and the data type for each attribute. For example,

> CREATE TABLE STUDENT
>   (STUDENT_NAME (CHAR(20) VAR NOT NULL)
>   AGE (INTEGER)
>   DEGREE_EXPECTED (CHAR(4))
>   MATRIC#(CHAR(6) NOT NULL UNIQUE));

constructs the schema for the relation

> STUDENT (STUDENT_NAME, AGE, DEGREE_EXPECTED,
>   MATRIC#).

The following statement expands the STUDENT relation with an additional column for GRADE_POINT_AVG:

> EXPAND TABLE STUDENT
>   ADD COLUMN GRADE_POINT_AVG (DECIMAL (3,2));

The following statement removes the definition of the student relation from the database description:

> DROP TABLE STUDENT;

Defining Views

SQL also includes facilities to form a relation's subset defining a *view,* which is a window on the base relation. When values change in the base relation, they also change in the views defined for that base relation.

For example, the following statement creates a view of the STUDENT relation that includes only the students with a grade-point average greater than 2.5:

> DEFINE VIEW MIS_STUDENTS AS
>   SELECT STUDENT_NAME,
>   AGE, MATRIC#, GRADE_POINT_AVG
>   FROM STUDENT
>   WHERE GRADE_POINT_AVG > 2.5;

The SELECT clause is a SQL query expression that here specifies a RESTRICT on STUDENT (where GRADE_POINT_AVG > 2.5), followed by a PROJECT of four columns (STUDENT_NAME, AGE, MATRIC#, and GRADE_POINT_AVG). The view's columns have the same names as do the base relation's corresponding columns. A variation of view definition changes the column names.

Many relational systems prohibit updating any view that does not correspond directly to a base relation. A view that results from a JOIN of two base relations cannot be updated, nor can a view that results from a PROJECT of a base relation be updated.

Domains and Assertions

Domains have been supported in some versions of SQL as a type of assertion. For example, the following statement limits the valid set of values for GRADE_POINT_AVG in the STUDENT relation:

> ASSERT A1 ON STUDENT:
>   GRADE_POINT_AVG BETWEEN 0 AND 4.00;

Assertions can also be used to specify referential integrity constraints. For example, if DEPARTMENT_NAME were a foreign-key attribute in STUDENT, with home relation DEPARTMENT, then the referential integrity constraint could be specified in the following statement:

> ASSERT A2:
>   (SELECT DEPARTMENT_NAME FROM STUDENT)
>   IS IN
>   (SELECT DEPARTMENT_NAME FROM DEPARTMENT);

MAPPING FROM LOGICAL DATA MODELS

The approach to database design introduced in Chapter 2 first develops a logical data model using a technique (see Chapter 3) independent of any DBMS. It then maps the logical data model to the model supported by the DBMS to be used for implementation. Relational DBMSs support the relational model.

The mapping from a logical data model to a relational model is relatively straightforward as long as no category relationships are encountered. The resulting relational model, however, loses some of the semantic information explicit in the logical data model. Because they are not in the DBMS's native model, these semantics must be enforced by application-program code rather than by the DBMS (often they are not enforced at all).

ENTITIES, ATTRIBUTES, AND CONNECTION RELATIONSHIPS

The basic rules for mapping entities, attributes, and connection relationships from a logical data model to a relational database are

- An entity is represented by a relation.
- Each attribute of an entity is represented by an attribute in the relation.
- A connection relationship is represented by the presence of a foreign-key attribute in the child relation.

It is relatively simple to develop a set of relations that corresponds to a data model in which

- nonspecific relationships have been resolved.
- keys have been migrated (forming foreign-key attributes).
- no rolenames are used.

Figure 4.8 shows such a data model and its corresponding relations. The data model has no many-to-many relationships or zero-or-one-to-many relationships. Each entity has been translated into a relation, which a column for each of the entity's attributes, and the relationships appear not as separate relations but as foreign-key attributes in the entity relations.

The mapping of a data model in which nonspecific relationships have not been resolved and in which keys have not been migrated to form foreign-key attributes is not so straightforward. Just representing the entities by relations excludes structural information about the relationships, as the foreign-key attributes are needed to show logical associations across relations.

One alternative for regaining this information is to introduce a relation for each relationship. Such a relation would contain just the keys of the entities being related, and the key of the resulting relation would be determined by the relationship's cardinality. Figure 4.8(b) lists the relations that result from ap-

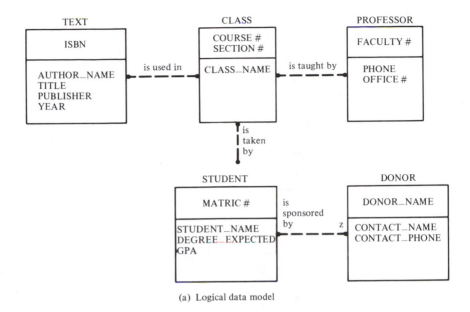

(a) Logical data model

TEXT (AUTHOR_NAME, ISBN, TITLE, PUBLISHER, YEAR)
CLASS (COURSE #, SECTION #, CLASS_NAME)
PROFESSOR (FACULTY #, PHONE, OFFICE #)
STUDENT (MATRIC #, STUDENT_NAME, DEGREE_EXPECTED, GPA)
DONOR (DONOR NAME, CONTACT_NAME, CONTACT_PHONE)
IS_USED_IN (ISBN, COURSE #, SECTION #)
IS_TAUGHT_BY (COURSE #, SECTION #, FACULTY #)
IS_TAKEN_BY (COURSE #, SECTION #, MATRIC #)
IS_SPONSORED_BY (MATRIC #, DONOR_NAME)

(b) Relations, one per entity and one per
relationship

FIGURE 4.8. Corresponding logical data model and relations.

plying this alternative to the data model of Fig. 4.8(a), which is an early version of the resolved and migrated model shown in Fig. 4.9(a).

Another alternative for regaining the structural information is to go through an intermediate step of resolving the many-to-many and zero-or-one-to-many relationships and migrating keys to form foreign-key attributes. Then the entities can be represented by relations, and the relationship information will be carried by the foreign-key attributes, as shown in Fig. 4.9(b).

The relations that correspond to the data model of Fig. 3.14, which resolves the many-to-many relationship of the model in Fig. 3.13(a), are

CLASS_SECTION (DEPARTMENT#, COURSE#, SECTION#,
CLASS_NAME)

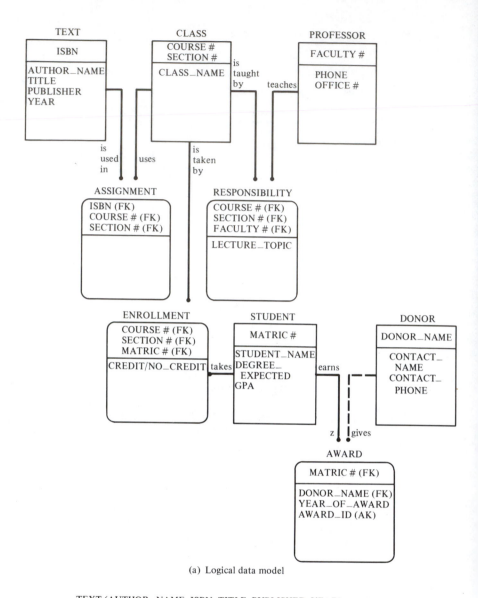

(a) Logical data model

TEXT (AUTHOR_NAME, <u>ISBN</u>, TITLE, PUBLISHER, YEAR)
CLASS (<u>COURSE #</u>, <u>SECTION #</u>, CLASS_NAME)
PROFESSOR (<u>FACULTY #</u>, PHONE, OFFICE #)
ASSIGNMENT (<u>ISBN</u>, <u>COURSE #</u>, <u>SECTION #</u>)
RESPONSIBILITY (<u>COURSE #</u>, <u>SECTION #</u>, <u>FACULTY #</u>, LECTURE_TOPIC)
STUDENT (<u>MATRIC #</u>, STUDENT_NAME, DEGREE_EXPECTED, GPA)
ENROLLMENT (<u>COURSE #</u>, <u>SECTION #</u>, <u>MATRIC #</u>, CREDIT/NO_CREDIT)
DONOR (<u>DONOR NAME</u>, CONTACT_NAME, CONTACT_PHONE)
AWARD (<u>MATRIC #</u>, DONOR_NAME, YEAR_OF_AWARD, AWARD_ID)

(b) Relations, one per entity

FIGURE 4.9. Corresponding logical data model and relations.

STUDENT (<u>MATRIC#</u>, STUDENT_NAME, BIRTH_DATE,
ADDRESS, GPA)
ENROLLMENT (<u>MATRIC#</u>, <u>DEPARTMENT#</u>, <u>COURSE#</u>,
<u>SECTION#</u>)

The relations that correspond to the data model of Fig. 3.15(b), which resolves the zero-or-one-to-many relationship of the model in Fig. 3.15(a), are

CLASS (<u>DEPARTMENT#</u>, <u>COURSE#</u>, COURSE_LEVEL)
COUNSELOR (<u>COUNSELOR_ID</u>, FACULTY#,
APPOINTMENT_DATE,
TRAINING_DATE)
TEACHING_ASSISTANT (<u>MATRIC#</u>, COUNSELOR_ID,
DEPARTMENT#, COURSE#,
HOURS_PER_MONTH)

Nonkey attributes have been added to the entities.

Not all of the semantic information in the logical data model has been captured in the corresponding relational model. Most obviously, relationship cardinalities have disappeared: the relational model is not able to indicate that a CLASS_SECTION relation instance has a maximum of forty-five related EN-ROLLMENT instances or that a STUDENT's MATRIC# key value can appear as a foreign-key attribute value in a maximum of seven ENROLLMENT instances. Nor can it indicate that a STUDENT's MATRIC# key value can appear in only one TEACHING_ASSISTANT instance or that a MATRIC# value must appear in at least one LETTER_OF_RECOMMENDATION instance.

If rolenames are used, then foreign-key attributes can be obscured. For example, in the relations

PART (<u>PART#</u>, DESCRIPTION, SIZE, BIN#)
COMPONENT (<u>ASSEMBLY#</u>, <u>COMPONENT#</u>, QUANTITY)

it is not obvious that ASSEMBLY# and COMPONENT# are rolenames in the COMPONENT entity for the foreign-key attribute PART# from the PART entity. And if the foreign-key attributes cannot be identified, then the relationships in the model cannot be detected.

Category Relationships

A category relationship is not handled conveniently in the relational model. Representation is like that of connection relationships, with each entity mapping directly to a relation and relationships shown by foreign-key attributes. The category hierarchy of Fig. 3.19(b) is represented by the following relations:

EMPLOYEE (<u>SOCIAL_SECURITY#</u>, EMPLOYEE_NAME, BIRTH_
DATE, #_DEPENDENTS, ADDRESS, STATUS)

STUDENT (SOCIAL_SECURITY#, STUDY_YEAR,
                    EXPECTED_DEGREE_YEAR, EXPECTED_DEGREE,
                    HOURLY_RATE)
STAFF (SOCIAL_SECURITY#, EXEMPTION_CODE,
                    BENEFIT_PLAN, MONTHLY_SALARY)
FACULTY (SOCIAL_SECURITY#, RANK, ANNUAL_SALARY,
                    FACULTY_CLUB_DUES)

The first problem with this representation of the category is that the hierarchical structure has been lost. From the set of relations, it is not clear which (if
any) relation represents the generic entity and which the subtype entities. It
therefore is not clear which relations should implicitly inherit attributes from
which other relations. The logical data model says that the STUDENT, STAFF,
and FACULTY entities all inherit all of the attributes of the EMPLOYEE entity.
An alternative is to inherit explicitly the generic attributes:

STUDENT (SOCIAL_SECURITY#, EMPLOYEE_NAME,
                    BIRTH_DATE, #_DEPENDENTS, ADDRESS,
                    STATUS, STUDY_YEAR,
                    EXPECTED_DEGREE_YEAR, EXPECTED_DEGREE,
                    HOURLY_RATE)
STAFF (SOCIAL_SECURITY#, EMPLOYEE_NAME,
                    BIRTH_DATE, #_DEPENDENTS, ADDRESS,
                    STATUS, EXEMPTION_CODE, BENEFIT_PLAN,
                    MONTHLY_SALARY)
FACULTY (SOCIAL_SECURITY#, EMPLOYEE_NAME,
                    BIRTH_DATE, #_DEPENDENTS, ADDRESS,
                    STATUS, RANK, ANNUAL_SALARY,
                    FACULTY_CLUB_DUES)

This approach also obscures the hierarchical structure, as it is not clear whether
STUDENT, STAFF, and FACULTY entities all are subtypes of a single generic
entity.

The second problem with category relationships is in the relational operators.
To list all the attribute values of the student entity instances, the following
operations can be used:

R1 := SELECT (EMPLOYEE) (STATUS = 'student');
ANSWER := R1 |X| STUDENT;

Now, however, try to list the full set (i.e., home and implicitly inherited) of all
the employees' attribute values, without knowing the entire set of values for the
STATUS attribute. Or try to list the full set of attribute values of the employees
whose STATUS = *input-status* (a variable). The following syntax cannot be
processed by any of the relational DBMSs:

R2 := SELECT (EMPLOYEE) (STATUS = *input-status*);
ANSWER := R2 |X| *input-status*;

The syntax analyzer expects the names of two relations as the operands of the JOIN; here *input-status* is the name of a variable.

Identifier Dependencies

The relational model represents identifier dependency in its databases' schemas. If one relation is identifier dependent on another, then the primary key of the independent is completely contained (as a foreign-key attribute) in the dependent relation's primary key. For example, in the following, the relation MONTHLY_BUDGET is identifier dependent on the relation DEPARTMENT, but the relation EMPLOYEE is not:

> DEPARTMENT (DEPARTMENT#, DEPARTMENT_NAME, LOCATION)
> MONTHLY_BUDGET (DEPARTMENT#, MONTH, YEAR, AMOUNT)
> EMPLOYEE (DEPARTMENT#, EMPLOYEE#, EMPLOYEE_NAME)

The relational model is not able to represent identifier dependency if role-names are used for the foreign-key attributes. For example, the relations corresponding to the model of Fig. 3.16(b) are

> CITY (CITY_CODE, LONGITUDE, LATITUDE, AIRPORT_NAME)
> FLIGHT_SEGMENT (DEPARTURE_CITY_CODE, ARRIVAL_CITY
> CODE, FLIGHT#,
> SCHEDULED_DEPARTURE_TIME,
> SCHEDULED_ARRIVAL_TIME, AIRCRAFT_TYPE)

It may not be clear from these relations that the FLIGHT_SEGMENT relation has two foreign-key attributes: DEPARTURE_CITY_CODE and ARRIVAL_CITY_CODE both are rolenames for CITY_CODE, which is the key of CITY. Without knowing that these are rolenames, it is not possible to identify the identifier dependency.

Many of the relational DBMSs' schema definition languages specify neither keys nor rolenames, and so the identification dependencies are not explicit.

Referential Integrity Constraints

The relational model theoretically assumes that if a foreign-key attribute cannot have a null value, then the referential integrity constraint (and therefore existence dependency) always will hold. The value of a foreign-key attribute must be matched by a value of the corresponding primary-key attribute in the home relation, and a row of the dependent relation that is not directly related to a row of the home relation should not exist in the database.

The DBMSs that implement the relational model, however, usually do not enforce referential integrity constraints. Most do not even provide the assertion facility (see our discussion of schema definition languages) to specify referential integrity constraints. But if they did enforce referential integrity, they would

- upon tuple insertion, verify that foreign-key attribute values are represented in the set of primary-key attribute values of the home relation.
- upon tuple deletion, verify that the primary-key attribute value is not represented in any foreign-key attribute value of a dependent relation.

If the referential integrity constraint is enforced, it is usually through the applications code, and this is one area in which future relational DBMS products should excel.

The Mapping Process

A proven sequence of events in database design is first to build a logical data model and then to map that data model to a form that can be implemented by a DBMS. The steps of mapping to a relational database are to

1. construct a data model of the subject area.
2. resolve the many-to-many and zero-or-one-to-many relationships.
3. migrate the primary keys, forming foreign-key attributes in dependent entities.
4. define a relation for each entity, with the entity's attributes becoming the relation's columns.
5. tune the relation structures to enhance physical performance.

The last step will be addressed in Chapter 10, on the physical design of relational databases, but it may include

- combining relations (e.g., collapsing one-to-zero-or-one relationships).
- spliting relations (e.g., when some attributes in a relation are accessed far more frequently than others are).
- specifying access paths (e.g., constructing indexes on primary keys or other attributes).
- assigning relations to physical space (e.g., clustering relations that are typically used together).

Sometimes instead of building the data model first, a data model may be constructed that corresponds to an already-existing set of relations in a database. This may be done to help clarify what information is actually contained in the database. The graphic representation of a logical data model is a convenient way to identify the relationships carried by the foreign-key attributes of a set of relations. Additionally, the questions asked in building a logical data model should elicit any category relationships that may be hidden in the relational database.

INTRODUCTION TO COMMERCIAL RELATIONAL DATABASE MANAGEMENT SYSTEMS

Numerous commercial database management systems call themselves *relational*. The parent of them all is System R, which was developed in the 1970s at the IBM San Jose Research Laboratory. This experimental system investigated implementation of not only the relational model's structures and operations but also data protection facilities in a relational environment. The System R work led to many research publications concerning shared access, concurrency control, backup and recovery, transaction control, and user-interface facilities. The project was also the forerunner of the IBM San Jose Research Laboratory's System R* project, which has studied relational data management in distributed computer networks.

System R led to two major licensed program products from IBM, SQL/Data System (SQL/DS) and Database 2 (DB2). SQL/DS became commercially available in 1982 and runs on IBM's intermediate range of computers, including the System/370, 303x, 43xx, and compatible DOS/VSE processors. DB2 became commercially available in 1984 and runs on IBM's larger range of computers, including the MVS/XA and MVS/370 environments. Two companion products are the Query Management Facility (QMF), which provides interactive access to DB2 and SQL/DS databases, and Data Extract (DXT), which offers a method of selectively extracting data from existing IMS/VS databases or sequential or VSAM files, to be loaded into DB2 or SQL/DS databases.

Two of the earliest commercial implementations of the relational model were ORACLE, from Oracle Inc. (formerly Relational Software, Inc.) and INGRES, from Relational Technology, Inc. ORACLE is rooted in the System R work; INGRES grew from research work at the University of California, Berkeley, on a system by the same name—INGRES. Both INGRES and ORACLE were initially implemented on Digital Equipment Corporation Vax machines. Berkeley INGRES runs on the UNIX operating system; ORACLE and Relational Technology INGRES run on the VMS operating system. ORACLE now also runs on IBM computers with the MVS operating system. Both ORACLE and INGRES are also available for various multiuser microcomputers running the UNIX operating system.

There are many other database management systems that support a tabular view of data. Among these products for mainframes are Cullinet's IDMS/R, Software AG's ADABAS, and Computer Corporation of America's Model 204. Relational products for micros include Unify Corporation's Unify, Relational Database Systems, Inc.'s Informix, Pacific Software Manufacturing Company's Sequitur, Microrim Inc.'s R:base, and others.

Relational model support is now commercially available on dedicated computers called *database machines,* which are hardware- and software-specialized to handle efficiently database storage and access. The prominent entries in this marketplace today are Britton-Lee's IDM and Teradata's DBC/1012.

CLOSING COMMENTS

The development of the relational model was a landmark sequence of events in data management research. The relational model's simplicity and separation of user and implementation concerns have made it attractive for nearly fifteen years, first to the research community and now to the commercial marketplace.

The best features of the relational model are its

- simple, tabular view of data.
- complete set of data manipulation operators.
- separation of logical model from physical implementation concerns.

The basic weaknesses of the relational model are

- semantic overloading, in that a single tabular structure is used to represent a variety of logical data-modeling constructs.
- overzealousness in the characterization of commercial database management systems as "relational," even though they do not enforce some of the important constraints of the relational model, like referential integrity.
- the relational operators which are at a procedural, programmer level and need to be overlaid by a higher level of commands that are easier for nonprogrammers to use.
- inefficient implementation, relative to some other designs, for some types of data structures.

The first problem can be addressed by using a logical data-modeling technique along with the relational model. The second problem is not really the relational model itself, but the industry's use of terminology. There has been much work on the third problem. The fourth problem is being resolved through database hardware and software specialization, which will be discussed in Chapter 10. Commercial relational DBMSs continue to have performance problems in large, complex database environments.

TERMS

alternate key	home relation
attribute	identifier dependency
category relationship	instance table
connection relationship	intension of a relation
data definition language	JOIN
domain	logical data model
existence dependency	NATURAL JOIN
extension of a relation	null
foreign-key assertion	primary key
foreign-key attribute	primary-key assertion

PROJECT	SELECT
referential integrity	SQL
relation	System R
schema	tuple
schema definition language	view

REVIEW EXERCISES

1. Define each of the terms in the preceding list.

2. Consider the following relations:
   - BUYER (BUYER_ID, BUYER_PHONE, BUYER_RATING)
   - PURCHASE_ORDER (PO#, PART#, PO_$_VALUE, PART_QUANTITY)
   - PART (PART#, PART_NAME, PART_TYPE, PART_SIZE)
   - SUPPLIER (SUPPLIER#, SUPPLIER_NAME, SUPPLIER_CITY, TIME_ZONE)
   - SUPPLY (PART#, SUPPLIER#, BUYER_ID)

   Using PROJECT, SELECT, and JOIN, write the appropriate sequence of operators to answer each of the following questions:
   a. What are the buyers' phone numbers?
   b. What are the names of parts whose size = 'small'?
   c. What are the po#'s of purchase orders whose po$ value is between $100 and $999?
   d. What are the names of parts purchased on po# 1234?
   e. What are the names of parts supplied by suppliers in Albuquerque?
   f. What are the names of parts supplied by suppliers for which the buyer's rating is 'A-OK'?

3. Consider the following relations:
   - STUDENT (MATRIC#, STUDENT_NAME, MAJOR_DEPT, YEAR, GPA)
   - TEACHER (DEPT, FACULTY#, TEACHER_NAME)
   - ENROLLMENT (MATRIC#, COURSE#, GRADE)
   - RESPONSIBILITY (FACULTY#, COURSE#)

   Using PROJECT, SELECT, and JOIN, write the appropriate sequence of operators to answer each of the following questions:
   a. What are the names of teachers who are responsible for courses in which students whose name is Jones are enrolled?
   b. What are the GPAs of students who are enrolled in courses that are the responsibility of teachers in the MIS department and who have grades of C in those courses?

4. Consider the following relations and their instance tables:

R (STUDENT, COURSE)		S (COURSE, TEACHER)	
Joe	32	32	North
Ellen	32	43	Jones

Marge	51	43	Smith
Ellen	43	51	Elgin
Jan	43	65	Elgin
		51	Marlin

a. Show the instance table of the NATURAL JOIN of R and S.
b. Show the instance table of PROJECT (R) (COURSE).
c. Show the instance table of SELECT (S) (COURSE>43).

5. Construct the set of relations that corresponds to the data model in Fig. 4.10.
6. Construct the set of relations that corresponds to the data model in Fig. 4.11.
7. Construct the set of relations that corresponds to the data model in Fig. 4.12.
8. Construct the set of relations that corresponds to the data model in Fig. 4.13.

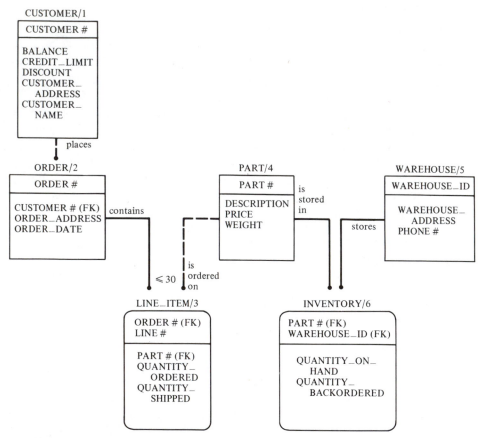

FIGURE 4.10. Logical data model for Exercise 4.5.

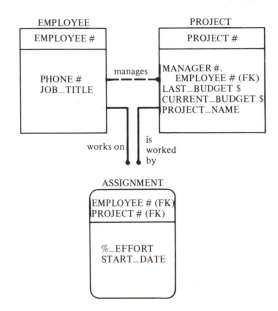

FIGURE 4.11. Logical data model for Exercise 4.6.

9. List the types of semantic information that can be lost when a logical data model is translated into a set of relations.

10. Extend the SQL schema definition capabilities introduced here to specify compound keys, rolenames, and other semantic information from a logical data model.

11. Compare the SQL schema definition capabilities introduced here with those of the relational database language proposed by the ANSI/X3H2 committee.

12. Compare the proposed standard for SQL with the original Sequel 2 language (see D.D. Chamberlin, et al. in the reference list at the end of this chapter).

13. One approach to relational database design is first to build a logical data model and then translate that model into a set of relations. Why might a designer want to build a logical data model from an existing set of relations?

14. Leaf through several issues of the computer trade magazines and list the data management packages advertised as being ''relational.''

15. Describe two or more of the commercially available relational database management systems, and compare their capabilities.

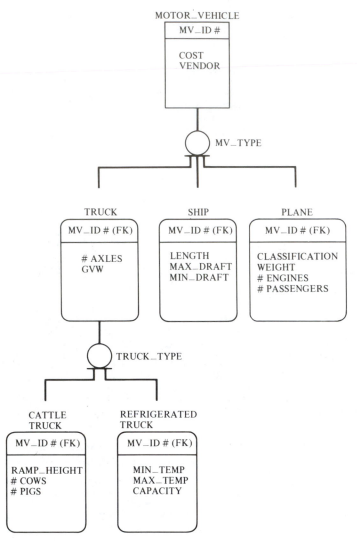

FIGURE 4.12. Logical data model for Exercise 4.7.

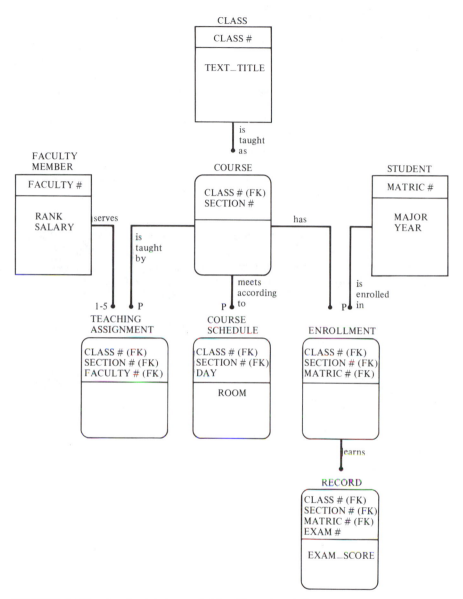

FIGURE 4.13. Logical data model for Exercise 4.8.

REFERENCES

ANSI/X3H2 Committee. (Working Draft) *American National Standard Database Language SQL (X3H2-84-117)*, ANSI/X3/SPARC Project 363D, October 1984.

Astrahan, M. M., et al. System R: relational approach to database management, *ACM Trans. Database Systems* 1 (June 1976):97–137.

Brodie, M. L., and J. W. Schmidt, (eds.) Final report of the relational database task group, *ANSI/X3/SPARC/DBSSG, ACM SIGMOD Record* 12 (July 1982).

Chamberlin, D. D., et al. SEQUEL 2: A unified approach to data definition, manipulation, and control, *IBM Journal of Research and Development* 20 (November 1976):560–575.

Codd, E. F. Extending the database relational model to capture more meaning, *ACM Trans. Database Systems*, 4 (December 1979):397–434.

————. A relational model for large shared databases, *Communications ACM*, 13 (June 1970):377–387.

Date, C. J. A formal definition of the relational model, *ACM SIGMOD Record* 13 (September 1982).

INGRES Demonstration and Introduction. Berkeley, Calif.: Relational Technology.

ORACLE Relational Data Base Management System, Introduction. Menlo Park, Calif.

Ross, R. G. The significance of DB2, *Database Newsletter* 11 (September-October 1983).

Sibley, E. H. *A Functional Specification of the Relational DBMS, National Technical Information Service Report No. NBS-GCR-82-372*, January 31, 1982.

Stonebraker, M., et al. The design and implementation of INGRES, *ACM Trans. Database Systems*, 1 (September 1976):189–222.

Williams, R., et al. R*: An overview of the architecture, *Computer Science Research Report RJ3325 (40082)*, IBM Research Division, December 2, 1981.

Zaniolo, C., and M. A. Melkanoff. On the design of relational database schemata, *ACM Trans. Database Systems* 6 (March 1981):1–47.

Normalization

Normalization is a process developed in conjunction with the relational data model, though it is applicable to logical data modeling in general. It can be useful in answering two major data questions: "What is a good logical database design?" and "What is a good physical database design?"

OBJECTIVES

Relational normalization is a process for identifying "stable" attribute groupings, with high interdependency and affinity. Normalization incorporates principles of semantic data modeling and results in extensible logical database designs. It can also lead to flexible physical database designs, while keeping separate the logical and physical considerations.

DEPENDENCIES

Normalization is based on concepts of dependencies among attributes, and it enforces a set of rules governing the structure of data meanings. These rules, based on dependency conditions, help stabilize the definitions of meanings and predict the representations of facts.

The two most important types of attribute dependencies for our purposes are *functional dependency* and *multivalued dependency*.

Functional Dependency

Consider the following relation:

> TEACHER (TEACHER_NAME, FACULTY#, RANK,
> DEPARTMENT_ NAME, COLLEGE_NAME, PHONE,
> BIRTH_DATE, HIRE_DATE)

Assume that each FACULTY# value has associated with it one, and only one, value for BIRTH_DATE. But because two teachers can have exactly the same birthday, each BIRTH_DATE value may be associated with more than one FACULTY# value. BIRTH_DATE is thus said to be functionally dependent on FACULTY#. This is sometimes denoted FACULTY# → BIRTH_DATE and is read "FACULTY# functionally determines BIRTH_DATE."

Consider relation R with attributes A and B. Attribute B is said to be *functionally dependent* on attribute A if, and only if, each value of A in the rows of R has associated with it at any one time precisely one value of B in R. That is,

- the rows of R with a given value of A all must have the same value of B.
- when two rows of R have the same value of B, they need not have the same values of A.

Multivalued Dependency

Consider the relation

> RESPONSIBILITY (FACULTY#, COURSE#, COMMITTEE_NAME)

Assume that each FACULTY# value has associated with it one or more COURSE# values. The set of COURSE# values associated with a given FACULTY# value, however, is the same for every COMMITTEE# that is also associated with that FACULTY#.

Assume that FACULTY# = 12345 appears in three rows in the RESPONSIBILITY relation, with COURSE# values: 100, 200, and 300. To add that FACULTY# = 12345 serves on COMMITTEE# = 12 would require three FACULTY#, COURSE#, COMMITTEE# rows to be added to the RESPONSIBILITY relation:

12345, 100, 12
12345, 200, 12
12345, 300, 12

The set of COURSE# values associated with a given FACULTY# value (here 12345) must be exactly the same for every COMMITTEE# value. Thus COMMITTEE# = 12 cannot appear with FACULTY# = 12345 and only one of the COURSE# values in the set {100, 200, 300}.

COURSE# is said to be multivalued dependent on FACULTY#, which is sometimes denoted FACULTY# $\rightarrow\rightarrow$ COURSE# and is read "FACULTY# multivalued determines COURSE#."

Consider now relation R with attributes A, B, and C. Attribute B is said to be *multivalued dependent* on attribute A if, and only if, the set of values of B in R matching a given ⟨A, C⟩ pair of values in R is independent of the value of C. That is, all of the following are true:

- Not all the rows of R with a given value of A need to have the same value of B. (The B-values in these rows are referred to as "the set of B-values determined by the A-value.")
- Whenever two rows of relation R have the same values of A, they need not have the same values of B, but their values of B must be elements of the set of values determined by the value of A.
- Changing the value of C in a row of R cannot affect the value of B in that row.
- When two rows of relation R have the same values of B, they do not necessarily need the same values of A.
- Consider two values of C: C1 and C2. The set of values of B in rows of R with a given value of A and with C-value C1 must be exactly the same as the set of values of B in rows of R with that same A-value and with C-value C2.

FIRST NORMAL FORM

Relational theory uses the term *normal forms* to describe the extent to which attributes have been grouped into stable relations. Numerous normal forms have been proposed, each trying to achieve a more stable grouping of attributes. Of primary interest to us are six normal forms, the first normal form through the fifth normal form and the Boyce/Codd normal form.

A relation is in *first normal form (1NF)* if, and only if, every attribute in every row can contain only a single value. A 1NF relation cannot have any row that contains a repeating group of attribute values.

Consider the following relation:

> FACULTY_1 (TEACHER_NAME, FACULTY#, STUDENT_NAME, MATRIC#, DEPARTMENT_NAME, COURSE#, TEXT, GRADE, COMMITTEE#, MEETING_DAY, MEETING_TIME)

It is not possible to determine whether this relation is in 1NF without either looking at an instance table or answering the question, For a given row of this

FACULTY_1

TEACHER NAME	FACULTY #	STUDENT NAME	MATRIC #	DEPARTMENT NAME	COURSE #	TEXT	GRADE	COMMITTEE #	MEETING DAY	MEETING TIME
Smith	12751	Jones	469213	MIS	231	One	A	12	M	9
		Green	532162	MIS	231	One	B	20	W	8
		Adams	112146	CSC	201	Two	B			
Wondra	21936	Jones	469213	GEOL	512	Four	A	0	∅'	∅
Kientz	51326	Sandy	513251	MIS	531	One	A	12	M	9
								20	W	8
								18	W	9
Hayward	31962	Winn	219623	CSC	200	Two	A	5	F	8
		Jason	319216	GEOL	512	Four	B			

FIGURE 5.1. Instance table for the FACULTY_1 relation.

FACULTY_1

TEACHER NAME	FACULTY #	STUDENT NAME	MATRIC #	DEPARTMENT NAME	COURSE #	TEXT	GRADE	COMMITTEE #	MEETING DAY	MEETING TIME
Smith	12751	Jones	469213	MIS	231	One	A	12	M	9
Smith	12751	Green	532162	MIS	231	One	B	20	W	8
Smith	12751	Adams	112146	CSC	201	Two	B	20	W	8
Wondra	21936	Jones	469213	GEOL	512	Four	A	0	∅	∅
Kientz	51326	Sandy	513251	MIS	531	One	A	12	M	9
Kientz	51326	Sandy	513251	MIS	531	One	A	20	W	8
Kientz	51326	Sandy	513251	MIS	531	One	A	18	W	9
Hayward	31962	Winn	219623	CSC	200	Two	A	5	F	8
Hayward	31962	Jason	319216	GEOL	512	Four	B	5	F	8

FIGURE 5.2. Instance table for the FACULTY_1 relation in 1NF.

relation, can there be multiple values of any attribute? An instance table for the FACULTY_1 relation is shown in Fig. 5.1. The relation is not in 1NF, as there are multiple values of STUDENT_NAME (and several other attributes) in the row for FACULTY# = 12345.

Producing 1NF

To normalize a relation to 1NF, it is necessary to "flatten" the rows, so that no row contains repeating attributes. Figure 5.2 shows an instance table for the FACULTY_1 relation modified to be in 1NF. Note that the schema for the relation has not been changed.

The primary key for the example relation is FACULTY#, DEPARTMENT_NAME, COURSE# MATRIC#, as all four attributes are needed to identify the rows.

Objectives of 1NF

The two main reasons to use 1NF relations rather than unnormalized relations are that the semantics of a 1NF relation are more explicit—no attribute can have more than one value in any given row—and that the relational operators are applicable only to flat, that is, 1NF, relations. The schema of an unnormalized relation gives no clues to which attributes can have multiple values. By contrast, knowing that a relation is in 1NF means that no attribute can have multiple values in a row.

SECOND NORMAL FORM

A relation is in *second normal form (2NF)* if, and only if, it is in 1NF and every nonkey attribute is fully functionally dependent on the primary key. That is, a 2NF relation cannot have any attribute that is functionally dependent on only *part* of the primary key. It is not possible to tell whether a relation is in 2NF just by looking at its schema; rather, it is necessary to know what the functional dependencies are.

Consider again the FACULTY_1 relation, which is now in 1NF:

FACULTY_1 (TEACHER_NAME <u>FACULTY#</u>, STUDENT_NAME,
         MATRIC#, <u>DEPARTMENT_NAME</u>, <u>COURSE#</u>,
         TEXT, GRADE, COMMITTEE#, MEETING_DAY,
         MEETING_TIME)

Assume that the following functional dependencies hold:

        FACULTY# → TEACHER_NAME
        FACULTY# → COMMITTEE#

FACULTY# → DEPARTMENT_NAME, COURSE#
FACULTY# → MEETING_DAY
FACULTY# → MEETING_TIME
MATRIC# → STUDENT_NAME
MATRIC#, DEPARTMENT_NAME, COURSE# → GRADE
DEPARTMENT_NAME, COURSE# → TEXT

We can now determine that the FACULTY_1 relation is not in 2NF, as there are nonkey attributes that are not determined by the entire primary key. For example,

- TEACHER_NAME is functionally dependent on only part of the key: FACULTY#.
- STUDENT_NAME is functionally dependent on only part of the key: MATRIC#.
- GRADE is functionally dependent on only part of the key: MATRIC#, DEPARTMENT_NAME, COURSE#.
- TEXT is functionally dependent on only part of the key: DEPARTMENT_NAME, COURSE#.

Producing 2NF

A relation can be resolved into 2NF by dividing it into component relations, each of which meets the 2NF test. The relation R ($\underline{A}$, $\underline{B}$, C, D) with dependencies

$$A \rightarrow C$$
$$A, B \rightarrow D$$

should be split into two relations,

$$R1\ (\underline{A}, C)$$
$$R2\ (\underline{A}, \underline{B}, D)$$

Resolving the relation FACULTY_1 gives the following four relations:

FACULTY_2 (FACULTY#, TEACHER_NAME, COMMITTEE#,
                      MEETING_DAY, MEETING_TIME, DEPARTMENT_
                      NAME, COURSE#)
STUDENT (MATRIC#, STUDENT_NAME)
COURSE_STUDENT (DEPARTMENT_NAME, COURSE#,
                      MATRIC#, GRADE)
COURSE (DEPARTMENT_NAME, COURSE#, TEXT)

In each relation, all of the nonkey attributes are dependent on the entire primary key.

Note that DEPARTMENT_NAME, COURSE# is a compound foreign-key attribute in FACULTY_2, which shows a one-to-many relationship between

FACULTY_1

| FACULTY # |
| MATRIC # |
| DEPARTMENT_NAME |
| COURSE # |

TEACHER_NAME
STUDENT_NAME (0)
TEXT (0)
GRADE (0)
COMMITTEE # (0)
MEETING_DAY (0)
MEETING_TIME (0)

FIGURE 5.3. Logical data model corresponding to 1NF FACULTY_1 relation.

COURSE and FACULTY. DEPARTMENT_NAME, COURSE# also is a compound foreign-key attribute in the COURSE_STUDENT relation, which shows a one-to-many relationship between COURSE and COURSE_STUDENT. COURSE_STUDENT has another foreign-key attribute, MATRIC#, which shows a one-to-many relationship between STUDENT and COURSE_STUDENT. Figure 5.3 shows a data model diagram for the FACULTY_1 relation, and Figure 5.4 shows a data model diagram for the set of 2NF relations.

A 1NF relation with a single-attribute key is always a 2NF relation (unless there are ''off-beat'' nonkey attributes in the relation that are not at all dependent on the key). No nonkey attribute can be dependent on only part of the key, as there is only one attribute in the key.

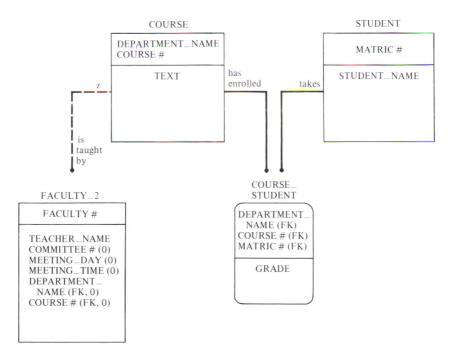

FIGURE 5.4. Logical data model of FACULTY_1 normalized to 2NF.

Objectives of 2NF

The two main reasons to use 2NF relations rather than 1NF relations are that the semantics of a 2NF relation are more explicit—all attributes are dependent on the entire primary key—and that a database designed with 2NF relations will avoid certain undesirable update anomalies present in 1NF relations.

The schema of a 1NF relation gives no clues to which attributes are dependent on which other attributes. By contrast, knowing that a relation is in 2NF means that no attribute is dependent on only part of the key.

Updating the facts in a 1NF relation can cause anomalies that are avoided in a 2NF relation. These situations occur when inserting new rows, deleting rows, and modifying rows.

Consider again the FACULTY_1 relation, which is in 1NF. It is not possible to insert a new row for a teacher who does not yet have students enrolled in the course that he teaches; MATRIC# is part of the primary key and therefore cannot have a null value. Similarly, a row for a new student cannot be inserted unless he is enrolled in a class.

If the FACULTY_1 row for a given teacher is deleted and it happens to be the only row for a particular student, then information about that student will also be lost, even though the intention was to delete the teacher information. A MATRIC# cannot exist in the relation without being associated with a FACULTY#, a DEPARTMENT_NAME, and a COURSE#, as all four of these attributes are the primary key. If it is necessary to change a student's name, then every FACULTY_1 row in which that student appears must be modified; otherwise the relation will contain contradictory data. The student may appear in several rows, because she may be taking several courses. Splitting the FACULTY_1 relation into FACULTY_2 and STUDENT avoids these problems. Similar arguments can be made for splitting off the COURSE_STUDENT and COURSE relations.

THIRD NORMAL FORM

A relation is in *third normal form (3NF)* if, and only if, it is in 2NF and no nonkey attribute is "transitively dependent" on the primary key. That is, a 3NF relation cannot have any nonkey attribute that is dependent on another nonkey attribute.

For example, the preceding relation FACULTY_2,

FACULTY_2 (FACULTY#, TEACHER_NAME, COMMITTEE#,
    MEETING_DAY, MEETING_TIME, DEPARTMENT_
    NAME, COURSE#)

is not in 3NF if the following functional dependencies hold in addition to the ones already introduced:

$$COMMITTEE\# \rightarrow MEETING\_DAY$$
$$COMMITTEE\# \rightarrow MEETING\_TIME$$

Two of the nonkey attributes (MEETING_DAY and MEETING_TIME) are dependent on another nonkey attribute (COMMITTEE#). Assume that the other nonkey attributes are not interdependent.

Producing 3NF

A relation can be resolved into 3NF by dividing it into component relations, each of which meets the 3NF test. The relation R (A, B, C) with dependencies

$$A \rightarrow B$$
$$B \rightarrow C$$
$$A \rightarrow C$$

should be split into two relations,

$$R1 (\underline{A}, B)$$
$$R2 (\underline{B}, C)$$

Resolving the FACULTY_2 relation gives

COMMITTEE (COMMITTEE#, MEETING_DAY, MEETING_TIME)
FACULTY_3 (FACULTY#, TEACHER_NAME, COMMITTEE#,
          DEPARTMENT_NAME, COURSE#)

Note that the COMMITTEE# attribute has been retained in the FACULTY_3 relation; it is a foreign-key attribute to the COMMITTEE relation. Without COMMITTEE# in FACULTY_3, it is not possible to know to which committee a teacher is assigned. Figure 5.5 shows a data model for the resulting set of 3NF relations.

A 2NF relation with only one (or no) nonkey attributes must always be a 3NF relation. No nonkey attribute can be dependent on another nonkey attribute unless there are at least two nonkey attributes in the relation.

Objectives of 3NF

The two main reasons for preferring 3NF relations over 2NF relations are that the semantics of a 3NF relation are more explicit—all attributes are dependent only on the primary key—and that a database designed with 3NF relations will avoid certain undesirable update anomalies present in 2NF relations.

The schema of a 2NF relation gives no clues to which nonkey attributes might be dependent on which other nonkey attributes. By contrast, knowing that a

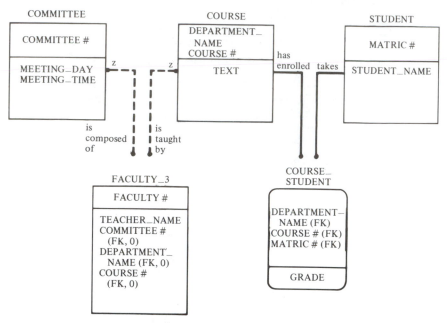

FIGURE 5.5 Logical data model normalized to 3NF.

relation is in 3NF means that no nonkey attribute is dependent on another nonkey attribute.

Anomalous situations arise when updating the facts in a 2NF relation that are avoided in a 3NF relation. These situations occur when inserting new rows, deleting rows, and modifying rows and are quite similar to the anomalies that arise in updating 1NF relations.

Consider the FACULTY_2 relation, which is in 2NF. It is not possible to insert facts about the meeting day and time for a new committee until there are teachers assigned to that committee; that is, committee data cannot exist unless they have an associated FACULTY#.

If the FACULTY_1 row for a given teacher is deleted and it happens to be the only row for a particular committee, then the data about that committee will be lost, even though the intention was to delete the teacher data, because a COMMITTEE# cannot exist in the relation without being associated with a FACULTY#.

If it is necessary to change a committee's meeting time, then every FACULTY_1 row in which that committee appears must be modified; otherwise the relation will contain contradictory data. The committee may appear in several rows, because there may be many teachers assigned to it.

Splitting the FACULTY_2 relation into FACULTY_3 and COMMITTEE avoids these problems.

BOYCE/CODD NORMAL FORM

The *Boyce/Codd normal form (BCNF)* is a stronger form of 3NF, in which an attribute or set of attributes on which some other attribute is fully functionally dependent is called a *determinant*. A relation is in BCNF if, and only if, every determinant is a candidate key.

BCNF differs from 3NF in that it requires full functional dependence on the candidate keys, whereas 3NF requires full functional dependence on only the primary key. They are equivalent rules unless the relation has more than one candidate key, and if there is only one candidate key, then it must be the primary key.

The relations COMMITTEE and FACULTY_3 are in both 3NF and BCNF, given the set of assumed functional dependencies. But if TEACHER_NAME is introduced as a candidate key for the FACULTY_3 relation, then it is no longer in 3NF. COMMITTEE#, DEPARTMENT_NAME, and COURSE# are determined by a nonkey attribute—TEACHER_NAME—as well as by the primary key—FACULTY#. BCNF accommodates this anomaly because TEACHER_NAME is a candidate key.

Consider also the following relation:

APPROVED_DEALER (CITY, CAR, DEALER_NAME)

with dependencies

DEALER_NAME → CITY	Each dealer is in only one city.
CAR, CITY → DEALER_NAME	For each car, each city that sells that car has only one approved dealer.

Assume that each car can be sold in many cities and each city can have many approved dealers.

The candidate keys are CITY, CAR and CAR, DEALER_NAME. The following instance table illustrates the attribute dependencies:

APPROVED_DEALER (CITY, CAR, DEALER_NAME)

CITY	CAR	DEALER_NAME
Tucson	Jeep	Galloway
Chicago	Jeep	O'Brien
Tucson	Mercedes	Galloway
Chicago	Mercedes	Cox

The APPROVED_DEALER relation is not in BCNF, as DEALER_NAME is a determinant but not a candidate key.

Producing BCNF

If a relation has several overlapping candidate keys, then it must be decomposed (separated) in order to attain BCNF. Two candidate keys overlap when both are compound and share an attribute.

The relation R (A, B, C) with dependencies

$$A, B \rightarrow C$$
$$C \quad \rightarrow B$$

and candidate keys A, B and A, C should be split into two relations:

$$R1 (B, \underline{C})$$
$$R2 (\underline{A}, \underline{C})$$

Resolving the APPROVED_DEALER relation gives

DEALER_LOC (<u>DEALER_NAME</u>, CITY)
PRODUCT (<u>DEALER_NAME</u>, <u>CAR</u>)

A 3NF relation with only one candidate key (which must also be the primary key) must always be a BCNF relation. A 3NF relation with only nonoverlapping candidate keys must always be a BCNF relation, which in turn always satisfies the 3NF rules.

Objectives of BCNF

The two main reasons for preferring BCNF relations over 3NF relations are that the semantics of multiple candidate keys are more explicit—all attributes are dependent only on the candidate keys—and that a database designed with BCNF relations will avoid certain undesirable update anomalies present in 3NF relations.

Defining all candidate keys of a relation is important when establishing uniqueness assertions. These assertions should be enforced when inserting, deleting, and modifying rows in the relation. All candidate keys, not just the primary key, must have unique values.

Anomalous situations arise when updating facts in a 3NF relation that are avoided in a BCNF relation. These anomalies occur when the relation has overlapping candidate keys.

For example, in the APPROVED_DEALER relation, it is not possible to delete the fact that Jeep is sold in Chicago without losing the fact that O'Brien is a dealer in Chicago. CAR is part of the key, regardless of which candidate key is designated as the primary key. A city and dealer fact cannot exist without an associated car fact, as CAR cannot be null. Similarly, it is not possible to insert the fact that Munson is a dealer in Tucson without designating a CAR fact.

The problem is that DEALER_NAME is a determinant but is not a candidate key, thus the relation is not in BCNF. Splitting the APPROVED_DEALER relation into DEALER_LOC and PRODUCT avoids these problems.

FOURTH NORMAL FORM

A relation is in *fourth normal form (4NF)* if, and only if, whenever there is a multivalued dependency on a determinant, all the attributes are functionally dependent on the determinant. A 4NF relation cannot have more than one multivalued dependency.

For example, consider again the FACULTY_3 relation:

FACULTY_3 (FACULTY#, TEACHER_NAME, COMMITTEE#,
          DEPARTMENT_NAME, COURSE#)

The dependencies so far indicate that a teacher is assigned to one committee and teaches one course. Let us now change the situation so that a teacher may be assigned to many committees and teach many courses, thus introducing two multivalued dependencies:

FACULTY# $\rightarrow\rightarrow$ COMMITTEE#
FACULTY# $\rightarrow\rightarrow$ DEPARTMENT_NAME, COURSE#

The relation now must have as its key FACULTY#, COMMITTEE#, DEPARTMENT_NAME, COURSE#.

The relation is not in 4NF, as it contains more than one multivalued dependency. In fact, it is not even in 2NF, because there is a nonkey attribute that is dependent on only part of the key. Splitting out the attribute that is dependent only on FACULTY# gives two relations:

FACULTY (FACULTY#, TEACHER_NAME)
FACULTY_4 (FACULTY#, COMMITTEE#,
          DEPARTMENT_NAME,
          COURSE#

FACULTY is now in 4NF, for the following reasons:

- It contains only single-valued attributes.
- Each nonkey attribute is dependent on the entire key.
- There are no dependencies among the nonkey attributes.
- There are no multivalued dependencies.

FACULTY_4 is in BCNF but is still not in 4NF. The dependencies imply that the set of COMMITTEE# values associated with a given FACULTY# value is totally independent of the set of DEPARTMENT_NAME, COURSE# values associated with that FACULTY# value. There is no dependence between COMMITTEE# and DEPARTMENT_NAME, COURSE#. Note that if this were not the case, then there would not be two multivalued dependencies.

Producing 4NF

A relation like this can be resolved into 4NF by splitting it into component relations, each of which meets the 4NF test. The relation R ($\underline{A}$, $\underline{B}$, $\underline{C}$) with dependencies

$$A \twoheadrightarrow B$$
$$A \twoheadrightarrow C$$

should be divided into two relations,

$$R1\ (\underline{A},\ \underline{B})$$
$$R2\ (\underline{A},\ \underline{C})$$

Resolving the FACULTY_4 relation produces two relations:

FACULTY_COMMITTEE (FACULTY#, COMMITTEE#)
FACULTY_COURSE (FACULTY#, DEPARTMENT_NAME, COURSE#)

Note that FACULTY# is a foreign-key attribute in both FACULTY_COMMITTEE and FACULTY_COURSE. COMMITTEE# is a foreign-key attribute in FACULTY_COMMITTEE, and DEPARTMENT_NAME, COURSE# is a compound foreign key in FACULTY_COURSE. These foreign-key attributes represent the connection relationships in the set of relations. Figure 5.6 shows a data model for the complete set of 4NF relations.

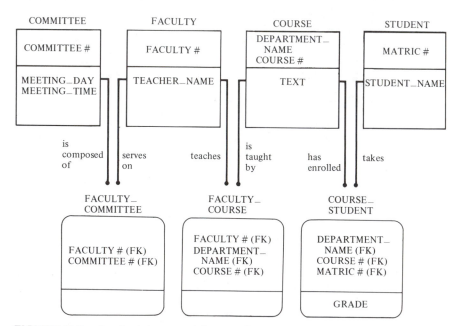

FIGURE 5.6. Logical data model normalized to 4NF. Note that multivalued dependencies have been added.

Objectives of 4NF

The two main reasons for preferring 4NF relations over BCNF relations are that the semantics of a 4NF relation are more explicit—all dependencies are related—and that a database designed with 4NF relations will avoid certain undesirable update anomalies present in 3NF relations.

The schema of a BCNF relation gives no clues to whether there are multi-valued dependencies among the primary key's components, nor is it clear which components of the primary key are independent of one another. By contrast, knowing that a relation is in 4NF means that no component of the key is independent of any other component.

Anomalous situations arise when updating a BCNF relation that are avoided in a 4NF relation. These situations occur when inserting new rows, deleting rows, and modifying rows and are quite similar to the anomalies that rise in updating 1NF, 2NF, and 3NF relations.

Consider the FACULTY_4 relation, which is in BCNF. Assume that the teacher with FACULTY# = 12345 teaches five courses and serves on four committees. It is not possible to insert data about the assignment of the teacher to another committee without actually inserting five rows, one for every course that the teacher teaches. The same set of DEPARTMENT_NAME, COURSE# values must exist in the relation for every COMMITTEE# value associated with the FACULTY#. If a committee assignment for the teacher is deleted, then that deletion actually means the removal of five rows, one for each course taught by the teacher. The same set of COMMITTEE# values must exist in the relation for every DEPARTMENT_NAME, COURSE# value associated with the FACULTY#.

If it is necessary to change a COURSE# for a course taught by this teacher, then that change must be reflected in four rows, one for each committee on which the teacher serves. Again, the same set of DEPARTMENT_NAME, COURSE# values must exist in the relation for every COMMITTEE# value associated with the FACULTY#.

Splitting the FACULTY_4 relation into FACULTY_COMMITTEE and FACULTY_COURSE avoids these problems.

FIFTH NORMAL FORM

A relation is in *fifth normal form (5NF)* if it cannot be split into smaller relations and then rejoined without changing its facts and meaning. It is in its most elementary form, representing its data by using the fewest attributes possible. A relation that is in 5NF is also in 4NF.

Because the properties of 5NF tend to be obscure, this last normal form is explained by means of an example. Consider the relation

DOG_SHOW (JUDGE, BREED, EVENT)

This relation is in 5NF unless it can be split into

ASSIGNMENT   (JUDGE, BREED)
ENTRY   (BREED, EVENT)
QUALIFICATION   (JUDGE, EVENT)

and these three relations can be rejoined to form a three-attribute relation with exactly the same instance table as the original DOG_SHOW relation had.

If DOG_SHOW is in 5NF, then the combined three attributes are necessary in order to express valid semantics. If it is in 5NF, then the DOG_SHOW relation can be interpreted as including the assertions that

• a person is qualified to judge only certain events for certain breeds.
• only certain breeds can enter certain events.

A valid instance table for the DOG_SHOW relation is given in Fig. 5.7. Edwin can judge the conformation event for Great Danes and the obedience event for poodles but is not qualified to judge obedience in Great Danes or conformation of poodles. Great Danes may enter the obedience and conformation events but may not enter the tricks event.

By contrast, if the DOG_SHOW relation is not in 5NF and can be decomposed into the three relations ASSIGNMENT, ENTRY, and QUALIFICATION and recombined without semantic change, then the operative assertion will be

> if   a person is qualified to judge an event
>   and a breed is allowed to enter an event
> then the person is qualified to judge that breed
>   in the event.

Valid instance tables for the ASSIGNMENT, ENTRY, and QUALIFICATION relations and the result of joining these relations are shown in Fig. 5.8. Note the differences between the combined relation here and the DOG_SHOW relation in Fig. 5.7. Data models of the DOG_SHOW relation and the ASSIGNMENT, ENTRY, and QUALIFICATION relations are shown in Fig. 5.9.

When a relation is in 5NF, there can be no further decomposition without destroying some of the facts and meaning. No combination of joining relations with fewer attributes can present the same data. A relation that is in 4NF and has only two attributes in its primary key must also be in 5NF, because there is no way to decompose it without losing data.

DOG_SHOW

JUDGE	BREED	EVENT
Edwin	Great Dane	Conformation
Edwin	Poodle	Obedience
Miller	Great Dane	Obedience
Miller	Poodle	Tricks
Miller	St. Bernard	Tricks
White	Great Dane	Conformation
Green	Poodle	Tricks
Green	Poodle	Obedience

FIGURE 5.7. Instance table for DOG_SHOW relation.

ASSIGNMENT

JUDGE	BREED
Edwin	Great Dane
Edwin	Poodle
Miller	Great Dane
Miller	Poodle
Miller	St. Bernard
White	Great Dane
Green	Poodle

ENTRY

BREED	EVENT
Great Dane	Conformation
Great Dane	Obedience
Poodle	Obedience
Poodle	Tricks
St. Bernard	Tricks

QUALIFICATION

JUDGE	EVENT
Edwin	Conformation
Edwin	Obedience
Miller	Obedience
Miller	Tricks
White	Conformation
Green	Tricks
Green	Obedience

(a) Instance tables for the three
binary relations projected from
the DOG_SHOW relation (Fig. 5.7).

JUDGE	BREED	EVENT
Edwin	Great Dane	Conformation
Edwin	Great Dane	Obedience
Miller	Great Dane	Obedience
Green	Great Dane	Obedience
White	Great Dane	Conformation
Edwin	Poodle	Obedience
Edwin	Poodle	Tricks
Miller	Poodle	Obedience
Green	Poodle	Obedience
Miller	Poodle	Tricks
Green	Poodle	Tricks
Miller	St. Bernard	Tricks
Green	St. Bernard	Tricks
White	Great Dane	Obedience

(b) Relation resulting from joining
the instance tables in (a).

FIGURE 5.8. Projections and rejoining of binary relations from DOG_
SHOW relation of Fig. 5.7.

Objectives of 5NF

The three main reasons for preferring 5NF relations over 4NF relations are that
the semantics of a 5NF relation are more explicit—there are no unrelated dependencies among groups of attributes—that a database designed with 5NF
relations will avoid certain undesirable update anomalies present in 4NF relations, and that 5NF relations are in their most granular form and there seems to
be little advantage in further decomposition.

Both 4NF and 5NF deal with multivalued dependencies, although 4NF recognizes only pairings of attributes by multivalued dependencies, and 5NF recognizes that multivalued dependencies can exist among three or more attributes.

Anomalous situations arise when updating a 4NF relation that are avoided in
a 5NF relation. These situations occur when inserting new rows, deleting rows,
and modifying rows and are quite similar to the anomalies that arise in updating

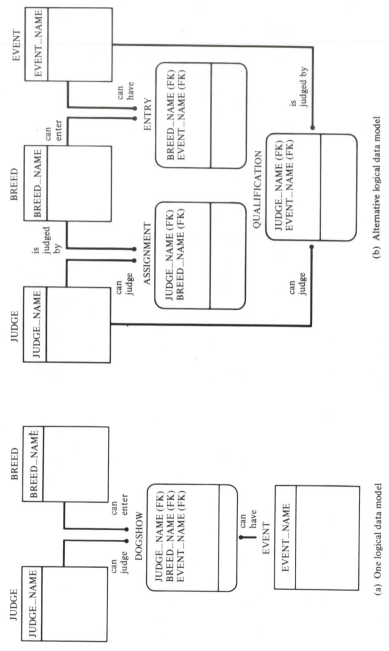

(a) One logical data model

(b) Alternative logical data model

FIGURE 5.9. Two logical data models representing different semantics.

1NF, 2NF, 3NF, and BCNF relations. In 4NF, the anomalies are caused by redundancies in the relation's instance table.

Consider the DOG_SHOW relation that is in 4NF but not in 5NF. Assume that judge Bob is assigned to three events, each of which allows four different breeds to be entered. The fact that Bob is assigned to the trick event is recorded four times, but this replication is removed when the DOG_SHOW relation is split into its three component relations.

THE NORMALIZATION PROCESS

The two approaches to relational normalization are *synthesis* and *decomposition*.

Synthesis

The synthesis approach starts with a set of attributes and a statement of dependencies and combines the attributes in such a way that a set of normalized relations results. Much of the work on this approach was published before the development of Boyce/Codd and the fourth and fifth normal forms. The approach therefore addresses the synthesis of 3NF relations.

Decomposition

The decomposition approach starts with a set of relations (perhaps just one) and a statement of dependencies and splits these initial relations into a set of normalized relations. The explanation of the normal forms in this chapter used the decomposition approach.

The decomposition approach is generally preferable to the synthesis approach, because the synthesis algorithms deal only with patterns of stated dependencies (i.e., with syntax) rather than with semantics. The decomposition approach, by contrast, deals with attributes in the context of relations, which supply a semantic framework.

The assumption that all attributes can be considered as being in one universal relation has undesirable implications, as it is necessary to identify the initial groupings of attributes into relations that have some semantic sense as entities before applying decomposition procedures. Chapter 8 discusses obtaining these initial relations.

APPLICATIONS OF NORMALIZATION THEORY

We saw earlier that relational normalization has basically one objective, to obtain stable groupings of attributes into relations and that there are two primary motivations for this objective, extensible logical database designs and flexible physical database designs.

Logical Data Modeling

Relational normalization helps answer a question that arises in logical data modeling: What is a well-defined entity? If the objective of normalization is restated as obtaining "stable" groupings of attributes into entities, then the applicability of relational normalization to logical database design becomes more obvious. Each relation in a normalized model represents an entity; therefore, relational normalization becomes a logical data-modeling tool. Principles of normalization can be applied to help determine in which entity an attribute should reside.

Each successive form of normalization increases the semantic explicitness of the resulting relations, and more semantic information is conveyed by the relational schema just by knowing that it is in a particular normal form. If a logical data model's entities conform to the rules of normalization, then the model should convey more semantic information than if the concepts of normalization were not applied.

The primary practical difficulty encountered in applying relational normalization to building logical data models is identifying the functional and multivalued dependencies in the real world. Normalization relies completely on valid statements of dependencies; yet users can have difficulty developing these statements.

The value of relational normalization as a part of logical data modeling should not be interpreted as an endorsement of the relational model as an approach to logical data modeling. In fact, some important data-modeling concepts are quite difficult to represent in the relational model. One example of a concept that is not well treated by the relational model is the category relationship. Furthermore, the normalization rules are not the only rules that can be applied to identify "stable" entities, although these other rules are beyond the scope of this text. The utility of relational normalization for logical data modeling thus is primarily in the area of the intensions (i.e., schemas) of relations.

Physical Database Design

Much of the justification for the relational normal forms is the avoidance of various update anomalies. These are cases when storing facts in the database is adversely affected by the relations' structure. The utility of relational normalization for physical database design is principally in the extensions (i.e., population) of relations.

It may at first seem inefficient to split a table into several tables to meet the constraints of the normalization rules, although such decomposition actually can improve performance by reducing the number of rows in each table. More importantly, the integrity of the data can be maintained more efficiently if the relations in the database are designed to meet the rules of normalization.

But there is more to the physical design of relational databases than identifying the base relations. For example, indexes and search strategies can be selected, and the distribution of relations into physical files can be specified. The application of normalization principles to reduce data replication can lead, however, to more efficient, more flexible physical relational databases.

CLOSING COMMENTS

Relational normalization is a rigorous, exact approach to grouping attributes into stable relations and can be applied to logical design of all databases, regardless of whether they will be implemented with a relational database management system.

The questions most commonly asked when splitting an un-normalized relation into normalized relations are

- (1NF) Can any attribute have multiple values? If yes, then "flatten" the relation into 1NF.
- (2NF) Is any attribute dependent on only part of the key? If yes, then split the relation until all attributes are dependent on their entire key.
- (3NF) Is any attribute dependent on a nonkey attribute? If yes, then split the relation until all attributes are dependent only on their key.
- (BCNF) Does the relation contain any dependencies on other than the candidate keys? If yes, then split the relation until all attributes are dependent only on the candidate keys.
- (4NF, 5NF) Does the relation contain independent multivalued dependencies? If yes, then split the relation until no independent dependencies remain.

Perhaps the simplest way to phrase the normalization rules is

- Each nonkey attribute is dependent on the entire key and nothing but the key.
- No relation contains unrelated dependencies.

TERMS

Boyce/Codd normal form (BCNF)	instance table
candidate key	intension of a relation
decomposition	key
determinant	multivalued dependency
extension of a relation	normalization
fifth normal form (5NF)	primary key
first normal form (1NF)	second normal form (2NF)
foreign-key attribute	synthesis
fourth normal form (4NF)	third normal form (3NF)
functional dependency	

REVIEW EXERCISES

1. Define each of the terms in the preceding list.

2. Consider the following relation:
Q (EMP#, FIRST_NAME, LAST_NAME, DEPT#, JOB_CODE, COURSE#, JOB_NAME, DATE, SALARY, CHILD_NAME, CUSTOMER#, CUSTOMER_NAME, QUANTITY, DESCRIPTION)

a. In which normal form is relation Q?

b. Assuming the following dependencies, split Q into 4NF:
EMP# → FIRST_NAME, LAST_NAME
EMP# → JOB_CODE, JOB_NAME
EMP# → COURSE#
EMP#, DATE → SALARY
EMP#, CUST# → QUANTITY, DESCRIPTION
JOB_CODE → JOB_NAME
CUSTOMER# → CUSTOMER_NAME
EMP# →→ CHILD_NAME
EMP# →→ DATE, SALARY

c. Assuming that each of your relations is an entity, draw a logical data model diagram to represent the result of normalizing Q.

3. Consider the following relation:
STUDENT (MATRIC#, NAME, MAJOR_DEPT#, DEPT_NAME, COURSE_ID, DESCRIPTION, SECTION#, GRADE, TEACHER, MEETING_TIME, MEETING_PLACE)

a. Assuming the following dependencies, split STUDENT into 4NF:
MATRIC# → NAME
MATRIC# → MAJOR_DEPT#
DEPT_NAME, COURSE_ID → DESCRIPTION
DEPT_NAME, COURSE_ID, SECTION# → TEACHER
DEPT_NAME, COURSE_ID, SECTION# → MEETING_TIME
DEPT_NAME, COURSE_ID, SECTION# → MEETING_PLACE
MATRIC#, DEPT_NAME, COURSE_ID, SECTION# → GRADE

b. Assuming that each of your relations is an entity, draw a logical data model diagram to represent the result of normalizing STUDENT.

4. Consider the following relation:
R (CLASS, SECTION, STUDENT, MAJOR, EXAM, YEAR, INSTRUCTOR, RANK, SALARY, TEXT, DAY, ROOM)

a. In which normal form is R?

b. Assuming the following dependencies, split R into 4NF:
CLASS, SECTION → INSTRUCTOR
CLASS, SECTION, DAY → ROOM
STUDENT → MAJOR, YEAR

> INSTRUCTOR $\rightarrow$ RANK, SALARY
> CLASS, SECTION $\rightarrow\rightarrow$ STUDENT, MAJOR, EXAM, YEAR
> CLASS, SECTION $\rightarrow\rightarrow$ DAY, ROOM
> CLASS, SECTION, STUDENT $\rightarrow\rightarrow$ EXAM

    c. Assuming that each of your relations is an entity, draw a logical data model diagram to represent the result of normalizing R.

5. For each of the following relations, what are the corresponding 4NF relations? Assume the following dependencies:

$A \rightarrow B$
$A \rightarrow C$
$A \rightarrow\rightarrow D$
$A \rightarrow\rightarrow E$
$B \rightarrow L$
$B \rightarrow C$
$F \rightarrow G$
$H \rightarrow F$
$A, F \rightarrow K$
$A, F \rightarrow H$

    a. R1 ($\underline{A}$, B, $\underline{F}$, G)
    b. R2 ($\underline{A}$, B, C)
    c. R3 ($\underline{A}$, B, $\underline{D}$, $\underline{E}$)
    d. R4 ($\underline{A}$, C, $\underline{G}$)
    e. R5 ($\underline{A}$, $\underline{F}$, H, K)
    f. R6 ($\underline{B}$, L)

6. Consider the following relations:

R1 (A, B, C, D)
R2 (A, B, E)
R3 (A, C, D, F)

Assuming the following dependencies, give an equivalent set of 4NF relations. Your answer should have three relations.

$A \rightarrow B$
$A, C, \rightarrow D$
$A \rightarrow E$
$B \rightarrow C$
$D \rightarrow F$
$B \rightarrow D$

7. In addition to functional and multivalued dependencies, several other types of dependencies have been proposed in the relational literature. What are these dependencies, and how do they differ from functional and multivalued dependencies?

8. In addition to 1NF, 2NF, 3NF, BCNF, 4NF, and 5NF, several other normal forms have been proposed in the relational literature. What are these forms, and how do they differ from the six normal forms?

9.   Describe how each of the automated data-modeling tools introduced in Chapter 3 addresses normalization.

10.   Are the normalization principles used in your organization as part of the database development process?

REFERENCES

Aho, A. V., C. Beeri, and J. D. Ullman. The theory of joins in relational databases, *ACM Trans. on Database Systems* 4 (September 1979):297–314.

Armstrong, W.W. Dependency structures of data base relationships, *Proc. IFIP Congress, 1974.*

Beeri, C., R. Fagin, and J. H. Howard. A complete axiomatization for functional and multivalued dependencies in database relations, ACM SIGMOD Conf. on Management of Data, Toronto, August 1977, pp. 47–61.

Bernstein, P. A. Synthesizing third normal form relations from functional dependencies, *ACM Trans. on Database Systems* 1 (December 1976):277–298.

Bernstein, P. A., and C. Beeri. An algorithmic approach to normalization of relational database schemas, *Tech. Rpt. CSRG-73,* Computer Systems Research Group, Dept. of Computer Science, University of Toronto, September 1976.

Brown, R. G. *Logical Database Design Techniques.* Mountain View, Calif.: The Database Design Group, July 14, 1982.

Codd, E. F. Extending the database relational model to capture more meaning, *ACM Trans. Database Systems* 4 (December 1979):397–434.

———. Normalized data base structure: A brief tutorial, Proc. 1971 ACM SIGFIDET Workshop on Data Description, Access and Control, 1971.

———. A relational model for large shared databases, *Communications ACM* 13 (June 1970):377–387.

Date, C. J. Further normalization, chap. 14 in *An Introduction to Database Systems.* Third ed. Reading, Mass.: Addison-Wesley, 1981, pp. 237–272.

Fagin, R. The decomposition versus the synthetic approach to relational database design, Proc. 3rd Intl. Conf. on Very Large Data Bases, Tokyo, 1977, pp. 441–446.

———. Functional dependencies in a relational database and propositional logic, *IBM Journal of Research and Development* 21 (November 1977).

———. Multivalued dependencies and a new normal form for relational databases, *ACM Trans. Database Systems* 2 (September 1977):262–278.

Kent, W. Consequences of assuming a universal relation, *ACM Trans. on Database Systems.* 6 (December 1981):539–556.

———. A simple guide to five normal forms in relational database theory, *Communications ACM* 26 (February 1983):120–125.

Schmid, H. A., and J. R. Swenson. On the semantics of the relational data model, *Proc. of ACM SIGMOD Conf. on Management of Data,* San Jose, Calif., May 1975, pp. 211–223.

Mapping to the Network Data Model

Relational and network data model developments have proceeded in parallel. The relational model has its roots in the research world and has been extended through the database research literature, whereas the network data model grew from efforts to provide commercial database management services. The network model does not have the firm theoretic basis that the relational model enjoys, but it does have a reputation for being able to handle the implementation of and access to large, real databases. The network data model is important because nearly all the major computer hardware/software vendors have developed a commercial database management product to support it, the most notable exception being IBM.

The two main forces behind network databases are the CODASYL committees and Cincom Systems, Inc. The first group developed the CODASYL data model, and Cincom is the vendor of the TOTAL database management system.

THE CODASYL COMMITTEE

The CODASYL data model was developed by an organization named CODASYL: Conference on Data Systems Languages. Approximately half of its members are representatives of hardware and software vendor companies. The other half of its members are representatives of the user community, including the United States armed forces and organizations from the public and private sectors.

The CODASYL organization evolved through a number of committees, including the Data Base Task Group (DBTG), the Data Definition Language Committee (DDLC), the Programming Language Committee, the COBOL Committee, the Systems Committee, the FORTRAN Data Manipulation Language Committee, the End Users Facilities Committee, and the Common Operating Systems Control Language Committee. Several have had major impacts on the CODASYL data model, and all are run under the guidance of the CODASYL Executive Committee.

The DBTG published its principal report in 1971, which specified the fundamentals of today's commercial CODASYL-compatible database management systems. The task group was the forerunner of the DDLC, which concentrated on the structural aspects of databases. The committee's efforts on a data definition language (DDL) were documented in its *Journals of Development*, published approximately every three years, the major publications being the 1973 and the 1978 reports. The DDLC was disbanded in 1984, in part because the data definition language had been picked up for standardization by the X3H2 committee of the American National Standards Institute (ANSI).

The data manipulation aspects of CODASYL databases are the responsibility of the programming language committees, and their results are documented primarily in the *COBOL Journal of Development* and the *FORTRAN Journal of Development*. In these documents, data manipulation language (DML) commands are added to both the COBOL and FORTRAN languages.

The X3H2 work addresses both the data definition and data manipulation aspects of the database language. Rather than being separated into distinct documents, the network DDL and DML are one language in the X3H2 publications.

FUNDAMENTALS OF THE CODASYL MODEL

The three main aspects of the CODASYL model are its *structure, assertions,* and *operators*. The CODASYL model's structure is more complex than that of the relational model, as CODASYL databases are represented as networks of interconnected record types. Assertions are tied directly to the operators and their effects on various structures.

STRUCTURE

The structural components of the CODASYL data model are the data items and data fields, record occurrences and record types, set types, keys, and areas.

Data Items and Data Fields

A *data item* is an occurrence of the smallest unit of named data and is represented in the database by a value. A data item is essentially the same as a field in a file, for example, "Flyswift Airlines," "Igor," and 12345.

A data item represents an attribute value, whereas a *data field* is an attribute, for example, airline name, employee name, and zip code. A data field has associated with it a data type, which determines its format. The CODASYL data types are programming-language-like and include COBOL pictures, binary, decimal, fixed, float, real, complex, bit, character, and implementor defined. There is no explicit concept of a domain in the CODASYL data model. A data field is characterized by its mode of representation (i.e., by its data type) rather than by its valid set of values.

Record Occurrences and Record Types

A *record occurrence* is an instance of a named collection of zero, one, or more data items, like a record in a file. The format of a record occurrence is determined by its *record type,* and a *record type description* tells the name of the record type and its data fields. There may be an arbitrary number of record occurrences of a given record type in a database. A record type can be used to represent an entity, and when it does, each record occurrence represents an entity instance.

A CODASYL database contains many different record types, which can be physically implemented in a single physical file. The database schema describes the record types and their interrelationships.

Set Types

Record interrelationships are represented in a CODASYL database by sets. A *set type* represents a named, one-to-many relationship among record types. Each set type has one record type declared to be its owner record type, and one or more record types declared as its member record types. A *set occurrence* must contain one occurrence of its owner record type and may contain zero, one, or more (i.e., many) occurrences of its member record type.

Figure 6.1(a) illustrates a logical data model with a one-to-many relationship, named EMPLOYS, between two entities: TEACHING_UNIT and TEACHER. Figure 6.1(b) shows the schema of the corresponding CODASYL structure. A set type is represented by an arrow connecting the owner record type to the member record type.

An example of a set type with multiple member record types is shown in Fig. 6.2(a). Here each DEPARTMENT record occurrence has associated with it in

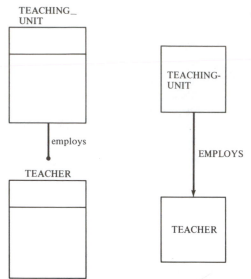

FIGURE 6.1. One-to-many connection relationship.

(a) Logical data model   (b) CODASYL schema

the HAS-MAJORS set type many GRADUATE-STUDENT record occurrences and many UNDERGRADUATE-STUDENT record occurrences. Two possible corresponding logical data models are shown in Figs. 6.2(b) and 6.2(c). The first uses two connection relationships, and the second also introduces a category relationship.

The member record occurrences in a set are sequenced in a predefined order. When the member record occurrences of a set are retrieved, they are accessed in that order. Set ordering distinguishes the representation of relationships in the CODASYL data model from the relational model. There is no concept of ordering of tuples in a relation (unless explicitly requested in formatting results of a request). Note that there is also no concept of sequencing in the instances of an entity in a logical data model (see Chapter 3).

Some set types are known as *value-based sets*. In an occurrence of one of these sets, the value of one or more specified data fields in the owner record occurrence must match the value of one or more specified data fields in each member occurrence. For example, the set EMPLOYS introduced in Fig. 6.1(b) would be value based if the value of DEPARTMENT-NAME, COLLEGE-NAME in each TEACHER record had to match the DEPARTMENT-NAME, COLLEGE-NAME value in the TEACHING-UNIT record with which it is associated.

The data fields in the owner and member record types need not have the same name in order to be used as the basis for a value-based set. Rather, a value-based set exists whenever the following constraint holds:

If record type O with data fields O1, O2, . . . , On is the owner and record type M with data fields M1, M2, . . . , Mm is the member in set

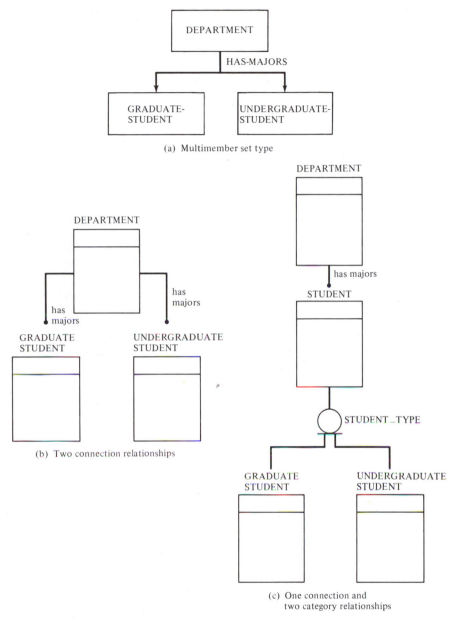

(a) Multimember set type

(b) Two connection relationships

(c) One connection and
two category relationships

FIGURE 6.2. Logical data model-CODASYL structure correspondence.

type S, then set type S is value based if the value of Oj = the value of Mi for each owner and member in each occurrence of the set, where Oj and Mi are collections of data fields in record types O and M, respectively.

This constraint is much like the key migration rule in a logical data model, according to which attributes from the independent entity in a relationship mi-

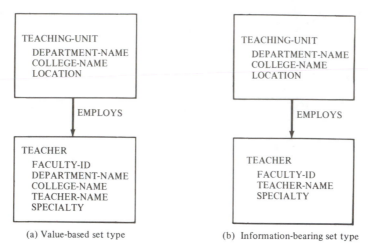

(a) Value-based set type   (b) Information-bearing set type

FIGURE 6.3. Two versions of set types.

grate into the dependent entity. It is also like the referential integrity constraint of the relational model, which requires that the value of a foreign key be represented as the value of the home relation's primary key.

If a set is not value based, then it is said to be *information bearing*. There is no logical connection made based on a foreign-key-like construct; rather, the logical connection exists solely because the set type exists. An information-bearing set is also called an *essential set*.

Figure 6.3 illustrates two versions of the EMPLOYS set type. Figure 6.3(a) is value based, whereas Fig. 6.3(b) is information bearing. If the EMPLOYS set were removed from the schema in Fig. 6.3(a), the logical relationship between TEACHING-UNIT and TEACHER would continue to exist. In fact, the structure would be exactly the same as if there were two relations, TEACHING_UNIT and TEACHER. The foreign-key DEPARTMENT_NAME, COLLEGE_NAME in TEACHER, would match the primary key of the home relation, TEACHING_UNIT. By contrast, if the EMPLOYS set were removed from the schema in Fig. 6.3(b), the logical relationship between TEACHING-UNIT and TEACHER would be lost. The result is the same as when translating each entity of a logical data model into a relation before the keys migrate through the relationships.

Keys

The CODASYL data model supports two kinds of keys: *identifiers* and *sort keys*. A record type can be declared to have identifying data fields, which may or may not be unique. If they are unique identifiers, then these keys are essentially the same as the candidate keys defined in Chapter 3. There is no require-ment that a primary key be identified for any record type. Or a set type can be declared to have a sort key, whose value determines the order of member records in the set's occurrences. These keys need not have unique values. No analogous type of key was introduced in Chapter 3.

The early CODASYL data model (1973) additionally supported *search keys*, which were used to specify physical access paths, but they were removed from later versions of the data model so as to achieve better logical-physical sepa-ration. They are still used in various commercial CODASYL DBMSs.

Areas

Some CODASYL DBMSs support a structure called *areas*, or named collections of one or more record types. Areas have sometimes been called *realms*.

Areas are used to define subsets of a database. They sometimes compartmen-talize a database for security protection. In addition, operators may be available to scan an area for occurrences of a particular record type, without accessing the contents of other areas.

An area can be declared to be temporary, which means that it is copied from the database and is local to the execution of the program that opens it. No changes that the program makes in the area are reflected in the database, and they disappear when the program terminates. Temporary areas are useful for testing program logic.

Usually an area is implemented as a physical file. Some people believe that this kind of physical structure should not be declared in a data definition language and should not be part of a logical model. The 1978 *Journal of Development* reflects some of this contention over areas and is itself inconsistent in its treat-ment of areas: Although every record type must be declared to reside in some area, there is no way to define an area and no other use of areas.

The area structure does not appear in more recent releases of some CODASYL DBMSs. It is used, however, in others.

Representation

The CODASYL data model is represented by a diagram resembling a logical data model diagram. Figure 6.4 illustrates a CODASYL data model that cor-responds directly to the logical data model of Fig. 4.10. Each record type is represented by a box containing the record type's name, and each set type is represented by an arrow from the owner record type to the member record type. Data-field names are not shown in these diagrams, although they may be written into the appropriate record type boxes.

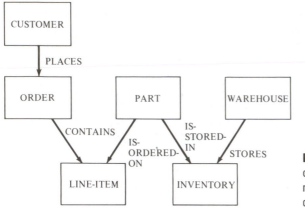

FIGURE 6.4. CODASYL data model corresponding directly to the logical data model of Fig. 4.10.

OPERATORS

The CODASYL data model's operators are part of its Data Manipulation Language (DML). The DML operators process records one at a time, which is the main distinction between these operators and those of the relational model, which process entire relations at one time. The operators were intended to be used in application programs written in COBOL, FORTRAN, or other similar languages, which are oriented toward record-at-a-time operations. For example, a COBOL READ from a file retrieves just one record, and a FORTRAN WRITE to a file creates just one record.

The syntax of the CODASYL data manipulation operators varies slightly in the *Journals of Development* and in the various CODASYL-compatible commercial database management systems. One representative notation has been adopted here.

The CODASYL data manipulation language is a procedural language in which the programmer specifies how to walk through the database, not just what data are wanted from the database.

The seven CODASYL data manipulation operators are FIND, GET, MODIFY, STORE, ERASE, CONNECT, and DISCONNECT. Correct use of the operators requires an understanding of the target database schema structure. They are used by the programmer to traverse through the record and set structures of the database.

Currency

Currency is a technique for leaving "place-holders" in a database. These place-holders are essential to proper navigation through the database structure. Each program that is accessing a CODASYL database has available to it a group of currency indicators (or logical pointers) that indicate the most recently referenced records in various structures of the database.

The following are the currency indicators that a CODASYL database management system makes available to each execution of a program or *run-unit:*

- Current of run-unit: the record occurrence most recently referenced.
- Current of record type: for each record type, the record occurrence most recently referenced.
- Current of set type: for each set type, the record occurrence (owner or member) of the set occurrence most recently referenced.
- Current of area: for each area, the record occurrence most recently referenced.

Currency indicators are updated by the database management system during the successful execution of certain data manipulation operators. If a database had 100 record types and 102 set types, then the database management system would maintain

- one record as the current of run-unit.
- 100 records as the current of their respective record types.
- 102 records as the current of their respective set types.

The value of a currency indicator is a logical pointer known in CODASYL terminology as a *database key*. CODASYL database keys usually are implemented as physical addresses.

Selecting Record Occurrences

The FIND statement is used to select a database record occurrence, and its typical format is

FIND record-selection-expression

which may be followed by a phrase to suppress the update of currency indicators. When this phrase is not specified, the record referenced by the record-selection-expression becomes the current record of the run-unit, the current record of its record type, the current record of all set types in which it participates, and the current record of all areas in which it resides.

There are several formats for record-selection-expressions, which support record selection both directly and relative to other records in the database. The ways to identify a record occurrence are (see Fig. 6.5) by its position, currency indicator, key value, or address.

The ways of locating a record by position are illustrated in the following examples. The database structure accessed is that of Fig. 6.4. Throughout, "selects" here implies that the currency indicators have been changed.

FIND FIRST CUSTOMER RECORD OF PERSONNEL AREA.
Selects the first occurrence of CUSTOMER that appears in the PERSONNEL area.

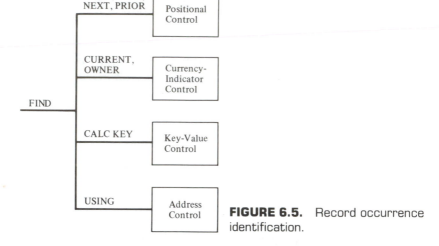

FIGURE 6.5. Record occurrence identification.

FIND NEXT CUSTOMER RECORD OF PERSONNEL AREA.
> Selects the next occurrence of CUSTOMER that appears in the PER-SONNEL area, relative to the current CUSTOMER record in that area.

FIND 5 CUSTOMER RECORD OF PERSONNEL AREA.
> Selects the fifth occurrence of CUSTOMER that appears in the PER-SONNEL area. Any integer or integer-valued identifier may be specified.

FIND PRIOR CUSTOMER RECORD OF PERSONNEL AREA.
> Selects the previous occurrence of CUSTOMER that appears in the PERSONNEL area, relative to the current CUSTOMER record in that area.

FIND LAST CUSTOMER RECORD OF PERSONNEL AREA.
> Selects the final occurrence of CUSTOMER that appears in the PER-SONNEL area.

An area FIND generally is processed by a sequential scan of the file that implements the area.

Positionally controlled FINDs can also be specified within a set type. For example,

```
FIND FIRST ORDER RECORD OF PLACES SET.
FIND NEXT ORDER RECORD OF PLACES SET.
FIND 12 ORDER RECORD OF PLACES SET.
FIND PRIOR ORDER RECORD OF PLACES SET.
FIND LAST ORDER RECORD OF PLACES SET.
```

Processing each of these commands first identifies the current of the PLACES set, determining which of the occurrences of that set is of interest. Then the first, next, twelfth, prior, or last member of the set is selected.

Another set-oriented, positionally controlled FIND resets the currency from a member occurrence in a set to its owner. This type of record-selection-expression can be relative to the current of run-unit:

```
FIND OWNER IN PLACES SET.
```

which will give an error condition if the current of run-unit is not a member in the PLACES set. A FIND OWNER command also can be relative to another currency indicator. For example,

```
FIND OWNER IN PLACES OF CURRENT OF ORDER RECORD.
FIND OWNER IN PLACES OF CURRENT OF PERSONNEL AREA.
FIND OWNER IN CONTAINS OF CURRENT OF IS-ORDERED-ON SET.
```

The last option is useful in traversing the many-to-many relationships formed by two set types with a common base record.

The non-set-oriented options for locating a record by means of the currency indicator are illustrated in the following examples:

```
FIND CURRENT CUSTOMER RECORD.
FIND CURRENT OF PLACES SET.
FIND CURRENT OF PERSONNEL AREA.
```

Each of these resets the current of run-unit to be the current of the specified record, set, or area.

Records can also be selected by their key values. Assume that CUSTOMER was declared to have a search key or CALC key of CUSTOMER#. (CALC keys will be discussed shortly; for now consider them to be identifiers.) The following statements locate the CUSTOMER record with CUSTOMER# = 123456:

```
MOVE 123456 TO CUSTOMER#.
FIND CUSTOMER.
```

Finally, records can be selected by their addresses. Assume that the programmer knows a particular CUSTOMER record's database key value (i.e., logical address). That value has been stored in a programmer-defined field named TARGET-RECORD-ADDRESS, which must have a data-type database-key. The following statement locates the corresponding CUSTOMER record:

```
FIND CUSTOMER USING TARGET-RECORD-ADDRESS.
```

Thus there are many ways to specify which record of a database is to be selected. Record-selection-expressions are positional (i.e., FIRST, NEXT, PRIOR, LAST, nth, OWNER), by currency, by key value, and by logical address. Each selects just one record occurrence, and so the programmer must iterate through a sequence of FIND NEXTs in order to select all of the member record occurrences of a set.

Fetching Data-Item Values from Records

The FIND statement establishes the values of various currency indicators, and it locates a record of interest. The GET statement fetches values from data items of the run-unit's current record. These values can then be moved into program variables or manipulated directly by the programmer.

For example, the following sequence of statements first locates the CUSTOMER record with CUSTOMER# = 12345 and then makes available the data items in that record:

```
MOVE 12345 TO CUSTOMER#.
FIND CUSTOMER.
GET.
```

The programmer instead could have said GET CUSTOMER, which more clearly documents the action. GET always fetches the run-unit's current record and never changes its currency.

Changing Data-Item Values in Records

The MODIFY statement replaces the contents of one or more data items in the run-unit's current record. For example, the following statements change the values of the CREDIT-LIMIT and DISCOUNT data items in the CUSTOMER record with CUSTOMER# = 12345. Assume that a previous statement (e.g., the preceding FIND) has already made that record the current record of the run-unit.

```
ADD 1000 TO CREDIT-LIMIT.
MOVE SPECIAL-DEAL TO DISCOUNT.
MODIFY.
```

The programmer instead could have said MODIFY CUSTOMER. MODIFY always works on the run-unit's current record and never changes its currency.

Adding New Record Occurrences

The STORE statement causes a record occurrence to be placed into the database. The values of the record's data items should have been moved previously to those data items. For example, the following sequence of statements creates a new CUSTOMER record in the database:

```
MOVE 98765 TO CUSTOMER#.
MOVE 250 TO CREDIT-LIMIT.
MOVE 0 TO DISCOUNT.
MOVE '1200 S. PALO VERDE' TO CUSTOMER-ADDRESS.
MOVE 'ELLIE BEANE' TO CUSTOMER-NAME.
STORE CUSTOMER.
```

The STORE statement has an optional phrase to suppress the update of the currency indicators. If that phrase is not used, the newly stored record will become the current of the run-unit, the current of its record type, the current of any set types in which it participates as owner or member, and the current of the area in which it resides.

Deleting Record Occurrences

The ERASE statement deletes one or more records from the database and has sometimes also been known as the DELETE statement. The ERASE statement always acts on the run-unit's current record; the programmer must use a currency-establishing statement (e.g., a FIND) to make the desired record current. For example, the following sequence of statements first locates the CUSTOMER record for CUSTOMER# = 55555 and then deletes it:

```
MOVE 55555 TO CUSTOMER#.
FIND CUSTOMER.
ERASE.
```

The programmer instead could have said ERASE CUSTOMER. ERASE always works on the run-unit's current record.

An optional ALL phrase on the ERASE statement can also be used to delete any records owned by the erased record. If the ALL option is not specified, then various assertions will determine whether owned record occurrences will be affected by the ERASE.

Establishing Set Linkages

The CONNECT statement causes the run-unit's current record to become a member in the one or more set types in which it is declared to participate. The record is inserted into each set in accordance with its set-ordering criteria. For example, consider again the schema of Fig. 6.4. Assume that the proper values have been moved to the data items of LINE-ITEM. The following sequence of statements first stores the new record occurrence in the database, establishing the run-unit's currency, and then places the record into the two sets:

```
STORE LINE-ITEM.
CONNECT TO CONTAINS, IS-ORDERED-ON.
```

The programmer instead could have said CONNECT LINE-ITEM TO CONTAINS, IS-ORDERED-ON. The CONNECT statement need not immediately follow the STORE statement, although the new record occurrence does not become part of the set until the CONNECT has occurred.

CONNECT always works on the run-unit's current record. The currency indicator for each set type to which the record is connected is modified so that that record becomes the current of the set type. No other currency indicators are changed.

Removing Set Linkages

The DISCONNECT statement removes the run-unit's current record from one or more sets. For example, the following sequence of statements first loops through the LINE-ITEM records that are members in the CONTAINS set with the ORDER owner having ORDER# = AB1213 and then disconnects each LINE-ITEM record from this set and the IS-ORDERED-ON set if the QUANTITY-ORDERED < 10:

```
MOVE 'N' TO END-OF-SET.
MOVE 'AB1213' TO ORDER#.
FIND ORDER.
FIND FIRST LINE-ITEM IN CONTAINS SET.
IF ERROR-COUNT > 0
    MOVE 'Y' TO END-OF-SET.
PERFORM FIND-NEXT-LINE-ITEM UNTIL END-OF-SET = 'Y'.
```

The referenced paragraph is

```
FIND-NEXT-LINE-ITEM.
   IF QUANTITY-ORDERED < 10
       DISCONNECT LINE-ITEM FROM CONTAINS, IS-ORDERED-ON.
   FIND NEXT LINE-ITEM IN CONTAINS SET.
   IF ERROR-COUNT > 0
       MOVE 'Y' TO END-OF-SET.
```

ERROR-COUNT is a status indicator that is discussed in the next section.

DISCONNECT always works on the run-unit's current record. The currency indicator for each set type from which the record is disconnected will be modified if the record is the current of that set type. No other currency indicators are changed. DISCONNECT does not delete any records from the database. It removes set linkages, but the subject records continue to exist.

Another variation of the DISCONNECT specifies that a record be disconnected from all the sets in which it participates as a member.

Changing Set Linkages

The RECONNECT statement moves a record from being a member in one set occurrence to being a member in another occurrence of that same set. For example, the following sequence of statements changes an employee from being employed by the ''operations'' department to being employed by the ''development'' department:

```
MOVE 12751 TO EMP-NO.
FIND EMPLOYEE.
MOVE "development" TO DEPT-NAME.
FIND DEPARTMENT.
RECONNECT EMPLOYEE IN EMPLOYS.
```

RECONNECT is used when a record occurrence must remain a member of a particular set but it is necessary to change its owner. The record is logically moved from one set occurrence into the other.

Status Indicators

The preceding examples refer to a field named ERROR-COUNT, which is one of several indicators that a CODASYL database management system makes available to return the status of each requested operation. Two of the more useful indicators are the ERROR-COUNT, which is zero if the last operation was executed successfully and greater than zero otherwise, and ERROR-STA-TUS, which has a value that indicates the condition resulting from the last operation.

ERROR-COUNT will be greater than zero in the following situations, among others:

- Attempt to FIND NEXT record in a set, when the last record in the set is already the run-unit's current record.
- Attempt to FIND PRIOR record in a set, when the first record in the set is already the run-unit's current record.
- Attempt to FIND a record based on a key value, when there are no records of the specified type with that key value.
- Attempt to INSERT into a set, when the current of run-unit is not of the type that is a member in that set.
- Attempt to DISCONNECT from a set, when the current record of the run-unit is not of the type that is a member in the set.

It is good programming practice in a CODASYL database environment to test the ERROR-COUNT after every attempted operation.

Other Operators

Other operators in the CODASYL data manipulation language support security control, shared-access control, backup and recovery operations, and database open and close activities. The manuals for a target database management system should be consulted for details, as each commercial system uses the operators slightly differently.

ASSERTIONS

A CODASYL database management system offers several kinds of assertions to the database designer, including uniqueness constraints, retention constraints, insertion constraints, and check conditions.

Uniqueness Constraints

Uniqueness constraints are assertions that prevent the occurrence of records with duplicated values of specified data items, either within a record type or within the members of a set occurrence. In the CODASYL data definition language, a uniqueness constraint is specified by including a DUPLICATES ARE NOT ALLOWED phrase with the definition of the record key or of the member of a set type. These assertions are enforced by the database management system when either record occurrences are inserted or data items are modified.

Retention Constraints

Retention constraints are assertions that control the actions to be taken when a record has been deleted. Each set type must have a retention constraint specified for its members. There are three options:

- Fixed: once a record has become a member of an occurrence of the set type, it must remain a member of that set until it is deleted from the database.
- Mandatory: once a record has become a member of an occurrence of the set type, it must remain a member of some set of that type until it is deleted from the database.
- Optional: a record, having become a member of an occurrence of the set type, need not remain a member of that set or any other occurrence of that set type.

When an attempt is made to delete the owner in a set, the retention constraints are examined by the database management system to determine the effects on the members of that set. Various database management systems may handle retention differently.

The ANSI/X3H2 committee introduced an ERASE statement that can specify either WITH FULL CASCADE or WITH PARTIAL CASCADE. For example, consider the schema of Fig. 6.6. Assume that the set type EMPLOYS has mandatory retention; set type HAS has fixed retention; and set type SPONSORS has optional retention. The interpretation is that an employee can change departments but must be affiliated with a department; a budget record can be associated with only one department; and a club may or may not have a department sponsor.

The effect of the statement

```
ERASE DEPARTMENT WITH PARTIAL CASCADE
```

is to

- be prohibited if the DEPARTMENT record occurrence has any EMPLOYEE members in the EMPLOYS set (because it has mandatory retention).
- also erase any BUDGET members in the HAS set (because it has fixed retention; the BUDGET records could never be affiliated with another DEPARTMENT occurrence).

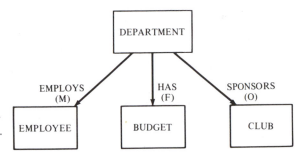

FIGURE 6.6. Set type retentions: EMPLOYS is mandatory. HAS is fixed. SPONSORS is optional.

- disconnect any CLUB members in the SPONSORS set (because it has optional retention; the CLUB records can exist without being affiliated with a DEPARTMENT occurrence).

The effect of the statement

```
ERASE DEPARTMENT WITH FULL CASCADE
```

is to delete the DEPARTMENT record and all the members that it has in any sets.

The net effect is that the retention constraints provide part of a technique for the designer to specify whether or not the member record type is existence dependent on the owner record type. The retention constraint by itself cannot specify existence dependency, because it goes into effect only after the candidate-dependent record has become a member in the set. The record can exist without being associated with an owner if it has never been associated with an owner.

Insertion Constraints

Insertion constraints are assertions that control the actions to be taken when a new record is stored. Each set type must have an insertion constraint specified for its members. There are three options:

- Manual: a record can be inserted as a member in an occurrence of the set type only by an explicit CONNECT statement.
- Automatic: a record can be inserted as a member in an occurrence of the set type only when the record is initially stored in the database. The owner record is identified by the application program logic.
- Structural: a record can be inserted as a member in an occurrence of the set type only when the record is initially stored in the database. The owner record has values of specified data items equal to those of the record being inserted.

When an attempt is made to store a record, the insertion constraints are examined by the database management system to determine in which sets the

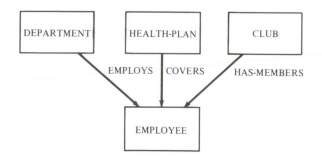

FIGURE 6.7. Set type insertions: EMPLOYS is automatic. COVERS is structural. HAS-MEMBERS is manual.

record becomes a member. For example, consider the schema shown in Fig. 6.7. Assume that the set type EMPLOYS has automatic insertion; set type COVERS has structural insertion on HEALTH-PLAN-CODE in HEALTH-PLAN equal to HEALTH-PLAN-CODE in EMPLOYEE; and HAS-MEMBERS has manual insertion. The insertion of an EMPLOYEE record occurrence will cause

- the EMPLOYEE to be connected in the EMPLOYS set to the current record of the DEPARTMENT type.
- the EMPLOYEE to be connected in the COVERS set to the HEALTH-PLAN record with the matching HEALTH-PLAN-CODE value.

The EMPLOYEE record will not be connected to any CLUB record in the HAS-MEMBERS set. If such a connection is to be made, it must be specified explicitly by a CONNECT statement in the program code.

The combination of automatic insertion and mandatory/fixed retention gives the existence dependency assertion. When a candidate-dependent record is stored in the database, it is automatically connected to an occurrence of the independent record type, and it must thereafter remain connected to an occurrence of the independent record type.

The combination of structural insertion and mandatory/fixed retention gives the referential integrity assertion. Not only is there existence dependency, but also the foreign key in the dependent record must always match the primary key in the independent record. Although the CODASYL model does not refer to primary and foreign keys, the structural insertion provides a means for specifying them.

Check Conditions

Check conditions are assertions about the valid values of the data items in a record type. They may be determined by the data item itself (e.g., SALARY < 100,000), by the data item in combination with other data items from the record type (e.g., IF JOB-CODE < 60 THEN SALARY < 50,000), or by the data item in combination with data items from an owner record type (e.g.,

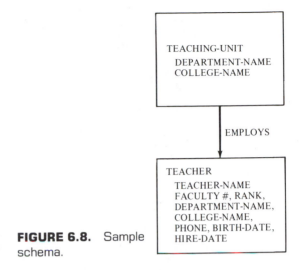

FIGURE 6.8. Sample schema.

HEALTH-PLAN-CODE IN EMPLOYEE = HEALTH-PLAN-CODE IN HEALTH-PLAN). Check conditions are enforced by the database management system when the record in the database has been modified.

SCHEMA DEFINITION

The *schema definition language* for a CODASYL database must be able to create, modify, and delete descriptions of record types, data items, and set types. (We ignore areas here, because they seem destined to be phased out of the model.) Because the data definition language used to describe CODASYL database schemas has evolved over time, the specification of the CODASYL data model depends on which of the *Journals of Development* is used as the source. Here we use both the 1973 publication, which is the basis for most of the commercial CODASYL-compatible database management systems, and the draft work of the ANSI/X3H2 committee on a network database language.

Record Types, Data Items, and Set Types

An incomplete description of the schema shown in Fig. 6.8 is

```
RECORD NAME IS TEACHER.
02   TEACHER-NAME      PICTURE X(20).
02   FACULTY#          PICTURE 9(5).
02   RANK              PICTURE X(5).
02   DEPARTMENT-NAME   PICTURE X(8).
02   COLLEGE-NAME      PICTURE X(8).
02   PHONE             PICTURE 9(5).
02   BIRTH-DATE        PICTURE X(8).
02   HIRE-DATE         PICTURE X(8).
```

```
RECORD NAME IS TEACHING-UNIT.
02   DEPARTMENT-NAME      PIC X(8).
02   COLLEGE-NAME         PIC X(8).
SET NAME IS EMPLOYS
     OWNER IS TEACHING-UNIT
     MEMBER IS TEACHER.
```

The set definition statement also has phrases for defining members' insertion and retention characteristics, ordering set member record occurrences, and specifying uniqueness constraints.

A partial description of the schema shown in Fig. 6.2(a) is

```
RECORD NAME IS DEPARTMENT.
02  DEPARTMENT-NAME          PICTURE X(10).
. . .
RECORD NAME IS GRADUATE-STUDENT.
02  G-STUDENT-NAME           PICTURE X(20).
. . .
RECORD NAME IS UNDERGRADUATE-STUDENT.
02  U-STUDENT-NAME           PICTURE X(20).
. . .
SET NAME IS HAS-MAJORS
     OWNER IS DEPARTMENT
     MEMBER IS GRADUATE-STUDENT
                UNDERGRADUATE-STUDENT.
```

This schema includes a multimember set type.

Value-based Sets

The 1973 *CODASYL Data Definition Language Committee Journal of Development* does not provide a facility for declaring *value-based sets;* rather, they exist implicitly when a program enforces the match of data-field values across owner and member record occurrences. But the 1978 *Journal of Development* does provide for declaring value-based sets. For example, the preceding EMPLOYS set could be (incompletely) declared as follows:

```
SET NAME IS EMPLOYS
     OWNER IS TEACHING-UNIT
     MEMBER IS TEACHER
             INSERTION IS AUTOMATIC
             RETENTION IS OPTIONAL
             STRUCTURAL CONSTRAINT IS
                 DEPARTMENT-NAME OF TEACHER =
                 DEPARTMENT-NAME OF TEACHING-UNIT,
                 COLLEGE-NAME OF TEACHER =
                 COLLEGE-NAME OF TEACHING-UNIT.
```

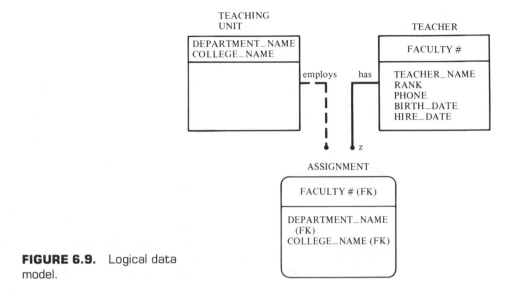

FIGURE 6.9. Logical data model.

The ANSI/X3H2-proposed language provides for declaring valued-based sets through the INSERTION IS STRUCTURAL phrase. For example,

```
SET NAME IS EMPLOYS
     ORDER IS SORTED
     OWNER IS TEACHING-UNIT
     MEMBER IS TEACHER
          INSERTION IS STRUCTURAL
               DEPARTMENT-NAME OF TEACHER =
               DEPRATMENT-NAME OF TEACHING-UNIT
               AND COLLEGE-NAME OF TEACHER =
               COLLEGE-NAME OF TEACHING-UNIT.
          RETENTION OPTIONAL.
```

This is an example of a value-based set in which the member has no existence dependency on the owner record type, as indicated by the RETENTION OPTIONAL phrase. A corresponding logical data model is given in Fig. 6.9.

To define the set to have referential integrity, the DEPARTMENT-NAME and COLLEGE-NAME data fields in TEACHER need to be defined to be NOT NULL, with RETENTION MANDATORY in the set.

Set Ordering

The CODASYL data description language makes available the following options for ordering set member record occurrences:

```
FIRST
LAST
NEXT
PRIOR
IMMATERIAL or DEFAULT
SORTED
```

These options determine the position of a new member in the set. For example, assume that the preceding EMPLOYS set type is declared by

```
SET NAME IS EMPLOYS
    ORDER IS FIRST
    OWNER IS TEACHING-UNIT
    MEMBER IS TEACHER.
```

The insertion of a new occurrence of TEACHER in the EMPLOYS set would place it first in the collection of all TEACHER occurrences associated with the TEACHING-UNIT. If the TEACHER with FACULTY# = 34567 were inserted in the set owned by the TEACHING-UNIT with DEPARTMENT-NAME = 'COMP SCI' and COLLEGE-NAME = 'ENGR,' it would logically precede the other TEACHER occurrences in that set.

ORDER IS FIRST is appropriate for last-in, first-out (LIFO) relationships, and the set's member records are accessible in reverse chronological order. ORDER IS LAST places a new member occurrence logically after all existing members in a set and is appropriate for first-in, first-out (FIFO) relationships. The member records of the set are accessible in chronological order.

When a set type is declared with ORDER IS NEXT, a new occurrence of a member record type is inserted next to that set's current record, that is, next to the most recently referenced member record occurrence. For example, assume that the EMPLOYS set type is declared by

```
SET NAME IS EMPLOYS
    ORDER IS NEXT
    OWNER IS TEACHING-UNIT
    MEMBER IS TEACHER.
```

Assume too that the most recently accessed occurrence of TEACHING-UNIT is for DEPARTMENT-NAME = 'GEOLOGY' and COLLEGE-NAME = 'GEOSCI.' This establishes the current occurrence of the set type EMPLOYS. Assume that the most recently referenced record occurrence in that set is for the teacher with FACULTY# = 42137. The insertion of a new occurrence of TEACHER in the EMPLOYS set places it immediately after the current of the set, that is, after the record with FACULTY# = 42137.

ORDER IS PRIOR inserts the new member occurrence logically just before the set's current record. ORDER IS NEXT and PRIOR are used when the programmer or user wants to have complete control over the sequencing of member records. The program positions the currency indicator at the appropriate member record (establishing the set's desired current record) and then requests the insertion of the new member record in the set.

ORDER IS IMMATERIAL (1973 *Journal of Development*) or SYSTEM-DEFAULT (1978 *Journal of Development*) or DEFAULT (ANSI/X3H2 draft network language) is used when ordering member record occurrences in a set that is not to be controlled by their order of insertion in the database. A set type with ORDER IS IMMATERIAL does not superimpose sequencing on the logical relationship but more closely represents a logical data model relationship than do set types with specified record sequencing.

ORDER IS SORTED allows the specification of data fields whose values will determine the sequencing of member occurrences in the set. For example, assume that the EMPLOYS set type was declared by

```
SET NAME IS EMPLOYS
    ORDER IS SORTED BY DEFINED KEYS
    OWNER IS TEACHING-UNIT
    MEMBER IS TEACHER.
```

in which the declaration of TEACHER includes a sort key, as follows (without its data fields):

```
RECORD NAME IS TEACHER
    KEY IS ASCENDING FACULTY#
        DUPLICATES ARE NOT ALLOWED.
```

The resulting position of a new occurrence of TEACHER in the EMPLOYS set does not depend on the set currency. The insertion sequences the member records by their FACULTY# data items, and the retrieval is also in that sequence. Sort keys are one or more data fields in the member record type, and ordering can be declared to be by ascending or descending sort key values.

Record Placement

In database management systems that use the 1973 data definition language, LOCATION MODE specifies how occurrences of records are stored and how they can be accessed. The ORDER phrase in a set declaration specifies the logical placement of record occurrences in sets. By contrast, the LOCATION MODE phrase in a record declaration specifies physical placement of records in the database files.

The three options for the LOCATION MODE of a record type are

- CALC, which indicates that record occurrences are to be randomized in storage using the value of a specified data field, known as the *CALC key*.
- VIA, which indicates that record occurrences are to be stored as physically close as possible to their owner in a specified set type.

- DIRECT, which indicates that record occurrences will be located at addresses supplied when their storage is requested.

If a record type has LOCATION MODE CALC, then its CALC key will serve as a direct-access key. Assume that the STUDENT record type is declared as follows:

```
RECORD NAME IS STUDENT
     WITHIN ALL-COLLEGE AREA
     LOCATION MODE IS CALC USING MATRIC#
          DUPLICATES ARE NOT ALLOWED.
02   MATRIC#      PIC 9(5).
02   STUDENT-NAME PIC X(20).
     etc.
```

The record for the student with MATRIC# = 12345 is stored by the following sequence of statements:

```
MOVE 12345 TO MATRIC#.
MOVE 'JOHN SMITH' TO STUDENT-NAME.
     etc.
STORE STUDENT.
IF ERROR-COUNT > 0
     THEN DISPLAY 'ATTEMPT TO STORE STUDENT WITH
          DUPLICATE MATRIC# ' MATRIC#.
```

The database manager uses the MATRIC# value to find an open location for the record and calculates a storage address from the MATRIC# value using a technique called *hashing* (see Chapter 9).

The record stored is retrieved by

```
MOVE 12345 TO MATRIC#.
FIND STUDENT.
IF ERROR-COUNT > 0
     THEN DISPLAY 'NO STUDENT WITH MATRIC# ' MATRIC#.
```

It is not possible to use this kind of direct FIND to locate the student with STUDENT-NAME = 'JOHN SMITH', as a record type can have only one CALC key.

If a record type has LOCATION MODE VIA, then one of the set types in which it participates as member is specified. Occurrences of the member record are then clustered physically with their owner in that set. Assume that the STUDENT record type is declared as follows:

```
RECORD NAME IS STUDENT
     WITHIN ALL-COLLEGE AREA
     LOCATION MODE IS VIA HAS-MAJORS SET.
02   MATRIC#      PIC 9(5).
02   STUDENT-NAME PIC X(20).
     etc.
```

In order to store a STUDENT record, the correct owner in the HAS-MAJORS set type must be identified. For example, the record for the student with MA-TRIC# = 12345, who is majoring in MIS, is stored by the following sequence of statements. It is assumed that DEPARTMENT has CALC key DEPART-MENT-NAME and that the owner of the HAS-MAJORS set is determined by the current of the DEPARTMENT record type.

```
MOVE 'MIS' TO DEPARTMENT-NAME.
FIND DEPARTMENT.
IF ERROR-COUNT > 0
    THEN DISPLAY 'ATTEMPT TO STORE STUDENT IN
        NONEXISTENT DEPARTMENT ' DEPARTMENT-NAME
ELSE
    MOVE 12345 TO MATRIC#
    MOVE 'JOHN SMITH' TO STUDENT-NAME
    etc
    STORE STUDENT
    IF ERROR COUNT > 0
    THEN DISPLAY 'ATTEMPT TO STORE STUDENT WITH
        DUPLICATE MATRIC# ' MATRIC#.
```

The student record is stored as close as possible to the DEPARTMENT record with DEPARTMENT-NAME = 'MIS'.

That record is retrieved by

```
MOVE 'MIS' TO DEPARTMENT-NAME.
FIND DEPARTMENT.
IF ERROR-COUNT > 0
    THEN DISPLAY 'ATTEMPT TO FIND NONEXISTENT
        DEPARTMENT ' DEPARTMENT-NAME
    ELSE PERFORM LOOP-THRU-STUDENTS.
```

The referenced paragraph is

```
LOOP-THRU-STUDENTS.
    MOVE 'N' TO EOS-HAS-MAJORS.
    FIND FIRST STUDENT IN HAS-MAJORS SET.
    IF ERROR-COUNT > 0
        THEN MOVE 'Y' TO EOS-HAS-MAJORS.
    PERFORM FIND-NEXT-STUDENT UNTIL EOS-HAS-MAJORS = 'Y'.
```

The referenced paragraph is

```
FIND-NEXT-STUDENT.
    IF MATRIC# = 12345
        THEN DISPLAY 'HAVE FOUND STUDENT WITH MATRIC# '
                MATRIC#
        ELSE FIND NEXT STUDENT IN HAS-MAJORS SET
            IF ERROR-COUNT > 0
                THEN MOVE 'Y' TO EOS-HAS-MAJORS.
```

Note that the record has not been found directly, as it does not have a CALC key. Instead, each record of the HAS-MAJORS set for the target DEPARTMENT occurrence must be examined to determine whether it is the desired one. If the DEPARTMENT of the desired STUDENT is not known, the logic is even more complex.

Later Data Definition Languages

The LOCATION MODE phrase caused criticism of the 1973 Data Definition Language, as it ties logical considerations of record access to physical characteristics of how the record locations are determined. The 1978 Data Definition Language thus removed the LOCATION MODE phrase and introduced a second language, the Data Storage Definition Language (DSDL). The reason was to improve data independence by separating the definitions of logical and physical aspects of databases. Proposals for the DSDL included statements to perform the LOCATION MODE functions.

The work of the ANSI/X3H2 committee on a Network Database Language has followed the approach of improved logical-physical separation.

MAPPING FROM LOGICAL DATA MODELS

Mapping from a logical data model to a CODASYL data model is relatively straightforward. The resulting model, however, loses some of the semantic information that is explicit in the logical data model.

Entities, Attributes, and Connection Relationships

The basic rules for mapping entities, attributes, and connection relationships from a logical data model are

- Each entity is represented by a record type.
- Each attribute of an entity is represented by a data field in the record type.
- Each connection relationship is represented by a set type.

It is relatively simple to develop the CODASYL structure corresponding to a logical data model in which many-to-many relationships have been resolved. Figure 6.10 shows such a case. The logical data model has no many-to-many relationships, and each entity has been translated into a record type, with a data field for each of the entity's attributes. The relationships appear as set types with mandatory retention; the parent entity is the owner record type; and the child entity is the member record type.

Mapping a logical data model with many-to-many relationships to a CODASYL data model requires that each of those relationships first be resolved

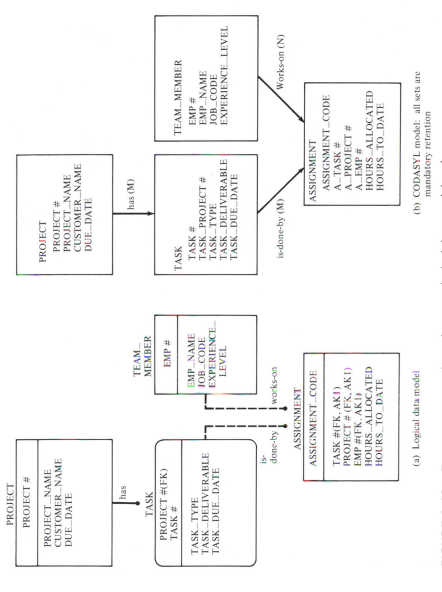

FIGURE 6.10. Direct correspondence between logical data model and CODASYL model.

(a) Logical data model

(b) CODASYL model: all sets are mandatory retention

into two one-to-many relationships. Then each one-to-many relationship can be represented directly by a set type, as a CODASYL data model cannot directly represent many-to-many relationships.

Each zero-or-one-to-many relationship of a logical data model can be resolved into two relationships: One is one-to-many, and the other is one-to-zero-or-one, as shown in Fig. 6.11(a) and (b). If there are no attributes in the intersection entity (ASSIGNMENT in the figure) other than the two foreign keys, then the structure is usually represented by a set type with RETENTION OPTIONAL,

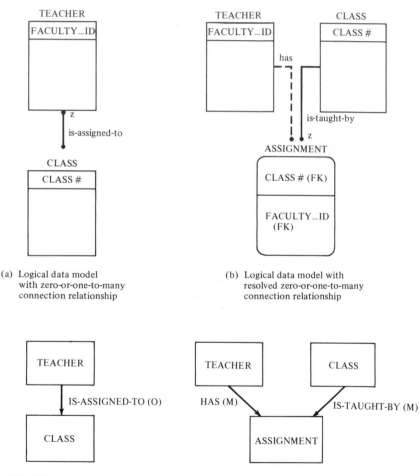

(a) Logical data model with zero-or-one-to-many connection relationship

(b) Logical data model with resolved zero-or-one-to-many connection relationship

(c) CODASYL structure used when ASSIGNMENT entity in (b) has no attributes other than the two foreign keys. Note that the IS-ASSIGNED-TO set type has optional retention

(d) CODASYL structure used when ASSIGNMENT entity in (b) does have attributes in addition to the two foreign keys (e.g., FUNDING-SOURCE). Both set types have mandatory retention. Note that IS-TAUGHT-BY will not be prevented from having more than one ASSIGNMENT for a class by the DBMS, even though that is a semantic constraint of the data model.

FIGURE 6.11. Logical data models and CODASYL structures.

as shown in Fig. 6.11(c). This allows member records to exist without being tied to an owner record and reflects the independence of the two original entities (TEACHER and CLASS in the figure).

On the other hand, if the intersection entity does have attributes in addition to the two foreign keys, then the structure is represented by two set types, each with RETENTION MANDATORY, as shown in Fig. 6.11(d). These additional attributes can be foreign keys from other relationships, as well as attributes owned by the entity. Note that the semantics of the one-to-zero-or-one relationship will not be enforced by the database management system, which always interprets a set type to be a one-to-many relationship.

Each one-to-zero-or-one relationship (Fig. 6.12[a]) can be represented by a set type (Figs. 6.12[a] and [b]) or by a single record type (Fig. 6.12[c]). When collapsed into one record type, the data items that correspond to the attributes of the dependent entity may have null values.

The CODASYL models corresponding to the logical data models with many-to-many and zero-or-one-to-many relationships in Figs. 3.14 and 3.15(b) are shown in Figs. 6.13 and 6.14(a) and (b). (The relations for these logical data models are shown in Chapter 4.)

Note that not all of the semantic information in the logical data model has been captured in the corresponding CODASYL data model. Most obviously, the relationship cardinalities have disappeared. The CODASYL model is also not able to indicate that a CLASS record is owner of a maximum of forty-five ENROLLMENT records or that a STUDENT is owner of a maximum of seven

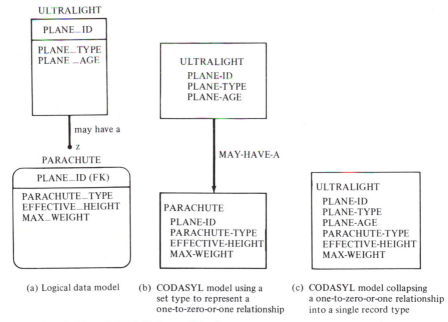

(a) Logical data model

(b) CODASYL model using a set type to represent a one-to-zero-or-one relationship

(c) CODASYL model collapsing a one-to-zero-or-one relationship into a single record type

FIGURE 6.12. CODASYL models for one-to-zero-or-one relationships.

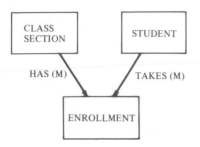

FIGURE 6.13. CODASYL model corresponding to logical data model of Fig. 3.14.

ENROLLMENT members. It also cannot indicate that a class has a maximum of one teaching assistant.

Foreign keys need not be represented in member record types, but if they are then the set will be value based. If they are not, then the set will be information bearing. Arguments for conserving storage space favor making sets information bearing, whereas arguments for minimizing record accesses favor making sets value based.

To preserve database integrity, it is recommended that value-based sets be used, especially with a database management system that supports INSERTION IS STRUCTURAL or the STRUCTURAL CONSTRAINT. The database manager then will ensure that member records are associated with the correct owner records. Without this automatic enforcement, the application programmer is responsible for correctly relating owners and members. When sets are information bearing, the correctness of relationships cannot be automatically traced.

Category Relationships

There are at least three approaches to handling category relationships in the CODASYL model:

- one or more set types per category relationship.
- redefined data aggregates within the generic entity's record type.
- explicit inheritance of the generic attributes within the record type of each subtype entity.

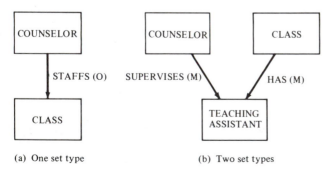

(a) One set type   (b) Two set types

FIGURE 6.14. CODASYL model alternatives corresponding to logical data model of Fig. 3.15.

None of these is entirely satisfactory.

In the first approach, each entity maps directly to a record type, and the relationship is represented by a set type with multiple member record types, one per subtype entity. Consider again the category relationship of Fig. 3.19(b). Using this first approach, that hierarchy corresponds to the CODASYL model shown in Fig. 6.15(a). The member record types should have INSERTION STRUCTURAL and RETENTION FIXED or MANDATORY, depending on whether an entity can change subtypes.

A variant of this approach is to introduce one set type per subtype entity. Using this approach, the example hierarchy corresponds to the CODASYL model shown in Fig. 6.15(b). Note that the set types here have RETENTION FIXED, and a given member record occurrence cannot switch owners.

The main problem with this approach is the loss of the one-to-one nature of the generic entity's relationship to the subtype entity. A CODASYL set type is always one-to-many. The database manager will not automatically enforce the category constraint that each generic record occurrence be related to, at most, one of the subtype occurrences, as each set occurrence can have many member records.

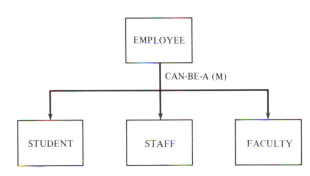

(a) Using a multimember set type to represent a category hierarchy

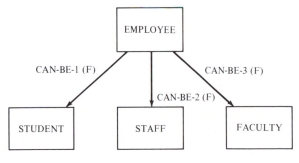

FIGURE 6.15. Using one or more set types to represent category relationships.

(b) Using multiple set types to represent a category hierarchy. Note that the set types have fixed retention

The second approach to representing a category relationship is to use a redefined data aggregate within the generic entity's record type. For example, a definition of the record type corresponding to the category relationship of Fig. 3.19(b) could be

```
RECORD NAME IS EMPLOYEE
   . . .
   02   SOCIAL-SECURITY-NUM PIC 9(9).
   02   EMPLOYEE-NAME        PIC X(24).
   02   BIRTH-DATE           PIC X(8).
   02   NUM-DEPENDENTS       PIC 9(2).
   02   ADDRESS              PIC X(40).
   02   STATUS               PIC X.
   02   STUDENT-STATUS.
        03   STUDY-YEAR                 PIC 9.
        03   EXPECTED-DEGREE-YEAR       PIC 99.
        03   HOURLY-RATE                PIC 99V99.
        03   FILLER                     PIC X(3).
   02   STAFF-STATUS REDEFINES STUDENT-STATUS.
        03   EXEMPTION-CODE             PIC X.
        03   BENEFIT-PLAN               PIC X.
        03   MONTHLY-SALARY             PIC 9(4)V99.
        03   FILLER                     PIC X(2).
   02   FACULTY-STATUS REDEFINES STUDENT-STATUS.
        03   RANK                       PIC X.
        03   ANNUAL-SALARY              PIC 9(5).
        03   FACULTY-CLUB-DUES          PIC 99V99.
```

The record type EMPLOYEE contains the generic data fields, including the subtype discriminator, and it also contains an area of storage that can have one of three formats for any particular record occurrence. It can be formatted according to STUDENT-STATUS or STAFF-STATUS or FACULTY-STATUS. The FILLER fields are inserted because the three subtypes' data areas are not equal in length.

This structure retains the category's hierarchical structure and also explicitly represents the inheritance of attributes from the generic entity.

There are, however, the following problems with this approach to representing category relationships:

• Category networks cannot be represented using this approach. A redefined area can be part of only one record type.
• A relationship in which only one of the subtype entities participates cannot be distinguished from a relationship in which the generic entity participates. A set type must have an entire record as its owner or member; part of the record definition cannot be singled out for inclusion.
• A relationship among subtype entities cannot be represented explicitly. A set type may have the same record type for both its owner and member, but it cannot distinguish between the redefined areas as having owner and member roles.

- Representation of nested categories is awkward. If the aforementioned STUDENT_EMPLOYEE were a generic entity for two subtypes (GRADUATE_STUDENT_EMPLOYEE and UNDERGRADUATE_STUDENT_EMPLOYEE), then its category redefinition structure would need to be included in the STUDENT-STATUS area.

A third approach to representing category relationships is to map each entity to a record type, with explicit inheritance of attributes. For example, definitions of the record types corresponding to the category relationship of Fig. 3.19(b) could be

```
RECORD NAME IS STUDENT-EMPLOYEE
     . . .
02    STUDENT-SOCIAL-SECURITY-NUM  PIC 9(9).
02    STUDENT-EMPLOYEE-NAME        PIC X(24).
02    STUDENT-BIRTH-DATE           PIC X(8).
02    STUDENT-NUM-DEPENDENTS       PIC 9(2).
02    STUDENT-ADDRESS              PIC X(40).
02    STUDENT-STATUS               PIC X.
02    STUDY-YEAR                   PIC 9.
02    EXPECTED-DEGREE-YEAR         PIC 99.
02    HOURLY-RATE                  PIC 99V99.
RECORD NAME IS STAFF-EMPLOYEE
     . . .
02    STAFF-SOCIAL-SECURITY-NUM    PIC 9(9).
02    STAFF-EMPLOYEE-NAME          PIC X(24).
02    STAFF-BIRTH-DATE             PIC X(8).
02    STAFF-NUM-DEPENDENTS         PIC 9(2).
02    STAFF-ADDRESS                PIC X(40).
02    STAFF-STATUS                 PIC X.
02    EXEMPTION-CODE               PIC X.
02    BENEFIT-PLAN                 PIC X.
02    MONTHLY-SALARY               PIC 9(4)V99.
RECORD NAME IS FACULTY-EMPLOYEE
     . . .
02    FACULTY-SOCIAL-SECURITY-NUM  PIC 9(9).
02    FACULTY-EMPLOYEE-NAME        PIC X(24).
02    FACULTY-BIRTH-DATE           PIC X(8).
02    FACULTY-NUM-DEPENDENTS       PIC 9(2).
02    FACULTY-ADDRESS              PIC X(40).
02    FACULTY-STATUS               PIC X.
02    RANK                         PIC X.
02    ANNUAL-SALARY                PIC 9(5).
02    FACULTY-CLUB-DUES            PIC 99V99.
```

This approach loses the relationship's hierarchic structure, for it is not clear that STUDENT-EMPLOYEE, STAFF-EMPLOYEE and FACULTY-EMPLOYEE all are subtypes of a single generic entity. Understanding the relationship among these record types depends on the data names chosen, and many CODASYL database management systems require that data fields have unique names.

Dependencies

The CODASYL data model does not explicitly represent identifier dependency and does not require that a primary key be designated for any record type. Furthermore, it does not require that foreign keys be shown, because the set types can be information bearing.

The referential integrity constraint is explicitly represented using a set type with INSERTION IS STRUCTURAL and RETENTION IS MANDATORY or FIXED on the members. The value of a data field in the member must be matched by a value of a data field in the owner; these data fields will be the foreign key and primary key, respectively. An instance of the member record type should not exist in the database unless it is participating in the set type.

Existence dependency is almost represented by participation in a set type with RETENTION IS MANDATORY or FIXED. Both of these require that once a record occurrence is a member of the set, it must remain a member of that set type until it is erased from the database. Neither, however, specifies that the record type cannot exist before being inserted in the set. Thus, existence dependency is not truly represented.

The Mapping Process

As stated in Chapter 4, the recommended sequence of events in the database design is first to build a logical data model and then to map that data model to a form that can be implemented by a database management system. The steps for mapping a logical data model to a structure that can be implemented by a CODASYL database manager are

1. Construct a logical data model of the subject area.
2. Resolve the many-to-many and the zero-or-one-to-many relationships.
3. Migrate the primary keys, forming foreign keys.
4. Map each entity to a record type, with the entity's attributes becoming the record type's data fields.
5. If the intersection entity produced by resolving a zero-or-one-to-many relationship has no attributes other than the two foreign keys, then represent the zero-or-one-to-many relationship by a set type with INSERTION IS MANUAL and RETENTION IS OPTIONAL.
6. Map each one-to-many relationship to a set type with INSERTION IS STRUCTURAL and RETENTION IS MANDATORY.
7. Map each one-to-zero-or-one relationship to a set type or a single record type. The set type mapping is generally preferable if the dependent entity participates in other relationships.
8. Map each category structure to one of the preceding alternatives.
9. Tune the structure to enhance physical performance.

The last step will be addressed in Chapter 11, on the physical design of network databases. It may mean, among other things,

- combining record types and removing set types (e.g., collapsing one-to-zero-or-one relationships into a single record type, or even one-to-many relationships into a single record type with a repeating group).
- splitting record types (e.g., when some data fields are accessed far more frequently than are others in a record type).
- making set types information bearing rather than value based.
- removing value-based set types and leaving the relationship to be represented by the presence of the foreign key.
- specifying access paths (e.g., identifying LOCATION MODEs on record types or completing the Data Storage Definition Language description of the database).
- assigning record types to physical space (e.g., specifying areas for record types).

Instead of building the logical data model first, a logical data model may sometimes be constructed that corresponds to an already-existing CODASYL database structure. This may be done to help elicit what information is actually contained in the database. But a common trap in starting with the database structure is to rely on that structure to convey a logical model. In fact, the database structure may have been designed with a heavy bias toward physical implementation. Combined record types, collapsed set types, and split record types can obscure entities. A diagram of a CODASYL schema looks so much like a logical data model that it may be tempting just to map directly record types to entities and set types to relationships. There actually may be relationships that are not represented by set types and entities that are buried in record types, and record types that do not represent entities at all.

The resulting logical data model should always be reviewed with experts in the area that it represents. Sometimes the experts who helped design the database structure were database experts, and its users made few contributions.

INTRODUCTION TO COMMERCIAL CODASYL DATABASE MANAGEMENT SYSTEMS

Commercial CODASYL database management systems have earned a reputation for being able to handle large production databases. These systems are mature products and provide good data protection through shared access, concurrency control, backup and recovery, and transaction control facilities.

The CODASYL database managers have their roots in a system called the Integrated Data Store, developed primarily by Charles W. Bachman, then at the General Electric Company. This system became IDS and then IDS-II, offered by Honeywell.

Nearly all of the major mainframe vendors have developed CODASYL or CODASYL-like database management systems, which execute on their CPUs and operating systems. Table 6.1 lists some of these systems, including several from software vendors, who have developed database management systems for execution on other vendors' CPUs and operating systems. Most prominent among these is Cullinet, whose product, IDMS and its newer version, IDMS/R, runs on IBM CPUs and operating systems. IDMS/R is distinguished in that it supports in a single environment both the CODASYL data model and the relational data model.

TABLE 6.1 Database Management Systems in the CODASYL Family

Package	Vendor	Hardware
DBMS-10 DBMS-20 DBMS	Digital Equipment Corporation	DEC System 10 DEC System 20 Vax, PDP 11
DMS-11	Burroughs Corporation	Burroughs mainframes
DMS-90 DMS-1100	Sperry-Univac	Univac mainframes
IDMS IDMS/R IDMS-11	Cullinet Software, Inc.	IBM DEC
IDS-II	Honeywell	Honeywell mainframes
Seed	International Data Base Systems, Inc.	DEC, IBM, CDC mainframes
MicroSeed	MicroSeed, Inc.	various microcomputers
MDBS-III	Micro Data Base Systems, Inc.	various microcomputers

The other software-only vendors are Micro Database Systems, Inc., International Data Base Systems, Inc., and its offshoot MicroSeed, Inc. MDBS-III and MicroSeed are targeted for microcomputers. Seed was developed primarily in FORTRAN and runs on a variety of CPUs and operating systems, including systems from DEC, IBM, CDC, and several microcomputer vendors.

A noticeable omission from this list is IBM, as it has never provided a CODASYL-compatible database management system. This is probably because of its tremendous investment in IMS (a hierarchic system described in Chapter 7) and in the development of relational DBMS.

The CODASYL-compatible database management systems comprise a relatively small share of the marketplace, compared with the share belonging to IBM's IMS or Cincom's TOTAL.

THE TOTAL NETWORK MODEL

TOTAL manages data structured in networks, but its data model is not the same as CODASYL's.

Structure

TOTAL databases are represented as networks of interconnected record types. Our discussion of CODASYL data items, data fields, record occurrences, and record types applies directly to a TOTAL database. The record interrelationships, however, are represented by designating two types of records, *master records* and *variable records*. These types are also called *master files* and *variable files*, because each TOTAL record type is implemented in its own file.

Each master record has a primary key, its *control key*, which can be used to access the master records directly. Variable records do not have keys and can be accessed only through their relationships to master records.

Master and variable records contain data fields, and the format of every master record in a file is the same. By contrast, there can be several formats for the variable records in a file. If there are several formats, then the variable record is called a *coded record*. For example, a variable record called STUDENT can be coded in two formats, one for GRADUATE STUDENT and one for UNDER-GRADUATE STUDENT.

Figure 6.16 illustrates a TOTAL schema corresponding to the one-to-many relationship of Fig. 6.1. A master file is represented by a box, and a variable file is represented by a circle. Their relationship is represented by a line and is called a *linkage path*. The relationship between a master file and a variable file is always one-to-many. Each TEACHING-UNIT record in the example is associated with many TEACHER records; each TEACHER record is associated with one, and only one, TEACHING-UNIT record.

A master record can be related to more than one variable record. Figure 6.17(a) shows a TOTAL schema with two one-to-many relationships. Each DEPARTMENT record is associated with many GRADUATE-STUDENT records and many UNDERGRADUATE-STUDENT records. Each of those variable records is associated with one, and only one, DEPARTMENT record.

This structure could alternatively be represented by a DEPARTMENT master record and a coded STUDENT record, as shown in Fig. 6.17(b). The difference between this approach and the approach of Fig. 6.17(a) is that the coded records will be intermingled, and so a request to list all the graduate students for a department must use program code to separate them from the undergraduate students.

FIGURE 6.16. A one-to-many connection relationship in a TOTAL schema (same structure as Fig. 6.1).

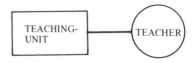

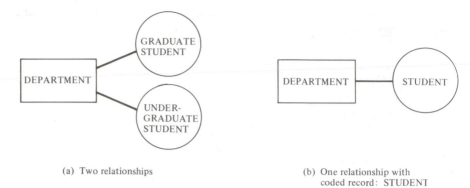

(a) Two relationships

(b) One relationship with
coded record: STUDENT

FIGURE 6.17. TOTAL structures corresponding to Fig. 6.2.

A variable record can be related to more than one master record. Figure 6.18 illustrates a TOTAL schema with three one-to-many relationships that share the same variable file. Each DEPARTMENT record, each HEALTH-PLAN record, and each CLUB record is associated with many EMPLOYEE records, but each EMPLOYEE record is associated with only one DEPARTMENT record, one HEALTH-PLAN record, and one CLUB record.

A TOTAL schema can have only two levels, and so in order to represent a three-level logical hierarchy (Fig. 6.19[a]), the structure shown in Fig. 6.19(b) must be used. Each BUILDING record is associated with many OFFICE records; there is not only a variable OFFICE record but also a master OFFICE' record. Each master is associated with many EMPLOYEE records. Rather than replicating the OFFICE data, the variable OFFICE record acts as a logical pointer to the master OFFICE' record. The OFFICE' record contains data fields for the OFFICE entity, and the OFFICE record contains the key for the OFFICE entity, which can be used to access OFFICE' directly.

Figure 6.20 is a TOTAL schema to represent the logical data model of Fig. 4.10, which appeared in Fig. 6.4 as a CODASYL schema. It has four master files and three variable files.

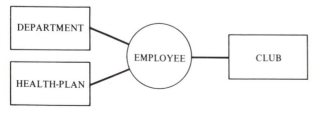

FIGURE 6.18. TOTAL schema with three one-to-many relationships, sharing a common variable file (same structure as Fig. 6.7).

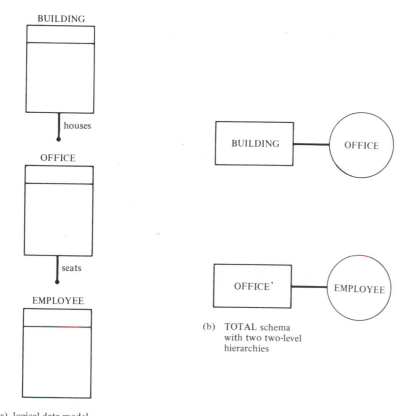

(a) logical data model
    with three-level hierarchy

(b) TOTAL schema
    with two two-level
    hierarchies

FIGURE 6.19. Corresponding structures.

FIGURE 6.20. TOTAL
schema corresponding di-
rectly to the logical data
model of Fig. 4.10.

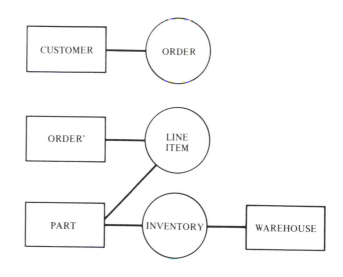

Operators

The TOTAL operators process records one at a time. Just as for the CODASYL operators, these commands were intended to be used in application programs written in COBOL, FORTRAN, and other similar languages. Cincom Systems has introduced higher-level languages that are more appropriate for the end user.

The basic TOTAL data manipulation functions include

READM	reads a record in a master file.
READV	reads the next record in a chain in a variable file.
READR	reads the previous record in a chain in a variable file.
RDNXT	reads the physically next record in a file.
ADD-M	adds a new record to a master file.
ADDVC	adds a new variable record to the end of all its associated chains.
ADDVA	adds a new variable record after the current one.
ADDVB	adds a new variable record before the current one.
DEL-M	deletes a record from a master file.
DELVD	deletes a record from a variable file.
WRITM	updates in place an existing record in a master file.
WRITV	updates in place an existing record in a variable file.

The functions to access master records are invoked using statements of the form

```
CALL "DATBAS" USING FUNCTION,
                    STATUS,
                    DATASET,
                    CONTROL-KEY,
                    ELEMENT-LIST,
                    USER-AREA,
                    "ENDP".
```

FUNCTION is the name of the operator, e.g., "READM."
STATUS will contain the returned status indicator.
DATASET is the name of the file to be manipulated, e.g., "DEPART-MENT."
CONTROL-KEY contains the record's key value.
ELEMENT-LIST is the names of the fields to be manipulated.
USER-AREA is the name of the program data structure to receive a record, e.g., "WS-DEPARTMENT."

The CALL statements to access variable records require two more parameters:

REFERENCE indicates the relative position of the variable record in its file/chain, e.g., "17" or "LKEM."
LINKAGE-PATH names the master-variable path to be processed, e.g., "ORDER-LINE-ITEM."

Assertions

TOTAL enforces several kinds of assertions, including uniqueness constraints, retention constraints, and insertion constraints.

Uniqueness constraints in TOTAL apply to the values of the master records' keys. Key uniqueness is enforced on the insertion and modification of the master records.

Retention constraints in TOTAL apply to attempts to delete master records. If a master record has associated variable records, the deletion will be prohibited. All variable records associated with a master must be deleted before the master is deleted.

Insertion constraints apply to attempts to add variable records. Because each variable record must contain as a foreign key the control key of any master record with which it is associated, TOTAL can determine whether or not the master exists. If the master does not exist, the variable record cannot be inserted. Thus TOTAL enforces referential integrity between the master and the variable records.

If an entity is represented by both a master and a variable record (e.g., OFFICE' and OFFICE in Fig. 6.19[b]), then TOTAL will not validate that each variable record has a corresponding master. Rather, that must be checked by the application program code.

Mapping from Logical Data Models

Mapping from a logical data model to a TOTAL network model is relatively straightforward. Because the semantics of the TOTAL network model can be derived directly from those of the CODASYL network model, we shall present here only the steps of the mapping process:

1. Construct a logical data model of the subject area.
2. Resolve the many-to-many relationships and the zero-or-one-to-many relationships.
3. Migrate the primary keys, forming foreign keys.
4. Map each parent entity to a master record type, with the entity's attributes becoming the record type's data fields and its primary key becoming its control key.
5. Map each child entity to a variable record type. If the entity does not also participate as an independent entity, then the entity's attributes will become the record type's data fields. If the entity also does participate as a parent entity, then only the entity's primary key and foreign keys will become the record type's data fields.
6. Map each one-to-many connection relationship to a master-variable linkage path.
7. Map each one-to-zero-or-one connection or category relationship to a master-variable linkage path.
8. Tune the structure to enhance physical performance.

The last step will be discussed further in Chapter 11 on the physical design of network databases, but it may involve, among other things:

- combining record types and collapsing linkage paths (e.g., collapsing the variable records for the subtype entities of a category structure into a single coded variable file).
- splitting record types (e.g., when some data fields are accessed far more frequently than are others in a record file).

In summary, a TOTAL network model differs from a CODASYL network model in the following ways:

- TOTAL supports only two-level hierarchies, whereas CODASYL supports arbitrary levels of parent-child relationships.
- TOTAL and CODASYL support slightly different operators.

CLOSING COMMENTS

Many major databases and off-the-shelf applications software packages have been developed using network database management system support.

The best features of the network model are

- easy-to-understand graphic display of database structures.
- availability of commercial implementations that will execute on a wide variety of CPUs and operating systems.
- availability of commercial implementations that provide the data protection features necessary for production environments.

The second and third points are not really features of the model itself, but implementations of the model. They do, however, indicate that the network model is practical in production environments and attractive enough for large investments by many companies.

The basic weaknesses of the network model are

- no natural ability to represent some of the common logical data model structures (e.g., categories).
- the data manipulation operators are at a procedural, programmer level and need to be overlaid by a higher level of commands that are easier for nonprogrammers to use.
- until recently, there has been relatively poor separation of the descriptions of a database's logical and physical aspects.

The first problem can be addressed by using a logical data–modeling technique in conjunction with the network data model. A logical data–modeling technique should be used when designing the database structure. The second problem is being addressed by many of the DBMS vendors, and the third problem is being tackled in the ANSI/X3H2 committee's work on standardizing a network database language.

For several years in the late 1970s and early 1980s, the question, "Which is better, the relational model or the network model?" was debated at database conferences and in industry publications. The question, of course, was never settled with a single answer acceptable to all parties, but this may be because the wrong question was being asked. More important is the question, "How should the relational model and the network model coexist?" By strengthening the network model's explicit logical data–modeling capabilities and superimposing an optional relational view, the best of both approaches can cooperate to provide better data management capabilities. This is exactly the approach now being offered by the two major vendors of network database management systems: Cullinet (with IDMS/R) and Cincom Systems (with TIS and SUPRA, full-system extensions of TOTAL).

TERMS

ANSI/X3H2
area
CALC key
CASCADE
category
check condition
CODASYL
coded record
connection
control key
currency
database key
data definition language (DDL)
Data Definition Language
  Committee (DDLC)
data manipulation language (DML)
Data Storage Definition Language
  (DSDL)
data field
data item
data type
essential set
existence dependency
hashing

identifier
information-bearing set
insertion constraint
LOCATION MODE
master record
member record type
owner record type
realm
record occurrence
record type
referential integrity
retention constraint
schema
search key
set occurrence
set type
sort key
status indicator
temporary area
TOTAL
uniqueness constraint
value-based set
variable record

REVIEW EXERCISES

1. Define each of the terms in the preceding list.
2. Compare the representations of category relationships in the relational, CODASYL, and TOTAL data models.

3.   Compare the semantic richness of the relational, CODASYL, and TOTAL data models.

4.   Consider the CODASYL database schema shown in Fig. 6.21, and write CODASYL data manipulation statements to do each of the following:
      a. List all the students in the Dump Dorm.
      b. List all the students.
      c. List the grades for students in classes taught by Bozo.
      d. List the names and grades for students in classes taught by Bozo.
      e. List the names and grades for students whose adviser is Bozo.

5.   Develop a CODASYL database structure for the logical data model shown in Fig. 6.22. Make all the sets value based.

6.   Develop a CODASYL database structure for the logical data model shown in Fig. 6.22. Make all the sets information bearing.

7.   Discuss the differences among RETENTION IS MANDATORY, OPTIONAL, and FIXED. Illustrate by examples when it would be appropriate to use each.

8.   Using the DDL of a CODASYL database management system, describe the schema shown in Fig. 6.23. Run the DDL statements through the system's DDL processor. Write a small program to perform the following operations on the database:
      a. Print the NUM_REQ of all parts owned by product 143 for factory F1.
      b. Print the names of all distributors owned by warehouses that are owned by factory F2.
      c. Delete all data about the warehouse with LOCCODE_10.
      d. Delete all data about factory F3.
      e. Delete all products costing more than $45.
      f. Modify product 260 to cost $85.
      g. Modify the cost of all products to be 10 percent greater.
      h. Add distributor D11 to warehouse with LOCCODE_20.

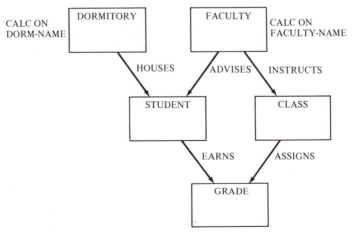

FIGURE 6.21.   CODASYL schema for Exercise 6.4.

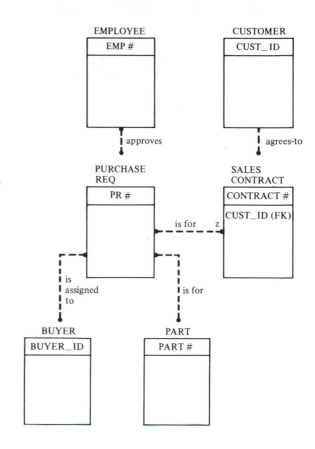

FIGURE 6.22. Logical data model for Exercises 6.5, 6.6, and 6.9 (most nonkey attributes omitted).

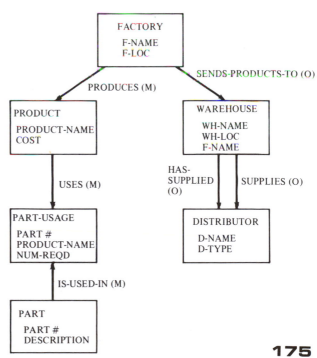

FIGURE 6.23. CODASYL model for Exercises 6.8 and 6.10.

175

    i. Add to factory F2: product 45 with cost $45, and with requirements for 26 of part P14 and 31 of part P17.

    Load the database with the suitable test data, and run your requests.

9.   Develop a TOTAL network database structure for the logical data model shown in Fig. 6.22.

10.   Develop a TOTAL network database structure corresponding to the CODASYL schema of Fig. 6.23.

11.   Compare the semantics of a TOTAL linkage path and a CODASYL set type.

12.   Compare the features of Cullinet's IDMS/R and Cincom's TIS and SUPRA.

13.   Describe the features of Software AG's ADABAS. ADABAS is an inverted-file DBMS that supports specification of network relationships among record types.

REFERENCES

American National Standards Institute, X3H2 Committee. (Draft Proposed) *Network Database Language (X3H2-84-1),* January 1984.

Bachman, C. W. Data structure diagrams, *Database* 1 (Summer 1969).

———. The programmer as navigator. *Communications ACM* 16 (November 1973):653–658.

BCS/CODASYL DDLC Data Base Administration Working Group. Draft specification of a data storage description language, *CODASYL Journal of Development* 1980, App. A.

Cardenas, A. F. *Data Base Management Systems.* Boston: Allyn & Bacon, 1979.

CODASYL Data Base Task Group. *April 1971 Report.* New York: ACM, 1971.

CODASYL Data Description Language Committee. *Data Description Language Journal of Development,* Document C13.6/2:113. U.S. Government Printing Office, Washington, D.C.: 1978.

CODASYL Programming Language Committee. *CODASYL COBOL Journal of Development.* Ottawa: Dept. of Supply and Services, Government of Canada, Technical Services Branch, 1981.

Loomis, M. E. S. The 78 CODASYL model: A comparison with preceding specifications, *Proceedings ACM SIGMOD International Conference on Management of Data,* Santa Monica, Calif., May 1980. New York: ACM, 1980, pp. 30–44.

Taylor, R. W., and R. L. Frank. CODASYL data-base management systems, *ACM Computing Surveys* 8 (March 1976):67–103.

Mapping to the Hierarchical Data Model

The hierarchical approach to modeling data is as old as files containing repeating groups of records, predating both the network and the relational approaches. In the 1960s, IBM and North American Aviation embarked on a joint development project, that led to an IBM product called Data Language/I or, simply, DL/I. DL/I became the basis for IMS, which remains the most widely used of all database management systems. IMS has evolved through versions of the OS/360 IBM operating system into IMS/VS, which runs under OS/VS.

The hierarchical model is also a basis for System 2000 from the SAS Institute. System 2000 began as System 2000, from MRI, and then was marketed by Intel Corporation. Its physical implementation structure is different from that of IMS, but its logical data model is similar.

The hierarchical data model has been supported now for over twenty years, and it promises to continue to be prominent in the database management world.

FUNDAMENTALS OF THE HIERARCHICAL MODEL

The three main aspects of the hierarchical data model are structure, operators, and assertions. The structure of a hierarchical data model is simple. The user sees data as trees of interconnected record types. The assertions are tied directly to the operators and determine the operators' effects on records in a hierarchy.

Because of its widespread influence, we shall use IMS as our example of a hierarchical database management system, though we shall simplify its data definition language and data manipulation language to keep from burdening the reader with the details of a particular commercial product.

STRUCTURE

The structural components of the hierarchical data model are data items and data fields, segments and segment types, hierarchical relationships, hierarchical sequence, and logical pointers and logical databases.

Data Items and Data Fields

A *data item* is an occurrence of the smallest unit of named data and is represented in the database by a value. A data item is essentially the same as a field in a file, for example, 12345 and "Maple".

A data item represents an attribute value, whereas a *data field* is an attribute, for example, part number and street name. The terms *data item* and *data field* have the same meaning in the hierarchic data model as they did in the network data model (see Chapter 6).

A data field is associated with a data type, which determines its format. The IMS data types are character, packed decimal, and hexadecimal. Each data field also has a length, expressed in bytes. System 2000 data types also include money and date. There is no explicit concept of a domain in IMS.

Segments and Segment Types

A *segment* is an instance of a named collection of data items. It is sometimes also referred to as a *record* and is like a record in a network data model. A segment's format is determined by its *segment type,* and a *segment type description* tells the name of the segment type and its fields. There may be an arbitrary number of segments of a given type in a database. A segment type can be used to represent an entity, and when it does, each segment represents an entity instance.

A hierarchical database typically contains several different segment types, which can be physically implemented in a single physical database. The database definition (or schema) describes a database's segment types and their interrelationships.

Hierarchical Relationships

Segment interrelationships are represented by one-to-many associations. Each of these relationships has one segment type declared to be the parent, and one segment type declared to be the child. One occurrence of the parent segment is related to zero, one, or many occurrences of the child segment.

Figure 7.1 shows a relationship between two segment types, TEACHING-UNIT and TEACHER. The corresponding logical data model is given in Fig. 6.1(a), in which the relationship is represented by a line connecting the segments. Contrast this figure with Fig. 6.1(b), which gives a CODASYL schema for the same logical data model, and with Fig. 6.16, which is the corresponding TOTAL network model. Hierarchical models are drawn with the parent segment on top, so that there is no question about which end of the relationship arc is the parent and which is the child.

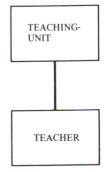

FIGURE 7.1. One-to-many relationship in the hierarchical model (same structure as Fig. 6.1).

The hierarchical parent–child relationship more closely represents the semantic one-to-many relationship of a logical data model or a TOTAL linkage path than does a CODASYL set. In a CODASYL set type with OPTIONAL RETENTION, a member record occurrence can exist in the database without being associated with an owner. In a hierarchy, a child cannot exist without a parent; that is, if a parent is deleted, then so must be its children.

Tree Structures

An example of a tree of hierarchical relationships is shown in Fig. 7.2. Each DEPARTMENT segment can have associated with it many GRADUATE-STUDENT and UNDERGRADUATE-STUDENT segments. This tree corresponds to the logical data models of Figs. 6.2(b) and (c). Corresponding CODASYL and TOTAL networks are given in Figs. 6.2(a) and 6.17, respectively.

Each tree schema has one segment type known as its root, and in Fig. 7.3, DEPT is the root. A root segment may have many child segments, all of which depend on the root for their existence. A segment that has a parent is called a *dependent segment*. All segments in a tree except the root are dependent segments, as each has a parent. In Fig. 7.3, BUDGET, EMP, and TASK all are dependent segments. A segment type that does not have at least one child segment type is called a *leaf segment*. In Fig. 7.3, BUDGET and TASK are leaf segments.

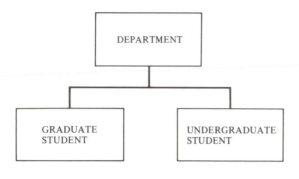

FIGURE 7.2. Two one-to-many relationships in the hierarchical model (same structure as Fig. 6.2).

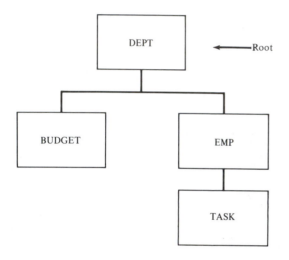

FIGURE 7.3. Another hierarchy.

Within a tree occurrence, segments of the same type are called *twins* and must have the same parent segment occurrence. Segments of different types but on the same level of the tree are called *siblings*. In Fig. 7.3, the BUDGET segments for a DEPT segment are twins. Each of these BUDGET segments is a sibling of each of the EMP segments for that same department. Note that a BUDGET segment cannot be a sibling of a TASK assignment. Similarly, BUDGET segments for different departments are not twins, and BUDGET segments and EMP segments for different departments are not siblings.

Each segment type of a tree lies on a hierarchical path. That path is defined by parent–child relationships from the root to the segment type. No segment type can lie on more than one hierarchical path in a tree. The hierarchical paths in the tree of Fig. 7.3 are

```
DEPT - BUDGET
DEPT - EMP
DEPT - EMP - TASK
```

Hierarchical Sequence

The segments of a tree have an ordering predefined by a *hierarchical sequence*. This sequence is a result of both the value of a designated *sequence field* in each segment and the relative positioning of segment types in the tree.

The root of a tree must have a sequence field with unique values. The dependent segment types usually also have sequence fields. Sequence fields of dependent segments may be defined as unique within occurrences of a parent.

Each segment occurrence in a tree has a hierarchical sequence-key value that identifies it. The hierarchical-sequence-key value of a segment is a code identifying its segment-type code and sequence-field value, prefixed by the hierarchical-sequence-key value for its parent. This scheme carries all the way up to the root of the tree. For example, the hierarchical-sequence-key values for various segments in the tree of Fig. 7.4 are

> segment type = TASK, sequence field (TASK#) value = 49,
>   parent (EMP) sequence field (EMP#) value = 12751;
> segment type = TASK, sequence field (TASK#) value = 75,
>   parent (EMP) sequence field (EMP#) value = 12751;
> segment type = EMP, sequence field (EMP#) value = 12751,
>   parent (DEPT) sequence field (DEPTCODE) value = MIS;
> segment type = BUDGET, sequence field (MO) value = 12,
>   parent (DEPT) sequence field (DEPTCODE) value = MIS;
> segment type = BUDGET, sequence field (MO) value = 11,
>   parent (DEPT) sequence field (DEPTCODE) value = MIS;
> segment type = DEPT, sequence field (DEPTCODE) value = MIS.

In practice, the hierarchical-sequence-key value is a string of concatenated segment-type codes and sequence-field values.

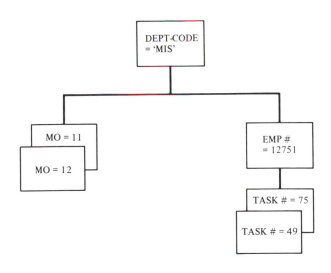

FIGURE 7.4. Sample occurrence of the tree of Fig. 7.3.

The segments of every hierarchic database can be ordered in a hierarchical sequence, which for a database orders segment occurrences by ascending values of their hierarchical-sequence keys. Hierarchical sequence is especially important because certain data manipulation statements use it to access the database. Hierarchical sequence does not restrict data access, except that a command to access the "next" segment will fetch the segment that is next in the hierarchical sequence.

IMS database storage is controlled by the hierarchical sequence of segments. This close association between the effects of certain data manipulation statements and the control of data storage reveals the relative lack of logical-physical data independence in IMS databases.

In IMS or DL/I terminology, a tree occurrence is called a *data base record,* and a set of data base records is called a *data base.* (Henceforth, we shall return to the single word, *database.*) An IMS environment may have many hundreds of tree structures and therefore many hundreds of databases. The term *database* connotes a smaller logical scope in IMS than it does in other database environments.

Representation

We have seen that a hierarchical data model is represented by a diagram that resembles a logical data model diagram. Each segment type is represented by a box containing its name, and each parent–child relationship is represented by an arc between the segment types. Parent segments are drawn above their children. Data-field names generally are not shown in these diagrams, although they may be written into the appropriate segment-type boxes.

Logical Pointers

One distinction between the hierarchical model and the network models (including the CODASYL model) is that no segment in a hierarchy can have more than one parent. This restriction significantly constrains the hierarchic model's capability to represent the semantics of data relationships. Fortunately, a "workaround" in the form of logical pointers has been introduced into the hierarchical model, enabling it to represent networks.

The logical data model of Fig. 6.10(a) has a network structure: there is a many-to-many relationship between TASK and TEAM-MEMBER. This network is represented directly in the CODASYL structure of Fig. 6.10(b), and a representation of the same data using the hierarchical model is shown in Fig. 7.5. There are two trees: PROJECT—TASK—ASSIGNMENT and TEAM-MEMBER—ASSIGNMENT. The trees overlap; they both contain ASSIGNMENT information. If it were desirable to access ASSIGNMENT information by both TASK and TEAM-MEMBER, then the ASSIGNMENT information would be replicated in the two trees, but replication can mean inconsistency.

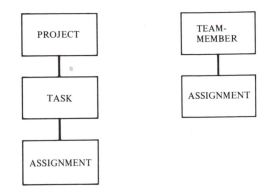

FIGURE 7.5. Hierarchical model corresponding to the logical data model of Fig. 6.10.

An alternative is to use a logical pointer; which connects a segment in one tree to a segment in another tree. In one tree, the segment has no data but is instead a pointer segment that points to the segment in the other tree that actually contains the data. Logical pointers are typically represented as dashed arrows.

For example, Fig. 7.6(a) shows a logical pointer from the ASSIGNMENT segment in the PROJECT tree to the ASSIGNMENT segment in the TEAM tree, which indicates that the ASSIGNMENT facts are stored in the TEAM tree. If ASSIGNMENT data are to be accessed for a TASK in the PROJECT tree, then the TEAM tree must also be accessed. Figure 7.6(b) shows an alternative structure in which the ASSIGNMENT segment in the TEAM tree points to the ASSIGNMENT segment in the PROJECT tree.

Either structure is correct. The structure chosen, however, will affect the database's performance. It generally is more expensive in disk accesses to jump to another tree than it is to stay within a tree.

The logical data model of Fig. 4.10 has a network structure: there are many-to-many relationships between ORDER and PART and between PART and

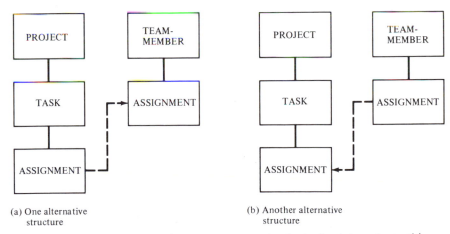

(a) One alternative structure

(b) Another alternative structure

FIGURE 7.6. Two alternative structures using logical pointers to avoid the data replication of Fig. 7.5.

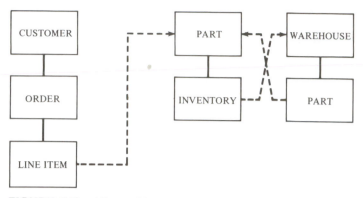

FIGURE 7.7. Hierarchies to represent the network of Fig. 4.10. Note the three logical pointers.

WAREHOUSE. The network is represented directly in the CODASYL structure shown in Fig. 6.4 and in the TOTAL structure shown in Fig. 6.20. A representation of the same information using the hierarchical model is shown in Fig. 7.7. There are three trees: CUSTOMER—ORDER—LINE-ITEM, PART—IN-VENTORY, and WAREHOUSE—PART. The logical pointers suggest that (1) LINE-ITEM data are more frequently accessed through CUSTOMER and OR-DER than they would be through PART and that (2) INVENTORY data are more frequently accessed through PART than through WAREHOUSE.

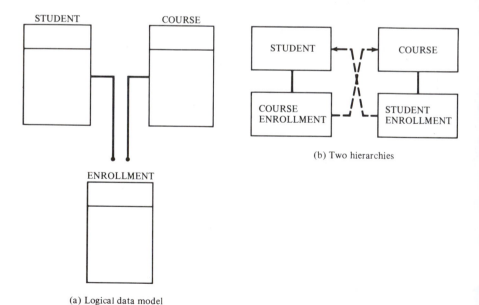

FIGURE 7.8. Correspondence between many-to-many logical relationship and two hierarchies, each with a logical pointer to the root of the other.

Consider another example. The logical data model of Fig. 7.8(a) can be represented using the hierarchical model shown in Fig. 7.8(b). Each of the hierarchies has a logical pointer to a segment in the other.

Logical Databases

The IMS hierarchical model has a feature called *logical databases,* which allow several users to see the same physical databases in different ways without introducing redundancy. Logical databases structures can also cross physical database boundaries; that is, a logical pointer field in one physical database can point to a segment in another physical database.

Logical databases allow two physical databases to be combined into a single logical database. The programmer then may ignore the pointer field connecting the physical databases or the boundaries between the physical databases, and the user can retrieve from the logical databases as if it were one physical database. A logical database does not exist on its own but, rather, as a structure superimposed on one or more physical databases.

Consider the example shown in Fig. 7.9. The physical databases in Fig. 7.9(a) are linked by a logical pointer field in the DRIVER segment. This linkage avoids duplicating the employee data in two databases. The CARPOOL logical database in Fig. 7.9(b) includes the CAR segment from the DRIVING physical database, the intersection data from the DRIVER segment of the DRIVING database, the EMP segment of the PERSONNEL database, and the SKILLS segment from the PERSONNEL database. (It could also have been designed to include the JOBS segment.)

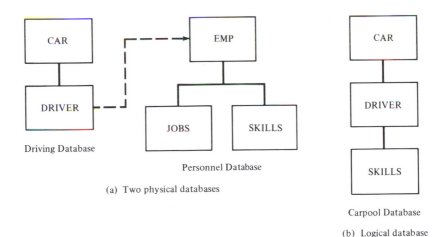

(a) Two physical databases

(b) Logical database constructed from the two physical databases

FIGURE 7.9. Examples of physical and logical database hierarchies.

Thus a logical database imposes a structure on the data that may be different from the basic structure represented by the underlying physical databases. The transformations that are used to define a logical database have some restrictions, two of which are (1) the logical database must itself be a hierarchy, and (2) the root of a logical database must be the same as the root of some physical database. Any segment type of the physical database record hierarchy and all its dependents can be omitted, and any subset of the fields of a physical database record can be included. The fields themselves can be rearranged.

In IMS terminology, a physical database is called a *PDB;* a logical database is called an *LDB*. An LDB is similar in concept to a relational view and a CODASYL subschema.

OPERATORS

The hierarchical model's operators process segments one at a time. The hierarchic and the CODASYL models' operators are at similar levels, and both are distinguished from the relational operators, which process entire relations at once.

Here we use derivatives of the IMS data manipulation language, because they represent the hierarchic model's operators. A programmer accesses an IMS database using a language called *Data Language/I* (DL/I), which is invoked using subroutine calls. These calls are available to PL/I, COBOL, and Assembler Language programs. As in CODASYL and TOTAL database environments, predefined data items are used to hold status information to enable communication between the program and the database management system.

There are three basic DL/I operators: GET, INSERT, and DELETE. Correct usage of the operators requires a thorough understanding of the target database structure. Each references the definition of an LDB known to the program, and each operation can access only one logical database.

Segment Search Arguments

Segment search arguments (SSAs) are used to designate segments. An SSA is a character string giving the name of a segment, which may be followed by a condition. The condition is a set of triples of the form

field comparison-operator value

connected by AND and/or OR booleans. For example, the following are possible SSAs for the LDB shown in Fig. 7.9(b):

```
'CAR      (SERIAL   =123456)'
'CAR      (COLOR    =YELLOW OR COLOR    =BLUE)'
'CAR      (AGE      >10      )'
'DRIVER   (EMPID    =12751   )'
'DRIVER   (EMPNAME  =SMITH   )'
```

The field in an SSA need not be a sequence field; any field can be specified. The comparison-operator may be $=$, $not=$, $<$, $<=$, $>$, or $>=$.

An SSA supplies values for locating individual segments, and a DL/I statement specifies one SSA per segment in the hierarchic path to the desired segment.

Fully Concatenated Key

The fully concatenated key of a segment is the concatentation of all sequence fields of segments on the hierarchical path leading to that segment. It is like the full hierarchical-sequence-key value for a segment, except that it does not include the segment-type names. A fully concatenated key completely defines the position of a segment in a database. For example, the fully concatenated keys of the two TASK segments in Fig. 7.4 are

```
MIS       12751      49
MIS       12751      75
```

Whenever a segment is accessed by a program, IMS carries the segment's fully concatenated key into the program. The most recently referenced fully concatenated key is similar to the run-unit currency indicator in a CODASYL database. It is, however, completely logical, whereas the CODASYL implementations of database keys are typically relative physical addresses.

Selecting Segment Occurrences

The GET statement is used to select a segment occurrence. There are several types of GET statements:

```
GET UNIQUE (GU)
GET NEXT (GN)
GET NEXT WITHIN PARENT (GNP)
```

Each of the operators selects one segment and moves it into a work area in the user's program. The examples used in this section refer to the database shown in Fig. 7.10.

GET UNIQUE selects a segment with a particular value for the segment search argument supplied with the command. For example,

```
GU    PART(PART#=123)
```

selects the PART segment whose sequence field PART# has the value 123.

```
GU    PART(PARTNAME='WIDGET')
      WORKORDR(WO#='453A')
      TASK(TYPE='MANUAL')
```

FIGURE 7.10.   Example of a hierarchy.

selects a TASK segment. Note that the segment search arguments need not refer to sequence fields.

```
GU    PART(PART#=123)
      WORKORDR(ENDDATE='110185')
```

selects a WORKORDR segment whose ENDDATE value is '110185' and whose parent PART has PART# value 123. If there happen to be multiple segment occurrences in the database with the same segment search argument, then the first encountered will be returned. If the segment search argument specifies a fully concatenated key, then by definition only one segment occurrence will qualify.

GET NEXT selects the next segment in the hierarchic sequence, relative to the current segment, that is, relative to the most recently selected segment. Consider, for example,

```
GU    PART(PART#=123)
      WORKORDR(ENDDATE='110185')
      TASK(MACHINE='VMC')
GN
```

The GU causes the TASK segment for the specified MACHINE value and the specified WORKORDR and PART parents to be read. The GN reads the next TASK segment in the database for that parent. The TASK segment may have a different MACHINE value. If there are no more TASK segments for the parent, then the next segment in the hierarchical sequence is read, regardless of its type. In this example, it could cause a read of an EMP segment (if there are any for the WORKORDR) or a read of a WORKORDR or even a read of a PART (if there were no EMPs or WORKORDRs intervening).

A GET NEXT may also specify a qualified read. For example, the sequence

```
GU    PART(PART#=123)
      WORKORDR(DEPT='FABR')
GN    WORKORDR(DEPT='REWORK')
```

reads first the WORKORDR segment in the 'FABR' department for the specified part and then the WORKORDR segment in the 'REWORK' department for that part.

The programmer can write a loop of GN commands to read a sequence of segments. Parents and segment types (if not specified) will be switched, if necessary, to read the next segment. The reading can continue to the end of the database.

GET NEXT WITHIN PARENT also specifies that the next segment in the hierarchical sequence relative to the current one be read but does not continue to the next segment type. Rather, an end-of-parent status code is returned. For example,

```
GU    PART(PART#=123)
      WORKORDR(ENDDATE='110185')
      TASK(MACHINE='VMC')
GNP
```

will read only TASK segments that are children of the PART and WORKORDR segments initially selected by the GU command.

Changing Data-Item Values in Segments

Each of the statements in the preceding section is used to retrieve segment occurrences. Variations of those retrieval statements are used to prepare segment updates. Each request to modify or delete segments from the database must be preceded by a retrieval request that establishes which segment occurrences will be changed.

Three statements are used for positioning:

```
GET HOLD UNIQUE (GHU)
GET HOLD NEXT (GHN)
GET HOLD NEXT WITHIN PARENT (GHNP)
```

These have the same effects as do the corresponding retrieval commands (GU, GN, and GNP), except that the selected segment can subsequently be changed or deleted.

Data items in a segment occurrence are changed using the REPLACE (REPL) command, which must be preceded by program statements that move new values into the data items. The segment is updated when the REPL is executed. For example,

```
GHU PART(PART#=123)
MOVE 'GADGET' TO PARTNAME
REPL
```

first locates the PART segment occurrence with the specified PART# value, moves the new value for one of its data items (PARTNAME) into the work area, and then replaces the segment occurrence, using the new data-item value. The values of other data items remain unchanged.

Adding New Segments

New segments are added to a database using the INSERT (INSRT) command. The programmer first moves the data-item values into a work area. The INSERT statement specifies the target location of the new segment occurrence by giving its parent-segment names and their sequence-field values. For example, to create a new TASK segment, with parents WORKORDR and PART, the following statements can be used:

```
MOVE  'AUTOMATED' TO TYPE OF TASK.
. . . move data values to other data items in the segment
INSRT      PART(PART#=123)
           WORKORDR(WO#='453a')
           TASK
```

The specified sequencing of the inserted segment determines where in the set of children it will reside. If the TASKs are sorted, then the values of the sort fields will be used to locate the new segment.

Note that a retrieval with a GET HOLD is not necessary before an insertion. INSRT creates a new segment; there is no target segment on which to position.

Deleting Segments

A segment is deleted by first positioning on the segment using a GET HOLD and then using a DELETE (DLET) statement. For example,

```
GHU   PART(PARTNAME='WIDGET')
      WORKORDR(WO#='453A')
      TASK(TYPE='MANUAL')
DLET
```

first selects a TASK segment and then removes it from the database.

```
GHU   PART(PART#=123)
DLET
```

first locates the PART segment occurrence with the specified PART# value and then deletes that segment.

When a segment is deleted, its child segments are also deleted. A delete at the root of a hierarchy will delete all segments subordinate to that root. It is important that this deletion be done carefully, as DLET is a powerful command.

Establishing Relationships

The relationships among segments are established automatically when a new segment is inserted in the database. The relationships are clearly defined by the database's schema description, as a child segment cannot exist in the database without being related to its parent.

Note that hierarchical-model relationships have mandatory retention. By contrast, in a CODASYL set with optional retention, a child (member) record can exist without being related to a parent (owner). The programmer can decide when the member will be inserted in the set. A child in a hierarchical database is associated with its parent when the child is created, and there can be no delay.

Status Indicators

A status indicator called STATUS is filled in by the database management system and is available to the programmer as part of the program communication block (PCB). STATUS contains a two-byte value, which is filled in after each DL/I call. If STATUS is blank, then the operation has been completed successfully. Other values represent error conditions or exceptional situations, for example, segment not found on a GU, end of database on GN, and end of children on GNP. STATUS is used to control looping through children of a parent.

It is good practice for the programmer to check the value of STATUS after each DL/I operation. The indicator serves the same function as does the ERROR-STATUS field of CODASYL systems.

ASSERTIONS

The definition of a physical database includes rules for inserting, deleting, and replacing each of its segments. These rules provide the uniqueness, retention, insertion, and modification assertions for the database.

Uniqueness Constraints

Each segment in an IMS database has a unique sequence-key value that determines its location in the database's hierarchical sequence. These sequence fields within the hierarchical paths provide uniqueness constraints, and an attempt to add a segment occurrence that would violate the requirement for unique sequence-key values will be rejected.

Retention Constraints

Retention constraints in a hierarchical database are dictated by the database's hierarchical structure. The rule that guides retention is "No child may exist without being related to its parent." One of the implications of this rule is "The deletion of a parent causes deletion of its children."

One of the database designer's tasks is selecting deletion assertions that implement appropriate actions in conjunction with the deletion rule. The most important choice is whether an attempt to delete a parent with children should be prohibited or allowed (with consequent deletion of the children). For example, depending on the deletion rule specified, a request to delete a PART segment from the logical database of Fig. 7.10 may either

- delete the specified PART segment and any WORKORDR, TASK, and EMP segments that are in its hierarchy of children.
- be disallowed if it has any WORKORDR, TASK, or EMP segments in its hierarchy of children.

If the second deletion rule is used, the implication is that the child segments need to be deleted first. Deletions may safely proceed from the bottom of the tree to the top.

The deletion rules and implications become more complex with logical databases that combine multiple physical databases. Consider again the example of Fig. 7.9(b). Depending on the deletion rule specified, a request to delete a DRIVER segment from the CARPOOL logical database may either

- delete the corresponding EMP segment in the PERSONNEL database if there are no other references from DRIVER segments to that EMP segment.
- not affect the PERSONNEL database.

A request to one of the base physical databases to delete an EMP segment from the PERSONNEL database may either

- be rejected if there are any DRIVER segments that point to it.
- make the EMP segment data inaccessible in the PERSONNEL physical database but still allow it to be accessed from the CARPOOL logical database until all the corresponding DRIVER segments have been deleted.

It is important that the programmer of database updates understand the deletion rules that are in effect.

Insertion Constraints

Like the retention constraints, insertion constraints in a hierarchical database are dictated by the database's hierarchical structure: "No child may exist without being related to its parent." One of the implications of this rule was introduced in the preceding section. The other implication is, "A child cannot be inserted without associating it with its parent.'' Insertion of a child segment requires specification of its parent segments in the hierarchy.

Like deletion, insertion becomes more complex with logical databases that combine multiple physical databases. Consider again the example of Fig. 7.9(b). Depending on the insertion rule specified, a request to insert a DRIVER segment into the CARPOOL logical database may either

- update the corresponding fields in the EMP segment if it exists in the PER-SONNEL database.
- be rejected if there is no corresponding EMP segment in the PERSONNEL database.
- insert an EMP segment in the PERSONNEL database.

Modification Constraints

Modification constraints pertain to requests to replace facts in a segment of a logical database that combines multiple physical databases. For example, a request to modify facts in the DRIVER segment of the CARPOOL logical database may either

- replace values in the corresponding physical EMP segment.
- be rejected if the data fields are in the physical EMP segment.

Changing values in a physical segment will cause them to be changed in any pointer segments that refer to that segment. In the example, the EMP segment can be pointed to by physical databases other than the DRIVING database, though these other databases may not be known to the programmer requesting the update.

SCHEMA DEFINITION

As is usual with database management systems, the schema definition statements are stored in a system library and are invoked (extracted) by the programmer. They need not be rewritten by each programmer who needs to access the database. Indeed, to require that they be rewritten would remove some of the benefits of using a database management system, including relieving programmers of the need to describe data over and over again, which leads to errors, inconsistencies, and replication of data resources. Making libraries of schema definition statements is one relatively simple technique for giving the data administrator (rather than the programmers) control over data descriptions.

Today's implementations of the hierarchical model are usually two-schema structures, and the physical databases are defined by internal schemas, called *Data Base Definitions* (DBDs). The logical databases are defined by external schemas, which are described in program communication blocks (PCBs).

There is no conceptual schema. The collection of DBDs for physical databases, though showing all the data in the IMS data resource, does not show the relationships among the DBDs. The collection of all DBDs for logical databases typically gives a highly redundant picture of the relationships among physical DBDs.

Internal Schemas

Internal schemas correspond to physical databases. Each physical database (PDB) and physical database record (PDBR) describes aspects of physical storage. The internal schema is defined using a data base description (DBD), which is a set of assembly-language macroinstructions showing the structure of each database record. For example, the following DBD describes the physical database structure of Fig. 7.10:

```
DBD        NAME=PARTS
SEGM       NAME=PART, BYTES=40
FIELD      NAME=PARTNAME,BYTES=6,START=1
FIELD      NAME=(PART#,SEQ),BYTES=4,START=7
FIELD      NAME=DESCRP,BYTES=24,START=11
FIELD      NAME=PSIZE,BYTES=6,START=35
SEGM       NAME=WORKORDR,PARENT=PART,BYTES=20
FIELD      NAME=(WO#,SEQ),BYTES=4,START=1
FIELD      NAME=ENDDATE,BYTES=6,START=5
FIELD      NAME=STRTDATE,BYTES=6,START=11
FIELD      NAME=DEPT,BYTES=4,START=17
SEGM       NAME=TASK,PARENT=WORKORDR,BYTES=49
FIELD      NAME=(MACHINE,SEQ),BYTES=3,START=1
FIELD      NAME=TYPE,BYTES=10,START=4
FIELD      NAME=TIMEREQ,BYTES=6,START=14
FIELD      NAME=TNOTES,BYTES=30,START=20
FIELD      NAME=URGNCY,BYTES=2,START=20
SEGM       NAME=EMP,PARENT=PART,BYTES=49
FIELD      NAME=(SOCNO,SEQ),BYTES=9,START=1
FIELD      NAME=EMPNAME,BYTES=30,START=10
FIELD      NAME=ASSGDATE,BYTES=6,START=40
FIELD      NAME=RATING,BYTES=4,START=46
```

The database is named by the DBD macro. Each segment is described by a SEGM macro, followed by a set of FIELD macros. A SEGM macro names a segment and gives its parent's name and its total length in bytes. In the preceding example, PART is the root segment; no parent is specified. WORKORDR is a child of PART; TASK is a child of WORKORDR; and EMP is a child of WORKORDR.

Each field is described by a FIELD macro following the segment's description. A FIELD macro names a field and gives its length in bytes, its starting position in the segment, and its type (character, hex, packed decimal). The default type is character. One field in a segment is the sequence field for the logical ordering of occurrences. In the preceding example, PART# is the sequence field for PART, WO# for WORKORDR, MACHINE for TASK, and SOCNO for EMP. Overlapping fields can be defined, as each field is described by its starting position and length. For example, TNOTES and URGNCY overlap within the TASK segment.

The sequence of statements in a DBD indicates which fields are in which segments. The sequence also defines the database's structure. Segments must be defined top to bottom, left to right. In Chapter 12 on the physical implementations of hierarchical databases, we shall see that this structure is important to determining relative access times to physical segments.

Note that names in IMS are limited to a maximum of eight characters, which can lead to rather cryptic names in a large database environment. Thus it is important in these environments that data-naming standards be used to ensure the understanding of these relatively short names.

External Schemas

The logical databases (LDB) and logical database records (LDBR) describe data as they appear to application programs and thus correspond to external schemas. (Note, however, that an application program also can access a physical database directly.) Logical databases are defined by DBDs (which also define physical databases.) If a logical database includes data from just one physical database, then it need not have an additional DBD.

External schemas are copied into a program through a PCB (program communication block). The set of PCBs for one application program is called a *Program Specification Block* (PSB), and the segments included in the external schema (i.e., in the logical database) are called *sensitive segments*. The LDB is not aware of the existence of any other segments, as they are hidden. Note that this feature not only provides for some data security but also protects the external schema from certain changes in the physical database structure, for example, those changes that add segment types to the physical database.

The fields included in the external schema are similarly called *sensitive fields*. A sensitive field cannot be in a hidden segment. Note that the sequence field for a sensitive segment is generally made known to the external schema.

Mappings Between External and Internal Schemas

The correspondence between logical databases and physical databases is accomplished in an application program via a program communication block (PCB), which is again a collection of assembly-language macros. For example:

```
PCB       TYPE=DB,DBDNAME=WORKDB,KEYLEN=8
SENSEG    NAME=PART,PROCOPT=G
SENSEG    NAME=WORKORDR,PARENT=PART,PROCOPT=R
```

defines an external schema containing the top two segments of the hierarchy of Fig. 7.10. The PCB macro names the database description for the logical database record, which may be the name of a physical database's DBD if the logical database does not combine the physical databases. It also gives the length of the fully concatenated key in the logical database. This key is used for communication between the database manager and the program.

The PCB macro is followed by a SENSEG macro for each segment in the logical database. A SENSEG macro lists the name of a segment to be included in the external schema, and the value of the SENSEG PROCOPT parameter indicates the type of processing available. Retrieval only is G (get), modify is R (replace), delete is D, and insert is I.

It is sometimes necessary to include segments for which the program needs (or is authorized to use) only the sequence-key value, but none of the other fields. These segments have *key sensitivity,* indicated by PROCOPT = K. For example,

```
PCB        TYPE=DB,DBDNAME=TASKDB,KEYLEN=11
SENSEG     NAME=PART,PROCOPT=K
SENSEG     NAME=WORKORDR,PARENT=PART,PROCOPT=K
SENSEG     NAME=TASK,PARENT=WORKORDR,PROCOPT=R
```

gives an application program access to the TASK segment contents, but not to PART or WORKORDR data.

The sequence-key value is needed to form the fully concatenated key of dependent segments, and the program accesses the database as if the key-sensitive segment(s) did not exist.

MAPPING FROM LOGICAL DATA MODELS

Mapping from a logical data model to a hierarchical database structure can be relatively straightforward, unless the logical data model contains networks and category relationships. The resulting hierarchical model usually loses some of the semantic information that is explicit in the logical data model.

Entities, Attributes, and Connection Relationships

The basic rules for mapping entities, attributes, and connection relationships from a logical data model are

- An entity is represented by a segment type.
- Each attribute of an entity is represented by a data field in the segment type.
- A connection relationship is represented by a parent–child relationship.

It is relatively simple to develop the hierarchical database structure if the logical data model is completely hierarchical. Each zero-or-one-to-many relationship is represented by a parent–child relationship. Relationship cardinality cannot be represented more precisely than "many," and any cardinality constraints must be enforced by program logic.

In order to create a simpler, more efficient, and more flexible physical database structure, two or more entities may be combined into a single segment. This combining is usually for entities between which there is a one-to-zero-or-one relationship. An entity may also be duplicated in more than one segment, generally when the logical data model contains networks.

Nonhierarchical Relationships

Only rarely is a logical data model hierarchical. More likely, a logical data model contains a complex set of networked relationships. Mapping from these to the hierarchical data model is not straightforward, as there is no one right way to do it.

Many possible hierarchical databases may be derived from one logical data model, their variations being caused largely by performance considerations. The logical structure of a hierarchical database is a determining factor in its physical structure, which in turn is a factor in the database system's resulting performance. Mapping a logical data model to a hierarchical database structure takes into account performance requirements.

Consider the logical data model shown in Fig. 7.11. It is a network and cannot be mapped directly to a hierarchy. It can, however, be mapped indirectly to two hierarchies, as shown in Fig. 7.12(a). One hierarchy has root DEPT, with child EMP, which has child TASK. The other hierarchy has root PROJ, with child TASK. To avoid replicating the TASK data in both hierarchies, logical pointers have been used. The TASK segment in the DEPT hierarchy has a logical pointer to the TASK segment in the PROJ hierarchy, which is where the TASK data are stored.

An alternative structure, which reverses the logical pointer, is shown in Fig. 7.12(b). Here the TASK segment in the PROJ hierarchy has a logical pointer to the TASK segment in the DEPT hierarchy, which is where the TASK data are stored.

Which is the correct structure? Both represent the same logical data model; however, their performance characteristics are different. Generally it takes more time to follow a logical pointer than to follow parent–child pointers within a hierarchy. Thus the structure of Fig. 7.12(a) would be more appropriate if the TASK data were more commonly accessed with PROJ data than with DEPT and EMP data. And the structure of Fig. 7.12(b) would be more appropriate if the TASK data were more commonly accessed with the DEPT and EMP data than with the PROJ data.

Thus one step in mapping the logical data model to the hierarchical data model is deciding which segments will contain logical pointers to other hierarchies. These decisions should be based on data volumes and access patterns.

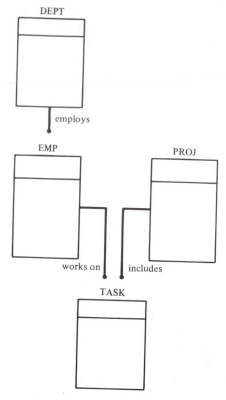

FIGURE 7.11. Data model containing resolved many-to-many relationship.

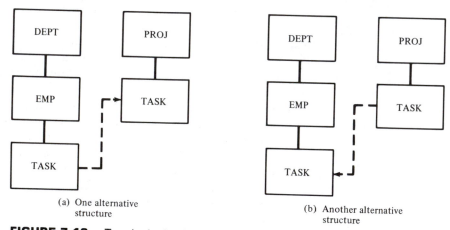

(a) One alternative structure

(b) Another alternative structure

FIGURE 7.12. Two logical pointer alternatives for representing the network of Fig. 7.11.

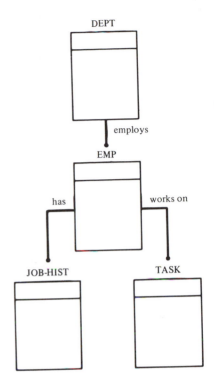

FIGURE 7.13. Another logical data model.

Consider now the logical data model of Fig. 7.13, which is an embellishment of the DEPT-EMP-TASK part of our current example. This logical data model is a hierarchy, but even so, there are decisions to be made in mapping it to a hierarchical database. Figure 7.14 shows two alternative structures that differ from each other in the order of the JOBHST and TASK segment types.

Which is the correct structure? Both represent the same logical data model; however, as in the preceding example, their performance characteristics are different. Generally it takes more time to access the child segments on the right side of a hierarchy than to access the child segments on the left side of a hierarchy. Thus the structure of Fig. 7.14(a) would be more appropriate if the JOBHST data were more commonly accessed than the TASK data were, and the structure of Fig. 7.14(b) would be more appropriate if the TASK data were more commonly accessed than the JOBHST data were.

Thus another step in mapping the logical data model to the hierarchical data model is deciding the left-to-right order of segment types for a parent segment. These decisions should be based on data volumes and access patterns.

Consider the logical data model of Fig. 7.15, two alternative structures of which are shown in Fig. 7.16. One maps the hierarchy into one tall hierarchical database with root DEPT, and the other maps the hierarchy into two shorter

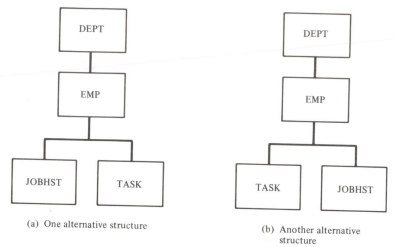

(a) One alternative structure

(b) Another alternative
structure

FIGURE 7.14. Two dependent-segment placement alternatives for representing the hierarchy of Fig. 7.13.

hierarchical databases, one with root DEPT, and the other with root JOB. The shorter hierarchies are connected by a logical pointer.

Which structure is correct? They are logically the same. But as in the other examples, their performance characteristics differ. Generally, it takes more time to access the segments at the bottom of a hierarchy than to access the segments at the top of a hierarchy. Thus the structure of Fig. 7.16(b) would be the more appropriate if there were a need to frequently access JOB data.

Another step in mapping the logical data model to the hierarchical data model, then, is deciding whether tall hierarchies should be split into several shorter hierarchies, connected by logical pointers. A hierarchical database environment that supports high-volume, relatively unpredictable, interactive accesses usually performs better when structured with many short hierarchies. By contrast, a hierarchical database environment that supports high-volume, predictable, batch accesses usually performs better when structured with fewer tall hierarchies. There are, of course, exceptions.

Category Relationships

The three approaches to handling category relationships in the CODASYL model also apply to the hierarchic model:

- One or more parent–child relationships per category relationship.
- Redefined data aggregates within the generic entity's segment type.
- Explicit inheritance of the generic attributes within the segment type of each subtype entity.

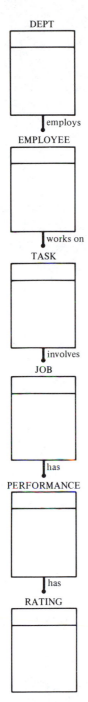

FIGURE 7.15. Another logical data model.

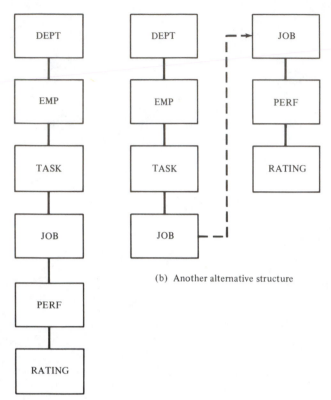

(a) One alternative
    structure

(b) Another alternative structure

FIGURE 7.16.   Two alternative structures for representing the data model of Fig. 7.15.

As with the CODASYL model, none of these approaches is entirely satisfactory.

In the first approach, each entity maps directly to a segment type, and the category relationship is represented by a parent–child relationship between each generic-subtype entity pair. Figure 7.17(a) shows this approach applied to the category relationship of Fig. 3.20(b).

The main problem with this approach is the loss of the one-to-one nature of the relationships between generic and subtype entities. A parent–child relationship is always one-to-many. The database manager will not automatically enforce the generalization constraint that each generic segment be related to at most one of the subtype segments; therefore each parent could have many children.

The second approach to representing a category uses a redefined data aggregate within the generic entity's segment type (Fig. 7.17[b]). The explanation of this approach in Chapter 6 on network data models also applies here. This structure retains the category's hierarchical structure and explicitly represents the inheritance of attributes from the generic entity.

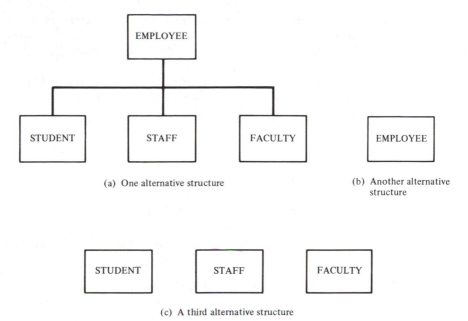

(a) One alternative structure

(b) Another alternative structure

(c) A third alternative structure

FIGURE 7.17. Three alternative structures for representing the category relationship of Fig. 3.21 (b).

The problems with this approach are as indicated in Chapter 6, on network models:

- Category networks cannot be represented.
- A relationship in which only one of the subtype entities participates cannot be distinguished from a relationship in which the generic entity participates.
- A relationship among subtype entities cannot be represented explicitly.
- Representation of nested categories is awkward.

A third approach to representing category relationships is to map each entity to a segment type, with explicit inheritance of attributes (Fig. 7.17[a]). No parent–child relationships are introduced between the entities in the generalization. The explanation of this approach in Chapter 6 on network data models also applies here. This structure loses the hierarchical structure of the category.

Of these three approaches, the second is probably the one most widely used.

Dependencies

The hierarchical data model implicitly assumes identifier dependency within a parent–child relationship. A fully concatenated key is composed of the full string of identifiers down the pertinent leg of the hierarchy.

The referential integrity constraint is implicitly enforced through parent–child relationships. The fully concatenated key of a child must have the appropriate foreign-key value for its parent, and no child can be inserted in the database without being related to a parent.

Existence dependency is also enforced in parent–child relationships. When a parent is deleted, its children must also be deleted, and when a child is inserted, its parent must be designated. No child can exist in the database without its parent.

The Mapping Process

Before designing a database using the hierarchical data model, the logical data model should be developed. That data model then can be mapped to a form that can be implemented by a hierarchical database management system. The basic steps of the mapping process are

1. Construct a data model of the subject area.
2. Resolve the many-to-many relationships and the zero-or-one-to-many relationships.
3. Migrate the primary keys, forming foreign keys.
4. Map each entity to a segment type, with the entity's attributes becoming the segment type's data fields.
5. Map each one-to-many relationship to a parent–child relationship.
6. Map each one-to-zero-or-one relationship to a parent–child relationship or a single record type. The parent–child mapping is preferable if the dependent entity participates in other relationships.
7. Map each category structure to one of the alternatives introduced in this chapter.
8. Identify the roots of the hierarchies in the database. These generally are entities that are not existence dependent on any other entities.
9. Draw the hierarchy of children for each root.
10. Identify the segments that apper in more than one hierarchy, and decide which of these segments will be logical pointer segments to other hierarchies rather than data segments.
11. Determine the left-to-right order of segment types for a parent segment.
12. Identify the hierarchies that are more than three segment types tall, and decide whether each of these should be split into shorter hierarchies, connected by logical pointers.
13. Tune the structure to enhance physical performance.

The last step will be addressed in Chapter 12 on the physical design of hierarchical databases. It may involve, among other things,

• splitting hierarchies into several physical databases.
• combining hierarchies into a single physical database.

- not representing all segment relationships.
- modifying the left-to-right positioning of children in a hierarchy.
- specifying indexes to be constructed on certain segment types.
- selecting the access method to be used for each hierarchy.

INTRODUCTION TO COMMERCIAL HIERARCHICAL DATABASE MANAGEMENT SYSTEMS

Commercial hierarchical database management systems are important, in that they manage nearly half, or perhaps more, of today's large production databases. They have been used for many years and are mature products.

The main hierarchical database management system product is IMS/VS from IBM.

IMS/VS has two features: the database feature is called *DL/I* or *DB,* and the data communications feature is called *DC*. Thus you may see references to IMS/VS-DB/DC or simply IMS DB/DC, referring to both capabilities. Using IMS/VS-DB, the application programmer can use DL/I commands in PL/I, COBOL, or Assembler Language programs to access IMS databases. IMS/VS-DC is a facility that allows on-line transactions to access IMS databases and is much like other on-line teleprocessing management systems.

An accompanying program product from IBM is the DB/DC Data Dictionary/Directory which stores basic descriptions of logical and physical databases, records, segments, and fields. It also has an extensibility feature that allows the database administrator to include additional descriptions.

IBM's IMS enjoys a large share of today's database management systems marketplace and is one of the oldest of the DBMS products.

The other hierarchical commercial DBMSs include IMAGE/3000 from Hewlett-Packard, System 2000 from SAS Institute (formerly from Intel Corporation), and FOCUS from Information Builders, Inc. (IBI). IMAGE/3000 and FOCUS logical structures are essentially the same as IMS structures.

The structure of System 2000 databases includes flexible indexes, which support a broad range of accesses to the data. Any field of any record can be specified to have an index, making retrievals on that field efficient. The data manipulation languages provided with System 2000 are less like programming languages than DL/I is. For example, typical System 2000 requests are

```
IF TIME-REQD GE 1000*
THEN PRINT WO#, PART#, TIME-REQD.
IF TIME-REQD GE 2000*
THEN ASSIGN URGENCY EQ 'T'.
PRINT WO#, PART#
WHERE (TIME-REQD GE 1000* AND
       URGENCY EQ 'T').
```

CLOSING COMMENTS

The hierarchical data model is a major force in today's data management environment. It is well entrenched, especially in the large data-processing shops supported by IBM mainframe computers.

The best feature of the hierarchical model is that it is supported by mature DBMS products that enforce a variety of data integrity constraints and can give excellent performance for some types of access.

The basic weaknesses of the hierarchical model are

- it is best suited to represent hierarchical data structures and thus requires some machinations to support natural many-to-many relationships.
- the data manipulation operators typically are at a procedural, programmer level and need to be overlaid by a higher level of commands that are easier for nonprogrammers to use.
- databases' logical and physical aspects are poorly separated.
- IMS is a complex package. In IBM's catalog of education, available IMS courses consume almost a man-year if taken in their entirety.

IBM's relational DB2 product interfaces with IMS environments, and various companion products bridge the two. The combination addresses the weaker points of both the hierarchical and relational models.

Although the industry is advocating relational data management, a tremendous legacy of data in hierarchical systems remains. These data are not going to be converted overnight but will continue to be the workhorses of the data industry for many years.

TERMS

child	physical database (PDB)
data base identification (DBD)	physical database record (PDBR)
data field	program communication block
data item	(PCB)
data type	program specification block (PSB)
dependent segment	root
DL/I	root segment
fully concatenated key	segment
hierarchical path	segment search argument (SSA)
hierarchical sequence	segment sequence field
hierarchical-sequence-key value	sensitive field
IMS	sibling segment
leaf segment	System 2000
logical database (LDB)	tree
logical database record (LDBR)	tree occurrence
parent	twin segment

REVIEW EXERCISES

1. Define each of the terms in the preceding list.

2. Compare the representations of category relationships in the relational, network, and hierarchical models.

3. Compare the semantic expressiveness of the relational, network, and hierarchical models.

4. Compare the semantics of an IMS parent–child relationship, a CODASYL set type, and a TOTAL linkage path.

5. Develop three alternative IMS structures for the logical data model in Fig. 6.22, and discuss their merits.

6. Develop an IMS structure corresponding to the CODASYL schema shown in Fig. 6.21.

7. Consider the hierarchy shown in Fig. 7.3, and write IMS data manipulation statements to do each of the following:
   a. List all the department names.
   b. List all the employee names.
   c. List the names of the employees in the 'MIS' department.
   d. Determine whether employee 'Jones' is in the 'operations' department.
   e. Total the budget figures for the 'marketing' department.
   f. List all tasks for employees in the 'marketing' department.
   g. List all tasks for employee 'Jones.'

8. Compare the features of IBM's IMS and SAS's System 2000.

9. Describe the power of IBM's IMS and DB2 used together.

REFERENCES

Date, C. J. *An Introduction to Database Systems*. Third ed. Reading, Mass.: Addison-Wesley, 1981.

IBM Corporation. *Information Management System/Virtual Storage General Information Manual*. IBM Form No. GH20-1260.

Kapp, D., and J. F. Leben. *IMS Programming Techniques: A Guide to Using DL/I*. New York: Van Nostrand Reinhold, 1978.

McGee, W. C. "The IMS/VS system," *IBM Systems Journal* 16 (June 1977).

A Practical Approach to Logical Data Modeling

In our discussion of a practical approach to building logical data models, we shall introduce modeling teams, outline the results of a modeling project, describe data collection and model review techniques, and consider possible types of logical data models.

Our approach is the Data Modeling Technique (DMT) of D. Appleton Company, Inc. (DACOM).[1] DMT has been used effectively in a variety of organizations, and the DMT graphic syntax was used in Chapters 3 through 7 as the example for diagramming logical data models.

The advantages of the Data Modeling Technique are that

- the models are developed by teams rather than individuals.
- users participate in the modeling process.
- the modeling graphics are easily understood by both users and data-processing personnel.

---

[1]DMT builds on concepts of the Logical Database Design Technique developed by Robert G. Brown of the Database Design Group, Inc. (DBDG). Automated support for the DMT became available in 1984 through a product named Janus, developed by DACOM and DBDG in conjunction with the Bank of America.

- the technique distinguishes the different levels of detail that should be of concern at particular stages of the logical data–modeling process.
- the resultant models can be used to develop physical database designs for a variety of DBMSs.

A DMT project produces a logical data model that has been reviewed and validated by subject experts. A logical data–modeling project usually is part of a larger project, which is either planning or implementing data resources. The intention of the data model determines the level of detail to be incorporated.

DATA-MODELING TEAMS

The most effective modeling efforts are conducted by teams of people, rather than by an individual. The result is models that reflect the synthesis of various points of view, rather than one person's perspective.

A logical data model is developed by a project team composed of

- a project manager, who is responsible for planning and controlling the work of the project team so that the project wil be completed within the budget and schedule limits.
- modelers, who gather information about the subject area being modeled and prepare the model diagrams and documentation.
- sources, who are subject experts providing information about the subject being modeled.
- reviewers, who are subject experts judging the validity of the model diagrams and documentation.

In most cases, these responsibilities may be distributed among several participants, though there must be a principal modeler and a project manager. Although the modelers' goal is to have the data model approved by the reviewers, the modelers report to the project manager, not the reviewers.

The modelers need not be expert in the subject being modeled, though they must be able to extract from the sources the information needed to model the area. The modelers are responsible for structuring the information that the sources provide. Typically each source will bring a different viewpoint to the modeling process. The modelers then synthesize these viewpoints and extract the semantics of the data.

The worst thing that can be done in the logical data–modeling process is to exclude input from the subject experts. Logical data–modeling projects should not be conducted solely by a data-processing department (unless it is the end user); rather, they should be conducted by users, with representation from the data-processing department. In some organizations, the data-processing group provides the modeling expertise.

OUTPUTS FROM A LOGICAL DATA–MODELING PROJECT

The two basic outputs from a logical data–modeling project are the data model diagrams and a glossary. Typically there are several *data model diagrams*, each of which represents a viewpoint, and one diagram that represents the integrated model. The intermediate models are commonly referred to as *views*, because they represent viewpoints rather than a neutral, integrated model. There also may be several levels of diagrams.

The other major product of a data-modeling project is a *glossary*, which defines the terms in the model diagrams. Each entity and attribute is listed with a succinct, accurate, agreed-upon definition.

The diagrams and glossary can be prepared manually or with software support. Software to capture definitions and data model structures is commonly called a *data dictionary system* (see Chapter 13).

Some modeling projects also produce *business rules*, which are statements of the business policies represented in a data model. They can be easily understood and verified by people not trained in data-modeling syntax.

COLLECTING MODELING DATA

Information for the data-modeling project can come from

- reading documents.
- observing the enterprise in operation.
- surveying subject-area experts, using questionnaires.
- talking with subject-area experts.
- using whatever is already known by the modeling team.

The most important of these is face-to-face interaction with subject-matter experts. Seldom will all the needed information be written, and so the modeling team project leader should be able to draw subject-matter experts into the modeling process. This can be difficult in organizations that traditionally have considered systems development to be the responsibility of data processing alone. Subject-matter experts can be interviewed either alone or in groups.

Interviews

Individual interviews should

- elicit facts about current operations.
- identify problems in current data availability.
- discuss solutions regarding future system capabilities.

Preparation for the interview includes

- selecting those to be interviewed.
- making appointments.
- establishing agendas.
- reviewing background information about those being interviewed.

People from different areas of responsibility and from various levels of the organization should be interviewed. Interviews with a few "indispensable" people can often yield much more information than can many interviews with people who are only vaguely familiar with the subject area.

Interviews should last for one-half to one hour. Interview agendas should include

- the scope, objectives, and viewpoint of the modeling project.
- the purpose of the interview.
- general questions about the subject area.
- specific questions about the subject area.

The interviewers should be familiar with the terminology used in the subject area. They should understand the pertinent parts of the organizational structure and have some idea of the functions performed by the persons being interviewed. If it is a followup interview, the results of the previous interviews should be reviewed.

Recording an interview is easier if most of the questions are decided before the interview. Recording is also easier if the interviewers work in pairs, with one person asking the questions and the other recording the answers. The interviewers also can record information in the form of model-diagram sketches.

After the interviews, the modeling team should synthesize the information, draft the model diagrams and the glossary, and then review them with the sources.

Group Modeling Sessions

A group modeling session brings together three to seven subject-matter experts to draft a portion of a logical data model. These experts generally represent a single functional area.

A group modeling session requires the same kind of careful preparation as interviews do. Sessions should be held in a room with a blackboard, whiteboard, or easel to record the model diagram sketches as they are created. A group modeling session is typically conducted by two members of the modeling team. A modeler asks the questions and sketches the evolving data model, and another team member records definitions and unresolved issues.

MANAGING A LOGICAL DATA-MODELING PROJECT

Before planning a data-modeling project, the project manager should discuss the model's scope, objectives, and viewpoint with the people who instigated the project. If the data-modeling project is part of a larger project to plan or implement data resources, then the manager should understand its needs. For example, it may be a larger data-planning project that uses high-level data models to define subsequent database implementation projects. Or the larger project may be a database implementation project that uses detailed data models to develop logical and physical database designs.

A model's scope determines the kinds of data needed by the project team. For example, a model's scope could be ''all data related to accounts,'' and its objective could be ''to help identify database implementation projects for the integrated automation of the bank's account data.'' Another model's scope could be ''marketing contracts and sales data,'' and its objective could be ''to support the logical design and physical implementation of a marketing contracts database that is logically integrated with the bank's other sales-related databases.''

The project manager prepares a project plan indicating the tasks to be performed and the budget and schedule for each. The model's scope, objectives, and viewpoint are the project manager's guide. The manager is also guided by the desired level of detail in the final data model, whether the model will be translated to a physical database design, and whether the model will be integrated with other available data models.

If a process or function model of the subject area is available, it can be used to identify the scopes of intermediate views and the strategy for integrating those views. For example, the node tree of Fig. 8.1 shows that ''Manage checking accounts'' comprises four activities, Open new accounts, Debit/credit accounts, Report account status, and Augment account services. Each of these activities could be the scope of a logical data model view. Each view will then be de-

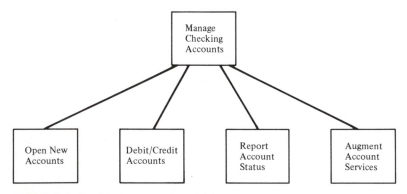

FIGURE 8.1. Node tree of activities.

veloped by the people who perform the pertinent activity and will model the data needed to support that activity. The four individual views together will represent the data needed to support the ''Manage checking accounts'' activity.

The project manager assigns people to act as modelers, sources, and reviewers, who usually are drawn from more than one department or organizational unit. Some data-processing departments offer a pool of expert data modelers, who can be assigned to users' data-modeling projects.

DEVELOPING DATA MODEL VIEWS

The four stages of creating a data model view are (1) developing an entity-relationship view, which represents the highest-level model of entities and relationships; (2) drawing up a key-based view; (3) producing a normalized, fully attributed view; and (4) adding transaction and volume details to support transformation to a physical database design.

Part of planning the project is determining the appropriate level of detail for the deliverable models. Entity-relationship views can be effective for communication to management; key-based views are effective for data-planning efforts; and fully attributed views are necessary for database implementation.

Developing Entity-Relationship Views

The modelers analyze the available material and draw up a view containing entities and relationships. This is done by interviewing users; studying pertinent procedures, forms, and reports; and attending group modeling sessions.

First, the subject experts are encouraged to discuss their area of expertise. The modelers ask:

> What kinds of data are needed for the activities conducted in this subject area? What kinds of data are produced from the activities?

The objective is to identify objects, concepts, persons, places, or events in the model's scope. The modeler lists the candidate entities as they are discovered; each candidate entity must have a noun name.

Each candidate entity is checked for identifiability. The modelers ask:

> How is one instance of this candidate entity distinguished from another?

Primary keys are not selected, but the existence of a primary key must be validated for each entity, as a check that it really is an entity. Some candidate entities are removed from the list. For example, EMPLOYEE is a reasonable candidate entity, as employees are distinguished from one another by social security number, or employee ID, or some other identifier. By contrast, PROBLEM might not be a reasonable candidate entity.

Entity relationships are identified with the help of sketched model diagrams. Sometimes an entity-versus-entity matrix (Fig. 8.2) is used to help decide which entity is related to which. An "X" is entered in the matrix for each pair of entities that are related.

The modelers and sources then determine the nature of each relationship and assign an appropriate name to each. The modeler asks two types of questions that will help identify category relationships, connection relationships, and additional entities:

Which entities are subtypes of which other entities? Are there categories of entities? Which entities are the same type of thing?

Which entities are different types of things but are associated with one another? What sentences can be made linking entity names by verbs?

For example, the first set of questions could help identify two subtype entities, SALARIED_ and HOURLY_EMPLOYEE, as categories of EMPLOYEE. And the second set of questions could help identify a WORKS_ON relationship between EMPLOYEE and PROJECT.

Each category relationship is sketched on the diagram with its generic and subtype entities, and each connection relationship is sketched on the diagram with its related entities and its verb name.

Basic terminators are then added to the connection relationships, and each end of a connection relationship line is attached to its entity with a symbol indicating "one" or "many." The modeler asks for example, "Can an employee work on many projects or on just one project?" "Can a project have many employees, or just one, working on it?" An entity-relationship diagram is shown in Fig. 8.3.

Entity	Tag #	1 Purchase Req.	2 Buyer	3 Vendor	4 Purchase Order	5 Requester	6 Part	7 Purchase Req. Item	8 Purchase Req. Line	9 Approver
Purchase Req.	1		X			X		X		X
Buyer	2	X			X					
Vendor	3				X		X			
Purchase Order	4		X	X						
Requester	5	X								
Part	6			X				X		
Purchase Req. Item	7	X					X		X	
Purchase Req. Line	8							X		
Approver	9	X								

FIGURE 8.2.   Entity—entity matrix, used to identify relationships.

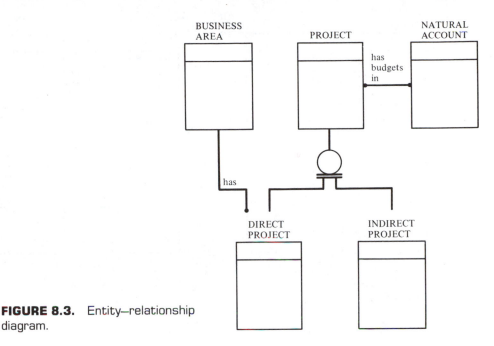

FIGURE 8.3. Entity–relationship diagram.

The modelers and sources then define each entity in the view. Preexisting models may be consulted to determine whether their definitions for same-named entities are appropriate. The difficulty of developing definitions should not be underestimated. It is commonly much more difficult to get people from different parts of an organization to agree on definition than to agree on entity and relationship names.

Developing Key-based Views

A key-based view is more detailed than an entity-relationship view, as it represents a closer understanding of data semantics. The modelers first resolve any nonspecific relationships in the entity-relationship view. A *nonspecific relationship* is one in which one entity does not depend on the other. The most common nonspecific relationships are many-to-manys, one-to-ones, and zero-or-one-to-manys. Many-to-manys and zero-or-one-to-manys are removed from the diagram by the introduction of intersection entities and specific relationships (see Fig. 8.4). One-to-ones are removed by either collapsing the entities into one entity or introducing a one-to-zero-or-one relationship.

The modelers then work top-down through the model, examining each entity and asking:

> What attribute has values that uniquely identify instances of this entity?
> Do some groups of attributes together have values that uniquely identify instances of this entity? Which is the primary identifier?

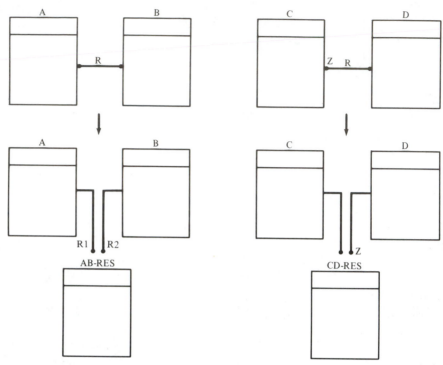

FIGURE 8.4. Resolutions of nonspecific relationships.

In this way, the modelers specify the primary key and any alternate keys.

The primary-key attributes are then migrated through the relationships into dependent entities, where they become foreign-key attributes, which in turn may be part of the primary key in the dependent entity.

Rolenames are assigned where appropriate. For each foreign-key attribute, the modelers ask:

Is there a better name to convey the meaning of this attribute and its role in establishing a relationship with the "home" entity?

The modelers look closely at the entities to which an attribute migrates more than once through different relationships. Here rolenames must be defined if the two appearances of the attribute are to be kept separate. The modelers ask:

Do these two appearances of attribute A always have matching values in every instance of this entity? Do these two appearances of attribute A in entity E have the same or different meanings?

Figure 8.5 illustrates the key-based view that results from refining the entity-relationship view of Fig. 8.3.

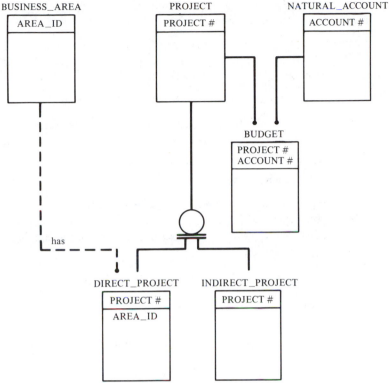

FIGURE 8.5. Key-based view, corresponding to Fig. 8.3.

Business rules then can be prepared. These statements read the relationships on the diagram, as follows:

- A category structure with generic entity A and subtype entities B, C, D, . . . produces the following business rule:

  A ⟨A⟩ can be a ⟨B⟩ or a ⟨C⟩ or a ⟨D⟩ or a . . .

  For example, "An ⟨employee⟩ can be a ⟨salaried employee⟩ or an ⟨hourly employee⟩."

- A many-to-many connection relationship R between entities A and B produces the following business rule:

  A ⟨A⟩ ⟨R⟩ many ⟨B⟩; a ⟨B⟩ ⟨R⟩' many ⟨A⟩.

  For example, "An ⟨employee⟩ ⟨can work on⟩ many ⟨projects⟩; a ⟨project⟩ ⟨can be worked on by⟩ many ⟨employees⟩."

- A one-to-many relationship R between entities A and B produces the following business rule:

  One ⟨A⟩ ⟨R⟩ many ⟨B⟩; each ⟨B⟩ ⟨R⟩' one ⟨A⟩.

For example, "One ⟨department⟩ ⟨employs⟩ many ⟨employees⟩; each ⟨employee⟩ ⟨is employed by⟩ one ⟨department⟩.

Business rules are tests of the quality of the model's names and of the validity of the model's relationships. If business rules are not meaningful, the model should be changed. Some of the business rules from Fig. 8.5 are

A ⟨project⟩ can be a ⟨direct project⟩ or an ⟨indirect project⟩.

A ⟨project⟩ ⟨has⟩ many ⟨budgets⟩, each ⟨budget⟩ is in one ⟨natural account⟩; a ⟨natural account⟩ ⟨has⟩ many ⟨budgets⟩; each ⟨budget⟩ is for one ⟨project⟩.

A ⟨business area⟩ ⟨has⟩ many ⟨direct projects⟩; each ⟨direct project⟩ ⟨belongs to⟩ one ⟨business area⟩.

The modelers and sources define both each of the new entities in the view and the newly introduced attributes. Existing models may be consulted to determine whether their definitions for the same-named entities and attributes are appropriate.

Developing Fully Attributed Views

The modelers and sources now can add nonkey attributes to the model, commonly through group sessions in which the subject experts talk about the kinds of information they need about each of the entities. The modelers ask questions that will help define the nonkey attributes. For example,

What do you need to know about this entity? What are the characteristics of instances of this entity? What are the properties of this entity? What kinds of facts do you need to keep about instances of this entity?

The modelers and sources then define each of the attributes and add them to the glossary. Existing models may be consulted to determine whether their definitions for same-named attributes are appropriate. As with entity definitions, attribute definitions may be quite difficult to decide on.

The modelers and sources also add precise cardinalities to the connection relationships. For each one-to-many relationship between entities A and B, the modelers ask:

Can this relationship be made more precise? Must an instance of A be related to at least one instance of B? Must an instance of A be related to exactly zero or one instance of B?

The relationship is indicated as having positive cardinality (one-to-one-or-many), exact cardinality (n), minimal cardinality (one-to-zero-or-one), or general cardinality (one-to-many).

New entities may be discovered while documenting the nonkey attributes and the precise relationship cardinalities. The modelers ask questions to confirm that the attributes have been placed in the correct entities and to uncover any hidden entities. These questions address

- attributes with multiple values.
- attributes with null values.
- interactions among primary-key attributes.
- interactions among nonkey attributes.

These questions are intended to give the modeling team the opportunity to reexamine its work and to detect any entities missed in the previous modeling efforts.

Attributes with Multiple Values

Chapter 3 stated that an entity instance should have only one value for each of its attributes. This "no-repeat" rule is applied to the attributes of each entity in the model as part of the validation that all entities have been discovered. The modelers ask

Can there be more than one value of this attribute for any instance of the entity?

If the answer is yes, a new dependent entity with a one-to-many connection relationship should be introduced to house that attribute.

For example, consider the PURCHASE_ORDER entity shown in Fig. 8.6(a).

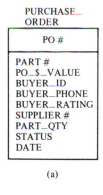

(a)

(b)

FIGURE 8.6. Removing attributes with multiple values.

If it were determined that the STATUS and DATE attributes could sometimes have more than one value for a given PURCHASE_ORDER instance, then a new entity and relationship would be introduced, and the repeating attributes STATUS and DATE would be moved to the new entity, as shown in Fig. 8.6(b). The removal of repeating-value attributes puts the PURCHASE_ORDER entity in the first normal form (see Chapter 5). Note that the primary key of PUR-CHASE_ORDER becomes a foreign-key attribute in the new entity.

The introduction of a new entity must always be followed by an identification of its primary-key and alternate-key attributes.

Attributes with Null Values

Another way to discover hidden entities is to determine which attributes can have null values. The modelers ask:

> Is there always one value of this attribute for any instance of the entity?
> Is there ever an instance of the entity that does not have a value for this attribute?

If the answer is yes, there may be a hidden entity subtype, and a new dependent entity should be introduced in a category relationship with the original entity as the generic.

For example, consider the STUDENT entity shown in Fig. 8.7(a). Assume that it has been determined that the THESIS_ADVISER, LAST_DEGREE, MAJOR_FIELD, and MINOR_FIELD attributes can sometimes not have values for a given STUDENT instance. The modelers may then discover that there really are two types of students, as shown in the category structure of Fig. 8.7(b). Two new entities—GRADUATE_STUDENT and UNDERGRADU-ATE_STUDENT—have been introduced, and the possibly null attributes THE-SIS_ADVISER, LAST_DEGREE, MAJOR_FIELD, and MINOR_FIELD have been moved to the new entities.

The introduction of a new entity must always be followed by an identification of its primary-key and alternate-key attributes. A subtype entity usually has the same primary-key attributes as its generic entity does.

The investigation of null-valued attributes can lead to the identification of additional attributes. For example, once graduate and undergraduate students have been distinguished, it may become clear that other facts about one (or both) of them need to be accommodated.

A null-valued attribute may indicate a category relationship for which only one subtype entity can be identified. Sometimes modelers choose not to break the null-valued attributes into separate entities, though this will limit the model's capability to express relationships in which either the generic entity or the subtype entity (but not both) participates.

If null-valued attributes are not moved to separate entities, they must be

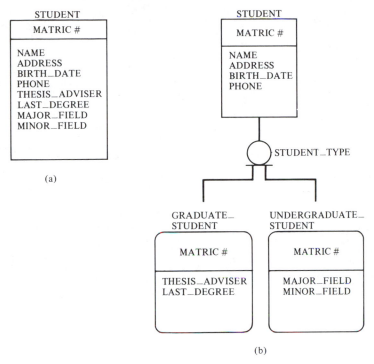

FIGURE 8.7. Using attributes with null values to identify categories.

flagged as allowing null values. This flag is an assertion that can later be enforced by a database management system.

Interactions Among Key Attributes

Hidden or missed entities can be uncovered by looking for interactions among the attributes of compound keys. For each entity with a compound key, the modeler asks:

Does any part of the key identify an additional entity?

If the answer is yes and if there is no entity with that key already in the model, then a new entity should be introduced. This new entity will participate in a one-to-many connection relationship with the original entity.

For example, consider the model shown in Fig. 8.8(a). PART#, SUPPLIER# is an alternate key for the PURCHASE_ORDER entity. Assume that further study has indicated that SUPPLIER# is an identifier of an additional entity—SUPPLIER—that is not part of the model. A new entity has been introduced in Fig. 8.8(b). Each of the nonkey attributes of PURCHASE_ORDER was ex-

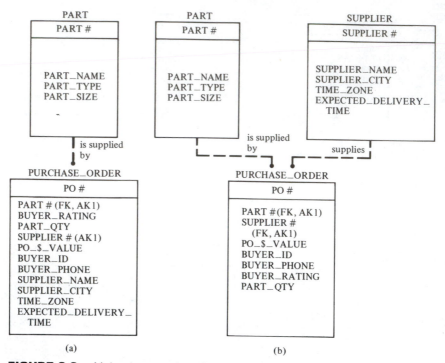

(a)   (b)

FIGURE 8.8. Using interactions between key attributes to identify hidden entities.

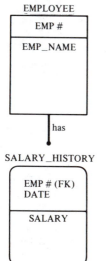

FIGURE 8.9. Example of a compound key that does not imply introduction of a new entity.

amined to determine whether it was really owned by PURCHASE_ORDER or by the new entity SUPPLIER.

Analysis of the interactions among key attributes here leaves the PART, SUPPLIER, and PURCHASE_ORDER entities in the second normal form (see Chapter 5). Each nonkey attribute depends on the entity's entire key.

Not every compound-key situation requires the presence of an entity identified by each component of the key. For example, in the model shown in Fig. 8.9, there would be no need to introduce an entity with primary key DATE, unless there were facts that should be recorded about DATE as an entity. The modelers ask:

> Is there at least one nonkey attribute of interest for this new candidate entity? Are there any facts that should be kept about the entity in addition to the fact that its key values exist?

If a new entity has no nonkey attributes, then it should be decided whether the candidate entity really identifies something about which facts are to be recorded.

Interactions Among Nonkey Attributes

Finally the modelers verify that no entities are hidden in the nonkey attributes, by looking for dependencies among the attributes. They ask:

> Does any nonkey attribute identify the other nonkey attributes? Does the value of any nonkey attribute determine the values of one or more of the others?

If the answer is yes and if the model does not already have an entity with that nonkey attribute as its primary key, then a new entity should be introduced. The new entity participates in a one-to-many relationship with the original entity, because its key appears in the original entity as a foreign key.

For example, consider the entity shown in Fig. 8.10(a). Careful examination reveals that BUYER determines the value for PHONE and RATING. The BUYER attribute thus would be better named BUYER_ID, as it is the identifier for a BUYER entity, which should be added to the model. The revised model is shown in Fig. 8.10(b).

The analysis of interactions among nonkey attributes leaves the BUYER and PURCHASE_ORDER entities in Boyce/Codd normal form (see Chapter 5). All the dependencies in each entity depend on candidate keys.

Checking the Normalization

Finally the normalization of the model is validated, generally with software support. The software looks for inconsistencies in the dependencies implied by the primary keys and the placement of nonkey attributes in entities. It detects

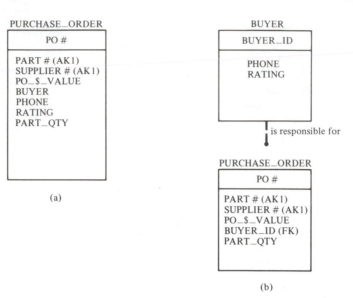

FIGURE 8.10. Using interactions between nonkey attributes to identify a hidden entity.

the same name appearing in a model with apparently different meanings, and it finds entities without primary keys and flags entities without nonkey attributes. Any errors are corrected, and the result is a normalized, fully attributed view.

Preparing for the Physical Database Design

The modelers and sources now add details of data usage to the model, in preparation for the physical database design. Their objective is to document the characteristics of model usage that will affect the physical structure of a corresponding database. The three main types of details added are *domains* for attributes, *data volumes* for entities, and *frequencies of access* to entities.

Domains must be specified for attributes before a physical database structure can be constructed. Typically the principal domain distinction made is between character and numeric values. Depending on the target database management system, more precise data types (e.g., date, money, time, floating point) may be specified.

Data volumes are estimated for the most important entities, and these estimates usually are based on known data volumes in existing files.

The patterns of access to the model's entities can be discovered in several ways. One of the most effective is to specify the logic of expected transactions in a formal, structured language, an example of which is shown in Fig. 8.11. Transaction frequencies can then be estimated and recorded, and the resulting volume and frequency totals can be calculated and added to the model. This

```
PERFORMANCE INFORMATION
     FREQUENCY 35 PER HOUR
     RESPONSE 5 SECONDS
     ACCESS
               * obtain property owner
          FETCH player
          FETCH property
          IF (95%) property not mortgaged
          THEN
                 IF (79%) property is residential
                 THEN
                         FETCH residential
                         IF (75%) no houses built on property
                             * see if player owns all properties in
                                 color group
                         THEN
                                 FETCH color-group USING residential
                                 REPEAT 3
                                     FETCH NEXT residential USING color group
                                     IF (67%) not property renter landed on
                                     THEN
                                             FETCH property USING residential
                                             FETCH ownership USING property
                                     ENDIF
                                 ENDR
                         ENDIF
                 ELSE
                         IF (14%) property is railroad
                     THEN
                         * see how many railroads used by property owner
                             REPEAT 4
                                 * use property type to just obtain railroads
                                 FETCH NEXT property USING property-type
                                     FETCH ownership USING property
                             ENDR
                             FETCH railroad fare table
                         ELSE
                             * property must be utility
                             REPEAT 2
                                 * use property type to just obtain utilities
                                 FETCH NEXT property USING property-type
                                 FETCH NEXT ownership USING property
                             ENDR
                             FETCH utility rate table
                         ENDIF
                 ENDIF
                 * obtain renter
                 FETCH player
                 * debit renter
                 REPLACE player
                 * credit property owner
                     REPLACE player
                     INSERT rent payment
          ENDIF
     ENDA
ENDP
```

FIGURE 8.11. Example of structured language to specify expected transactions against a logical data model. (Source: Brown, R.G. *Logical Database Design Techniques.* The Database Design Group, 1982.)

analysis is generally done with software, and the result is a *fully characterized view*.

INTEGRATING LOGICAL DATA MODEL VIEWS

Data views having different scopes and viewpoints can be merged into a neutral, integrated logical data model of the subject area. When integrating data model views, modelers must identify and resolve homonyms, synonyms, relationship inconsistencies, and attribute inconsistencies. While doing this, problems may surface that require collecting more modeling data or reexamining the component views. In fact, integrating two views may be more difficult than developing either one alone.

Views can be integrated at any level. The components may be entity-relationship diagrams, key-based views, fully attributed views, or fully characterized views. They should, however, be at the same level, as the integrated model will also be at that level.

First, the integrators make sure that they understand the scope of each of the component data views and of the integrated model. They study the statements of scope, objectives, and viewpoint that were prepared for each of the data views and then write statements of scope, objectives, and viewpoint for the integrated model. The views may be combined by software that identifies model overlaps and inconsistencies. The principal guideline is the rule of same name, same meaning.

Identifying and Resolving Homonyms

The model integrators determine when the same name is used in the component views to mean different things and consult the definitions to verify the meanings. When homonyms are detected, each must be given its own name. For example, if EMPLOYEE is used in two views, but with different meanings, then the names must be more specific. Perhaps one view should use SALARIED_EMPLOYEE, and the other should use EMPLOYEE.

The integrators also check the different definitions whenever a name appears in more than one view. Names like ACCOUNT#, PART#, VENDOR_NAME, ADDRESS, CITY should be suspect, as they may mean different things to different people.

Model glossaries can help find and resolve homonyms and also can help prevent them. Thus the developers of a new data view should consult the glossaries of definitions for previous data-modeling efforts, as a name should not be reused with a different meaning.

One way to avoid homonyms is to use precise descriptive names for entities and attributes. For example, CORPORATE_OFFICE_CITY_NAME is more precise than just CITY. Nonetheless, homonyms may occur when two entities or attributes have the same name but different meanings, when an entity and an attribute have the same name, and when two relationships between a pair of entities have the same name but different meanings.

Identifying and Resolving Synonyms

The model integrators determine when different names are used in the component views to mean the same thing and consult the definitions to verify the meanings. It is usually more difficult to identify synonyms than to identify homonyms. Synonyms are found by matching meanings; and homonyms are found by matching names. For example, investigation may reveal that DRAW-ING_CODE in one view is the same as SPECIFICATION_NUMBER in another view or that ENGINEERING_CHANGE_ORDER may mean the same thing as TECHNICAL_ORDER.

When synonyms are detected, one name is selected as the primary name; and the other name may be retained as an alias. Likewise, one of the definitions is retained.

Identifying and Resolving Relationship Inconsistencies

The model integrators next determine when the same relationship is represented by different cardinalities or by different dependencies in the component views. The final model can represent only one cardinality for a relationship; as its relationships will have one set of meanings. For example, the WORKS_ON relationship between EMPLOYEE and PROJECT may be one-to-many in one view and many-to-many in another view (Fig. 8.12). The integrators thus must find the correct cardinality and dependencies for the relationship.

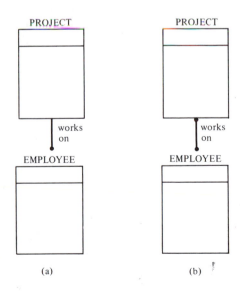

FIGURE 8.12. Two views of a relationship's cardinality.

(a)   (b)

Another possible inconsistency across views is a relationship that appears in one as an identifying relationship and in the other as a nonidentifying relationship (Fig. 8.13). In the identifying version of the INCLUDES relationship, the primary key of DIVISION appears as part of DEPARTMENT's primary key. But in the nonidentifying version of the relationship, DEPARTMENT's primary key does not include the key from DIVISION.

Identifying and Resolving Attribute Inconsistencies

The model integrators finally determine when the same attribute appears inconsistently in the component views. One source for attribute discrepancies is their domains.

Another possible attribute inconsistency appears in nonnull indicators. An attribute in the integrated model either allows or does not allow null values.

A third attribute inconsistency appears when an entity has one primary key in one view and a different primary key in the other view. One of the attributes is selected as the primary key for the entity in the merged view, and the other becomes an alternate key.

REVIEWING DATA VIEWS

At appropriate points in the model development process, subject experts should review the data views to ensure that they are complete and accurate. The two

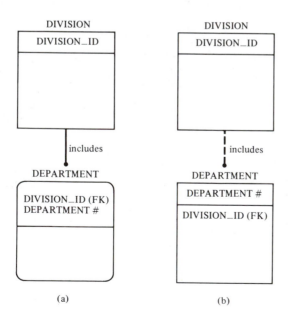

FIGURE 8.13. Two views of a relationship's identifier dependency.

methods are kit reviews and walkthroughs. A *kit review* requests feedback from individuals, and *walkthroughs* extract feedback from a group.

Kit Reviews

A kit review relies on the timely cycling of model documents between the modelers and the reviewers. A kit may contain diagrams, text, glossaries, business rules, decision summaries, background information, or anything packaged for review and comment.

The kit-review cycle proceeds as follows:

- The modelers select particular model documents for inclusion in a kit. They assemble the material and prepare a cover sheet to identify the kit and to indicate to the reviewers when their comments are due. Copies of the kit are distributed to each of the reviewers.
- Within the specified response period, the reviewer reads the kit and writes comments directly on the copy. Red ink is generally used to ensure that the comments can be easily found. The annotated kit is returned to the modelers.
- The modelers respond in writing directly on each reviewer's copy. The modelers may agree with the comment, note it on the working copy, and incorporate it in the next version of the model. If they disagree, the modelers note the disagreement on the kit. The modelers' responses are generally written in green or blue ink to distinguish them from the reviewers' comments. The reviewed kits are returned to the reviewers.
- The reviewer reads the modelers' responses. If satisfied, he or she files the kit. But if the reviewer does not agree with the modelers' responses, a meeting is arranged to resolve the differences.

This cycle continues until a model is created that represents the careful consideration of all the team members. The reviewers finally verify the model's technical accuracy, being responsible for finding errors and suggesting improvements.

Walkthrough Sessions

Walkthrough sessions can be effective when all the appropriate participants can be assembled. The modelers select the documents to be used in the walkthrough, usually the same as those in a review kit, and they prepare the presentation and handout materials. The project manager schedules the walkthrough, arranges for the necessary facilities (meeting room, overhead projector, and the like) and notifies the reviewers.

During the walkthrough, the modelers present the model and the reviewers comment on it. Corrections can be proposed at any step and may be noted for incorporation later or may be adopted immediately. But the modelers should be wary of getting so involved in correcting the model that they miss hearing the reviewers' comments.

A walkthrough is an orderly process, usually with the following steps:

- The entities and their definitions are reviewed. In a complex model, the generic entities and then the subtype entities are reviewed.
- The relationships are reviewed.
- The primary keys are reviewed for key-based views and fully attributed views.
- The relationship cardinalities are reviewed for fully attributed views.
- The nonkey attributes are reviewed for fully attributed views.

At each step, the reviewers verify that the model is accurate and complete.

CLOSING COMMENTS

This process of developing, integrating, and reviewing data models has been used successfully in a variety of organizations and is especially effective in modeling large subject areas that cannot be understood completely by a small group of individuals.

The process spans the breadth of the expressive capability of logical data–modeling techniques, from the preliminary listing of candidate entities through the detailed preparation for the physical database design. A single data-modeling technique that addresses all these various levels of detail can help build integrated systems that meet their users' requirements.

Building a logical data model at any level requires input from subject experts: their involvement and the modelers' expertise determine the quality of the final models.

TERMS

attribute	key-based view
business rule	kit
category relationship	modeler
connection relationship	nonkey attribute
data dictionary system	nonspecific relationship
data model diagram	normalization
Data Modeling Technique (DMT)	primary key
entity	project manager
entity-relationship view	relationship
fully attributed view	reviewer
fully characterized view	specific relationship
glossary	synonym
group modeling session	view
homonym	walkthrough session
interview	

REVIEW EXERCISES

1. Define each of the terms in the preceding list.
2. What roles are played by the members of a logical data-modeling project team?
3. What are the results of a logical data-modeling project?
4. Why might an organization start a logical data-modeling project?
5. Where can a modeling team find information about the logical modeling process?
6. What preparations must be made when interviewing subject-matter experts?
7. How does a group modeling session differ from an interview?
8. What does the manager of a logical data modeling project need to do?
9. Discuss the differences and similarities among the four levels of logical data model views.
10. Why may it be difficult to integrate two logical data model views?
11. What is the difference between a synonym and a homonym?
12. How does a walkthrough session differ from a kit review?
13. How does a walkthrough session differ from a group modeling session?
14. What do you think would be difficult about conducting a group modeling session?
15. Compare the logical data modeling approach presented in this chapter with another approach. What are the strong and weak points of each?
16. Survey the software available to support logical data modeling.

REFERENCES

Brown, R. G. *Logical Database Design Techniques*. The Database Design Group, 1982.

D. Appleton Company, Inc. *INFO Model-ER Reference Manual*. Manhattan Beach, Calif.: 1982.

D. Appleton Company, Inc. *Data Modeling Technique Reference Manual, PCFS-DMT-3.0*. Manhattan Beach, Calif.: 1985.

SofTech. *ICAM Architecture Part II*, Volume 5: *Information Modeling Manual (IDEF1)*, AFWAL-TR-81-4023. Materials Laboratory, Air Force Wright Aeronautical Laboratories, Air Force Systems Command, Wright-Patterson Air Force Base, Ohio, 45433, June 1981.

PHYSICAL DATABASE DESIGN

Part II consists of four chapters that discuss the principles of physical database design. Chapter 9 introduces physical database design by reviewing the basic building blocks of physical data structures, and Chapters 10, 11, and 12 describe the physical design of databases that implement the models introduced in Part I of the book: relational databases, network databases, and hierarchical databases.

Logical database design is usually the responsibility of data administrators, and physical database design is usually the province of database administrators. Both aspects of database design are essential: Without logical database design, there would be no match of the data repository to the business needs; and without physical database design, there would be no efficiency of implementation.

CHAPTER 9

Physical Structures

Implementing a database is mainly transforming a logical data model into a physical structure. The components of those structures embody the principles of two areas of the data management field, data structures and file organizations, and they can be applied to both centralized databases and distributed databases, which are implemented on networks of possibly heterogeneous computers.

BASIC CONCEPTS

Most databases are too large to be stored economically in a computer's main memory. Instead, they reside on secondary devices, which offer larger volumes of storage at lower costs per bit. Databases typically are stored on direct-access storage devices (e.g., rotating disks), rather than on serial-access devices (e.g., magnetic tape). A database's physical structure determines its layout or configuration in secondary storage.

Records and Files

The basic unit of data transfer between secondary storage and main memory is the *record*. All of a record's fields are read or written in one access to secondary storage. When a program requests that a record be read from secondary storage (typically using a READ statement), the data manager (1) ensures that the appropriate storage device is ready, (2) requests transfer of the record from the device into the program's buffer area, and (3) returns control to the program. The program waits until the record has filled the buffer, which is the program's holding area for data transferred to or from secondary storage. The same steps are followed when a program requests that a record be written (typically using a WRITE statement).

The most common technique for reducing the number of device accesses and the program wait time is to block records so that they may be read or written in a single access to the device. If there are n records per block, then only every nth READ by the program will cause a device access.

A *file* is a collection of blocks that are managed together. File design decisions concern which fields together form a record type, which record types are to be stored together in a file, and the file's blocking factor (i.e., the number of records per block).

Storage Devices

The two main ways of storing files are in serial-access storage devices or direct-access storage devices.

A *serial-access storage device* requires that records be accessed in physically consecutive order, and thus the time required to access record R2 after record R1 depends on the physical distance between them. Magnetic tape is the most widely used serial-access storage device. Serial-access storage is appropriate for files that will be accessed sequentially, that is, one record after another, through the entire file. For example, a file of names and addresses for printing mailing labels would be stored as a sequential file on a serial-access storage device.

A *direct-access storage device* offers access to records in any order, and thus the time required to access record R2 after record R1 does not depend only on their physical separation. Magnetic disk is the most widely used direct-access storage device. Direct-access storage is appropriate for files that will be accessed in an unpredictable order. For example, a file of credit data to support phone-in credit checks would be stored on a direct-access storage device.

Physical Databases

A *physical database* is a collection of files that together implement a logical data model. The files are integrated by the database's logical structure, and they can refer to one another. A user's request may draw data from several files in a single physical database, and depending on the database's organization, a file may contain records that implement one or more entities. The logical relationships among entities are implemented by interrecord and/or interfile references, which provide pathways to access one record from another.

The two types of files in a physical database structure are data files and index files. *Data files* store the facts that comprise the database. *Index files* (or *directories*) support access to the data files but usually do not themselves store facts other than key values. Meanings are provided by the database's logical structure, which in turn is used to determine which facts should be accessed and how they relate to one another.

DATA-FILE STRUCTURES

Data files have three main structures, based on whether the records have intrafile pointers, interfile pointers, or no pointers. Which of these alternatives is used helps determine how the logical relationships among entities will be implemented in the physical database.

A *pointer* is simply a stored address and is stored in a record so that accesses may proceed from that record to another. Figure 9.1 illustrates a linear linked list, in which each record points to the "next" record in a sequence. Note that the records' physical sequence need not match their logical sequence. The pointer is the key to being able to access records directly rather than serially. Regardless of where a record resides in storage, it can be reached directly by following a pointer to its location. One problem in designing a physical data structure is determining which records should point to which other records, and a challenge in managing data structures is making sure that the pointers point where they should.

A pointer value can be an absolute address or a relative address. An *absolute address* is the actual address of a record and can be used without modification to find the target record. If the record is on a magnetic disk, then the absolute address is generally a ⟨cylinder number, surface number, record number⟩ or a ⟨sector number, record number⟩.

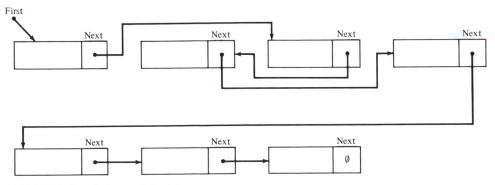

FIGURE 9.1. A linear linked list.

A pointer that is an absolute address provides very fast access, as almost no processing time is required to determine the target record's location. But the disadvantages of using absolute-address pointers in a database can outweigh the advantages:

- Absolute addresses are device dependent. Should it be desirable to upgrade or change the device in which the file resides, the absolute-address values will probably also need to be changed.
- Absolute addresses are address-space dependent. Should it be desirable to allocate to the file more (or less) space or to collect garbage space, the absolute-address values will probably also need to be changed.

A *relative address* indicates a record's location not by its specific location on a storage device but by the record's position in a file. For example, the relative address of the one-hundredth record in a file could be simply ⟨100⟩, and the relative address of the fourth record in the eightieth block allocated to a file could be ⟨80, 4⟩.

A relative address must be translated into an absolute address before the target record can be accessed. The processing required for this translation is generally minimal, and the flexibility gained by increased independence from physical device characteristics is attractive. Our examples will use relative addresses.

Intrafile Pointers

Some physical databases use *intrafile pointers* to show the relationships among records. Each record contains both data and pointer fields. A pointer field contains the address of the next record, and thus the records are said to form a *linked list* or a *chain*.

The order of records on a chain is determined by the application. For example, they could be sorted by the value of a field in the data, or they could be linked in the order in which they are created. The records' logical order need not be the same as their physical ordering.

Each linked list has a pointer to its first record, and the last record in a chain usually has a null pointer, indicating that there is no next record.

There can be many linked lists in a data file. For example, EMPLOYEE records could be linked so that all the records with DEPT# = 10 are in one chain; the records with DEPT# = 20 are in another chain; and so on. Figure 9.2 shows a doubly linked list. Each record has not only a pointer to the next record but also a pointer to the previous record. Figure 9.3 illustrates a file in which the records are linked in order by both SERIAL# and SIZE.

A file can contain records representing one or many entities. For now, assume that an entity is represented by a record type. The relationships among an entity's occurrences generally order those occurrences by the value of some field. For example, the EMPLOYEE records could be linked in ascending order of their SOCIAL_SECURITY_NUMBER field.

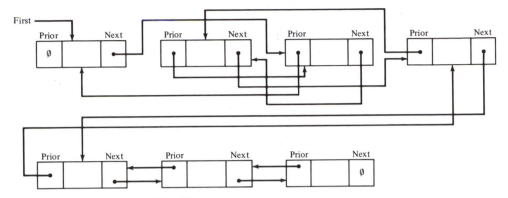

FIGURE 9.2. A doubly linked list.

If the file contains both EMPLOYEE records and DEPARTMENT records, then the relationships between their respective entities can be represented by linked lists. Each DEPARTMENT record can point to a chain of associated EMPLOYEE records, as shown in Fig. 9.4. Thus a file's pointers may connect records of the same or different types. Which records are connected is determined by the data's logical structure.

Interfile Pointers

Pointers across files, or *interfile pointers,* can also be used to represent relationships. A physical database can contain several files; typically all records of a given type appear on a single physical file. Each file contains one or several record types. The general case is modeled in Fig. 9.5.

Building on the preceding example, another file may contain PROJECT records, and the relationships among projects and departments can be represented by interfile pointers. Consider the data model in Fig. 9.6. Each department can have many projects, but each project is in only one department. This relationship can be implemented in at least three ways:

- Each PROJECT record can point to its DEPARTMENT record, as shown in Fig. 9.7.

Address	Serial #	Next Serial #	Size	Next Size	Color
1	34567	8	12	2	Blue
2	21922	4	14	$\emptyset$	Green
3	51362	5	10	4	Green
4	21923	10	10	1	Yellow
5	51466	6	3	10	Blue
6	61234	7	5	7	Pink
7	71911	$\emptyset$	6	8	Blue
8	51361	3	7	9	Green
9	12111	2	8	3	Yellow
10	21934	1	4	6	Purple

FIGURE 9.3. A file with two linked lists.

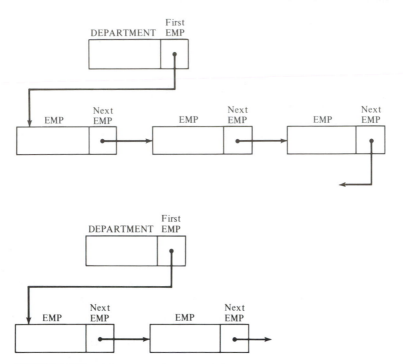

FIGURE 9.4. Interrecord-type pointers.

- Each DEPARTMENT record can point to a linked list of its PROJECT records, as shown in Fig. 9.8.
- Each DEPARTMENT record can have an array of pointers to its PROJECT records, as shown in Fig. 9.9.

Interfile pointers are basically the same as intrafile pointers and also need to indicate which file is being pointed to.

No Pointers

Some database management systems implement relationships without using pointers, an approach sometimes called *indirect addressing*. Rather than using pointer fields, which contain absolute or relative addresses, they use reference fields containing data values. For example, the relationship between an EMPLOYEE record and a DEPARTMENT record can be represented by matching the DEPT# values in the two records, which is exactly the approach taken with foreign-key attributes in a logical data model.

But using reference fields does not avoid having to translate the field values into record addresses, which is sometimes done by maintaining a separate table of ⟨access-key value, record address⟩ pairs. Rather than directly accessing the

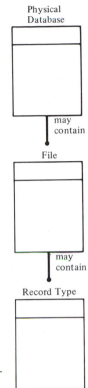

FIGURE 9.5. General relationships among physical data-bases, files, and record types.

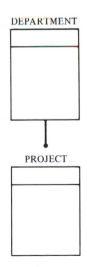

FIGURE 9.6. Logical data model showing relationship be-tween departments and projects.

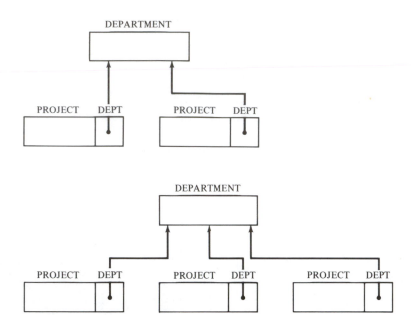

FIGURE 9.7. Each PROJECT points to its DEPARTMENT.

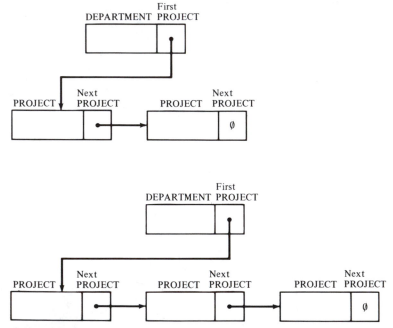

FIGURE 9.8. Each DEPARTMENT points to a linked list of PROJECTs.

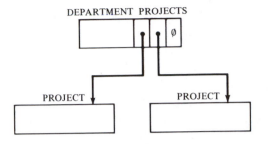

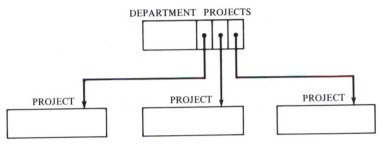

FIGURE 9.9. Each DEPARTMENT has an array of pointers to its PROJECTs.

employee's DEPARTMENT record by using a relative address stored in EM-PLOYEE, the DEPARTMENT record can be accessed indirectly via the ⟨DEPT#, record address⟩ index (Fig. 9.10). The DEPT# value stored in the EMPLOYEE

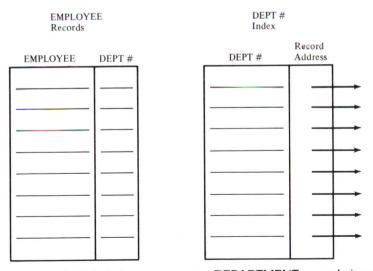

FIGURE 9.10. Indirect access to DEPARTMENT records is provided by accessing the DEPT# index from the EMPLOYEE-DEPT# values.

record is used to find the desired entry in the DEPT# index, which leads to the pertinent DEPARTMENT record.

FILE ORGANIZATIONS

One of the services of a database management system is to manage physical data structures, including interpreting relationships represented by intrafile pointers, interfile pointers, and without pointers. The programmer or user need not be aware of how the relationships are represented in the physical database structure, but only of the logical data structure.

In most computer configurations, a database management system works with the operating system to provide data management services. The database management system calls on operating system capabilities to perform *input/output (I/O)* to data stored on system devices.

These I/O services include

- maintaining directories so that files can be found.
- establishing pathways so that data can flow between secondary storage and main memory.
- coordinating communication between the secondary storage devices and the central processing unit.
- readying files for input or output.
- handling files when input or output is complete.

How these services are provided for any particular file is based on the file's structure and how it is being manipulated. A file's structure is called its *file organization*.

A file's organization determines the physical sequencing and configurations of its records. The records can be arranged either in some random order or in sorted order according to the value of some field. A file's organization also determines the types of operations needed to find records with particular field values. The operations may provide direct access to records based on a variety of fields, direct access based on a single field, or only sequential access to records.

The three fundamental file organizations used with data files are sequential, relative, and indexed sequential.

Sequential Files

The most basic way to organize the collection of records that form a file is to use *sequential file organization*. The records are written in physically consecutive order when the file is created, and they must be accessed in that same order when the file is later used (Fig. 9.11). A sequential file can be stored on a serial-access storage medium (e.g., magnetic tape) or a direct-access storage medium (e.g., hard magnetic disk).

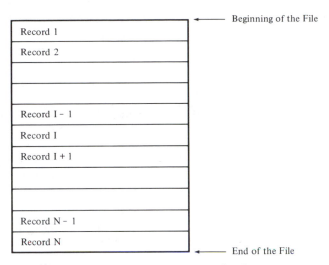

FIGURE 9.11. Sequential file organization.

Records often are supplied in sorted order when the file is created; such a file is called a *sorted file*. The field(s) whose values are used to determine the records' order is called the *sort key*. A sequential file can have only one sort key: the records cannot be in two orders because the logical sequence must be exactly the same as the physical sequence.

The nature of sequential files makes them suitable for batch processes, as it is much faster to access the "next" record than it is to access the record whose key value is x. On the average, half the records on the file must be read to find the one with the desired key value.

Sequential files are suitable for storing only archive, backup, and transport copies of databases. An archived copy records the state of the database at some time, say at year-end. A backup copy is used to restore the database as part of recovering from a system malfunction, and a transport copy is used to send a database from one machine or installation to another. Archive, backup, and transport copies are usually stored on magnetic tape.

Sequential file organization is attractive for these purposes because it can be used with inexpensive storage media and it has a low overhead (i.e., it stores only data, no indexes). Considerable processing may be required to load a nonsequential database structure from a sequential file, but presumably this is done infrequently. Archive processing, system recovery, and database installation are not everyday occurrences in most environments.

Relative Files

Relative file organization uses the value of a field in a record to determine its physical location in the file. The logical sequence of records need bear no relationship to their physical sequence (Fig. 9.12). If records appear physically in sorted order by some field, it is purely coincidental.

In contrast with sequential files, it is not necessary to access the records of a relative file in consecutive order. A relative file must be stored on a direct-access storage device, as the direct-access capabilities of a relative file cannot be exploited if it is stored on a serial device.

Relative file organization is based on maintaining a predictable relationship between a record's access-key value and its location in storage. The function used to translate a key value into a storage address is designated when the file is created. This function is used to find storage for the record when it is added to the file and to find the record when it is modified, retrieved, or deleted.

Relative files are commonly used to support interactive access. A particular record can be found rapidly if its access-key value is known. But finding a particular record based on a field other than the access key provides no performance advantage over a sequential file, as only the access key can be translated directly into a storage location.

Consider a company with eighty employees, each of whom is identified by a social security number. An extremely simple address calculation is *access-key = address*. Each EMPLOYEE record's location is thus uniquely determined by the record's SOCIAL-SECURITY-NUMBER value. Using this simple approach, however, results in a sparse data file. There are one million possible values for a nine-digit social security number, of which only eighty will be used by the company; yet space must be allocated for all, as it is difficult to predict which social security numbers will be contributed by new employees.

A more suitable calculation is to use the last two digits of each employee's social security number, as there are only one hundred possible values, which would accommodate all the employees.

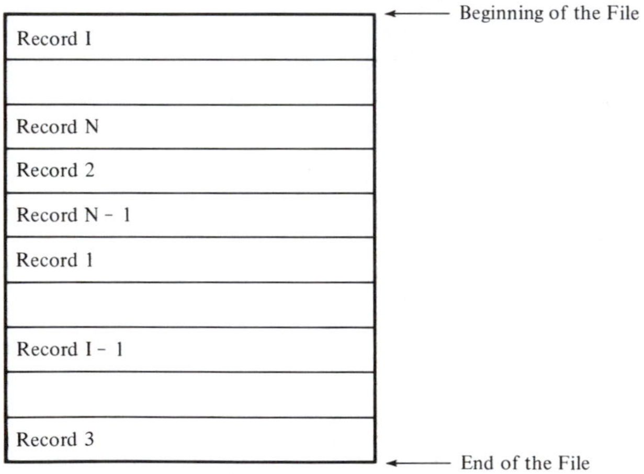

FIGURE 9.12. Relative file organization.

The address-calculation functions used by database management systems are much more complex than this one and are referred to as

- CALC algorithms.
- direct-addressing techniques.
- hash table methods.
- hashing.
- key-to-address transformation methods.
- randomizing techniques.
- scatter-storage techniques.

We shall use the term *hashing* and shall refer to the address-calculation function as a *hash function*.

Whatever function is used when records are stored must also be used when records are accessed for retrieval, modification, or deletion. If SOCIAL_SECURITY_NUMBER values are used by the hash function as the access-key values when EMPLOYEE records are stored, then the users must supply SOCIAL_SECURITY_NUMBER values when they wish to retrieve EMPLOYEE records. Access by the value of any other field requires a sequential search of the file. Pure relative files are not suitable for physical database structures, as databases require accessibility by many fields. The principles of relative files are, however, applicable to nearly all physical database structures.

Collisions

A problem arises in our simple example when two employees' social security numbers end in the same two digits, for example, 987654321 and 345678921. Two records cannot both be stored in the twenty-first position. When a hash function causes two unequal access-key values to calculate to the same address, a *collision* is said to occur, and the two access-key values are called *synonyms*.

Just as there are many possible hash functions, there also are various collision-resolution techniques. For example, using the preceding simple hash function, if record 987654321 arrives first, it will be stored in location 21, which is its *home address*. Thus when record 345678921 is to be added, its home address (21) is already full. If location 22 were empty, it could be stored there. But if location 22 were full, we might try location 23, then 24, and so on until we encounter an empty slot. This approach to collision resolution is called *linear probing*. The address space is searched sequentially from the home address, and the record is stored in the first available location.

Another approach to collision resolution is to apply a second address-calculation function, a technique called *double hashing*. If the first hash, which is always to the home address, results in a collision, a second function will be used to calculate a second-choice location.

The objective of an address-calculation technique and its accompanying approach to resolving collisions is to minimize the number of accesses required to find any given record. One good way to do this is to link the records with the same home location. For example, assume that record 345678921 finally was stored in location 59. When a user requested access to this record, the hash function would first lead to location 21. But this location would not hold the desired record, and so a linear probe would start until the target record was located. Many accesses later, the record would be encountered at location 59.

If, however, record 345678921 had been linked to its home location when it was stored, only two accesses would have been required: one to location 21 and then one to follow the pointer to the next synonym, at location 59 (Fig. 9.13). Even if our target record were the victim of several collisions when it was initially stored, following a linked list of synonyms would require many fewer accesses than would probing linearly through the file. Linking synonyms is called *synonym chaining*. One requirement of this technique is that a record must never be displaced from its home location by a record that is not its synonym.

Block Addressing

Another approach to handling the problem of collisions is *block addressing*, hashing to blocks of space that can accommodate multiple records, rather than hashing to individual record locations. For example, a file can be allocated one hundred blocks, each large enough to store ten records. The hash function generates addresses 0 through 99. Ten records can hash to the same block without causing a problematic collision. When a user wishes to access a particular record, the hash function is applied to the access-key value, giving the number of the home block. That block is then searched sequentially to find the record with the supplied access-key value.

When a block is full, the collision problem must be faced. The approaches to the block-overflow problem are basically the same as the approaches taken to resolve collisions with record-slot addressing. Space can be sought in the next block, using linear probing, or space can be sought in some other block, using double hashing. Sometimes an overflow block is allocated and is chained to the home block, or one set of overflow blocks accommodates synonym chains from all the home blocks.

One advantage of using blocks that can hold several records is that variable-length records can be accommodated relatively easily. Database management

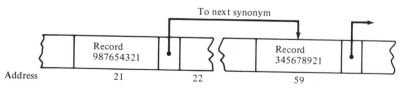

FIGURE 9.13. Synonym chaining.

systems typically use this approach, because a given file may contain different types of records, which usually also have different lengths.

With block addressing and variable-length records, finding available space in a block for a new record becomes more complex than just searching sequentially for the first open area. The space found must be large enough to accommodate the new record. Space in a block usually is managed by maintaining a linked list of the *holes*, which are the available spaces. Figure 9.14 shows a block containing records and a chain of holes.

When a new record hashes to a block, the hole chain is searched to find available space. It is convenient to order the list of holes in a block according to their increasing size. A sequential scan of the hole chain can stop when the first hole large enough to hold the new record is found. That hole is then taken off the hole chain, and the space is used to store the new record. Any leftover space can be put back into the hole chain, in the appropriate position for maintaining the sorted order of holes by increasing size.

Each block has a *header record* that includes a pointer to the first hole on the hole chain (see Fig. 9.14). The header also includes the size of the biggest hole in the block. If this hole is too small to satisfy a space request, then the search can proceed directly to the next block or an overflow block.

When a record is deleted, its space should be added to the hole chain. If this freed space is contiguous to an existing hole, then the spaces should be combined into one larger hole. A few large holes are preferable to many small holes, as

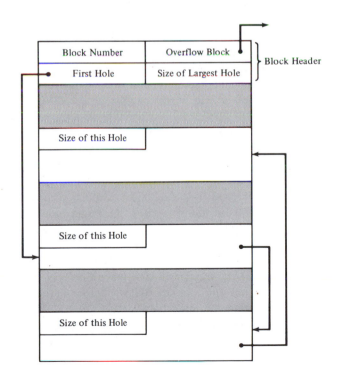

FIGURE 9.14. Block containing records and a chain of holes.

the probability of having to place a record outside its home block is higher with small holes. The process of recognizing deleted records and combining freed space is called *garbage collection*.

Indexed Sequential Files

Indexed sequential file organization combines access types supported by sequential and relative files. Records can be accessed both sequentially and directly by the access-key field's value.

An indexed sequential file is really two files. One is the data file; and the other is an index file of pointers into the data file (Fig. 9.15). The data file is commonly structured using block addressing. Within a block, the records are in sequential order according to the access-key field's value. Each data block has a pointer to the next block in the sorted sequence, though the data blocks themselves need not be in any particular physical sequence.

An index entry is an ⟨access-key value, address⟩ pair. The address is the location of a data block, and the corresponding access-key value is the first access-key value appearing in that data block.

Consider the file shown in Fig. 9.15. Assume that we want to locate the record for the employee whose name is Igor. The index would be searched first. In this simple table index, the access-key values would be searched until the first one greater than Igor is encountered. The pointer in the previous entry would then be followed to a data block which would be read sequentially until Igor's record is found or is determined not to be there.

If we wanted to access sequentially all of the EMPLOYEE records, we would follow the pointer to the first block, read the records there in sequence, then follow the pointer to the next block, read the records there in sequence, and then continue in this manner until the last block was read. The linked list of blocks provides a sequential path through the data records.

When a record is added to the file, it must be positioned so that the indexed sequential capabilities are maintained. The index is used to find the block where the record ought to reside. If there is room in that block, then the new record will be stored there. Other records in the block may need to be moved "down" in order to keep the block's contents in sequential order.

If there is not room in the home block, then a new block will be started, usually by splitting the home block into two blocks. Half the home-block records stay there; and half are moved into the new block. The new record is inserted in the appropriate slot to maintain sequentiality. When a block splits, the index file must be augmented so that the new block can be located. Figure 9.16 shows the example file adjusted to include a record for Mara. Note that there is an additional entry in the index.

A pure indexed sequential file is generally not a suitable structure for a physical database, as it provides direct access based on just one access-key, whereas

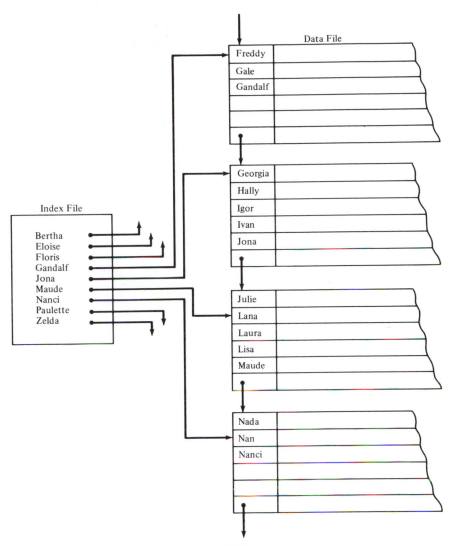

FIGURE 9.15. An indexed sequential file.

databases typically need to support direct access based on many different field values.

MULTIKEY FILE ORGANIZATION

The ability to search on many access keys is enabled by building multiple index files *(multikey file organization)* ''on top of'' the data file. The physical database then consists of one or more data files and many index files, and each data file

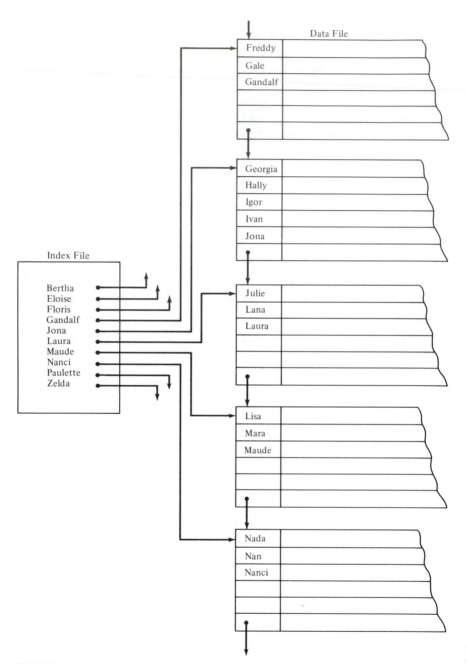

FIGURE 9.16. Indexed sequential file. One data block from Fig. 9.15 has been split, adding an entry to the index file.

contains either one or several record types. Each index file supports access by a particular field or group of fields.

Consider first a data file with one record type. One of the index files is usually a primary index and provides access based on a field (or group of fields) called the *primary key*. The primary key for a physical database record type uniquely identifies occurrences of that record and usually is the same as the primary key of the corresponding logical entity.

If the file structure also supports sequential access to the data records by means of the primary-key value, then it is an indexed sequential file organization. If it does not support sequential access by the primary-key value, then the data file may be a relative file.

A primary index is commonly used with address calculation in a relative file to avoid collision resolution. Rather than using synonym chaining to keep track of where records actually are stored, the primary index stores ⟨primary-key value, address⟩ pairs. To find a record using the primary index, first the primary-key value is located and then the indicated address is used to find the record on secondary storage.

To store a new record, first the home address is calculated using the hash function, and then any collisions are resolved. The record is stored, and the key value and address are placed into the index. Later accesses to the record can be handled directly by the index, without applying the hash function, resolving collisions, and detecting synonyms.

Multikey file organization augments primary-index support with one or more secondary indexes.

Secondary Indexes

An index that provides access on a field or fields other than the primary key is called a *secondary index* or an *alternate index*. The access field is called a *secondary key,* an *alternate key,* or an *inversion entry*.

Assume that it is necessary to access employee data not only directly by SOCIAL_SECURITY_NUMBER but also by DEPT# and by JOBCODE. Figure 9.17 sketches the data file and its associated primary and secondary indexes. To find the employee record for SOCIAL_SECURITY_NUMBER = 987654321, the primary index would be consulted, and to find the employee records for JOBCODE = 'DBA,' the appropriate secondary index would be searched.

A secondary index may have more than one target record for each secondary-key value, which can be accommodated in the following ways:

- One entry in the secondary index for each ⟨secondary-key value, address⟩ pair.
- One entry in the secondary index for each ⟨secondary-key value⟩, with an associated list of ⟨address⟩ entries, one for each qualifying record.

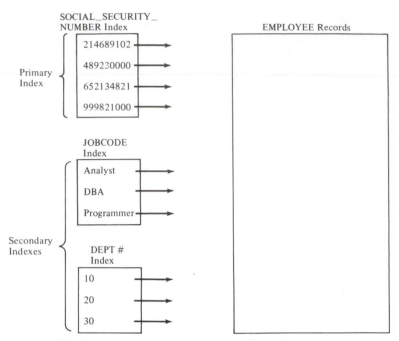

FIGURE 9.17. A data file with one primary index and two secondary indexes.

- One entry in the secondary index for the first ⟨secondary-key value, address⟩ pair, with a pointer in that target data record to the next data record with that secondary-key value, which has a pointer to the next data record with that same secondary-key value, and so forth.

The first two approaches do not affect the data file and are sometimes referred to as *inversion* structures. The third approach requires the data file to contain a linked list of records for each of the secondary-key values and is sometimes referred to as a *multilist* structure.

When a new employee's record is added, its storage location must first be determined using the system's hash function. If any collisions occur, they must be resolved. The record's SOCIAL_SECURITY_NUMBER value and the record's storage location can then be entered in the primary index. The new record must also be made accessible from the DEPT# and JOBCODE indexes. New entries are made in those indexes if an inversion approach has been used. With the multilist approach, the new record must be added to the appropriate linked lists for its DEPT# and JOBCODE values. A new entry will need to be made in a secondary index if this is the first employee with a particular DEPT# or JOB-CODE value.

Indirect Addressing

A secondary-index entry can use either *direct addressing* or *indirect addressing*. With direct addressing, the index entry is a ⟨secondary-key value, address⟩ pair, and with indirect addressing, the index entry is a ⟨secondary-key value, primary-key value⟩ pair. Figure 9.18 sketches the structure of the example files with indirect addressing. Contrast the structure shown with that of Fig. 9.17, which assumes direct addressing.

With indirect addressing, an access via a secondary index also requires an access to the primary index. For example, rather than having a secondary-index entry ⟨'DBA,' 59⟩ indicating that an employee with JOBCODE = 'DBA' is stored at location 59, the secondary-index entry would be ⟨'DBA,' 345678921⟩. This is a ⟨JOBCODE, SOCIAL_SECURITY_NUMBER⟩ pair. The primary index would then be searched for the entry ⟨345678921, 59⟩, which indicates that the target record is stored at location 59.

Nearly all database management systems support both primary and secondary indexes. Many of them use indirect addressing in their secondary indexes, and some of them claim not to use pointers. It should be understood, however, that an indirect address is a special type of pointer, an indicator or reference to another entry in an index or record in a data file.

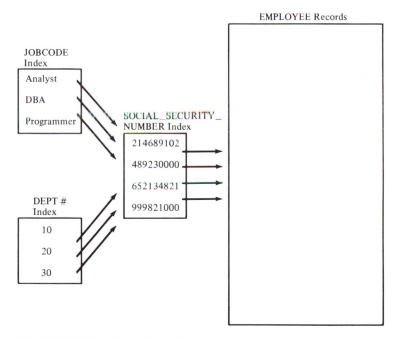

FIGURE 9.18. Data file with a primary index and two secondary indexes using indirect addressing.

Just as a relative address is one step removed from an absolute address, an indirect address is one step removed from a relative address. The primary index entries provide the indirect-to-relative address transformations. The benefit of indirect addressing is a level of independence between the index file entries and the data file's physical layout. With indirect addressing, spatial reorganization of the data file requires that new record locations be reflected in the primary index but not in the secondary indexes. The cost of indirect addressing is another file to access when locating data records.

INDEX STRUCTURES

The structures of index files all support rapid searches to a given access key value. The basic types are table indexes, binary search tree indexes, and B-tree indexes.

Table Indexes

In its simplest form, an index is implemented as a table or array of ⟨access-key value, address⟩ records, as shown in Fig. 9.19. If the records are not sorted, then a sequential search is necessary in order to find the record with a particular access-key value. On the average, half the entries need to be read to locate the desired entry. In the worst case, all the entries need to be read to determine that the desired access-key value is not in the index table.

If the index records are sorted by access-key values, then a *binary search* can be used to reduce the time required to find the correct entry. A binary search proceeds by successive probes into a sorted table. The first probe compares the access-key value in the middle of the table with the value sought. If the sought value is less, then the half of the table following the middle can be removed from further consideration. On the other hand, if the sought value is greater, then the half of the table preceding the middle need not be considered further. The second probe is to the access-key value in the middle of the retained half

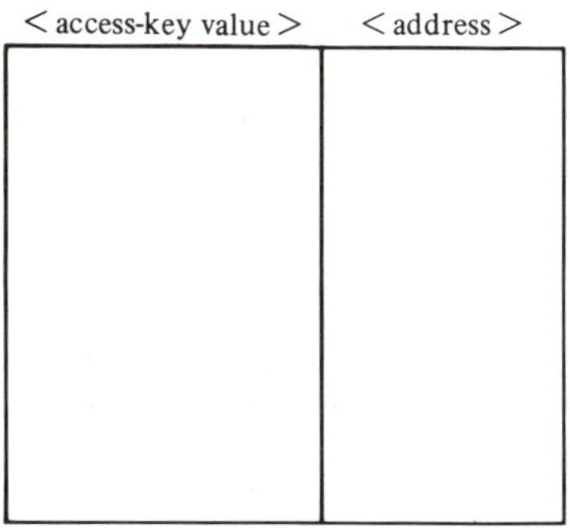

< access-key value >   < address >

FIGURE 9.19.   Tabular index array.

of the original table. Again, if the sought value is less than this probed record's access-key value, then the half of the (half-) table following the probe can be removed from further consideration. If the sought value is greater than this probed record's key value, then the half of the (half-) table preceding the probe need not be considered further. And so the probing process continues until the sought access-key value either is located or is determined not to reside in the table.

The table is cut in half over and over again until either the middle access-key value is the desired value, or the size of the remaining table is zero, implying that the sought access-key value is not in the table.

The maximum number of comparisons required for a binary search of a sorted table of N entries is $\log_2(N)$. If $N = 256$, then the worst case is eight comparisons. If $N = 1024$, then the worst case is ten comparisons. The average number of comparisons is half that, which is certainly better than if a sequential search were used, especially on a large table. The trade-off is the overhead of keeping the table records sorted by access-key value.

Binary Search Tree Indexes

One approach to gaining the benefits of binary search performance while avoiding the overhead of keeping table records in physically sequential order by access-key value is a *binary search tree index*.

A *tree* is a data structure in which each record branches (i.e., points) to one or more other records. These pointers can be used to access the records in some order other than their physical sequence. A *binary tree* is a special type of tree in which each record can branch to a maximum of two other records. Each of those records can then point to up to two more records.

There are several ways of organizing a tree offering convenient access to its records. One way is called a *binary search tree,* in which the records are arranged to simplify the search through the tree. A binary search tree is shown in Fig. 9.20. A search for a particular access-key value begins at the root, that is, at the "top" of the tree. If the target access-key value is less than the root's access-key value, the search will proceed down the tree's left branch, and if the target access-key value is greater than the root's access-key value, the search will proceed down the tree's right branch. These comparisons and search-direction selections are made at each node of the tree until the target access-key value is either found or determined not to be in the tree.

Each search step restricts the number of records remaining to those in the subtree of the selected branch. All access-key values in the left subtree must be less than the branch root's access-key value, and all access-key values in the right subtree must be greater than the branch root's access-key value. These two rules must hold for each record in the tree and must be enforced when a record is added to or removed from the tree.

Each record in a binary search tree index contains one additional pointer to

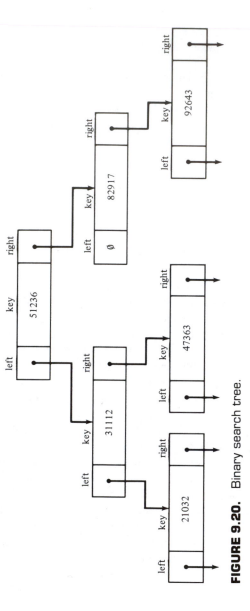

FIGURE 9.20. Binary search tree.

a data file (Fig. 9.21). Each record thus contains an access-key value and three pointers to (1) the data file record with the associated access-key value, (2) to the root of the left subtree, and (3) to the root of the right subtree.

The best binary search trees are bushy, with only the leaves (i.e., the "bottom" records) missing both left and right subtrees. With a bushy binary search tree, each access-key value comparison cuts the search space in half, in exactly the same way as does a binary search of an ordered table. The maximum number of comparisons is the same as the length of the tree's longest branch: The bushier the tree is, the shorter this longest branch will be.

B-Tree Indexes

To improve search performance, a more general form of the binary search tree is commonly used to structure an index. Rather than use binary (two-way) branching, m-way ($m > 2$) branching is used. If $m = 4$, then each comparison will reject three quarters of the remaining search space. In a binary tree, each comparison will reject just one-half of the remaining search space.

Each index record in an *m-way search tree* contains up to $m - 1$ access-key values and m pointers. The access-key values in each record are in sorted order, and all access-key values in the subtree pointed to by the i-th pointer are less than the ith access-key value. The subtree's access-key values pointed to by the mth pointer are greater than the last [i.e., the $(m - 1)$st] access-key value. Each subtree is also an m-way search tree, an arrangement that expands the structure of the binary search tree index records, in which $m = 2$.

A *B-tree of order m* is an m-way search tree with the following additional properties:

- Each record, except the root and the leaves, has at least $\lceil m/2 \rceil$ subtrees and no more than m subtrees, that is, is at least half "full."
- The root has either no subtrees or at least two subtrees, that is, the tree branches early.
- All leaves are on the same level, that is, at the same distance from the root.

These restrictions keep a B-tree "bushy."

Figure 9.22 shows a three-way B-tree. Each record contains up to two access-key values and three pointers, and each leaf is three branches from the root. To find access-key value 42, the following sequence of comparisons is made:

- Because 42 is less than the first access-key value (69) in record a, the first pointer out of record a is followed.
- Because 42 is greater than the first access-key value (19) in record b, the first pointer out of record b is not followed.
- Because 42 is less than the second access-key value (43) in record b, the second pointer out of record b is followed.
- Because 42 is greater than the first access-key value (26) in record e, the first pointer out of record e is not followed.

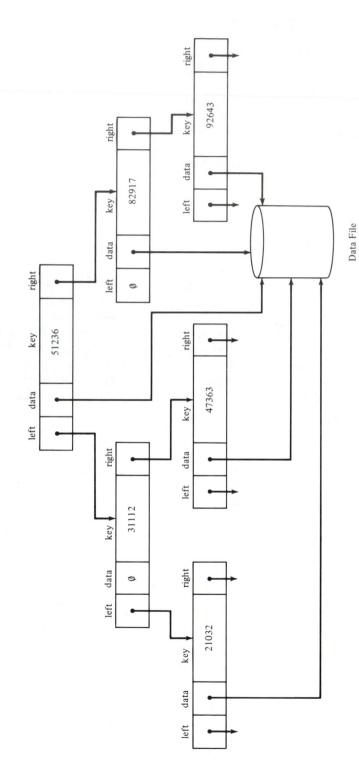

FIGURE 9.21. Binary search tree index.

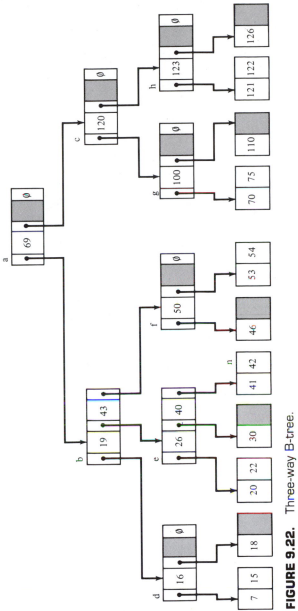

FIGURE 9.22. Three-way B-tree.

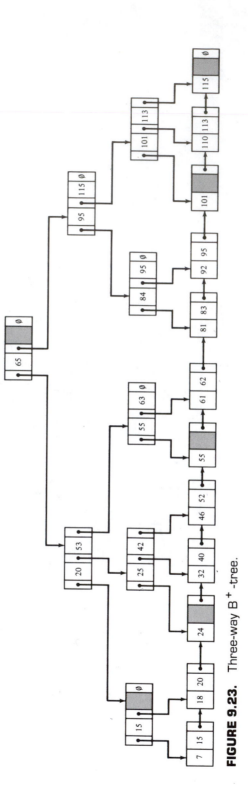

FIGURE 9.23. Three-way B⁺-tree.

- Because 42 is greater than the second access-key value (40) in record *e*, the second pointer out of record *e* is not followed.
- The third pointer out of record *e* is followed.
- Record *n* (a leaf) is searched sequentially to find 42 and its pointer to the corresponding data record.

When an entry is added to a B-tree, the tree structure rules must be followed. A new ⟨access-key value, pointer⟩ pair can be added to a record that is not full. If the appropriate index entry (the *home entry*) does not have room for another access-key value and pointer, then a new entry must be created. Half of the ⟨access-key value, pointer⟩ pairs in the home entry are moved to the new entry. The pointers in the next higher level of the index also must be adjusted to include a path to the new entry. If the parent index entry also is full, it will need to split. In the worst case, adding an entry to the B-tree will cause splits to crack all the way to the root of the tree, lengthening all of the search paths by one.

A variant on the B-tree is a *B⁺-tree*. In a B⁺-tree, the leaf entries are connected to form a linked list of access-key values in sequential order (Fig. 9.23). The access-key values in the leaves are the access-key values of the records in the data file, and the access-key values in the rest of the tree direct access to the leaves. Thus an access-key that appears in a nonleaf entry will also appear in a leaf if it corresponds to the access-key value of a record in the data file. B⁺-trees support both direct and sequential access by access-key values.

Both B-trees and B⁺-trees are commonly used by database management systems. They support relatively short access paths without suffering from too much overhead processing when records are inserted or deleted. Any number of B-trees or B⁺-trees can be constructed as indexes on top of a relative or indexed sequential file, thereby providing multikey access.

CLOSING COMMENTS

Database management systems use various combinations of the preceding physical structures to implement their logical data models. The performance characteristics of their databases are determined by how well these data structures support access to the data. This performance is affected by

- Data volumes: small databases usually perform better than do large databases.
- Usage patterns: a structure that is well suited to handling a wide variety of inquiry accesses usually performs relatively less well for update accesses, and vice versa.
- Transaction mixture: a data structure can usually be tuned to perform well with a known set of transactions. If the mixture changes, then the performance may also change.
- Growth requirements: a data structure that is suitable for a small database may perform relatively less well as the volume of records increases.

- Characteristics of the rest of the computer system: a computer that is heavily loaded doing other processing will house a database system with relatively worse performance than will a database system that runs on a dedicated machine with excess capacity.
- Buffer management policies: a data management strategy that swaps data and index records out of main memory when they are just about to be accessed again will perform relatively less well than will a strategy that generally keeps target records in main memory.

The database designer must create physical database structures that provide acceptable levels of performance. Database structures and transactions should be monitored so that changing requirements can be detected. The physical structures then can be refined to continue to perform adequately.

The database management system hides from the application programmer and the user the details of physical data structure management. For example, rather than explicitly following a pointer from one EMPLOYEE record to another, the programmer merely specifies FIND NEXT EMPLOYEE. Rather than executing a hash function, resolving collisions, and managing index entries, the programmer specifies STORE EMPLOYEE WITH SOCIAL_SECURITY_NUMBER = 345678921. The database management system manages the pointers. Using database management system services raises the programmer's level of concern from physical data structure management to logical application support.

TERMS

absolute address	chain
access key	collision
access technique	collision-resolution technique
address-calculation function	data file
alternate index	direct-access storage device
alternate key	direct-addressing technique
archive copy	directory
backup copy	double hashing
B-tree	doubly linked list
B$^+$-tree	file organization
binary search	garbage collection
binary search tree	hash function
binary search tree index	hashing
block	hash table method
block addressing	header record
blocking factor	hole
buffer	home address
bushy	index
CALC algorithm	indexed sequential file organization

index file
indirect addressing
interfile pointer
intrafile pointer
inversion entry
inversion structure
key-to-address transformation
    method
linear probing
linked list
main memory
multilist file organization
multilist structure
m-way search tree
null pointer
physical database
pointer
primary index
primary key

randomizing technique
record-slot addressing
relative address
relative file organization
scatter storage technique
secondary index
secondary key
secondary storage
sequential file organization
serial-access storage device
sort key
sorted file
subtree
synonym
synonym chaining
table index
transport copy
tree

REVIEW EXERCISES

1. Define each of the terms in the preceding list.

2. How do absolute addressing, relative addressing, and indirect addressing differ?

3. Write an algorithm to do a binary search.

4. Explain why a binary search cannot be performed on an unordered table.

5. Explain why a binary search cannot be performed on a linked list.

6. Show the sequence of pointer changes needed to delete a record from a linked list.

7. Often linked lists are implemented so that each record points to not just the next record but also to the previous record. Explain how this arrangement of pointers makes record insertion and deletion different from insertion and deletion in a linked list with only "next" pointers.

8. Write an algorithm to insert a new record into the appropriate position in a binary search tree.

9. Consider a binary search tree holding the access-key values 1 through 255. What is the maximum number of levels that this tree can have? Why? What is the minimum number of levels that this tree can have? Why?

10. Compare the file organizations introduced in this chapter with the file organizations available in various programming languages, for example, COBOL, FORTRAN, C, Pascal, and PL/I.

11.	Many address-calculation (i.e., hash) functions have been proposed in the data management literature. Describe and compare the division remainder technique, the mid-square technique, and the folding technique. Which is best?

12.	Explain why a B-tree with four-way branching will result in shorter search times for a given set of access-key values than will a binary search tree for those same access-key values.

13.	Show why a record must never be displaced from its home location by a non-synonym when synonym chaining is used.

14.	Describe extendable hashing techniques, which target at expanding address spaces.

15.	What are the factors to consider when determining whether sequential, relative, indexed sequential, or multikey file organization is the most appropriate?

16.	What are the factors to consider when determining whether an index file should be structured as a table or as a tree?

17.	What are the factors to consider when deciding which data fields should be secondary keys? Why not make every data field a secondary key?

18.	What are the factors to consider when deciding whether a secondary index should point to a primary index or directly to the data file?

19.	What complications are introduced when a data file can store several record types?

REFERENCES

Cohen, J. Garbage collection of linked data structures, *ACM Computing Surveys* 13 (September 1981): 341–367.

Comer, D. The ubiquitous B-tree, *ACM Computing Surveys* 11 (June 1979): 121–138.

Knuth, D. E. *The Art of Computer Programming,* vol. 3: *Sorting and Searching.* Reading, Mass.: Addison-Wesley, 1973, pp. 422–471.

Loomis, M. E. S. *Data Management and File Processing.* Englewood Cliffs, N.J.: Prentice-Hall, 1983.

Nievergelt, J. Binary search trees and file organization, *ACM Computing Surveys* 6 (September 1974):195–207.

Tenenbaum, A. M., and M. J. Augenstein. *Data Structures Using Pascal.* Englewood Cliffs, N.J.: Prentice-Hall, 1981.

Physical Design of Relational Databases

The physical design of relational databases is introduced by comparing several approaches to storing relational data. We use real systems as the basis for the alternatives, without giving all the details of those real systems. Rather, our intention is to show how the approaches relate to one another and what their implications are for physical database design.

One of the objectives in discussing various alternatives to physically implementing relational databases is to emphasize further the distinction between logical and physical design. There is almost never just one way to implement a logical design; it should be designed to support effectively the users' data needs. On the other hand, the physical design determines the cost of running the system and should be designed to fulfill the users' data needs efficiently. Efficiency is measured by the computer resources that the database system uses: compute time, accesses to secondary storage, communications traffic, storage space, and the like.

BASIC REQUIREMENTS OF A PHYSICAL RELATIONAL DATABASE

The physical implementation of a relational database must
1. Be translatable into tables.

2. Be accessible by the value of any attribute, not just by unique identifiers.
3. Be able to support select, project, and join operations.

Translatable into Tables

A variety of data structures can be used to implement logical relations, one being a simple table (i.e., an array) for each relation. In this case the physical structure mirrors the logical structure. Other data structures are linked lists and trees. Regardless of which underlying physical data structure is used, it must be invisible to the user; that is, the user must be able to view the data as if it were in tables, without concern for how the data are actually stored.

Accessible by Any Attribute

Whatever the underlying physical data structure, the user must be able to request access to the data by specifying the value of any attribute of the relation. For example, consider the relation TEACHER (TEACHER_NAME, FACULTY#, RANK, DEPARTMENT_NAME, COLLEGE_NAME, PHONE, BIRTH_DATE, HIRE_DATE) (Fig. 4.1). The user must be able to request the TEACHER rows with a particular value of TEACHER_NAME, or FACULTY#, or RANK, or any other attribute and must not be restricted to accessing data based on only uniquely identifying "key" attributes.

Support the Basic Relational Operators

The physical data structure must be able to support select, project, and join operations, without requiring the user to move around through the data structure using pointers and addresses. The database manager must be able to retrieve the subset of a table's rows that meet qualification criteria based on attribute values, retrieve a specified subset of a table's columns, and combine tables by matching the values of specified attributes.

The basic relational operators must be supported without the user's having to specify access paths through the physical data structure, and the user need not know which records point to which or how to get from one tuple to another.

The relational database management systems provide various languages for manipulating the tables. The specific operators SELECT, PROJECT, and JOIN need not be supported, but their capabilities must be provided.

BASIC LOGICAL-TO-PHYSICAL TRANSFORMATIONS

Several design issues concern mapping logical relations to physical relations. The most straightforward logical-to-physical transformation is to implement each table of the conceptual schema as a single base relation. But in order to improve the system's performance, the physical-database designer must determine whether any of the following logical-to-physical transformations would be more appropriate:

- Vertical partitioning: splitting a table into multiple base relations, with some of its attributes (i.e., columns) in one base relation and some in another (Fig. 10.1).
- Horizontal partitioning: splitting a table into multiple base relations, with some of its tuples (i.e., rows) in one base relation and some in another (Fig. 10.2).
- Joining: combining tables into a single base relation (Fig. 10.3).

These transformations result in base relations that do not correspond exactly to the starting tables.

Vertical Partitioning

Vertical partitioning projects some of a table's columns into one base relation and some into another. The column(s) for the primary key appear in both base relations so that the original logical table can be reconstructed.

Vertical partitioning can be appropriate if some of a table's columns are accessed much more frequently than the others are. Separating the infrequently accessed columns from the frequently accessed ones reduces the volume of data that must be copied to or from secondary storage in response to a request. Thus transactions that require the data only in the frequently accessed partition do not have to pull in the other partition's data.

Vertical partitioning can also be appropriate when some of a table's columns are accessed primarily by one set of users, and the other columns are accessed primarily by another group. This form of partitioning is especially useful when these user groups are geographically separated. The result is a distributed database, with some of the relations based at one computer and some at another (Fig. 10.4). For example, EMPLOYEE table columns containing compensation data could be stored in the Payroll Department's computer, and the other columns in the Personnel Department's computer.

An efficient distributed database stores the data where they will be accessed. Access to locally stored data avoids the costs of communicating with other computers and other partitions of the distributed database.

Another application of vertical partitioning is to enforce security constraints when the database management system protects only base relations. A user has access either to a base relation in its entirety or not at all. If some of a table's columns are accessible by users with one level of authorization, and the other columns are accessible by users with another level of authorization, then putting the columns into different base relations will enable the database manager to enforce the security constraints.

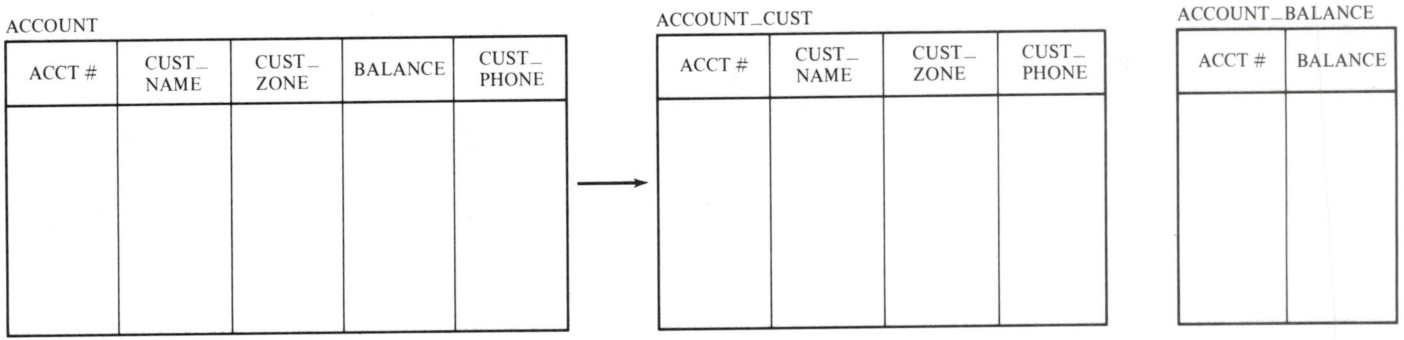

ACCOUNT

ACCT #	CUST_NAME	CUST_ZONE	BALANCE	CUST_PHONE

ACCOUNT_CUST

ACCT #	CUST_NAME	CUST_ZONE	CUST_PHONE

ACCOUNT_BALANCE

ACCT #	BALANCE

FIGURE 10.1. Vertical partitioning of relation ACCOUNT into two relations, ACCOUNT_CUST and ACCOUNT_BALANCE:
ACCOUNT_CUST = SELECT ACCT#, CUST_NAME, CUST_ZONE,
   FROM ACCOUNT
ACCOUNT_BALANCE = SELECT ACCT#, BALANCE FROM ACCOUNT

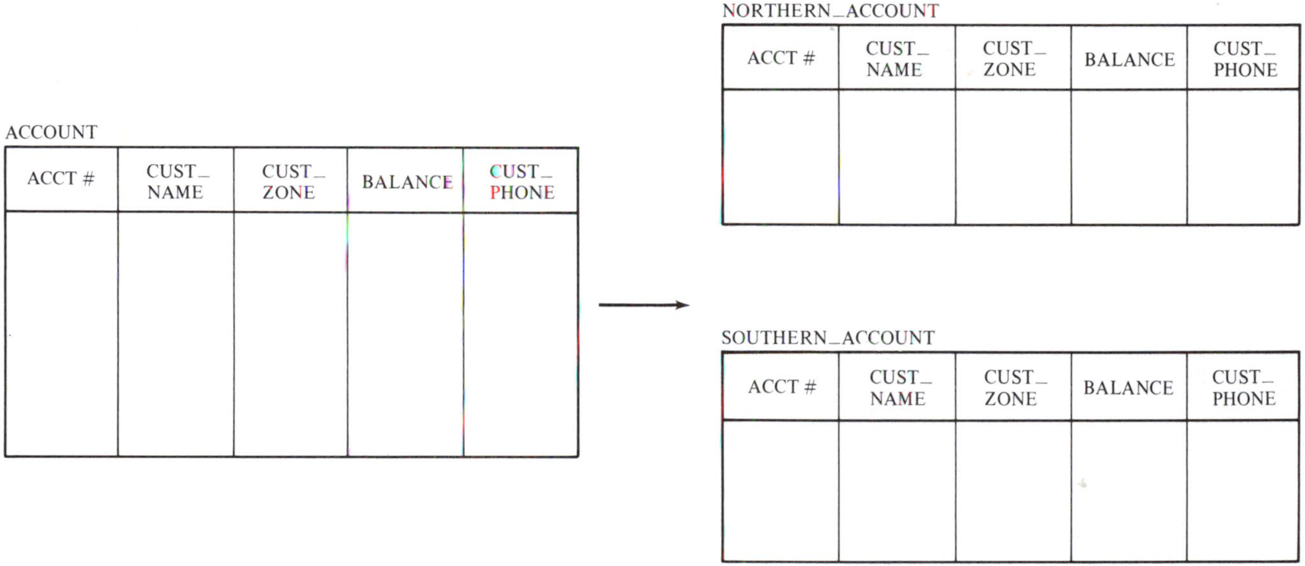

ACCOUNT

ACCT #	CUST_NAME	CUST_ZONE	BALANCE	CUST_PHONE

NORTHERN_ACCOUNT

ACCT #	CUST_NAME	CUST_ZONE	BALANCE	CUST_PHONE

SOUTHERN_ACCOUNT

ACCT #	CUST_NAME	CUST_ZONE	BALANCE	CUST_PHONE

FIGURE 10.2. Horizontal partitioning of relation ACCOUNT into two relations, NORTHERN_ACCOUNT and SOUTHERN_ACCOUNT.

NORTHERN_ACCOUNT = SELECT ALL FROM ACCOUNT WHERE
  CUST_ZONE = 'NCA' OR 'OR'
SOUTHERN_ACCOUNT = SELECT ALL FROM ACCOUNT WHERE
  CUST_ZONE = 'SCA' OR 'AZ' OR 'NV'

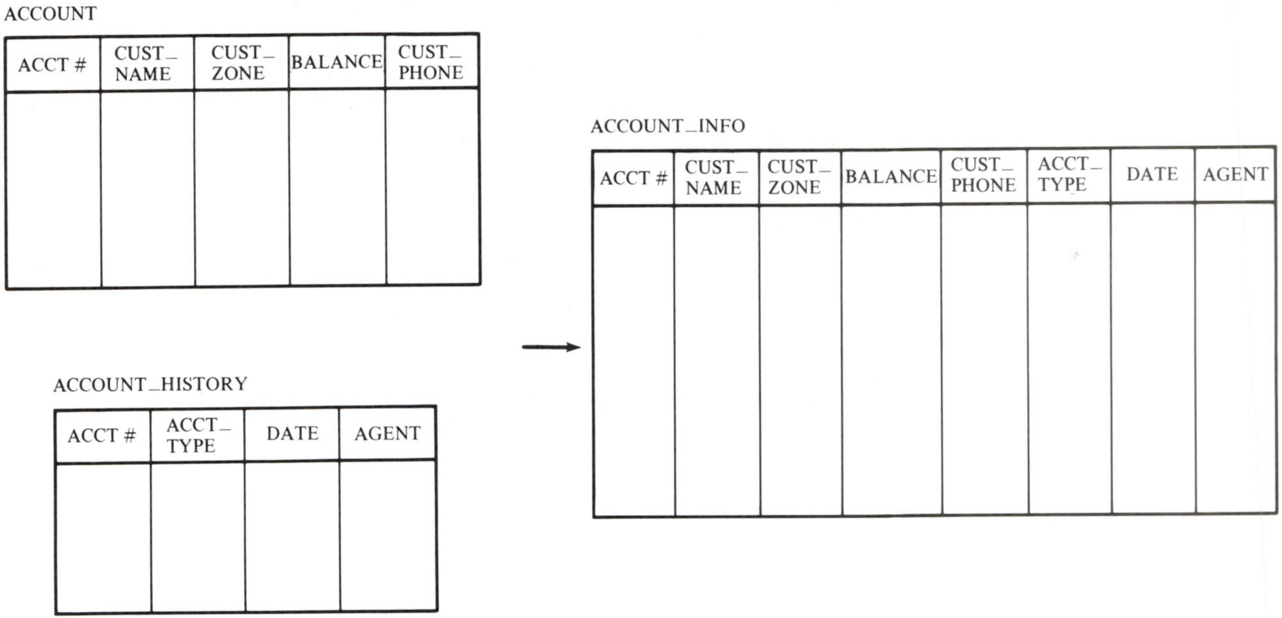

ACCOUNT

ACCT #	CUST_NAME	CUST_ZONE	BALANCE	CUST_PHONE

ACCOUNT_HISTORY

ACCT #	ACCT_TYPE	DATE	AGENT

ACCOUNT_INFO

ACCT #	CUST_NAME	CUST_ZONE	BALANCE	CUST_PHONE	ACCT_TYPE	DATE	AGENT

FIGURE 10.3. Joining of relations ACCOUNT and ACCOUNT_HISTORY to form relation ACCOUNT_INFO:

ACCOUNT_INFO = SELECT ALL FROM ACCOUNT, ACCOUNT_HISTORY
WHERE ACCOUNT .ACCT# = ACCOUNT_HISTORY .ACCT#

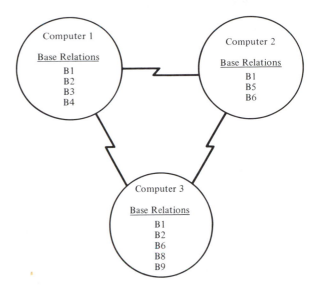

FIGURE 10.4. A distributed database with relations stored in multiple computers connected by a communications network.

Horizontal Partitioning

Horizontal partitioning puts some of a table's rows into one base relation and some into another. The original logical table can be reconstructed by forming the union of the two base relations (Fig. 10.2).

Horizontal partitioning can be appropriate if some of a table's rows are accessed much more frequently than the others are. Separating the infrequently and frequently accessed rows reduces the volume of data that must be copied to or from secondary storage in response to a request. Thus transactions that require the data only in the frequently accessed partition do not have to pull in the other partition's data.

Horizontal partitioning can also be appropriate when some of a table's rows are accessed primarily by one set of users, and the other rows are accessed primarily by another group. As with vertical partitioning, if the user groups are geographically separated, the result will be a distributed database. For example, the rows of the ACCOUNT table might be stored in San Francisco for Northern California accounts and in San Diego for Southern California accounts.

Joining

The rows of multiple tables can be combined in one base relation, a transformation that requires that the constituent tables be joinable, that is, that they share an attribute (Fig. 10.3). Usually the attribute is a primary-key attribute of one table and a foreign-key attribute in the other table.

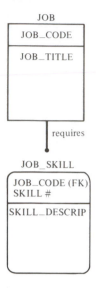

JOB

JOB_CODE
JOB_TITLE

requires

JOB_SKILL

JOB_CODE (FK) SKILL #
SKILL_DESCRIP

FIGURE 10.5. Sample data model.

JOB

JOB_ CODE	JOB_ TITLE
60	Secy II
70	Prgmr
80	Mngr

JOB_SKILL

JOB_ CODE	SKILL #	SKILL_ DESCRIP
60	463	Typing
60	231	Wd. Proc
70	231	Wd. Proc
70	801	C
60	333	Filing

FIGURE 10.6. Relations corresponding to data model of Fig. 10.5.

Joining is appropriate when the two tables are nearly always accessed together, with a join operation on the common attribute. For example, consider the data model of Fig. 10.5 and its corresponding relations in Fig. 10.6. If the JOB and associated JOB_SKILL rows were nearly always accessed together, then the base relation of Fig. 10.7 would be appropriate. Note that the JOB data are repeated for each JOB_SKILL row.

Physical joining can lead to both improved performance and difficulties in maintaining consistency, because it reduces the normalization level.

BASE_JOB_SKILL

JOB_ CODE	JOB_ TITLE	SKILL #	SKILL_ DESCRIP
60	Secy	463	Typing
60	Secy	231	Wd. Proc.
60	Secy	333	Filing
70	Prgmr	231	Wd. Proc.
70	Prgmr	801	C
80	Mngr	∅	∅

FIGURE 10.7. Base relation formed by joining the relations of Fig. 10.6.

Applicability of the Transformations

Whether or not a particular transformation is appropriate for a given table depends on several factors, including

- Width of the table (i.e., number of bytes in a row).
- Length of the table (i.e., number of rows).
- Patterns of access to the table:
  - Are some rows accessed much more frequently than others are?
  - Are some columns accessed much more frequently than others are?
  - Are some tables together accessed frequently?

All other factors being equal, we can make some generalizations about the influence of each of these factors:

- The wider the table is, the greater will be the probability that it should be partitioned vertically.
- The longer the table is, the greater will be the probability that it should be partitioned horizontally.
- The more skewed the patterns of access are to a subset of a table's rows, the greater will be the probability that it should be partitioned horizontally.
- The more skewed the patterns of access are to a subset of a table's columns, the greater will be the probability that it should be partitioned vertically.
- The more frequently two tables are accessed together, the greater will be the probability that they should be joined into one base relation.

User Views

In a three-schema environment, the user views (i.e., external schemas) are constructed by relational operations on the conceptual schema tables: selection of rows that meet certain qualification criteria, projection of certain columns, and joining of tables by matching attribute values. The mapping between the conceptual schema tables and the internal schema base relations is then used to locate the data for a particular user view.

In a two-schema environment, user views are mapped directly to base relations, as there is no conceptual schema. Each user view may join data in several base relations, and each base relation may support several user views.

The definition of views enables users' access to be restricted to subsets of the database, and different combinations of data can be used to support different applications.

IMPROVING PERFORMANCE

Each of these transformations between tables and base relations tries to improve the database's performance, by reducing the volumes of data transferred to or from secondary storage and by reducing the communications requirements in a network of computers.

Several other decisions must be addressed when developing an efficient physical database structure:

- Attribute access: Which attributes should have built-in fast access paths?
- Preconstructed joins: Which joins across base relations should have built-in fast access paths?
- Buffers: How large should the buffer spaces be for transferring base relations between main memory and secondary storage?
- Clustering physical relations: Which base relations should be stored together in the same file?

Attribute Access

Most of the relational database management systems allow the database designer to specify which attributes should have *built-in fast access paths*. These attributes are the ones for which users commonly specify values when they want to access certain rows of the table. The database designer analyzes patterns of access to the table, determining how frequently the following kind of access is specified:

```
SELECT list-of-attribute-names
   FROM table-name
 WHERE attribute-name-1 = value-1
    AND attribute-name-2 = value-2
    AND . . .
```

The more frequently that a particular attribute name appears in the WHERE clauses of retrieval and update requests, the more likely it is that it should have a built-in fast access path.

The presence of a built-in fast access path can significantly affect the database's performance. For example, in some systems, a request that takes hours without a fast access path may have a response time of seconds with a fast access path. Processing a request that qualifies rows based on attribute values for which there is no fast access path typically involves a sequential scan of the portion of the database containing the requested table.

In an attempt to improve performance for future requests, some database management systems will automatically construct and store a fast access path when a request qualifies rows on an attribute that does not already have a built-in one.

Built-in fast access paths are implemented either as index structures or by hashing on the values of the designated attribute. The index structures are commonly variants on B-tree structures (introduced in Chapter 9). The hash structures are address calculations to either particular slots or blocks in a file (also introduced in Chapter 9).

In most commercial database management systems, only one attribute of a base relation can have a built-in fast access path implemented by hashing. The values of this attribute determine the storage locations of the relation's rows. By contrast, many of a base relation's attributes can have built-in fast access paths implemented by index structures. Each index structure points into the set of rows of the relation, according to which rows have which attribute values.

The attributes that most often require built-in fast access paths are primary-key attributes, alternate-key attributes, and foreign-key attributes.

Primary-key attributes nearly always should have built-in fast access paths. The unique identifier of a table's rows is commonly used in requesting access to that table. If a base relation has a built-in fast access path implemented as a hash function, then that access path is nearly always implemented on the primary-key attributes.

If the primary key is compound, then the fast access path is built on the set of attributes making up the primary key. For example, if the primary key is DIVISION_CODE, DEPARTMENT_ID, then the hashing or indexing is on the combination of those two attributes. The primary-key access path would not be implemented correctly by one index on DIVISION_CODE and another on DE-PARTMENT_ID.

Alternate-key attributes should have built-in fast access paths if they commonly are used instead of the primary key for access to the table. For example, if EMPLOYEE# is the primary key of the EMPLOYEE table, but the alternate key SOCIAL_SECURITY# is commonly used to qualify rows, there should be one access path on EMPLOYEE# and another on SOCIAL_SECURITY#. Users then can easily access EMPLOYEE data based on either attribute.

Foreign-key attributes should have built-in fast access paths if their values are commonly used to qualify table rows and/or if the table is frequently joined with the table in which the foreign-key attributes appear as the primary key. The two tables can be joined more efficiently if there are indexes on the joining attributes.

Other attributes should have built-in fast access paths if all of the following conditions are true:

- Their values are commonly used to qualify table rows.
- Their values are not frequently updated.
- Their values are discriminatory.

But maintaining a built-in fast access path on an attribute whose values are frequently updated can be expensive. If an attribute is indexed, then each time that attribute value changes for a row, the index structure probably needs to be modified. If the rows are hashed, then changing the hash-attribute value almost always implies moving the row's record.

A *discriminating attribute* is one for which a relatively small percentage of the table rows have any particular value of that attribute. For example, in the EMPLOYEE relation, the attribute SEX_CODE is not a discriminating attribute, as there are only two possible values for the attribute and roughly half the rows have each value. Thus building an index on SEX_CODE would be expensive and would not significantly reduce the number of records scanned in response to a user's request. On the other hand, JOB_CODE probably is a discriminating attribute. If there are one hundred possible JOB_CODE values, then an index that supports direct access on JOB_CODE reduces a search to 1 percent of the records.

Preconstructed Joins

Another way to improve performance is to construct access paths to join tables before receiving the user's request for the join. Joining two large tables can be

DIRECTORY

B Value	R Pointer	S Pointer
b1	1	1
b1	2	1
b2	3	2
b3	4	3
b3	5	3
b4	Ø	4
b5	Ø	5

R

Address	A	B	C
1	a1	b1	c1
2	a2	b1	c2
3	a3	b2	c3
4	a4	b3	c3
5	a5	b3	c4

S

Address	B	D	E
1	b1	d1	e1
2	b2	d2	e2
3	b3	d3	e3
4	b4	d4	e4
5	b5	d5	e5

FIGURE 10.8. Directory containing join-attribute values with pointers to base tables. Relations R and S are joined on attribute B.

a resource-consuming process, as for each value of the join-attribute in one table, the other table's rows with the matching join-attribute value must be found. If the same join will be requested in the future, then retaining the correspondence between the two tables can avoid redoing the matches.

The correspondence between the joined tables can be retained in several ways, including

- a directory of join-attribute values, with pointers to the pertinent rows in each of the two tables (Fig. 10.8).
- linked lists, with a chain of pointers from each row in one table to the matching rows in the other table (Fig. 10.9).

Not all relational database management systems support preconstructed joins. The physical database designer must determine which joins should be preconstructed, based on their predicted benefits.

Buffers

Another design issue is the management of buffers for transferring base relations between main memory and secondary storage. Many relational database management systems give the database designer the capability to specify the size of each buffer and the number of buffers. Usually the size of a buffer is the same as the size of a page of main memory, which is determined by the operating system. The number of buffers should be large enough to keep in main memory the working set of rows used in servicing a request, the appropriate number depending on the request's characteristics and the database's contents.

S

B	D	E	1st R with B Value
b1	d1	e1	1
b2	d2	e2	3
b3	d3	e3	4
b4	d4	e4	Ø
b5	d5	e5	Ø

R

Address	A	B	C	Next R with B Value
1	a1	b1	c1	2
2	a2	b2	c2	Ø
3	a3	b2	c3	Ø
4	a4	b3	c3	5
5	a5	b3	c4	Ø

FIGURE 10.9. Linked list of preconstructed join on attribute B in base relations R and S.

Clustering Base Relations

A relational database management system uses operating-system file management capabilities for the actual storage and access to base relations. A file is an
address space, composed of a collection of same-sized pages, and may reside
in main memory or on secondary storage. Such files are used to store user data,
access-path data structures, internal directory data, and intermediate results generated while responding to requests.

Relational database managers differ in how they map base relations to files:

- One base relation, one file. Each file contains rows for one base relation, and
  the base relation appears only in that one file.
- N base relations, one file. Each file contains rows for many base relations,
  but each base relation appears only in that one file.
- N base relations, M files. Each file contains rows for many base relations, and
  each base relation may appear in many files.
- One base relation, N files. Each file contains rows for one base relation, but
  the base relation may appear in many files.

The scheme that is used is determined by the database management system, not
by the physical database designer. Knowing which approach is used by the
pertinent database management system helps the physical database designer decide what kinds of design alternatives are possible.

If a file can contain rows for more than one base relation, then the database
designer can cluster those data that are likely to be accessed together. For
example, if tuples from two base relations are frequently accessed together, say,
because of a common join between them, then the designer should consider
storing them in the same file. If the tuples are in the buffer space together (either
because they are on the same page or because all their pages are in the buffer),
then fewer accesses to secondary storage will be required to respond to the data
request. If tuples from two base relations are only infrequently accessed together,
then they should be stored in separate files. The objective is to cluster on a page
the tuples that are likely to be accessed together.

Another opportunity for physical clustering is to place on the same page the
rows that are likely to be accessed together. These rows can be from the same
relation or from many relations, assuming that a file can store more than one
relation. Physical clustering usually is done by the

- attribute value, so that rows with similar values for a designated attribute are
  stored together.
- time of storage, so that rows can be retrieved either in FIFO (first-in, first-
  out) or LIFO (last-in, first-out) sequence.
- association, so that children entity occurrences are stored close to their parent
  entity occurrence.

Sizing Files

Each file should be allocated enough space to accommodate its relations for the foreseeable future, plus at least 20 percent free space. Allocating additional space to the file can be expensive, especially if users are prevented from accessing the data while they are being reorganized. Too much space means paying for excess capacity, and too little space means finding space for new tuples and handling overflow from full pages.

ILLUSTRATIVE RELATIONAL DATABASE MANAGEMENT SYSTEMS

We shall now introduce several illustrative relational database management systems:

- System R (IBM Research Laboratory).
- INGRES (University of California, Berkeley).
- RDMS (Massachusetts Institute of Technology).

These all are research and development systems that have been important to the development of commercial software providing relational database support.

THE SYSTEM R APPROACH

The System R project at the IBM San Jose Research Laboratory was started in the mid-1970s, and it formed the basis for two products from IBM, the SQL/DS and DB2 relational database management systems. SQL/DS became available in early 1982. It runs on DOS/VSE on a variety of medium-sized IBM computers, including the S/370, 3031, 3033, 4311, and 4341. There are utilities available to dump from a DL/1 (hierarchical) database into a SQL database, but they do little data analysis; rather, mostly data reformatting.

The DB2 system became available in late 1984. It runs on MVS on a variety of medium- and large-sized IBM computers. There are utilities available to extract from an IMS (hierarchical) database into a DB2 database. As with the SQL/DS utilities, they are primarily concerned with data reformatting.

Architecture

The fundamental architecture of System R is shown in Fig. 10.10 and includes

- Relational Data Interface (RDI) between the user and the Relational Data System.
- Relational Data System (RDS).

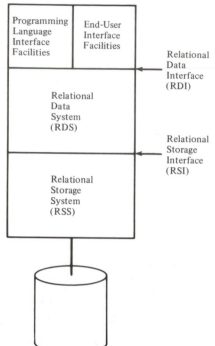

FIGURE 10.10. Basic architecture of System R [After Astrahan, M.M. et. al., 1976.]

- Relational Storage Interface (RSI) between the Relational Data System and the Relational Storage System.
- Relational Storage System (RSS).

The Relational Data Interface can be called directly from a programming language (PL/I, COBOL, FORTRAN, or assembler) or other user-interface software (e.g., SQL, QBE). The programmer or end user uses the language facilities of the Relational Data Interface, and the users interact with the portions (i.e., views) of the relational database that are of interest to their applications and are consistent with their access authorizations.

The Relational Data System supports the Relational Data Interface and performs the mapping between base relations and user views. It also provides authorization checking and enforcement, and some enforcement of integrity constraints.

The Relational Storage Interface is an internal interface that provides access to single rows of base relations. It delivers data a row at a time from the Relational Storage System to the Relational Data System, and vice versa.

The Relational Storage System manages storage devices, space allocation, storage buffers, transaction consistency and locking, deadlock detection, backout, transaction recovery, and system recovery. It maintains both indexes for fast access paths on selected attributes of base relations and pointer chains across relations, for fast access paths on prestructured joins.

File Structure

System R uses the approach of N base relations, one file. Each base relation is stored within a file's boundaries, and several base relations can be clustered in the same file. A single buffer therefore can contain rows from several tables. If this physical clustering matches the users' request needs, then performance can be better than if the tables were in two different files.

System R distinguishes between files that can be shared and those that are low-overhead files for temporary relations. There are no provisions for concurrent access to or recovery of the temporary files.

Page Structure

Each tuple is stored as a contiguous sequence of field values within a single page. There are two types of fields, stored-data fields and internal (or prefix) fields. The stored-data fields contain user data and can be either fixed or variable length, depending on how they were defined. The internal fields are used for storage management and row access and include the relation identifier, pointer fields linking this row to other rows, and additional internal information.

There are two types of pages; data pages and reserved pages. Data pages are used to store the rows of base relations, and the reserved pages are used to store internal directory entries and index entries. A data page has three sections; header, body, and slot pointers (Fig. 10.11). The header section contains the number of the page and other system data; the body section contains the row-field values; and the slot-pointer section contains pointers into the body section. There is one slot pointer per row stored on the page, and the slot-pointer value is the offset of the row location from the beginning of the page. For example, a slot-pointer value of 32 means that the corresponding row begins in the thirty-second byte of the page.

Tuple Identifier

Associated with each stored row is a tuple identifier, or TID. These identifiers are used by the Relational Storage System as a convenient means of addressing rows and are not intended for use by applications or end users.

A row's TID is the number of the page on which the row is stored and the number of the slot pointer. Thus the TID and the slot-pointer values together point to the row's location. The TID points to the slot pointer, and the slot pointer indicates the start of the row (Fig. 10.12).

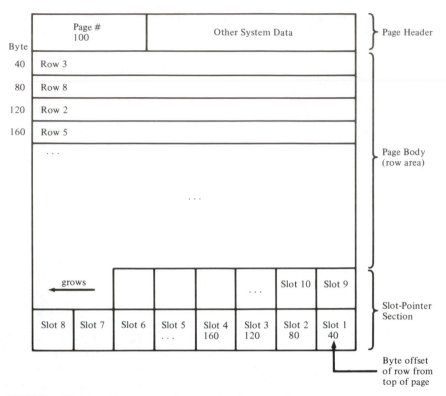

FIGURE 10.11. Data-page format for System R.

TIDs are used in the Relational Storage System to refer to rows from index structures and in pointer chains. The slot-pointer system allows the Relational Storage System to reorganize space on a page as needed, without affecting the TID values. Although their values may change, the slots themselves are never moved from their positions at the bottoms of the pages.

If a row is modified and becomes too large to fit in the available space on its page, then its TID value will point to a specially tagged record that in turn points to the overflow location. Access to a row via a TID value almost always involves access to just one page and never involves access to more than two pages.

Row	TID Value			Slot Value
	Page	Slot	Slot	Byte Offset
3	100	1	1	40
8	100	2	2	80
2	100	3	3	120
5	100	4	4	160

FIGURE 10.12. TID values and slot-pointer values.

Built-in Fast Access Paths

System R supports two types of built-in fast access paths: images, which support access by attribute values, and binary links, which support prestructured joins.

An *image* provides direct and sequential access for one or more attributes and is implemented by a multipage index structure similar to the B^+-tree introduced in Chapter 9. Each entry in the tree is an ⟨attribute value, pointer⟩ pair, and the pointer is to the index page containing attribute values less than or equal to the given one. Each leaf node is an ⟨attribute value, TID⟩ pointing to the pertinent row of the base relation. The leaves of the index tree are in a doubly linked list, thus the index tree supports both sequential and direct access to the rows by attribute value.

A *binary link* provides an access path between rows of one relation and related rows of another relation. For example, consider the two relations

```
DEPT (DEPT_CODE, DEPT_LOC, DEPT_TYPE)
EMP (EMP#, SOC_SEC#, DEPT_CODE, JOB_CODE, EMP_NAME)
```

One application of a binary link is to prestructure joins. For example, a binary link could chain each row of the DEPT relation to the set of EMP rows with the matching value of DEPT_CODE. Each DEPT row has a pointer to one of the EMP rows with the same DEPT_CODE value; and each EMP row has a pointer to another EMP row with the same DEPT_CODE value.

Another application of a binary link is to order the rows within a relation. For example, a binary link could chain each row of the DEPT relation to the row with the next greater DEPT_CODE value. These binary links are called *unary links,* because they chain rows within a relation, not across relations.

THE INGRES APPROACH

The INGRES (Interactive Graphics and Retrieval System) project at the University of California, Berkeley, became the foundation for the commercial INGRES relational database management system from Relational Technology, Inc. The commercial version executes on the Digital Equipment VMS and the UNIX operating systems.

Directory Structure

The relational database is described in a system catalog that is itself a set of relations. There are two system relations; RELATION and ATTRIBUTE. The RELATION relation has one row for each base and system relation in the database. The attributes of the RELATION relation include

REL ID   —   name of the relation.
OWNER   —   user id of the owner of the relation.

SPEC	—	code indicating the type of storage used for the relation.
INDEXD	—	flag indicating whether there is an index to the relation.
PROTECT	—	flag indicating whether there are access protections set for the relation.
INTEG .	—	flag indicating whether there are integrity constraints to be enforced for the relation.
SAVE	—	scheduled lifetime for the relation.
TUPLES	—	number of rows in the relation.
ATTS	—	number of attributes in each row.
WIDTH	—	number of bytes per row.
PRIM	—	number of pages in the primary file for this relation.

The ATTRIBUTE relation describes the columns of each base relation and system relation. There is one row in the ATTRIBUTE relation for each attribute in each relation in the database. The attributes of the ATTRIBUTE relation include

REL ID	—	name of the relation.
OWNER	—	user id of the owner of the relation.
ATT-NAME	—	name of the attribute.
ATT-NO	—	ordinal position of the attribute in the relation (e.g., 1, 2, 3, . . .).
OFFSET	—	number of bytes from the beginning of the row to the beginning of this attribute.
TYPE	—	data type for this attribute (e.g., integer, floating point, character).
LENGTH	—	number of bytes allocated to the attribute.
KEYNO	—	if the attribute is part of a key, then the sequence of this attribute within the key.

Other system catalog relations include

- INDEX, which has one row for each index structure in the database.
- PROTECTION, which describes security protection constraints.
- INTEGRITY, which describes data integrity constraints.
- VIEW, which describes user view (external schema) relations.

Because the directory is structured as a group of relations, INGRES can operate on its directory with the same facilities that are used for the user data.

File Structure

INGRES uses the approach of one base relation, one file. There is only one base relation per file, and each is stored within the file's boundaries. This allows each file's structure to be tailored to the characteristics of a specific relation. The storage scheme used for a file can be selected to correspond to the type of activity expected against that base relation.

INGRES supports a variety of file storage schemes: nonkeyed, hashed, compressed hashed, ISAM, and compressed ISAM.

The order of rows in a *nonkeyed file* is the same as their order of entry into the file. Each new row is appended to the last row in the file, and each row has a unique identifier (its *tuple identifier* or *TID*), which is its byte offset within the file.

A nonkeyed file requires little overhead and is suitable for very small relations. Note that a row's storage location is independent of any of its attribute values. This storage scheme is also used for transporting data into and out of other INGRES structures.

The other storage schemes are called *keyed storage structures,* and they all use the value of a row's primary key to determine its storage location.

Like each row of a relation in a nonkeyed storage structure, each row of a relation in a keyed storage structure has a tuple identifier (TID). In a keyed storage structure, a TID is a row's page number and line number. A line in INGRES is equivalent to a slot in System R. The systems use essentially the same page structure (compare Figs. 10.11 and 10.13). One difference is that INGRES has just one type of relation per page, whereas System R accommodates several types of relations per page. Other differences are in the ways the systems allocate overflow pages.

In the hashed storage scheme, the primary-key value is used to calculate the page number for storing the row (see Chapter 9).

The compressed hash storage scheme is like the hashed storage scheme, except that storage compression techniques are used. For example, trailing blanks are not stored in character-string fields. This scheme is useful for large relations of text data.

The ISAM storage scheme supports both sequential and direct access based on the relation's primary-key values (see Chapter 9). The compressed ISAM storage scheme adds storage compression techniques to the ISAM storage scheme.

All four of the keyed storage schemes, which provide built-in fast access paths by primary-key attributes, can also support built-in fast access paths by other attributes. These access paths are implemented by index structures and are described in the INDEX system relation.

THE RDMS APPROACH

The RDMS (Relational Data Management System) approach was developed in the mid-1970s at the Massachusetts Institute of Technology. RDMS was a basis for the MULTICS Relational Data Management System from Honeywell Information Systems, Inc.

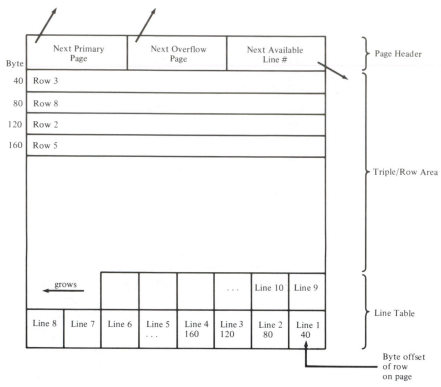

FIGURE 10.13. Data-page format for INGRES.

File Structure

An RDMS physical database is composed of two types of files: relations and dataclasses. A dataclass is a domain. As stated in Chapter 3, many attributes can draw their values from a single domain, and a domain determines a set of allowable values.

Because each dataclass is stored in its own file, the storage structure of that file can be tailored to the dataclass's characteristics. For example, two of the storage structure types are array and binary search tree. Arrays are suitable for storing relatively small sets of values whose sequence is immaterial. Each new value is appended to the array. Binary search trees (see Chapter 9) are suitable for storing alphanumeric values that need to be accessed directly as well as sequentially.

Each dataclass has an associated data-strategy-module (DSM) that governs the process of accessing and managing the storage structure of the dataclass file. For example, four of the data-strategy-modules are

- dsm_astring, for managing binary search trees.
- dsm_table, for managing arrays.

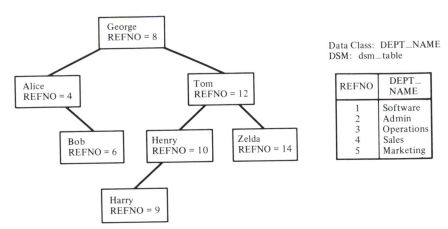

Data Class: EMP_NAME
DSM: dsm_astring

Data Class: DEPT_NAME
DSM: dsm_table

REFNO	DEPT_NAME
1	Software
2	Admin
3	Operations
4	Sales
5	Marketing

FIGURE 10.14. Two database files, one stored as a binary search tree and one as an array.

- dsm_integer, for managing integer storage.
- dsm_ciph_integer, for managing encrypted integer storage.

Figure 10.14 illustrates two dataclass files. The DEPT_NAME dataclass file is stored as an array and is managed by the dsm_table data-strategy-module. The EMP_NAME dataclass file is stored as a binary search tree and is managed by the dsm_astring data-strategy-module. Note that each entry in each dataclass file is assigned a reference number (REFNO), which will be used elsewhere to point to it.

Each relation is stored in its own file and is structured as a table of REFNO values. Each row of the table has one REFNO for each attribute in the relation. The REFNOs are either pointers into the appropriate dataclass files or actual integer values for an attribute.

Figure 10.15 shows a relation file. The relation has four attributes: EMP_NAME, CURRENT_DEPT_NAME, LAST_DEPT_NAME, and PERCENT_ASSIGNED. The REFNOs in the EMP_NAME column are pointers into the EMP_NAME dataclass file; the REFNOs in the CURRENT_DEPT_NAME and LAST_DEPT_NAME columns are pointers into the DEPT_NAME dataclass file; and the REFNOs in the PERCENT_ASSIGNED column are actual values.

Some of the advantages of this implementation approach are the following:

- Compactness: each domain (i.e., dataclass) value is stored only once rather than each time it is used as an attribute value.
- Uniformity and simplicity: data management of a relation amounts to handling REFNOs, which are guaranteed to be integer values.
- Efficiency: relational operations can be processed efficiently because of the dataclass files' tailored structures.

Relation: EMPLOYEE

EMP_ NAME	CURRENT_ DEPT_NAME	LAST_ DEPT_NAME	PERCENT_ ASSIGNED
8	1	0	100
4	1	3	80
14	5	4	50
12	5	3	100

FIGURE 10.15. Relation file: entries are REFNOs pointing into dataclass files.

The principal disadvantage of this implementation approach is that it requires a considerable amount of file manipulation to operate on relations and to display attribute values. Implementing this approach on an operating system with inefficient file manipulation can result in a very slow system, despite the tailored dataclass structures.

Directory Structure

The directory for an RDMS database is a table with three kinds of entries (Fig. 10.16): pointer to the system data file, pointers to dataclass files, and pointers to relation files. The system data file includes the names of all relations and all dataclasses and their associated data-strategy-modules. The dataclass and relation files are structured as indicated.

DATABASE MACHINES

Another alternative to implementing a relational database is to use a database machine, which is a computer with specialized hardware for database management system functions. The objective of a database machine is to provide database management system functions without tying up the resources of a general-purpose computer and to improve the performance of the database system in the process. The improvement may be a combination of faster access time, better throughput, lower overall hardware cost, simpler hardware and software maintenance, and increased function.

There are several ways to configure a system of database machines and general-purpose computers. A simple, prevalent configuration is shown in Fig. 10.17: a single general-purpose host and a single backend database machine. The objective of this configuration is to offload database processing from the host, an objective that is much the same as that of a frontend communications processor (Fig. 10.18), which offloads data communications processing.

A communications processor may be responsible for any of the following communications-related tasks:

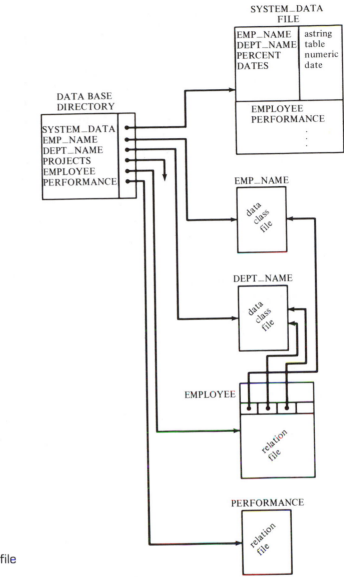

FIGURE 10.16. Interfile relationships.

- controlling the flow of message traffic in and out of the host.
- accommodating several speeds of transmission.
- accommodating several schemes of encoding messages.
- detecting and controlling message errors.
- polling terminals for message traffic.
- routing messages out of the host.

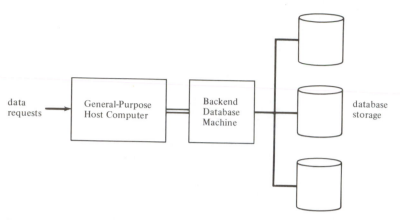

FIGURE 10.17. Simple configuration with database machine as backend to general-purpose host computer.

Giving this responsibility to a communications processor frees host resources to handle computing.

Similarly, a database machine may be responsible for any of the following database-related tasks:

- parsing and interpreting users' requests to retrieve or update data.
- selecting data access paths.
- managing physical storage.
- accessing data.
- preparing results for delivery to users.
- providing data recovery and security protection.
- enforcing data integrity constraints.

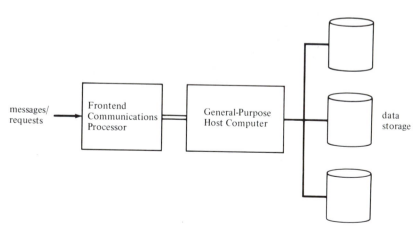

FIGURE 10.18. Use of a frontend communications processor to offload general-purpose host computer.

Giving this responsibility to a database machine also frees host resources to handle computing.

A database machine usually requires specialized software in the host computer. The software is part of the host-to-database machine interface. It may help parse and plan the execution of user requests or, at the other end of the spectrum, may do only minimal processing of requests.

The ideal database machine will

- make minimal processing demands on the host. A database call will be passed as simply as possible from the host to the database machine, in a form as close as possible to that received by the host from the user.
- send back only "relevant" data to the host machine, to minimize the time and cost of intermachine communication and the volume of data handled by the host.
- rely as much as possible on standard communication protocols for intermachine communication, so that specialized software for this communication does not have to be added to the host.

An ideal database machine does not rely on host services. A database-intensive environment can even be supported by a configuration in which there is no dependency on a host general-purpose computer (Fig. 10.19). A network of terminals, personal computers, or host computers directly accesses the database machine through the communications frontend. The database machine here serves as the database server for the network.

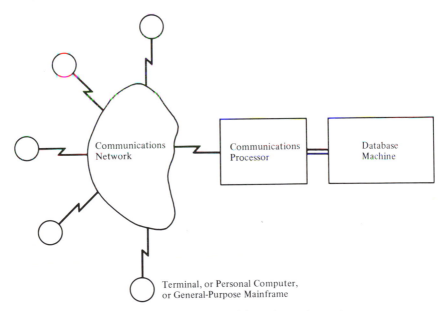

FIGURE 10.19. Database machine without host dependency.

Architecture

A representative architecture for a database machine is shown in Fig. 10.20. The database machine's controller communicates with several "slave" processors and storage devices via one or more communications channels. The data are distributed across storage devices so that they can be located and processed in parallel. Parallelism usually improves performance. In fact, the extent of parallel searching and processing is one of the most obvious differences between the approaches used by database machines and by general-purpose computers.

A database machine attempts to locate data more efficiently by bringing the association between data values and device addresses closer to the hardware level. Software database management systems track the mappings between values and addresses using index-structure techniques such as those introduced in Chapter 9. Database machines either use techniques based on content-addressable storage (devices whose controllers are able to find records directly by examination of their content, rather than by following pointers and addresses), or they speed up the index-management process by coding it into the hardware rather than into the software.

Data Distribution Techniques

For highly parallel processing, the data must be partitioned carefully for access by many processors. Database machines use different techniques for partitioning

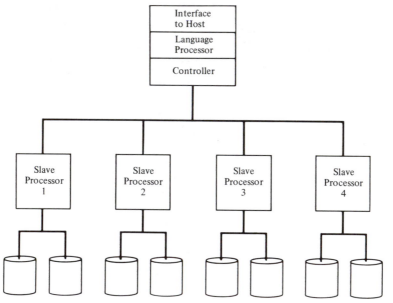

FIGURE 10.20.   Representative architecture of a database machine.

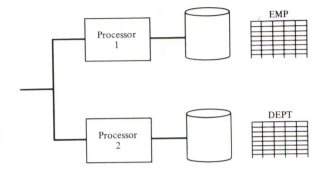

FIGURE 10.21. Distribution of whole relations to processors.

data across devices. To simplify our discussion of some of these techniques, assume that there are just two processors and two base relations; DEPT and EMP.

One way to distribute data is to store the DEPT rows at one processor and the EMP rows at the other processor (Fig. 10.21). This alternative does not provide much opportunity for parallelism, and any access to just the DEPT relation or just the EMP relation incurs no parallelism at all.

Another alternative is to use as many devices as possible to store the rows of any one relation, by using several files to store one relation. For example, store half the DEPT rows and half the EMP rows at one processor, and store the other DEPT and EMP rows at the other processor (Fig. 10.22). Now there is the potential for parallelism on an access to just the DEPT relation, to just the EMP relation, or on a join of the two relations.

The partitioning of a relation across devices can be horizontal (some rows accessed by one processor, some by another), vertical (some columns accessed by one processor, some by another), or a combination of horizontal and vertical partitioning. Horizontal partitioning is most commonly used.

Partitions should be distributed to devices in such a way that the load is fairly equal across the processors. If one processor becomes a bottleneck, say, because

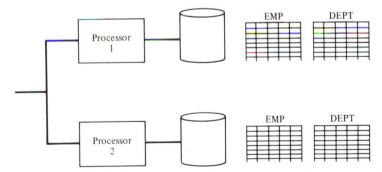

FIGURE 10.22. Distribution of partitions of relations to processors.

it has more data to access than do the other processors, then the opportunities for parallelism will diminish.

One way of distributing rows is to use block hashing (see Chapter 9) to the storage devices. Each device is treated as a block, and a second hash may be used to determine the storage addresses within the blocks.

Directory Structure

The system directory for a database machine needs to know not just which relations are stored on which devices, but also which partitions of which relations are stored where.

Database machine directories include indexes to facilitate locating partitions, and these indexes can be implemented

- in software or hardware at the controller to reduce the volume of data accessed and the number of processors servicing a request.
- in hardware in the communications bus to reduce the volume of data accessed and the number of processors servicing a request.

The rows of a partition can be searched sequentially, by using a local index available to the processor, or by using content-addressable storage.

Query Processing

Perhaps the most difficult part of implementing a database machine is developing the control strategies necessary to coordinate the many processors' actions. With parallel processors, the database machine must be able to coordinate the recovery of a request that spans processors and must be able to prevent interference when several requests update data in partitions involving multiple processors. These control strategies are similar to those required for managing distributed databases implemented on computer networks.

The User's View

From the user's point of view, interacting with a database machine should not be different from using a database management system in a general-purpose host computer. The languages and capabilities should be the same, and the logical data modeling activity is the same.

There is little consensus on the necessity of database machines. Some experts feel that the falling costs and improving performance of conventional hardware, coupled with improvements in database management software, have eclipsed the advantages claimed by the vendors of database machines. But other experts feel that the performance and cost trade-offs offered by database machines are essential to manage effectively the growing volumes of data that our society is amassing.

Commercial Database Machines

Database machines have only recently become available commercially. Their roots are in research systems developed at universities (including the University of Toronto, University of Florida, University of Utah, Ohio State University, and others) and in vendor laboratories.

Commercial database machines include the

- DBC/1012, from Teradata Corporation.
- IDM (Intelligent Database Machine), from Britton-Lee.
- iDBP Database Processor and iDIS Database Information System, from Intel.

The Teradata DBC/1012 provides backend database support for large IBM computers and includes microprocessor-based subsystems interconnected by an intelligent communications subsystem. The database machine can be expanded modularly by adding disk and processor subsystems. The DBC/1012 became available in 1984.

The Britton-Lee IDM products provide backend database support for a variety of medium- to large-sized computers, including the DEC VAX and PDP-11, and the IBM 43xx, 30xx, and 370. The IDM can also be interfaced, without a general-purpose host, to a network of one or more IBM PCs. There are several configurations of IDM products. The IDM first became available in 1981.

The Intel iDBP Database Processor is intended to integrate database management capabilities into small business or office systems application systems. Its use requires development of communications and end-user request interface software in a host mini- or microcomputer. The Intel iDIS Database Information System is a frontend database machine that provides an interface between distributed personal computers or terminals and a database on a host computer. It also supports development of a local relational database serving the personal computers.

DISTRIBUTED RELATIONAL DATABASES

The database described by a single logical data model may be implemented physically on several computers, connected by a communications network. The result is a distributed database. Not all of the data reside in one physical database; yet there is a logical model that ties the data together.

The data may be distributed in several ways, including

- whole partitions, in which a relation is stored in its entirety in one physical database.

- horizontal partitions, in which some of a relation's rows are stored in one physical database and some are stored in another.
- vertical partitions, in which some of a relation's columns are stored in one physical database and some are stored in another.
- overlapping partitions, in which some or all of the contents of one partition are replicated in another partition.

Why Distribute a Database?

The primary reason for a distributed database is an enterprize that is decentralized, yet needs to share information across the distributed sites. Distributed operations can lead to the following situations:

- Data may be generated at many sites, requiring fast local access and summary data crossing site boundaries.
- Data may be generated centrally, requiring fast remote access. Both the central and remote sites may need to update the data.
- Data may be generated at many sites, requiring fast access to both locally and remotely stored data.

In all of these situations, distributing the database can lead to better performance than centralizing the database in one location can, because distribution reduces data communications volumes, if most of the accesses are to locally stored data, and reduces the volume of data stored at any given machine, thereby reducing capacity requirements and improving responsiveness at that site.

Why Not Distribute a Database?

Despite all these reasons, distributed databases are not common today. Database management technology does not yet include commercially satisfactory solutions to problems of coordinating the actions of multiple processors against a single logical database. It must be possible for a single request to access or update data stored in multiple partitions of the database, without the user's having to specify which partitions are involved or where they are stored. To handle distributed update, there must be coordination to prevent updates in one partition from conflicting with updates in another, and there must be synchronization of recovery operations in the multiple partitions.

Most of what are today commonly referred to as *distributed databases* are really decentralized databases and have no single, integrated logical model of the data resource. They either cannot handle a user's request targeted at multiple partitions or require that the user specify which partitions are involved.

Basic Design Decisions

The basic decisions encountered in designing a distributed database are

- How should the data be partitioned across processors?
- Will redundancy of data across partitions be allowed?
- Which copy of data will be accessed in response to any given request?

These questions must be addressed, regardless of whether the distributed database is supported by the relational model, the network model, the hierarchical model, or some other model. In fact, each of the database's partitions may be represented locally using a different model.

CLOSING COMMENTS

There are a variety of approaches to physically implementing relational databases. Two alternatives are to use a software relational database management system or hardware specialized for database management. These alternatives can be combined to distribute relations across several computers as a distributed database.

All of the available software relational database management systems offer generally the same level of end-user support. They differ, however, in their approaches to locating data on storage and managing access to data. The approaches introduced in the text included one base relation per file, several base relations per file, several base relations in each of multiple files, and several files for a single base relation.

Database machines are computers specialized to manage databases. Today they all support the relational model and thus are candidates for physically implementing relational databases. Their objectives are to reduce the processing requirements for general-purpose computers and to improve the performance of database systems.

Distributed databases store partitions of the relations on multiple computers, connected by a communications network. A database is physically distributed to improve the database systems' performance in decentralized environments.

Chapter 4 discussed mapping logical data models to relational databases, which can be physically implemented using any of the kinds of database management support introduced in this chapter.

TERMS

backend processor	buffer
base relation	communications processor
B$^+$-tree	database machine

decentralized database   index
discriminating attribute   linked list
distributed database   page
file   pointer
frontend processor   preconstructed join
hashing   vertical partitioning
horizontal partitioning

REVIEW EXERCISES

1.   Define each of the terms in the preceding list.

2.   Design three or four relations to contain student and class information in a college database. Give an example of how vertical partitioning can be used to improve database performance, an example of how horizontal partitioning can be used to improve database performance, and an example of how joining to form a base relation can be used to improve database performance.

3.   Consider a database with two relations: ACCOUNT_CUST and AC-COUNT_BALANCE, as shown in Fig. 10.1. Assume that each has an index structured on its ACCT# attribute. Describe the sequence of steps required to process the following request:
```
SELECT CUST_NAME BALANCE
   FROM ACCOUNT_CUST ACCOUNT_BALANCE
   WHERE ACCOUNT_CUST.ACCT# = ACCOUNT_BALANCE.ACCT#;
```

4.   Describe a different sequence of steps to process the request in question 3. What are the trade-offs between the two approaches? How would a database management system determine which approach to use?

5.   Describe the sequence of steps required to process the following request, assuming that there is an index structured on the CUST_NAME attribute:
```
SELECT CUST_PHONE
   FROM ACCOUNT_CUST
   WHERE CUST_NAME = 'IGOR P. SPOTT';
```

6.   Describe the sequence of steps required to process the previous request, assuming that there is no index on the CUST_NAME attribute.

7.   What should a database designer consider when deciding whether or not to structure an index on a particular attribute of a relation?

8.   What must a database management system consider when determining whether or not to use an index structured on a particular attribute of a relation?

9.   What are the costs of establishing preconstructed joins in a relational database? What are the benefits?

10.   What must a database designer consider when determining whether or not to preconstruct a particular join?

11.   What are the trade-offs between using a directory of join-attribute values and

using linked lists to prestructure joins? What must a database designer consider when choosing between them, if the database management system supports both?

12. What are the costs of clustering certain records close to one another? What are the benefits?

13. What must a database designer consider when determining whether or not to cluster records?

14. Why are fast access paths more commonly built on foreign-key attributes than on attributes that are neither primary keys nor foreign keys?

15. What are the advantages of being able to store multiple relations in the same file? Are there any disadvantages? If so, what are they?

16. Compare the System R, INGRES, and RDMS approaches to storing relations. If you had available all three systems, how would you decide which to use for a particular database?

17. What are the advantages of using a database machine to manage a relational database? Are there any disadvantages? If so, what are they?

18. What are the advantages of using a distributed database to serve a set of data-processing requirements? Are there any disadvantages? If so, what are they?

19. The factors used to measure the performance of a database system include the number of disk accesses, main and secondary storage space requirements, CPU time, and pointer overhead requirements. What additional factors need to be considered when measuring the performance of a distributed database system?

20. What are the advantages of replicating data in a distributed database system? Are there any disadvantages? If so, what are they?

REFERENCES

Astrahan, M. M., et al. System R: Relational approach to database management, *ACM Trans. on Database Systems* 1 (June 1976): 97–137.

Hsiao, D. *Advanced Database Machine Architecture*. Englewood Cliffs, N.J.: Prentice-Hall, 1983.

Neches, P. M. Hardware support for advanced data management systems, *Computer* 17 (November 1984): 29–40.

RDMS. *Design Principles, RDMS Reference Guide*. Cambridge, Mass.: Massachusetts Institute of Technology, 1974.

Stonebraker, M., et al. The design and implementation of INGRES, *ACM Trans. on Database Systems* 1 (September 1976): 189–222.

Todd, S. PRTV: An efficient implementation for large relational databases, *Proc. International Conf. on Very Large Databases*. Framingham, Mass.: September 1975, pp. 554–556.

Physical Design of Network Databases

The implementation of network databases is introduced by comparing several approaches to storing network records and relationships. The chapter uses real systems as the basis for the alternatives, without giving all the details of those real systems. Rather, the intention is to show how the approaches relate to one another and what their implications are for physical database design.

All network database management systems support a specific approach to implementing the network model, usually an approach related to one of the schemes outlined in this chapter. The scheme used determines the questions that the physical-database designer must address and the performance characteristics that the implemented system will have with various types of data manipulation.

It is important to distinguish between logical and physical database designs: the effectiveness of a network model should not be altered by the database's physical implementation, and the user's view of the network database should not be affected by which physical structuring technique is used. As with a relational database, however, the different physical designs of a network database can deliver quite different performance.

BASIC REQUIREMENTS OF A PHYSICAL NETWORK DATABASE

The three requirements for the physical implementation of the network model are that it must

1. Represent one-to-many relationships between parent (owner) and child (member) record types.
2. Be accessible by the values of key attributes.
3. Be able to support basic traversal operators through the network of parent–child relationships.

Representation of Parent–Child Relationships

A variety of physical data structures can be used to implement the one-to-many relationships between parent and child record types. One of the structures is a linked list from each parent record, connecting it to its children records. Another structure is a set of pointers in each parent record, referencing the children records. Regardless of which underlying physical data structure is used, it should be possible to locate a parent record and its associated children and to locate a child record and its associated parent in a relationship.

Accessible by Key Attribute(s)

Whatever the physical data structure used to implement the parent–child relationships, various record types in the database must be accessible by their key attributes. These record types are sometimes referred to as *port* records.

Note that this requirement is less stringent than the similar requirement of a relational database management system, in which the user must be able to request access to the data by specifying the value of any attribute of any relation. In implementations of the network model, direct access is required by only some of the attributes, to only some of the record types.

Support of Basic Traversal Operators

The physical data structure must be able to support basic operators that traverse parent–child relationships. The supported operators should include

• selecting a particular record occurrence.
• selecting a record occurrence that has a specified relationship to the last record selected.

- deleting a record occurrence.
- modifying a record occurrence.
- inserting a record occurrence.

The specified relationship between designated record occurrences can be that

- they are of the same record type.
- one is the parent and one the child in a one-to-many relationship.
- they both are children of the same parent in a one-to-many relationship.

Note that these requirements are less stringent than those of a physical data structure to support the relational model. A relational database management system must be able to construct a table as the result of an operation on a table, and it must support access to a set of record occurrences in a single operation. By contrast, a network database management system need only support record-at-a-time access to the database.

BASIC LOGICAL-TO-PHYSICAL TRANSFORMATIONS

The design issues in mapping the logical record types of a network data model to base record types in a physical database structure are the same as those introduced in Chapter 10 for mapping logical tables to physical base relations.

The most straightforward logical-to-physical transformation is to implement each logical record type of a network model as a single base record type. But to improve the system's performance, the physical database designer must determine whether any of the following logical-to-physical transformations may be more appropriate:

- Vertical partitioning: splitting a logical record type into multiple base record types, with some of the data fields in one base record type and some in another

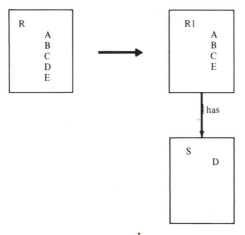

FIGURE 11.1. Vertical partitioning of record type R into two record types R1 and S, connected by an information-bearing set type (because the key of R1 is not stored in S).

FIGURE 11.2. Horizontal partitioning of record type R into two record types, R1 and R2. Some occurrences of R are stored as R1; some are stored as R2. R1 and R2 may reside in separate databases or different hosts.

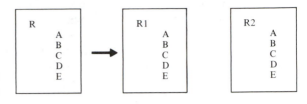

(Fig. 11.1). A variation of this transformation is not to represent physically some of the data fields of the logical record type.

- Horizontal partitioning: splitting a logical record type into multiple base record types, with some of the record occurrences in one base record type and some in another (Fig. 11.2).
- Joining: combining a logical record type with one or more other record types into a single base record type (Fig. 11.3).

These transformations result in base record types that do not correspond exactly to the starting logical record types. The reasons for using these transformations with a network database are approximately the same as for using them with a relational database.

Vertical Partitioning

As with a relational database, the reason to partition vertically a logical record type in a network is to separate into different base records those data fields that are not likely to be accessed together. The intention is to be able to bring into main memory from disk storage the data required to satisfy a user's request, without accessing much else.

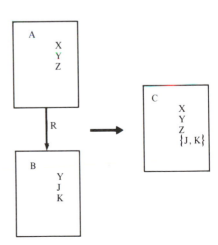

FIGURE 11.3. Joining of record types A and B to form base record type C. C contains a repeating group for the multiple J, K values that may exist for a given set of X, Y, Z values.

A variation of vertical partitioning is to omit physically some of the data fields of the logical record, most commonly done with foreign-key data fields. Because the data structure used to represent one-to-many relationships supports finding the parent of a given child record, it is not necessary to store in the child the value of the foreign-key data fields. The result is an information-bearing set. On the other hand, if the foreign-key data fields are represented, then the relationship is a value-based set.

The benefit of an information-bearing set is reduced space requirements, because the foreign-key data fields are not stored. The cost is the need to access the parent record to find the values of the foreign-key data fields. In many cases, the costs outweigh the benefits.

Horizontal Partitioning

The reason to partition horizontally a logical record type in a network is to facilitate physically clustering record occurrences that are likely to be accessed together. Into a horizontal partition should fall those record occurrences that will be accessed together. The other occurrences of the record type can be placed in another partition.

The database designer can specify which base record types are to be stored in which files. If each horizontal partition is a different base record type, then each can be placed in a separate file. The intention is to store record occurrences that will be accessed together onto the same page, without intermixing record occurrences that are not needed.

Joining

Joining record types in a network database typically means either

- collapsing a parent–child relationship that will always have, at most, one occurrence of the child for a given parent (e.g., a parent–child relationship caused by a category relationship).
- collapsing a one-to-many parent–child relationship by incorporating a repeating group of data fields into the parent record type.

Both of these types of joins are commonly used by physical database designers to improve network database performance.

Applicability of the Transformations

These transformations can be used with a network database in the same conditions that they can be used with a relational database. Those conditions are the following:

- The more bytes that are required to store an occurrence of a record type, the greater the probability will be that it should be partitioned vertically.
- The more occurrences there are of the record type, the greater the probability that it should be partitioned horizontally.
- The more skewed patterns of access there are to a subset of the occurrences of a record type, the greater the probability will be that it should be partitioned horizontally.
- The more skewed patterns of access there are to a subset of the data fields of a record type, the greater the probability will be that it should be partitioned vertically.
- The more frequently that occurrences of two record types are accessed together, the greater the probability will be that they should be joined into one base record type.

User Views

Regardless of the logical-to-physical transformations used, the user and programmer should be able to access the network database without knowing its physical structure. This capability may be offered by the subschema feature of a network database management system. A *subschema* describes the portion of the database available to a particular application. The subschema is derived from the schema, which describes the entire network database.

Most network database managers, however, require that a record type in a subschema map directly to a base record type in the schema. In contrast with the formation of views in a relational environment, the horizontal partitioning, vertical partitioning, and joining of base record types to form subschema record types are not supported by commercial network database management systems; programmers need to know the base record types and their relationships.

IMPROVING PERFORMANCE

Each of these transformations between logical record types and base record types has as its objective greater efficiency, by reducing the volumes of data transferred to or from secondary storage and by reducing communications requirements in computer networks.

There are other decisions in developing an efficient physical structure for a database to support the network model:

- Parent–child representation: What data structures should be used to represent the one-to-many relationships between parent and children record occurrences?
- Attribute access: Which attributes should have built-in fast access paths?
- Clustering of physical records: Which record occurrences should be stored together?

• Buffers: How large should the buffer spaces be for transferring base record types between main memory and secondary storage?

The last three decisions also are addressed when designing an efficient relational database.

PARENT–CHILD REPRESENTATIONS

A network database management system provides one or more techniques for representing the one-to-many relationships between parent and child record occurrences. If several techniques are offered, then the physical-database designer must select the approach that will deliver the best performance for the database system's expected activity.

The two main techniques for representing the one-to-many relationships between parent and child record occurrences are linked lists and indexes. To illustrate various alternative representations, consider the example data model shown in Fig. 11.4. There is a one-to-many relationship between PART and

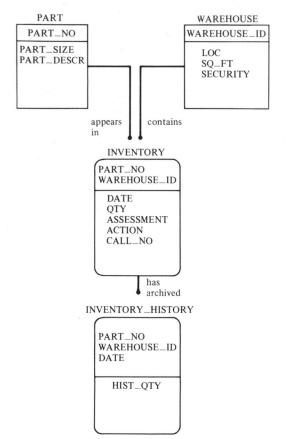

FIGURE 11.4. Example of a data model.

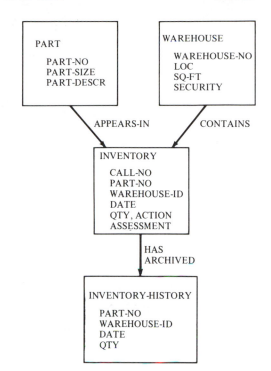

FIGURE 11.5a. CODASYL schema corresponding to data models of Fig. 11.4.

INVENTORY, another between WAREHOUSE and INVENTORY and another between INVENTORY and INVENTORY_HISTORY. The corresponding logical models for a CODASYL network database and for a TOTAL network database are shown in Figs. 11.5a and 11.5b, respectively.

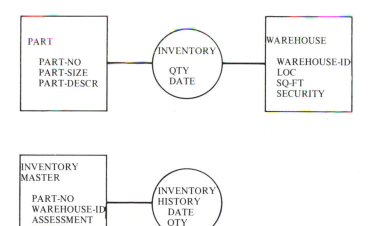

FIGURE 11.5b. TOTAL schema corresponding to data model of Fig. 11.4.

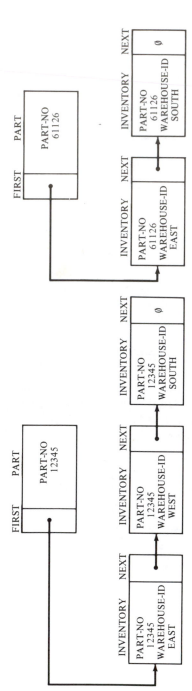

FIGURE 11.6. Basic linked list representing parent – child relationship between PART and INVENTORY.

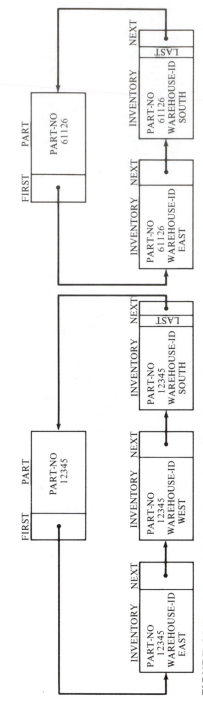

FIGURE 11.7. Linked list including pointer from last child of a set occurrence to the parent.

Linked Lists

A linked list representing the parent–child relationship between PART and IN-VENTORY is illustrated in Fig. 11.6. Each PART record occurrence has a pointer to its first associated INVENTORY record occurrence, and each IN-VENTORY record occurrence has a pointer to the next INVENTORY record occurrence with the same parent PART record.

This basic linked-list structure supports accessing the children of a given parent. A slight modification of the structure will enable it also to find the parent of a given child record. Figure 11.7 shows use of a pointer in the last child record to the set's parent.

Another modification of the basic linked-list structure will enable it to find more efficiently the previous child of a given parent record. Figure 11.8 shows a bidirectional linked list between the children of a parent. This structure also offers efficient access in reverse sequence to all the children of a parent.

The linked-list structure in Fig. 11.8 provides rapid access from a child record to its parent, for the first and the last children of the set. Another modification of the structure enables it to find more efficiently the parent record for any child record. Figure 11.9 shows a pointer from each child to its parent in the set.

If a network database management system offers this full spectrum of linked-list support for representing one-to-many relationships, then the physical database designer may need to consider the following questions:

- Should the linked list between children be bidirectional? The answer is determined by how frequently access from one child record to the previous child is required.
- Should each child have a pointer to the parent record? The answer is determined by how frequently access from a child to a parent is required.

Pointers to prior members can make the following kinds of data manipulation more efficient:

- supporting FIND PRIOR.
- inserting a new child in the set with the children sequenced in some sorted order.
- removing a child from the set.

These pointers do not speed up sequential access to the children in the set.

Assuming that prior and parent pointers are optional, the physical database designer must decide whether they will be used in each one-to-many set in the database. Not all of the sets need to use the same physical structures, but each occurrence (i.e., a parent record occurrence and its children) of the set must be structured physically in the same way as are all the other occurrences of that set.

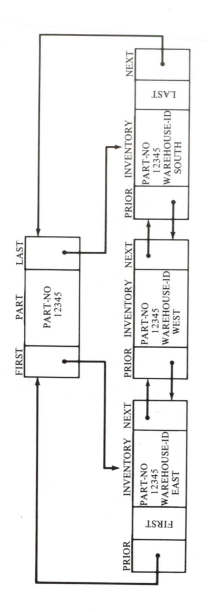

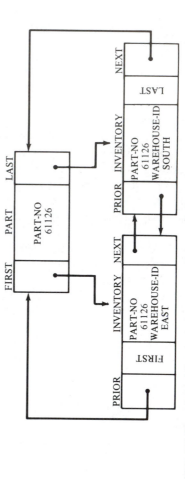

FIGURE 11.8. Linked list including bidirectional pointers between children records.

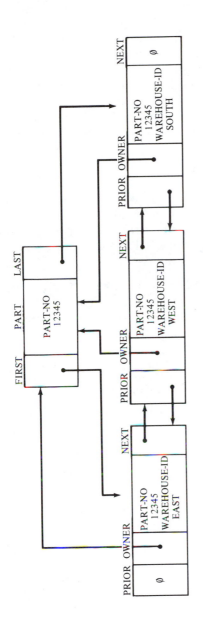

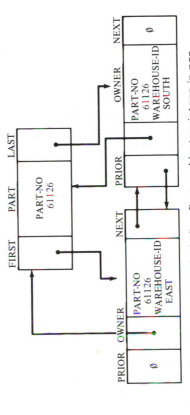

FIGURE 11.9. Linked-list structure including first and last pointers in parent records and prior, owner, and next pointers in children records.

Indexes

Another alternative for representing the parent–child relationship between PART and INVENTORY is illustrated in Fig. 11.10. Each parent PART record occurrence contains an array of pointers, one to each of its associated INVENTORY record occurrences. This basic index structure supports finding the children of a given parent. A modification of the structure enables it also to support finding the parent of any child record. Figure 11.11 shows a pointer in each child record to its parent in the set.

Another variation of the structure is shown in Fig. 11.12. The parent record does not contain an array of child pointers but instead contains a pointer to an index of child pointers. This index may be implemented as an array, a tree, or some other appropriate structure. Separating the index from the parent can be especially worthwhile when there are variable numbers of children, some parents having many and some just a few. It can also provide faster access to the children, depending on how the index is structured.

If a network database management system offers index support for representing one-to-many relationships, then the physical database designer may need to consider the following questions:

- How should the index be structured? The answer is determined by the expected numbers of children and the patterns of access to the children.
- Should the child pointers be in the parent records? The answer is determined in part by the index structure and the bounds on the number of children per parent.
- Should each child have a pointer to the parent record? The answer is determined by how frequently access from a child to a parent is required.

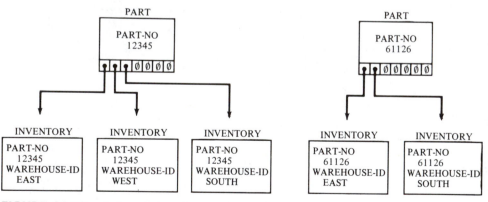

FIGURE 11.10. Indexed structure representing parent–child relationship between PART and INVENTORY.

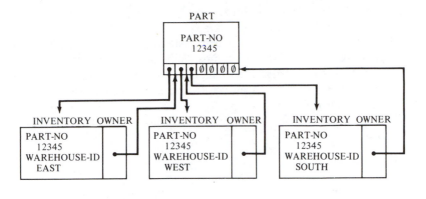

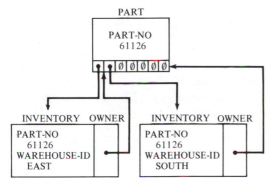

FIGURE 11.11. Indexed structure including arrays of pointers in parent records and parent pointers in children records.

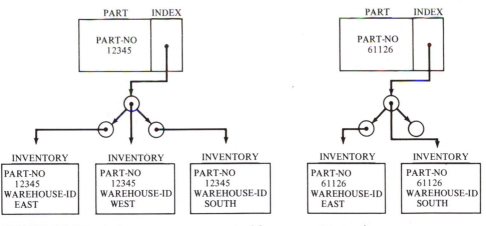

FIGURE 11.12. Index structure separated from parent records.

Linked Lists Versus Indexes

Some network database management systems provide both linked-list and index support for parent–child relationships. With these systems, the physical database designer must first determine which mode is more appropriate for each one-to-many relationship and then answer the pertinent questions about refining the use of either linked lists or indexes.

Linked lists can provide more efficient support for the following pattern of access:

Find a parent record.
Follow the pointer to the first child record.
Loop until the end of the set, each time following the pointer from the current child to the next child.

This kind of access with an array of child pointers in the parent requires the following:

Find a parent record.
Follow the first pointer, which leads to the first child record.
Loop until the end of the set, each time going back to the parent and following the next pointer, which leads to the next child.

By contrast, the array approach can provide more efficient support for the following pattern of access:

Find a parent record.
Follow the nth pointer to the nth child record.

This kind of access with the linked-list approach requires the following:

Find a parent record.
Follow the pointer to the first child record.
Loop n-1 times, each time following the pointer from the current child to the next child.

Thus, to determine whether linked lists or indexes are more appropriate for storing any particular one-to-many relationship, the physical database designer must know how the database will be accessed.

Regardless of whether linked lists or indexes are the underlying physical data structure, the programmer uses the same set of commands (FIND FIRST, FIND NEXT, FIND LAST, FIND nth, and FIND PARENT, and so forth) to access the database.

Other Data Structures

Sometimes the physical database designer decides that neither the basic linked-list nor the basic index structures supported directly by the network database management system are appropriate to represent a particular one-to-many relationship. The designer then can fashion a customized structure.

Some network database management systems make available the ''database key,'' or the logical address of a record when it is stored. These addresses are like the tuple identifiers (TIDs) introduced in Chapter 10. A database key is a page number and a line number, and the line number is either the byte offset on the page of the start of the record or the number of a field that contains the byte offset.

Using database keys, the designer can develop data structures that meet application needs exactly. For example, a data structure such as that illustrated in Fig. 11.13 might be appropriate. (We assume that this structure is not supported directly by the database management system.) The database designer has placed a pointer array on top of the system-supplied linked lists between the children records. Database keys are the pointers manipulated by database programmers to develop the index in each parent record to its children. The database keys for the pointer-array index reside in the data area of the stored record; and the pointers for the system-maintained linked lists reside in the ''overhead'' pointer areas of the stored records. The result is a customized data structure that provides efficient access to both individual children and the entire set of children.

ATTRIBUTE ACCESS

The network database management systems allow the physical database designer to specify which attributes should have built-in fast access paths. These attributes are the ones for which users commonly specify values when they want to access certain occurrences of a record type.

The built-in fast access paths in a network database are implemented using either hashing on one attribute group in a record type or index structures.

A record type that needs to be accessed directly rather than through a one-to-many relationship should have a built-in access path on one or more of its attributes. These record types are known as the *port* records of the database.

Any record type that is only a parent and never a child must either have a built-in attribute access path or be made the child in a set owned by a system-supplied record type called SYSTEM. There is only one occurrence of the SYSTEM record type, but it can be the owner of many set types. For example, SYSTEM could own the CUSTOMER records in a set type named ALL-CUSTOMERS and the PRODUCT records in a set type named ALL-PRODUCTS. Applications could quickly loop through all the PRODUCT records by following the ALL-PRODUCT set.

With nearly all commercial network database management systems, only one of the attribute groups of a base record type can have a built-in access path implemented by hashing. The values of these attributes determine the storage locations of record occurrences. By contrast, indexes can be built on several of the attributes of a base record type.

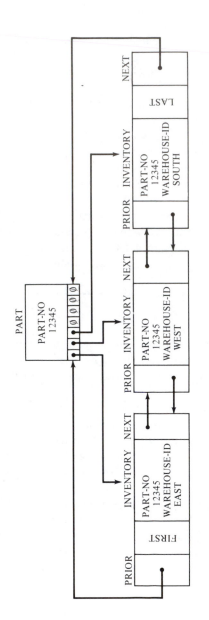

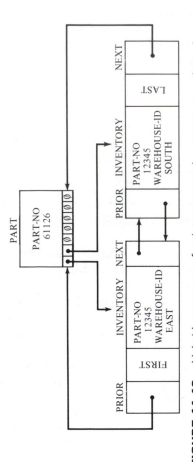

FIGURE 11.13. Hybrid structure of pointer arrays in parent records and linked lists between children records.

In the example (Fig. 11.5a), the record type PART could be hashed on PART-NO and have an index structure on PART-TYPE. The record type WAREHOUSE could be hashed on WAREHOUSE-ID. If INVENTORY records were accessed only in conjunction with their PART or WAREHOUSE parents, then the access paths provided by the internal representations of the APPEARS-IN and CONTAINS sets would suffice. On the other hand, if INVENTORY data need to be accessed direclty without PART or WAREHOUSE data, then either an index structure could be built on CALL-NO (or some other attribute), or INVENTORY records could be hashed. In either case, the internal representations of the one-to-many APPEARS-IN and CONTAINS relationships would be used to traverse from parent to child records.

Hashing is done on primary-key attributes, and index structures may be built on alternate-key attributes, foreign-key attributes, or other attributes.

CLUSTERING RECORDS

Like a relational database management system, a network database management system typically uses operating-system file management capabilities for the actual storage and access to base records. In some network database management systems, each record type is stored in its own file, and in others, the physical database designer determines which record types will be stored together in a file. In these systems, there are two opportunities for clustering records within an address space: clustering records of the same type or clustering child records with their parent record. The objective is to place on the same page those record occurrences that are likely to be accessed together. They then will be brought together into main memory in one access to secondary storage.

If the parent and child records of a one-to-many relationship are often accessed together, then physically clustering them can reduce the number of times that secondary storage must be referenced.

Consider again the PART-INVENTORY-WAREHOUSE example (Fig. 11.5a). Assume that the PART and WAREHOUSE records are hashed on PART-NO and WAREHOUSE-ID, respectively. If the INVENTORY data are most commonly accessed with the PART data, then the designer may specify that an INVENTORY record is to be stored as close as possible to its parent PART record. The intention is to put all of the INVENTORY records for a given PART record on the same page as that PART record. Note that this physical clustering implies that the INVENTORY records cannot be hashed. If hashing were used, there would be no attempt to locate an INVENTORY record near its parent PART. Note also that an INVENTORY record cannot be clustered with both the corresponding PART and WAREHOUSE parent records. The designer must determine which is the more probable access path. If access to INVENTORY data is more likely through PART than through WAREHOUSE, then the designer should specify placement of the INVENTORY records near the PART records.

PART	PART-NO 12345			
INVENTORY	PART-NO 12345	WAREHOUSE-ID EAST		
INVENTORY	PART-NO 12345	WAREHOUSE-ID WEST		
INVENTORY	PART-NO 12345	WAREHOUSE-ID SOUTH		
INVENTORY HISTORY	PART-NO 12345	WAREHOUSE-ID EAST	DATE 1/2/85	
INVENTORY HISTORY	PART-NO 12345	WAREHOUSE-ID EAST	DATE 7/1/84	
INVENTORY HISTORY	PART-NO 12345	WAREHOUSE-ID WEST	DATE 1/2/85	
INVENTORY HISTORY	PART-NO 12345	WAREHOUSE-ID WEST	DATE 7/1/84	
INVENTORY HISTORY	PART-NO 12345	WAREHOUSE-ID WEST	DATE 1/3/84	
INVENTORY HISTORY	PART-NO 12345	WAREHOUSE-ID WEST	DATE 7/1/83	
INVENTORY HISTORY	PART-NO 12345	WAREHOUSE-ID SOUTH	DATE 1/2/85	

FIGURE 11.14a.   Record clustering resulting from first storing a PART record, then all its INVENTORY records, and then all their INVENTORY-HISTORY records.

If INVENTORY-HISTORY were specified to be clustered via the HAS-AR-CHIVED set with INVENTORY, then we could expect to find the PART, INVENTORY, and INVENTORY-HISTORY records stored together. The records' relative locations would be determined by the order of adding them to the database. Figure 11.14a shows the result of storing first a PART record, then its associated INVENTORY records, and then their INVENTORY-HISTORY records. By contrast, Fig. 11.14b shows the result of storing first the PART record, then an INVENTORY record and its INVENTORY-HISTORY records, then another INVENTORY record and its INVENTORY-HISTORY records, and so on. Note the resulting displacement between the PART and INVEN-TORY records.

Clustering parent and child records is not, of course, an option when each record type is stored in its own file.

OVERHEAD

The physical database designer must balance the benefits to be gained by these various opportunities with the costs of carrying their accompanying overhead.

PART	PART-NO 12345			
INVENTORY	PART-NO 12345	WAREHOUSE-ID EAST		
INVENTORY HISTORY	PART-NO 12345	WAREHOUSE-ID EAST	DATE 1/2/85	
INVENTORY HISTORY	PART-NO 12345	WAREHOUSE-ID EAST	DATE 7/1/84	
INVENTORY	PART-NO 12345	WAREHOUSE-ID WEST		
INVENTORY HISTORY	PART-NO 12345	WAREHOUSE-ID WEST	DATE 1/2/85	
INVENTORY HISTORY	PART-NO 12345	WAREHOUSE-ID WEST	DATE 7/1/84	
INVENTORY HISTORY	PART-NO 12345	WAREHOUSE-ID WEST	DATE 1/3/84	
INVENTORY	PART-NO 12345	WAREHOUSE-ID SOUTH		
INVENTORY HISTORY	PART-NO 12345	WAREHOUSE-ID SOUTH	DATE 7/1/83	
INVENTORY HISTORY	PART-NO 12345	WAREHOUSE-ID SOUTH	DATE 1/2/85	

FIGURE 11.14b. Record clustering resulting from first storing a PART record, then an INVENTORY record and its INVENTORY-HISTORY records, then another INVENTORY record and its INVENTORY-HISTORY records, and so on.

For example, consider the options that could be selected for representing one-to-many relationships using linked lists. Each pointer introduced has the benefit of improving the accessibility of one record from another, but each also has the cost of being maintained. When a record is updated, it may be necessary to move it from one parent to another; when a record is deleted, no linkage may be allowed to continue to point to it; and when a record is inserted, all appropriate linkages must be established.

The more pointers there are, the more overhead will be incurred. This is true of pointers used to represent one-to-many parent–child relationships and those used to implement index structures. In general, the addition of pointer linkages improves the efficiency of processing retrieval-only requests, but it reduces the efficiency of processing update requests.

Other design issues that should be addressed are the management of buffers for transferring base records between main memory and secondary storage and the amount of space to be allocated to each file. These issues are the same with a network database management system as in a relational environment (see Chapter 10).

ILLUSTRATIVE NETWORK DATABASE MANAGEMENT SYSTEMS

We shall now introduce two representative network database management systems. One system implements the CODASYL network model, and the other implements the TOTAL network model.

A CODASYL NETWORK APPROACH

The Digital Equipment Corporation (DEC) has implemented CODASYL database management systems for a broad range of computers, including the large DEC System 10, the smaller DEC System 20, and the popular VAX machines. The system profiled in this section is referred to as DBMS (DataBase Management System) and is profiled from the System 10 and 20 offerings. It is similar to the VAX DBMS product and is representative of many of the CODASYL database management systems offered by other vendors.

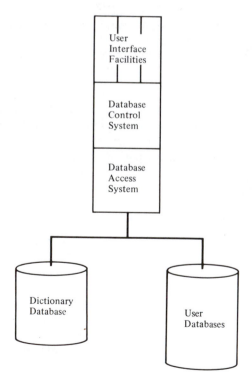

FIGURE 11.15. Architecture of a network database management system.

Architecture

The fundamental architecture of DBMS is shown in Fig. 11.15. Requests, written in programming language´or higher-level end user–oriented languages, are interfaced to the database control system.

A database description is stored in a dictionary file, which describes the database's logical and physical structure. The dictionary file is itself a database managed by the database control system. But rather than containing user data, it contains metadata. As stated early in this book, metadata is data about data.

A portion of a dictionary file's structure is shown in Fig. 11.16. The records in this database describe a user's database. Consider again the schema of Fig. 11.5a, whose metadata are stored in the records shown in Fig. 11.17. There are four record types in the user database; therefore there are four occurrences of the RECORD record in the dictionary. There are also three instances in which a record type has the role of owner record (i.e., three set relationships); therefore there are three occurrences of the OWNER record in the dictionary. Finally there are three instances in which a record type has the role of member record; therefore there are three occurrences of the MEMBER record in the dictionary.

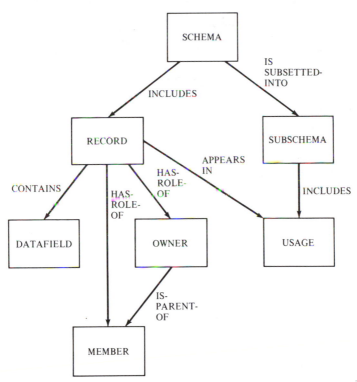

FIGURE 11.16. Sample structure of a dictionary database to support the network model.

RECORD records

RECORD-TYPE

PART	
WAREHOUSE	
INVENTORY	
INVENTORY-HISTORY	

OWNER records

RECORD-TYPE   SET-TYPE

PART	APPEARS-IN	
WAREHOUSE	CONTAINS	
INVENTORY	HAS-ARCHIVED	

MEMBER records

RECORD-TYPE   OWNER-RECORD-TYPE   SET-TYPE

INVENTORY	PART	APPEARS-IN	
INVENTORY	WAREHOUSE	CONTAINS	
INVENTORY-HISTORY	INVENTORY	HAS-ARCHIVED	

FIGURE 11.17. Metadata for the database of Fig. 11.5a, according to the dictionary structure of Fig. 11.16.

File Structure

Like the majority of database management systems that implement the CO-DASYL network model, this system can store occurrences of many different record types in a single file. The database designer can specify which record types are in which file. Recall that System R (a relational database management system) also can store rows from several tables in the same file.

Page Structure

Each data page has three sections: header, body, and line headers (Fig. 11.18). The structure is similar to that used by some relational database management systems, for example, System R and INGRES. (Compare Fig. 11.18 with Figs. 10.11 and 10.13.) The header section of the page contains

• the number of the page.
• the number of the highest line-header number used so far on the page.
• the offset of the first word in which there is no data.

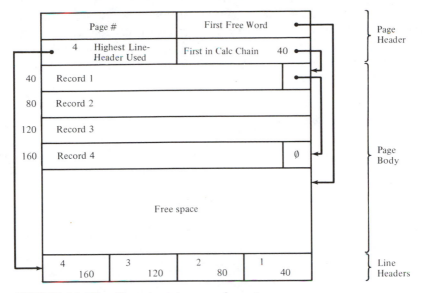

FIGURE 11.18. Sample data-page format.

- a "calc chain header," which is a pointer to the first record that hashed to this page.

The page body contains data records and has occupied space and free space, the latter being for the storage of new records.

Records that hash to the page are chained on the page. In Fig. 11.18, records 1 and 4 are hashed to the page, and records 2 and 3 have been stored on the page by some other technique, for example, to be clustered with record 1. When a data manipulation command results in a hash to the page, the linked list of synonym records is searched sequentially until the desired record is found. The database management system performs the search of the synonym chain; the programmer is not aware of any collisions.

The line headers contain pointers into the page body. There is one completed line header for each record occurrence stored on the page, each line header including

- the type of record it points to.
- the size of the record.
- the word offset on the page of the start of the data record.

Database Keys

Associated with each stored record occurrence is a *database key*, a logical address that is assigned by the database management system when the record is stored. Database keys are convenient means of addressing records but are not intended to be used by applications programmers or end users.

As stated earlier in this chapter, sometimes a physical database designer will access database keys to construct an unusual data structure (e.g., Fig. 11.13).

The database key in this system is a page number and a line-header number, and it points to a line header, which points to the corresponding record in the body of the page.

Set Representation

Like several other database management systems that implement the CODASYL network model, DBMS represents the one-to-many relationships between parent and child record occurrences as linked lists. This database management system always uses at least the basic structure of linking each parent record to the first associated child record in the relationship, then linking each child record to the next child record with the same parent, and finally linking the last child record to the parent (Fig. 11.7).

An example of this representation is

```
SET APPEARS-IN
    MODE IS CHAIN
    OWNER PART
    MEMBER INVENTORY.
```

The database designer can declare use of a bidirectional linked list between children (Fig. 11.8) by

```
SET APPEARS-IN
    MODE IS CHAIN
    OWNER PART
    MEMBER INVENTORY
        LINKED TO PRIOR.
```

Pointers from each child to its parent in the set (Fig. 11.9) can be declared by

```
SET APPEARS-IN
    MODE IS CHAIN
    OWNER PART
    MEMBER INVENTORY
        LINKED TO PRIOR
        LINKED TO OWNER.
```

The PRIOR and OWNER pointers are not interdependent, as either can be used without the other.

Record Structure

Each record occurrence is stored as a contiguous sequence of field values within a single page. There are two types of fields; stored-data fields and set-pointer fields. The *stored-data fields* contain user data, and the *set-pointer fields* are used for the internal representation of relationships between records.

For each set relationship in which the record type participates as an owner (parent), there is one set-pointer field in each occurrence of that record type, containing a pointer to the first member (child) record in that set. Like all other pointers that implement set relationships, the pointer value is a database key, that is, a page number and a line-header number. The pointer value is null for any record occurrence that does not have any associated members in the set. The pointer becomes nonnull when the first member is inserted in the set.

For each set relationship in which the record type participates as a member (child), there is one set-pointer field in each occurrence of that record type for each of the following:

- NEXT member pointer.
- PRIOR member pointer (if declared to be LINKED TO PRIOR).
- OWNER pointer (if declared to be LINKED TO OWNER).

These pointers all are null for any record occurrence that does not participate as a member in the set. The pointers will be made nonnull when (and if) the record is associated with a parent record occurrence and inserted in the set.

For example, consider the schema shown in Fig. 11.5a and the following declarations:

```
SET APPEARS-IN
      MODE CHAIN
      OWNER PART
      MEMBER INVENTORY
            LINKED TO PRIOR
            LINKED TO OWNER.
SET CONTAINS
      MODE CHAIN
      OWNER WAREHOUSE
      MEMBER INVENTORY
            LINKED TO PRIOR.
SET HAS-ARCHIVED
      MODE CHAIN
      OWNER INVENTORY
      MEMBER INVENTORY-HISTORY.
```

The format of the INVENTORY record is shown in Fig. 11.19 and contains a set-pointer field for each of the following purposes:

- NEXT pointer in the APPEARS-IN set.
- PRIOR pointer in the APPEARS-IN set.
- OWNER pointer in the APPEARS-IN set.
- NEXT pointer in the CONTAINS set.
- PRIOR pointer in the CONTAINS set.
- FIRST-MEMBER pointer in the HAS-ARCHIVED set.

INVENTORY RECORD

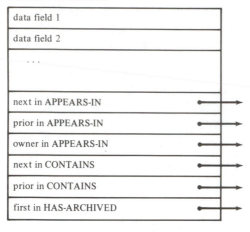

FIGURE 11.19. Sample record format, showing data area and pointer area.

The set-pointer fields are never seen by the end user or the programmer but are used by the database management system to support traversal through the database. The programmer can specify

```
FIND PRIOR INVENTORY IN CONTAINS SET.
```

without knowing whether or not there is a PRIOR set pointer to follow. If there is no PRIOR pointer, the FIND PRIOR statement is serviced by walking the linked list of children to the parent, then to the first child, and eventually to the desired record.

Some other CODASYL network database management systems provide the same set-pointer fields to support every set relationship. Each record occurrence contains a NEXT, PRIOR, and OWNER pointer for each set in which it may participate as a member. Each record occurrence contains a FIRST-MEMBER and LAST-MEMBER pointer for each set in which it may participate as an owner. In these systems, the designer cannot adjust the pointer-storage aspect of the database overhead.

Built-in Fast Access Paths

This database management system supports one type of built-in access path: direct access based on a key attribute's value. The access path is provided by hashing.

If occurrences of the PART record type were hashed by PART-NO value into the database, then the record type could be declared as follows:

```
RECORD TYPE PART
     PLACEMENT IS CALC USING PART-NO.
```

PART would be referred to as a "calc" record.

As stated in our discussion of page structures, the records that hash to a single page are chained together by a linked list. A programmer can say

```
MOVE 12344 TO PART-NO.
FIND PART.
```

and not have to know how the database management system follows the linked list to locate the correct record.

THE TOTAL NETWORK APPROACH

Cincom Systems, Inc., has implemented the TOTAL database management system for a large spectrum of computers. In fact, TOTAL runs on practically every large and small machine! One of the reasons that the database manager has proved to be so portable is its approach to physically implementing the TOTAL network model. A TOTAL database requires minimal file-management support from an operating system, and the kind of support required is found on nearly all computers.

File Structure

TOTAL stores each record type in its own data file. Recall that INGRES (a relational database management system) also stores each table in its own file. A TOTAL database has two types of files, single-entry data files and variable-entry data files.

A *single-entry data file* stores occurrences of one master record type. As seen in Chapter 6, a master record is like a parent (owner) record. A master record type can be the parent in relationships to many variable record types, each of which will be stored in its own variable-entry data file. Each record in a single-entry data file is identified by the value of a control field, known as its *control key*. No duplicate values are allowed for the control key. TOTAL locates a record in a single-entry data file by hashing on the value of its control key, and this hashing supports rapid direct access to master records.

A *variable-entry data file* stores occurrences of one variable record type. In contrast with a master record, a variable record can have many control fields, and there can be duplicate values for any control field in the file. So that the parent of a child can be located, each variable record contains the control key of each of its parents, one per one-to-many relationship. For example, each INVENTORY record of Fig. 11.5b has two control fields; one for the control key of its parent PART record and one for the control key of its parent WAREHOUSE record. A control-key value is used to hash into the parent's single-

PART Master Records

CONTROL KEY

12345	
31826	
21113	

INVENTORY Variable Records

PART CONTROL KEY	WAREHOUSE CONTROL KEY	
31826	WEST	
12345	SOUTH	
12345	EAST	
21113	EAST	
31826	NORTH	
12345	WEST	
42119	EAST	

FIGURE 11.20. Control keys in master and variable records.

entry data file and is not a direct pointer into the single-entry data file. Each control field corresponds to the control key of a master record (Fig. 11.20).

Parent—Child Representation

A variable-entry data file (containing children) is always accessed via a single-entry data file (containing parents). The linkage used is the internal representation of the one-to-many relationship between the corresponding master and

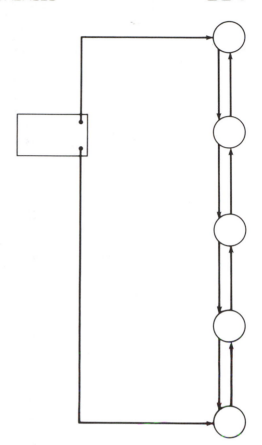

FIGURE 11.21. Linkage paths in a parent–child (master– variable) relationship.

variable record types. A TOTAL record type cannot be both a master (parent) and a variable (child) record.

TOTAL represents one-to-many relationships as linked lists, which are called *linkage paths*. Each parent record points to its first and last children in the relationship, and each child points to the prior and next child with the same parent (Fig. 11.21). With this structure, the files can support finding both all the children for a given parent and the next and prior children from any child in the relationship. Consider the schema shown in Fig. 11.5b and the linkage paths in Fig. 11.22.

Record Structure

As in nearly all systems, each record occurrence is stored as a contiguous sequence of field values. There are two types of fields in master records: stored-data fields and two linkage-path pointer fields per pertinent one-to-many relationship (one to the first variable record and one to the last in the relationship).

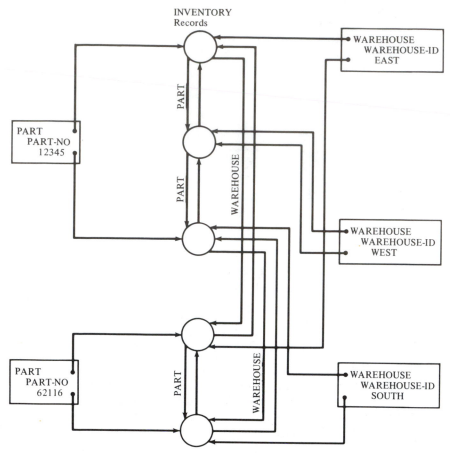

FIGURE 11.22. Some of the linkage paths in the database of Fig. 11.5b.

There are four types of fields in variable records: stored-data fields, format fields, one parent control-key field per pertinent one-to-many relationship, and two linkage-path pointer fields per pertinent one-to-many relationship (one to the prior variable record and one to the next in the relationship). The *stored-data fields* contain user data, and the *linkage-path pointer fields* implement one-to-many relationships. The *parent control-key fields* provide the capability to access the parent record in a one-to-many relationship. The *format fields* in variable records are needed because each variable-entry file may contain variations of the basic record's format, each containing different kinds of stored data.

The formats of the various records are shown in Fig. 11.23.

Each PART master record contains

- its control key.
- pointers to its first and last INVENTORY records.

Master Records

PART

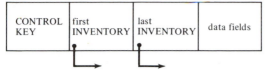

WAREHOUSE

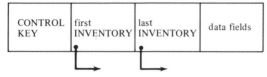

INVENTORY MASTER

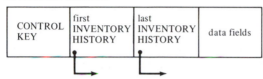

Variable Records

INVENTORY

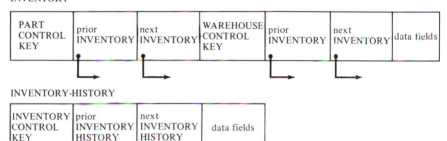

INVENTORY-HISTORY

FIGURE 11.23. Sample formats of TOTAL records.

Each WAREHOUSE master record contains

• its control key.
• pointers to its first and last INVENTORY records.

Each INVENTORY variable record contains

• the control key of its PART parent.
• pointers to the prior and next INVENTORY records with the same PART parent.
• the control key of its WAREHOUSE parent.

- pointers to the prior and next INVENTORY records with the same WARE-HOUSE parent.

Each INVENTORY-MASTER master record contains

- its control key.
- pointers to its first and last INVENTORY-HISTORY records.

Each INVENTORY-HISTORY variable record contains

- the control key of its INVENTORY-MASTER parent.
- pointers to the prior and next INVENTORY-HISTORY records with the same INVENTORY-MASTER parent.

Built-in Fast Access Paths

TOTAL supports one type of built-in access path: direct access based on the value of the control-key field of a master record type. This access path is provided by hashing. There are no built-in fast access paths to variable records, except through the linkage paths from master records.

DISTRIBUTED NETWORK DATABASES

The discussion in Chapter 10 of distributed relational databases also applies to distributed network databases. The data in different record types can be located at different host computers. A given record type can be partitioned so that some of its occurrences reside at one host and some at another. Relationships can occur between records that reside on different machines; and the pointers can include a host identifier as well as the page and line information needed by a given machine.

As with distributed relational databases, the reasons to develop a distributed network database are to tie together existing decentralized databases, to improve the performance of an existing centralized database, or to develop a database to support a decentralized environment.

The most difficult aspect of implementing a distributed database is developing the capability to coordinate data updates and controls across the hosts and data partitions.

CLOSING COMMENTS

There are a variety of approaches to physically implementing network databases. Nearly always, these databases are implemented with the support of a software database management system.

The various available network database management systems all provide basically the same level of data definition, manipulation, and control capabilities. They use well-known data-structuring techniques (linked lists and indexes) to implement the one-to-many relationships characteristic of a network database. They differ, however, in their ''add-on'' facilities to support end-user interfaces through natural languages, report writers, data dictionaries, communications control, and so forth.

TERMS

database key	metadata
file	page
hashing	pointer
horizontal partitioning	port record
index	subschema
information-bearing set	SYSTEM record
join	value-based set
linked list	vertical partitioning

REVIEW EXERCISES

1. Define each of the terms in the preceding list.
2. Draw an occurrence of a set that shows the use of PRIOR, NEXT, and OWNER pointers.
3. Draw an occurrence of a set that is implemented with a data structure that does not use PRIOR or NEXT or OWNER pointers. Explain your data structure.
4. For what kinds of processing is it more efficient to provide LINKED TO PRIOR in the implementation of a set relationship?
5. What should a database designer consider when selecting a data structure to implement a particular set type?
6. Under what circumstances should a database designer select the same kind of data structure to support every set type in a database?
7. For what kinds of processing is it more efficient to provide PLACEMENT IS CALC for a record type?
8. How is a particular record occurrence found if its record type is not declared to have PLACEMENT IS CALC?
9. In many systems the result of hashing a record is a page number, rather than a page number and a line-header number. What kinds of problems are avoided by this approach? Are any new problems encountered?

10. Two approaches for representing set relationships in CODASYL network databases were introduced in the text: linked lists (NEXT pointers, with optional PRIOR and OWNER pointers) and pointer arrays. Propose another approach. Compare the relative advantages and disadvantages of the three approaches.

11. Database management systems appear to need a way to identify record occurrences uniquely, for example, database keys in CODASYL network systems, control keys in TOTAL systems, and tuple ids (TIDs) in relational systems. These identifiers can be implemented as direct pointers or indirect ''pointers'' to occurrences. Compare the relative advantages and disadvantages of the two approaches.

12. Compare the CODASYL and TOTAL approaches to implementing one-to-many relationships.

13. How would a TOTAL database structure differ if a variable record were allowed to be the parent of other variable records?

14. Describe how additional built-in access paths could be implemented in a CODASYL database.

15. Describe how additional built-in access paths could be implemented in a TOTAL database.

16. A bidirectional linked list can be used to support efficient access to the previous child record of a given parent. Write the algorithm for finding the previous child record of a given parent if only basic linked lists with only forward pointers are used instead to represent a one-to-many relationship.

17. Chapter 10 introduced an approach to implementing relational databases that uses one file per domain of values (see the discussion of RDMS). Can this approach also be used to implement a network database? If so, how? If not, why not?

18. Some of the vendors of network database management systems are now also providing the capability for their databases to appear to be relational. Compare the physical data structures (file formats, page formats, record formats, and the like) used to implement the two kinds of database models. Explain what is different and what is similar about the approaches. Can one approach support both kinds of models?

19. You are responsible for designing a new database management system. This system is to support databases that can be viewed by application programmers as CODASYL-like and by end users as relational. Programmers will use a traditional navigational data manipulation language, with operators similar to those introduced in Chapter 6. End users will pose their requests using operators similar to those introduced in Chapter 4. Develop a first-cut design for this new database management system. Discuss the following:
- How is a database to be structured physically?
- How will the navigational operators be supported?
- How will the relational operators be supported?

REFERENCES

BCS/CODASYL DDLC Data Base Administration Working Group. Draft specification of a data storage description language, *CODASYL Journal of Development 1980,* app. A.

Cardenas, A. F. *Data Base Management Systems.* Boston: Allyn & Bacon, 1979.

Loomis, M. E. S. The 78 CODASYL model: A comparison with preceding specifications, *Proceedings ACM SIGMOD International Conference on Management of Data.* Santa Monica, Calif., May 1980; and New York: ACM, 1980, pp. 30–44.

Physical Design of Hierarchical Databases

The implementation of hierarchical databases is introduced by comparing several approaches to storing records and parent–child relationships. As in the preceding chapters, this chapter uses real systems as the basis for the alternatives, without all the details of those real systems. Rather, the intention is to show how the approaches relate to one another and what their implications are for physical database design.

All hierarchical database management systems support a specific approach to implementing the hierarchical model, usually an approach related to one of the schemes outlined in this chapter. The scheme used determines the questions that the physical database designer addresses and the performance characteristics that the implemented system will have with various types of data manipulation activity.

As was emphasized in preceding chapters, it is important to distinguish between logical and physical database designs. The effectiveness of a hierarchical model should not be altered by the database's physical implementation, and the user's view of the hierarchical database should not be affected by which physical structuring technique is used. As with relational and network databases, however, different physical designs of a hierarchical database can deliver quite different performance characteristics.

BASIC REQUIREMENTS OF A PHYSICAL HIERARCHICAL DATABASE

The three requirements for the physical implementation of the hierarchical model are that it must

1. Represent the one-to-many relationships of parent and child record types.
2. Be accessible through the root (top) record of a logical hierarchy of records.
3. Be able to support the basic traversal operators through the hierarchy of parent–child relationships.

Representation of Parent–Child Relationships

A variety of physical data structures can be used to implement the one-to-many relationships between parent and child record types. Because hierarchies are special cases of networks, any of the physical data structures used to represent parent–child relationships in a network database can also be used to represent parent–child relationships in a hierarchical database.

The two basic structures introduced in Chapter 11 were a linked list from each parent record to its set of children records and an index in each parent record, referencing the set of children records. Regardless of which underlying physical data structure is used, it should be possible to locate a parent record and its associated children. Note that this requirement is less stringent than the similar requirement of a network database management system, in which it must be possible to locate a child record and then to find its parent. In implementations of the hierarchical model, only top-down access is required in a hierarchy.

Accessibility to Root

Whatever the physical data structure used to implement parent–child relationships, each hierarchy in the database (or set of databases, to use the IMS scope for *database*) must be accessible by its top-most record. As in a network database, a record that can be accessed directly is called a *port* record.

Each port of a hierarchy has a uniquely identifying set of key attributes, whose values are used to determine which particular record occurrence (and therefore hierarchy occurrence) is requested by a user. This requirement is more specific than the similar requirement of a network database management system, in which it must be possible to access various record types by their key attributes. In implementations of the hierarchical model, these record types are at the tops of the hierarchies.

Support of Basic Traversal Operators

The physical data structure must be able to support the basic operators that traverse through the parent–child relationships. These supported operators should include

- selecting a particular record occurrence.
- selecting a record occurrence that has a specified relationship to the last record selected.
- deleting a record occurrence.
- modifying a record occurrence.
- inserting a record occurrence.

The specified relationship between designated record occurrences can be that

- they are of the same record type.
- one is the parent and one the child in a one-to-many relationship.
- they both are children of the same parent in a one-to-many relationship.

These requirements are the same as the requirements for a physical data structure to support the network model. A relational database management system must be able to construct a table as a result of an operation on a table, and it must support access to a set of record rows in a single operation. By contrast, both hierarchical and network database management systems need only support record-at-a-time access.

BASIC LOGICAL-TO-PHYSICAL TRANSFORMATIONS

The design issues in mapping the record types of a hierarchical data model to the record types in a physical database structure are basically the same as for designing network or relational databases.

A straightforward logical-to-physical transformation is to implement each logical record type (called a *logical segment* in IMS) of a hierarchical model as a single base record type (called a *physical segment* in IMS). To improve the system's performance, the physical database designer must determine whether any of the following logical-to-physical transformations may be more appropriate:

- Vertical partitioning: splitting a logical record type into multiple base record types, with some of the data fields in one base record and some in another (Fig. 11.1). A variation of this transformation is not to represent physically some of the data fields of the logical record type.
- Horizontal partitioning: splitting a logical record type into multiple base record types, with some of the record occurrences in one base record type and some in another (Fig. 11.2).

- Joining: combining a logical record type with one or more other record types into a single base record type. (Fig. 11.3).

These transformations result in base record types that do not correspond exactly to the starting logical record types. These transformations are also exactly the same as those in Chapter 11 for the network model. The reasons for their use and applicability are essentially the same.

As in the network model, a variation of vertical partitioning is not to represent physically fields whose values are implied by parent–child relationships. These fields are foreign-key data fields. Figure 12.1 shows a data model, a corresponding IMS hierarchical logical database structure, and a corresponding physical database structure. The foreign-key attribute DIV-CODE has been removed from the DEPT physical record type.

In IMS, each physical record includes certain control fields, one of which is the record's hierarchical-sequence key. Recall from Chapter 7 that the hierarchical-sequence key of a record (segment) is a code identifying the type of record and a identifying sequence-key value, prefixed by the hierarchical-sequence-key value for its parent. In effect, the foreign-key attributes are embedded in the hierarchical-sequence key. Deciding not to represent foreign-keys physically as user data fields does not affect the database management system's ability to determine foreign-key values using control fields.

User Views

As in the design of relational and network databases, regardless of the logical-to-physical transformations used, the user and programmer should be able to access the hierarchical database without knowing its physical structure. This capability is offered in IMS environments by the separation of logical records from physical records. For example, a logical record can be defined to partition vertically the records of a physical database.

IMPROVING PERFORMANCE

Each of these transformations between logical record types and base record types is done to improve efficiency by reducing the volumes of data transferred to or from secondary storage.

There are other decisions in developing an efficient physical structure for a database to support the hierarchical model:

- Parent–child representation: What data structures should be used to represent the one-to-many relationships between parent and children record occurrences?
- Attribute access: Which attributes should have built-in fast access paths?
- Clustering of physical records: Which record occurrences should be stored together?

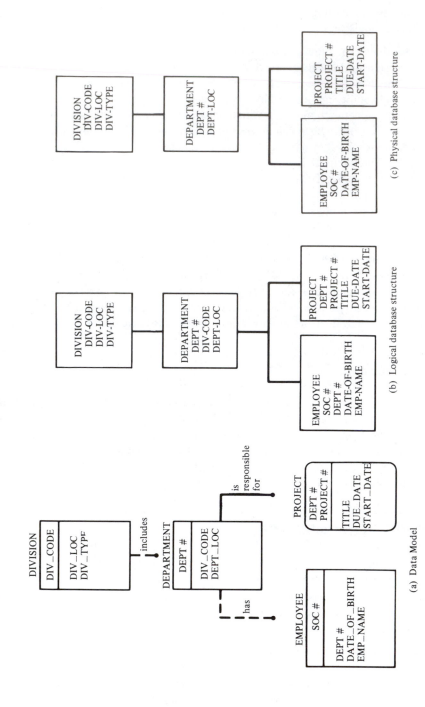

(a) Data Model

(b) Logical database structure

(c) Physical database structure

FIGURE 12.1. Hierarchies.

- Buffers: How large should the buffer spaces be for transferring base record occurrences between main memory and secondary storage?

These decisions are the same as those in Chapter 11 for improving the performance of a network database. The following is a summary of the points made in Chapter 11:

- The one-to-many relationships between parent and child record occurrences are implemented using either linked lists or indexes. Linked lists can consist of pointers from the parent to the first child, from each child to next child, from each child to prior child, and from each child to parent. Indexes can be arrays or trees of pointers from the parent to the set of children.
- Built-in fast access paths are implemented using either hashing on one attribute group in a record type or indexing on one or more attribute groups in a record type. Hashing supports direct access to record occurrences by transforming the values of a group of the record's attributes to storage addresses. Indexing supports indirect access to record occurrences by access to an array or tree of pointers structured according to the values of pertinent attribute groups.
- Record clustering can place together records of the same type on the same page or can be based on one-to-many parent–child relationships. In the latter case, each child record occurrence is stored as close as possible to its parent in the relationship.
- Buffer-size adjustments can improve the database system's performance. The number of buffers should be large enough to keep in main memory the working set of records used in servicing a user's request. This working-set size can vary, depending on characteristics of the data manipulation patterns.

ILLUSTRATIVE HIERARCHICAL DATABASE MANAGEMENT SYSTEMS

We shall now introduce two representative hierarchical database management systems, to explain the possible approaches to physical structures for implementing the hierarchical model and to compare physical structures to implement the hierarchical, network, and relational models. The two systems used here are IMS and System 2000.

IMS HIERARCHICAL APPROACH

The IMS family of database management systems was introduced in Chapter 7. These products from IBM were introduced in the 1960s and evolved through the 1970s. They today are among the most firmly entrenched of all software products, as thousands of companies rely on IMS and/or DL/I support to manage their production databases.

Architecture

The fundamental architecture of IMS is shown in Fig. 12.2. Requests to be processed by IMS are written in a nonprocedural language or are embedded in a program written in COBOL, PL/I, or assembler language. The program communicates with IMS through an Input/Output Area, which is a portion of main memory used to transfer data between the program and the accessed databases.

The program uses a Program Specification Block (PSB) to describe the segments of the databases that it accesses. As stated in Chapter 7, a PSB is formed from one or more Program Communication Blocks (PCBs), each of which corresponds to a logical database. A logical database is described by a Logical Database Definition (LDBD) and may map to one or more physical databases, each of which is described by a Physical Database Description (PDBD).

The dictionary that describes IMS logical and physical databases is the set of all PSBs and LDBDs (which describe external schemas) and PDBDs (which describe internal schemas). The IMS Control Program is responsible for mapping data to and from these various definitions. Another program product from IBM,

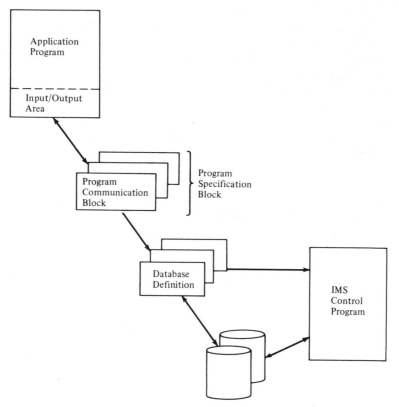

FIGURE 12.2. IMS-Application program communication architecture.

the DB/DC Data Dictionary, also provides dictionary services for IMS database environments.

File Structure

Each physical database is implemented as a separate file, which is referred to in IBM terminology as a *dataset*. A physical database can include several different base record types. Note that this is similar to the approach used by most of the CODASYL network database management systems but is different from the single-record-type-per-file approach used by the TOTAL network database management system. A particular access method is specified for each physical database, which determines the technique used to represent parent–child relationships and the technique used to provide access to hierarchies.

Parent–Child Representation

IMS represents the one-to-many relationships between parent and children records in a hierarchy using one of three techniques: (1) physical contiguity of the records in hierarchical sequence, (2) linked lists of the records in hierarchical

DEPT
DEPTCODE = 'GEOLOGY' ...
BUDGET
MO = 11 ...
BUDGET
MO = 12 ...
EMP
EMP # = 12751 ...
TASK
TASK # = 49 ...
TASK
TASK # = 75 ...
EMP
EMP # = 21346 ...
TASK
TASK # = 49 ...
TASK
TASK # = 56 ...
TASK
TASK # = 72 ...
DEPT
DEPTCODE = 'MIS' ...

FIGURE 12.3. Same physical ordering as hierarchical sequence.

sequence, and (3) linked lists of the records in child/twin sequence. The database designer selects one of these modes of representation for each physical database.

As stated in Chapter 11, each record occurrence in a hierarchy has a unique hierarchical-sequence-key value that is composed of a code identifying its segment-type code and its sequence-field value, prefixed by the hierarchical-sequence-key value for its parent. The hierarchical sequence for a database is its record occurrences, ordered by the ascending values of their hierarchical-sequence keys. The net effect of hierarchical sequence is to arrange a database's record occurrences in top-down, left-right order.

Consider the hierarchical structure shown in Fig. 7.4, which has four base record types: DEPT, BUDGET, EMP, and TASK. DEPT is the parent of BUDGET and EMP, and EMP is the parent of TASK. Figure 12.3 shows the use of physical contiguity to represent the parent–child relationships. The database's records are simply laid out in physically sequential order. Each record is preceded by the record that comes before it in the hierarchical sequence; and each record is followed by the record that comes after it in the hierarchical sequence. There are no pointer linkages between the records.

By contrast, Fig. 12.4 shows a linked list representing the parent–child re-

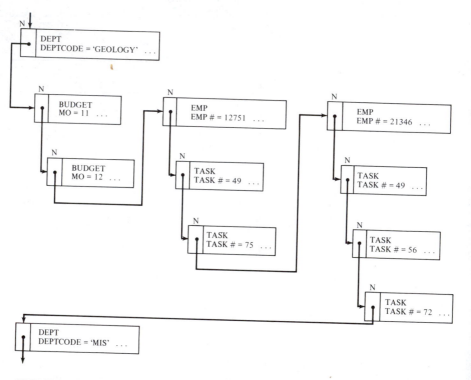

FIGURE 12.4. Hierarchical forward pointers representing parent – child relationships.

lationships of Fig. 7.4. Each record has a pointer to the next record in the hierarchical sequence. A DEPT record points to the first of its child BUDGET records, and this BUDGET record points to the next BUDGET record with the same DEPT parent. The last BUDGET record for this DEPT parent points to the first EMP record for this DEPT, and that EMP record points to the first TASK record for this EMP. That TASK record points to the next TASK record with the same EMP parent. The last TASK record for this EMP points to the next EMP record in the hierarchical sequence, which points to its first TASK record, and so forth. The last TASK record for the last EMP for this DEPT has a null pointer, because there is no next record in the hierarchical sequence for this DEPT's hierarchy of dependent records. An overhead cost of one pointer per record is incurred.

Figure 12.5 shows a modification of the linked-list structure of Fig. 12.4. Here a bidirectional linked list joins the records in hierarchical sequence. The pointers are referred to as *hierarchical forward and backward pointers*. The backward pointers make deletion and insertion of records into the hierarchical sequence more efficient but necessitate the cost of two pointers per record.

The other approach to representing parent–child relationships by linked lists is illustrated in Fig. 12.6. Each record has a pointer to both its first child in the hierarchy and its sibling in the hierarchy. These pointers are referred to as *physical child and physical twin pointers*. The DEPT record points to the first of its child BUDGET records, to the first of its child EMP records, and to the

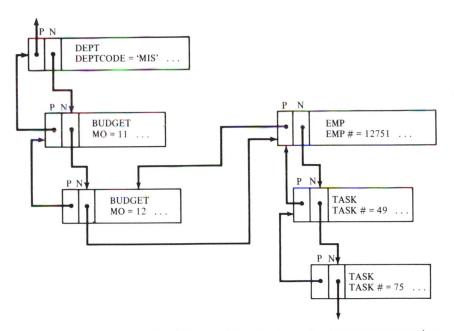

FIGURE 12.5. Hierarchical forward and backward pointers representing parent — child relationships.

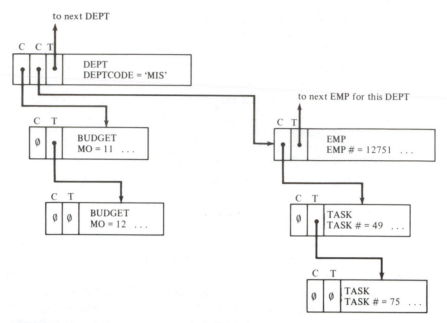

FIGURE 12.6. Physical child and physical twin pointers representing parent—child relationships.

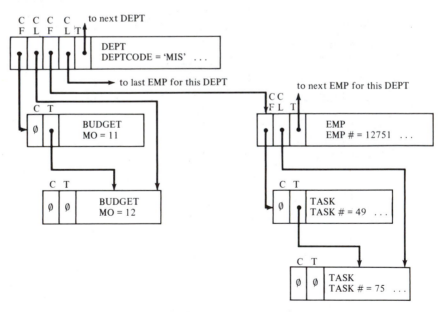

FIGURE 12.7. Physical child first, physical child last, and physical twin pointers representing parent—child relationships.

next DEPT record in the database. The DEPT record is called the *physical parent* of the BUDGET record and the EMP record, which are called its *physical children*. The two DEPT records are called *physical twins*.

Each BUDGET record has a pointer to the next BUDGET record for the same parent, that is, to its physical twin in the hierarchical sequence. The last BUDGET record for this DEPT record has a null physical twin pointer, as there is no next BUDGET for the same parent. Each BUDGET record also has a null physical child pointer, because BUDGET had no dependents in the hierarchy.

Each EMP record has a physical child pointer to the first of its dependent TASK records and a physical twin pointer to the next EMP for the same DEPT parent record. Each TASK record has a null physical child pointer and a physical twin pointer to the next TASK for that same parent EMP.

Figure 12.7 illustrates the option of having each physical parent point to both its first and last physical child. Figure 12.8 modifies this structure by having

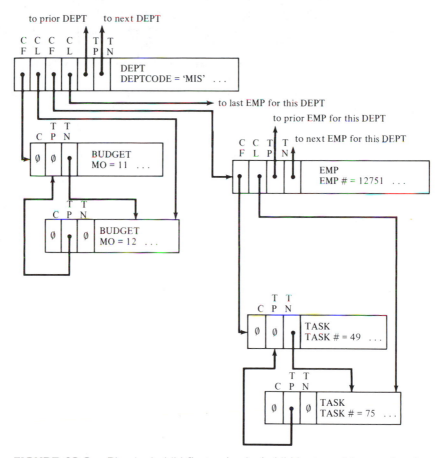

FIGURE 12.8. Physical child first, physical child last, and forward and backward physical twin pointers representing parent–child relationships.

both forward and backward physical twin pointers. These options add to the overhead carried in the database, though they streamline some retrieval and update operations.

Hierarchy Access

IMS provides access to hierarchy occurrences in a database by using (1) physically contiguous storage of hierarchies, (2) indexed access to the root record of each hierarchy, and (3) hashed access to the root record of each hierarchy. The technique used is determined by the access method used with the database.

Physically contiguous storage directly appends the records for one hierarchy to the records for the hierarchy preceding it in the hierarchical sequence. This mode of representation is provided by the Hierarchical Sequential Access Method (HSAM). HSAM is suitable for storing a database on magnetic tape or on a direct-access storage device, and it is commonly used to provide backup or archive copies of a database. Figure 12.9 illustrates the physically contiguous storage of example hierarchies.

Indexed and hashed access to hierarchies' root records support direct entry into a particular hierarchy of the database, given the value of the sequence field of the desired hierarchy's root record. Indexed access is supported by an indexed sequential data structure. The database is stored as three (and sometimes four) files. One file contains the hierarchies' data records and may be structured with either hierarchical pointers or physical child and twin pointers. The other files contain an index into the data file which in turn contains the root sequence values organized into a tree structure. This index may have an overflow-area file, one root-index file, and one primary-area index file, and it should provide rapid access to a particular hierarchy in the data file. Figure 12.10 shows a structure that supports indexed access to a hierarchical database.

By contrast, hashed access is supported by hashing on root-sequence values to find the storage location of the corresponding root records. There is no auxiliary index structure on the root-sequence values. The database is stored as one

DEPT DEPTCODE = 'MIS' ...	BUDGET MO = 11 ...	BUDGET MO = 12 ...
EMP EMP # = 12751		TASK TASK # = 49 ...
TASK TASK # = 75 ...	EMP EMP # = 21346 ...	
TASK TASK # = 36 ...	DEPT DEPTCODE = 'NAT'	BUDGET MO = 7
EMP EMP # = 00013 ...		TASK TASK # = 49

FIGURE 12.9. Physically contiguous storage of hierarchies.

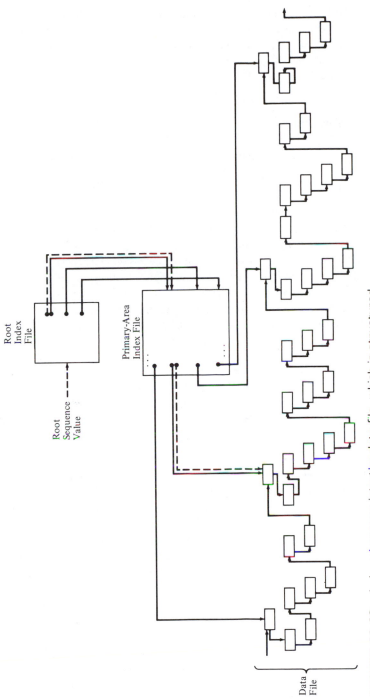

FIGURE 12.10. Indexed access into the data file, which is structured with hierarchical sequence pointers.

file, which has an addressable area and an overflow area. *Synonyms* (roots that hash to the same location and collide) are chained together in a linked list. Figure 12.11 illustrates a structure that supports hashed access to a hierarchical database and should provide rapid access to a particular hierarchy in the data file, without an auxiliary index structure.

Access Methods

There are four access methods used with IMS databases, and the one used determines the techniques to represent the database physically. The four access methods can be summarized as follows:

- Hierarchical Sequential Access Method (HSAM).
  - Physically contiguous parent–child representation.
  - Physically contiguous hierarchies.
- Hierarchical Indexed Sequential Access Method (HISAM).
  - Physically contiguous parent–child representation.
  - Indexed access to root records.
- Hierarchical Indexed Direct Access Method (HIDAM).
  - Linked-list parent–child representation.
    - Hierarchical sequence pointers.
    - Physical child and twin pointers.
  - Indexed access to root records.
- Hierarchical Direct Access Method (HDAM).
  - Linked-list parent–child representation.
    - Hierarchical sequence pointers.
    - Physical child and twin pointers.
  - Hashed access to root records.

In an HSAM database, all records and hierarchies are related by their physical adjacency. The database can be stored on a sequential-storage device and can be accessed for retrieval by reading sequentially through the records until the desired data are located. The database can be updated by rewriting it, making desired changes as the reload proceeds.

In a HISAM database, records in a hierarchy are related by their physical adjacency. Indexed access to the root records, and therefore into the hierarchies, is provided. The database must be stored on a direct-access storage device and can be accessed for retrieval by specifying a root record's sequence-field value and then reading sequentially through the dependent records until the desired data are located. The database can be updated in place to an extent.

In a HIDAM database, records in a hierarchy are related by hierarchical pointers and/or physical child and twin pointers. Indexed access to the root records, and therefore into the hierarchies, is provided. The database must be stored on a direct-access storage device and can be accessed for retrieval by specifying a root record's sequence-field value and then following either the

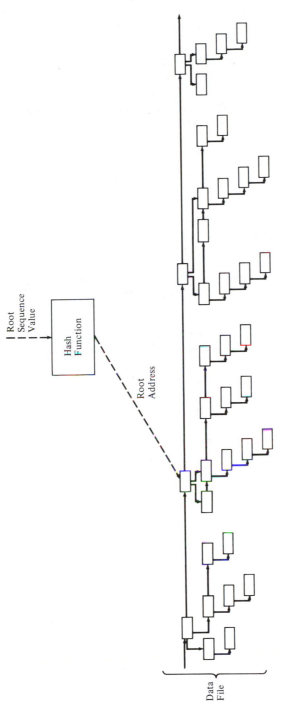

FIGURE 12.11. Hashed access into the data file, which is structured with physical child and physical twin pointers.

hierarchical pointers or the physical child and twin pointers through the dependent records until the desired data are located. The database can be updated in place.

In an HDAM database, records in a hierarchy are related by hierarchical pointers and/or physical child and twin pointers. Direct access to root records is supported by hashing the root's sequence-field value. The database must be stored on a direct-access storage device and is accessed for retrieval and update in the same way that a HIDAM database is, except that access to the root record is direct rather than through an index.

Record Structure

Each record occurrence is stored as a contiguous sequence of field values. There are two types of fields, stored-data fields and prefix fields. The stored-data fields contain user data, and the prefix fields include

- a segment code, indicating the type of the record.
- a delete byte, indicating the record's deletion status.
- pointer and counter area.

A *segment code* is a number used internally to identify a record type, in place of the record name. A segment code typically occupies less space than does the corresponding record name.

A *delete byte* indicates a variety of status information about the corresponding record. For example, it indicates whether the record has been deleted from the database, from a physical path, and from a logical path.

The *pointer and counter area* contains various overhead fields, which include any hierarchical and/or physical child and twin pointers and the hierarchical-sequence-field value for the record.

Attribute Access

Secondary index structures can be used to establish alternative entries into IMS databases. These entries use attribute values other than the sequence-field value of a root record.

An index can be specified on any data field of a root or dependent record type. The field need not have unique values across the occurrences of the record type. The index contains one pointer record for each target data record, and the pointer record contains the indexed field value and a pointer to the target data record.

Accessing the pointer records in an index sequentially and following their pointers into the data records result in a sequential ordering of those data records. That ordering is called a *secondary processing sequence,* in which the sequence corresponds to the hierarchical sequence for an alternative hierarchy of the records.

In this data structure, the target data record is considered to be a root record, even if it is not a root record in the physical database.

Secondary index structures thus can provide direct access to a database on fields other than the sequence-field value of the root record, and they also can be used to impose alternative hierarchical structures on a physical hierarchy of records.

SYSTEM 2000 HIERARCHICAL APPROACH

The System 2000 database management system was introduced briefly at the end of Chapter 7. It supports the hierarchical data model, with significant flexibility in its built-in fast access paths. Our discussion here of System 2000 addresses its physical data structure, in contrast with the approach used by IMS.

File Structure

A System 2000 database consists of the six following files (Fig. 12.12):

- Directory: contains names of data fields and pointers into the Unique Values Table.
- Unique Values Table: contains one entry per unique value of each key field, and pointers into the Multiple Occurrence Table and the Hierarchic Structure Table.
- Multiple Occurrence Table: contains one entry per replicated value of each key field, and pointers into the Hierarchic Structure Table.
- Hierarchic Structure Table: contains one entry per data record, with its parent–child relationship information.
- Data Table: contains data in fixed-length records.
- Overflow Table: contains expansions of data-field names and long data strings.

These files together represent parent–child relationships and provide built-in fast access paths on key fields.

Parent–Child Representation

The Data Table contains one entry for each user-data record, and the Hierarchic Structure Table (HST) has a corresponding entry which contains a pointer to each of the following (Fig. 12.13):

- the user-data record in the Data Table.
- the HST record for the parent of the user-data record.
- the HST record for the first child of the user-data record.
- the HST record for the sibling of the user-data record.

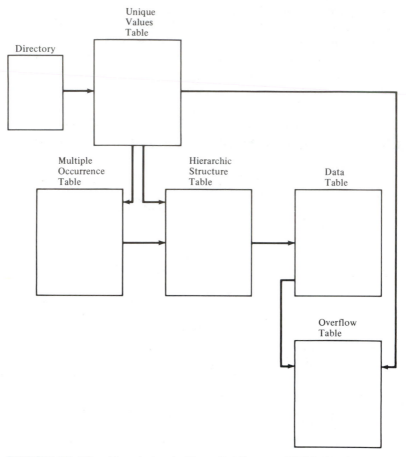

FIGURE 12.12. The six basic files of a System 2000 database.

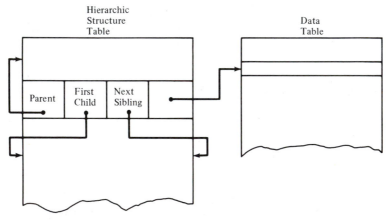

FIGURE 12.13. System 2000 Hierarchic Structure Table.

This structure is similar to that of the physical child and twin pointers of IMS, except that in System 2000 each record has a pointer to its parent and in System 2000 sibling rather than twin pointers are used. Siblings are record occurrences with the same parent, but they need not be of the same record type. Twins are record occurrences of the same type with the same parent.

Record Structure

Each record occurrence is stored in the Data Table as a contiguous sequence of field values, with pointers to the Overflow Table for string values that exceed a specified length. All characters up to that specified length are stored in the Data Table; the rest of the field is stored in the Overflow Table. Figure 12.14 shows a sample record layout.

Built-in Fast Access Paths

System 2000 supports one type of built-in fast access path: indexed access based on the value of any field specified by the database designer as a key field. Note that a key field is one through which the database designer wants to provide direct-access capability. Key fields need not have unique values.

The index structure is a combination of the Directory, the Unique Value Table, the Multiple Occurrence Table, and the Hierarchic Structure Table. The Directory is an index to the Unique Value Table (UVT).

Each entry in the Directory is a ⟨key-field name, UVT page number, data value⟩ triple. The data value is the highest data value to be found on the specified UVT page, which is part of the index for the named key field.

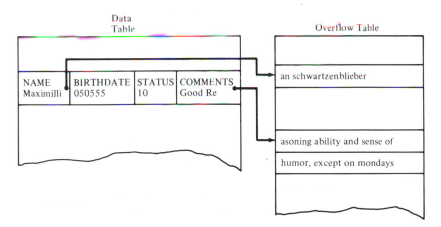

FIGURE 12.14. Example of use of Overflow Table records pointed to by Data Table record.

The Unique Value Table contains one entry for each unique value of each key field in the database. These entries are ordered sequentially. The Directory and UVT together are similar in many respects to an indexed sequential file. If the key-field values in the UVT were not sorted, then the Directory entries would not suffice for finding entries in the UVT.

The entry in the UVT is a ⟨key-field data value, table type, page number, line number⟩ quartet. If the key-field data value appears only in one record occurrence in the Data Table, then the UVT entry will point to a page and line in the Hierarchic Structure Table that is the location of the record pointing to that user-data record occurrence in the Data Table (Fig. 12.15).

If the key-field data value appears in many record occurrences in the Data Table, then the UVT entry will point to a page and line in the Multiple Occurrence Table (MOT). This MOT entry then has a pointer to each of the corresponding HST entries pointing to the Data Table entries for those record occurrences (Fig. 12.16).

To find a user-data record with a particular key-field value, for example, with CITY-NAME = 'Tucson,' the database management system executes the following steps:

1. Look in the Directory to determine whether CITY-NAME is a key field. If not, search the Data Table sequentially. If so, proceed to Step 2.
2. Find the entry in the Directory for the key-field CITY-NAME with the first data value greater than or equal to 'Tucson.' Follow its pointer a page in the Unique Values Table.
3. Find the entry on the Unique Values Table page for the value of 'Tucson.' Follow its pointer to either the Multiple Occurrence Table or the Hierarchic Structure Table.
4. If the pointer went to the Multiple Occurrence Table, then follow each of the pointers found there into the Hierarchic Structure Table. Execute Steps 5 and 6 for each of those entries in the Hierarchic Structure Table.
5. Follow the pointer into the Data Table from the entry in the Hierarchic Structure Table.
6. Access the other data fields for the record stored in the Data Table.

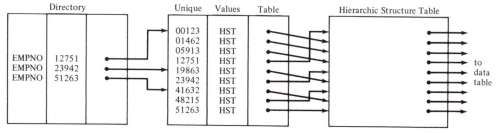

FIGURE 12.15 Structure used for attribute access: Directory + Unique Values Table + Hierarchic Structure Table + Data Table.

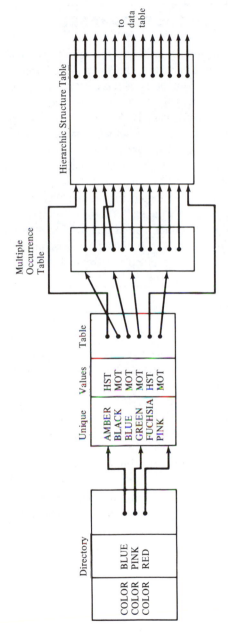

FIGURE 12.16. Structure used for attribute access: Directory + Unique Values Table + Multiple Occurrence Table + Hierarchic Structure Table + Data Table.

This processing retrieves data records based on key-field values with quite good performance. By contrast, updating key-field values can be relatively slow.

DISTRIBUTED HIERARCHICAL DATABASES

The discussion in Chapter 10 on distributed relational databases also applies to distributed hierarchical databases. The data in different record types can be located at different host computers. A given record type can be partitioned so that some of its occurrences reside at one host and some at another. A given physical hierarchy of records usually does not cross machine boundaries.

As with distributed relational and network databases, the reasons to develop a distributed hierarchical database are to tie together existing hierarchical databases, to improve the performance of an existing centralized database, or to develop a database to support a decentralized environment.

Nearly all the work in distributed hierarchical databases involves adding a relational layer on top of those databases. Users' requests for data are expressed as a global relational view, rather than as hierarchies. One result of the relatively recent marriage of relational capabilities to hierarchical databases may be to better manage and process distributed hierarchical databases.

CLOSING COMMENTS

This chapter discussed several approaches to physically implementing hierarchical databases. Some database management systems, such as IMS, support more than one approach. Other database management systems, such as System 2000, support just one approach.

The hierarchical database management systems have enjoyed many years of heavy-duty production usage. They offer very good performance for the kinds of activity that their databases were designed to support, but relatively poorer performance for unanticipated kinds of activity.

Hierarchical databases have been important data-processing assets since the late 1960s, although the prognosis is that the hierarchical database management systems have begun to die. For example, IBM is offering many relational accompaniments to IMS that may replace IMS in both decision-support and production environments.

TERMS

dependent segment	hierarchical sequence
file	hierarchical-sequence-key value
fully concatenated key	horizontal partitioning
hashing	index
hierarchical path	join

linked list	physical twin
logical database	physical twin pointer
logical database definition (LDBD)	pointer
logical database record	port record
page	program communication block
physical child	(PCB)
physical child pointer	program specification block (PSB)
physical database	root
physical database definition (PDBD)	sibling
physical database record	twin
physical parent	vertical partitioning

REVIEW EXERCISES

1. Define each of the terms in the preceding list.

2. What kinds of access to an IMS database are made more efficient by using both forward and backward hierarchical pointers instead of just forward hierarchical pointers? Are any kinds of access made less efficient?

3. What kinds of access to an IMS database are made more efficient by using both first and last physical child pointers instead of just first physical child pointers? Are any kinds of access made less efficient?

4. What kinds of access to an IMS database are made more efficient by using both forward and backward physical twin pointers instead of just forward twin pointers? Are any kinds of access made less efficient?

5. What kinds of access to an IMS database are made more efficient by using a physical hierarchical sequence to structure the database? Are any kinds of access made less efficient?

6. What kinds of access to an IMS database would suggest structuring the database using a physical hierarchical sequence?

7. What kinds of access to an IMS database would suggest structuring the database using hierarchical pointers?

8. What kinds of access to an IMS database would suggest structuring the database using physical child and twin pointers?

9. Compare the physical data structures representing a TOTAL database with those representing an IMS database.

10. Compare the physical data structures representing a CODASYL database with those representing an IMS database.

11. Compare the four basic access methods used to structure IMS databases. What kinds of retrieval and update patterns would suggest using each one?

12. What characteristics of the IMS and System 2000 data structures restrict them to representing hierarchies but not networks? How would you modify the IMS and System 2000 data structures to enable them to represent networks as well as hierarchies?

13. Compare the physical data structures used in IMS with those used in System 2000. How are they similar? How are they different?

14. Describe the processing steps required when a key-field value is changed in a System 2000 database.

15. You are responsible for designing a new database management system. This system supports databases that can be viewed by application programmers as IMS-like and by end users as relational. Programmers will use a traditional IMS-like navigational data manipulation language, with operators similar to those introduced in Chapter 7. Develop a first-cut design for this new database management system. How should a database be structured physically? How will the navigational operators be supported? How will the relational operators be supported?

16. Compare the data structures supporting hierarchical databases with those supporting network and relational databases. How are they similar? How are they different?

REFERENCES

Cardenas, A. F. *Data Base Management Systems*. Boston: Allyn & Bacon, 1979.
Inmon, W. H. *Effective Data Base Design*. Englewood Cliffs, N.J.: Prentice-Hall, 1981.
International Business Machines, Inc. *Information Management System Virtual Storage (IMS/VS) System/Application Design Guide,* Chapter 5, *Data Base Design Considerations,* SH20-9025.

DATABASE ADMINISTRATION AND PROTECTION

Part III consists of two chapters on the principles of database administration and protection. Chapter 13 introduces data dictionary/directory systems, which can improve data resource management and administration efforts. It discusses a framework for analyzing data dictionary/directory functions and configuration in database environments and then relates the commercially available product offerings to this framework.

Chapter 14 introduces the problems of protecting databases against various types of failure, potential conflicts from shared access, and security violations. It describes techniques for solving these problems and outlines the kinds of pertinent support that commercially available database management systems provide.

The focus of these chapters is on principles and techniques that are the foundation for the database administration and protection capabilities of today's and tomorrow's database management systems. The emphasis is on implications for database design, rather than on the design of database management systems themselves. The book closes with a brief chapter about trends in database management.

Data Dictionary/ Directory Systems

One of the most important tools for protecting and administering data resources is a data dictionary/directory system. Data dictionary/directory systems have a variety of names, such as *dictionary/directories*, *dictionaries*, and *directories*. Here they will be referred to generically as *data dictionary/directory systems* or, simply, *D/D systems*.

This chapter discusses the principal functions of a D/D system and the kinds of data that it contains. The chapter also introduces D/D system configurations and the possible range of interdependence between a D/D system and a database management system. It describes the roles of D/D systems in centralized and distributed database environments, in transferring from a process-driven orientation to a data-driven orientation and in supporting transaction processing and database-related design activities. These possibilities then are compared with the kind of support that today's commercially available D/D systems provide.

OBJECTIVES

A data dictionary/directory system is used to control access to data resources, to control the costs of developing and maintaining databases and software, and to prevent adverse effects from hardware and software changes. Commercially available D/D systems have been more or less successful, depending on their configurations and capabilities.

The heart of a D/D system is itself a database, called the *dictionary/directory* or simply, the *D/D*. This database contains *metadata,* which were mentioned in Chapter 2 as data that describe data. *Meta* is a Greek prefix that translates roughly into "behind," "after," or "along with." Thus metadata are the data behind the data, that is, the data that describe the data.

Scope

The useful scope of metadata extends beyond the programming-language description of fields to describe the users who can access the data (in order to control access to the data), the processes that manipulate the data (to control the quality of the data), and the hardware and software environment (to react to changes in that environment).

Users

At least six types of users can benefit directly from a D/D system:

- Data administrators, who use the D/D system to inventory the data resource, implement standards, design external schemas (user views), and build data models that evolve into the conceptual schema.
- Database administrators, who use the D/D system as an information source for designing, monitoring, and tuning physical database structures.
- Systems analysts and programmers, who use the D/D system to design the systems, to analyze system changes, and to reduce program coding.
- Operations staff, who retrieve information about jobs from the D/D.
- End users, who obtain from the D/D descriptions of the data about their external schemas.
- Data auditors, who examine the documentation provided by the D/D system.

Not all of these types of users actually benefit from D/D support in all enterprises. Often, the D/D is not available outside the data-processing function or cannot support the needs of this broad range of potential users. But part of data management is using tools like the D/D system to their full potential.

CONTENTS

The D/D database can contain metadata about the full range of data resources in an enterprise. A D/D's logical structure can be represented using entities, attributes, and relationships; any of the data-modeling techniques discussed in

Chapter 3 can be used. If the D/D system is closely aligned with a particular DBMS, then the D/D structure is most likely to be represented using the DBMS's "natural" data model. For example, Cullinet's Integrated Data Dictionary (IDD) structure is depicted as an IDMS (CODASYL) schema and Relational Technology's INGRES data dictionary structure is depicted as INGRES (relational) tables.

A typical D/D has the logical structure shown in Fig. 13.1. The entities in this model describe:

- Physical database structures: databases, subschemas, files.
- File structures: files, records, groups, fields.
- Activity: transactions, reports.
- Users.
- Equipment: processors, lines, terminals.
- Programs.

Figure 13.1 shows only a minimal set of relationships among these entities. Some D/Ds support many-to-many relationships among entities, and others further refine their treatment of database structures, activities, or programs.

Each entity in the typical D/D (and sometimes their relationships) can be described by numerous attributes, which characterize the particular type of entity. For example, the typical attributes of the transaction entity (frequency, expected volume of data, and so on) are quite different from the attributes of the field entity (data type, size, null/nonnull, and so on).

Many of the D/D systems offer an extensibility feature that allows the data administrator to expand the D/D's structure by defining additional entities, attributes, and relationships. These user-defined aspects of the D/D structure enable the vendor's standard package to meet the needs of a broader community of users. For example, a data administrator might add to the D/D system the capability to store and maintain data models.

To implement the three-schema approach, discussed in Chapter 2, a D/D must be able to describe all three types of schemas: conceptual, external, and internal and to include the mappings among these schemas. The model of Fig 13.1 does not include these entities; rather, they must be added using the extensibility feature of the D/D system.

There are no commercially available D/D systems that fully support all three schemas, but there has been considerable research interest in the area. Most commercial products describe only internal schemas and sometimes external schemas; they have no concept of a conceptual schema. They typically call external schemas *subschemas* and internal schemas *files*.

PRINCIPAL FUNCTIONS

The D/D's three principal functions are the glossary, catalog, and controller.

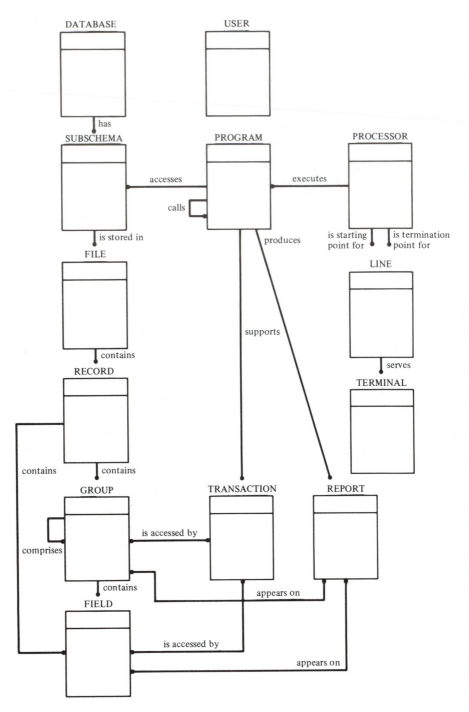

FIGURE 13.1. Logical structure of a D/D. The user entity can be related to all other entities, though these relationships are not shown.

Glossary

The D/D *glossary*

- loads and updates the D/D contents.
- reports the D/D contents, thus documenting the data resource. This reporting may be complete or a selected part of the D/D. A report can contain all the record types in a set of databases, with their data fields, listed in alphabetic sequence.
- analyzes D/D contents, documenting the effects of change to one part of the system on another part. For example, if zip code is changed to ten digits, which programs need to be changed and recompiled?
- creates, maintains, and reports new D/D structures, when extensibility has been used.

The glossary supports both data planning and development, and its effectiveness varies according to the scope of the metadata. Some database management systems have built-in D/D glossaries.

Some D/D systems can read metadata from source programs or libraries and use those metadata to load the D/D directly. This feature can be useful when initially establishing a D/D, as it avoids rekeying metadata that already exist in automated form. This feature, however, can capture only the metadata available from the sources. For example, a COBOL or FORTRAN program does not provide metadata about who has retrieval or update authority for the data elements, and the utilities that load a D/D from source programs typically do not analyze the metadata they find. For example, they generally do not identify which transactions or programs access a given data element or on which reports a given data element appears.

Catalog

The next principal function of a D/D system is as a *catalog,* which generates (1) data definition language (DDL) statements and (2) standard data manipulation logic. Both types of statements are copied directly into programs and transactions at compile-time. Generating data definitions and manipulation statements from a D/D is a major step forward in being able to control the effects of change and the costs of new development in the data environment. For example, once zip code is described to the D/D as having ten digits, then all programs and transactions whose DDL is generated by the D/D system will have that same understanding of the zip code's format. The data administrator can use the D/D system's glossary to determine which programs and transactions use zip code, as these are the programs and transactions that will need to be recompiled. The new description of zip code will be extracted directly from the D/D.

Catalogs are useful primarily for system development and maintenance. Many commercially available D/D systems, especially those tied closely to a particular

DBMS, have both a catalog and a glossary. Some database management systems also have built-in D/D systems with catalogs.

Controller

The third principal function of a D/D is as a controller, which directs the actual execution of the programs and transactions. Controllers (1) direct programs and transactions to the requested data's physical locations and (2) transform data requests from external schema form to conceptual schema form to internal schema form and then backwards for the response.

Controllers are useful for both system development and program execution. It may be helpful to consider the D/D controller as an extension of the conventional DBMS. Some database management systems have built-in D/D systems that provide the first part of the controller; none has a built-in three-schema transformation.

Controllers are especially valuable in a network of computers with several databases. In a distributed database environment, the conceptual-to-internal transform may decompose a request into several requests, each against a single database, and select a strategy to acquire and aggregate responses from the targeted databases into a single response for presentation to the user. Without the D/D controller in a distributed database environment, a programmer must figure out the interschema transforms and the decomposition/aggregation strategy.

The D/D controller is especially important to an environment that networks heterogeneous database management systems, for example, that supports the relational, hierarchical, and network models (procured from different vendors and running on different types of computers). The controller enables the user to request data from the distributed data resource without knowing in which database the desired data reside. This request can be in a neutral language independent of any of the individual DBMSs, as the user does not need to know which of the DBMSs is/are managing the data being requested.

There are no commercially available D/D systems today that provide the full controller function, but it is an area of considerable research interest. Perhaps the most capable of the commercial offerings is part of Tandem Corporation's Encompass system, which operates in a homogeneous environment of Tandem computers and database management services. This is not a separate D/D system. Pertinent research systems include the Common Data Model Processor subsystem of the Integrated Information Support System (IISS), developed by General Electric with funding by the Integrated Computer-Aided Manufacturing (ICAM) program of the U.S. Air Force, and the Multibase system developed by Computer Corporation of America (CCA) with funding from the U.S. Navy. Both of these developing systems operate in heterogeneous environments with various DBMSs.

FUNDAMENTAL CONFIGURATIONS

D/D systems depend on particular database management systems for data management services and on the D/D as a source of metadata. The three configurations are independent, DBMS application, and embedded.

Independent

A D/D system that takes the *independent* approach is autonomous; it does not rely on any particular database management system but manages its own database (the D/D). It is responsible for its own recovery protection, shared access control, access languages, query processing, space management, and the like. Example commercially available independent D/D systems are Data Catalogue 2 (from TSI International), Datamanager (from Management Systems and Programming, Ltd.), and Pride/Logik (from M. Bryce & Associates).

The principal advantage of the independent approach is that the D/D system can be used with a variety of DBMS packages (Fig. 13.2). The D/D system customer does not have to have a particular DBMS. The D/D system can be fit into an existing DBMS environment, and the environment can be extended in the future to include new DBMS services. This ability is particularly important for centralized D/D control in a network of heterogeneous DBMSs.

The main disadvantage of the independent approach is that DBMSs need not get their metadata from the D/D. They maintain their own schemas; thus there is metadata redundancy. The data administration must also take special precautions to coordinate the contents of the metadata sources.

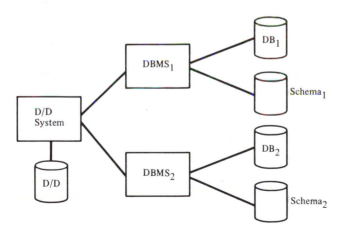

FIGURE 13.2. Independent D/D configuration.

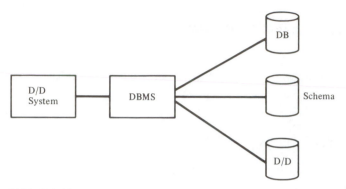

FIGURE 13.3.   DBMS-application D/D configuration.

DBMS Application

A D/D system that is a *DBMS application* relies on the data management support of a particular database management system. These systems may or may not be provided by the same vendor. The D/D appears to the DBMS as just another database (Fig. 13.3) and is accessed by the database management system in the same way that any other database is accessed. Many of the D/D system's functions are provided by DBMS utilities, and additional functions generally are provided by the D/D system's programs and transactions. The D/D system obviously depends on a particular DBMS, and in some cases, D/D systems using this approach can also describe data managed by other DBMSs.

DBMS-application D/D systems include the ADABAS Data Dictionary (from Software AG, dependent on its ADABAS DBMS), DB/DC Data Dictionary (from IBM, dependent on its IMS DBMS), IDD (from Cullinet, dependent on its IDMS DBMS), IDD (from Intel, dependent on its System 2000/80 DBMS), and UCC Ten (from UCC, dependent on the IBM IMS DBMS).

The primary advantage of a DBMS-application D/D system is that it uses the data management facilities already available in the environment; thus the D/D system code tends to be relatively compact. Another advantage is that the D/D system can be bought from the same vendor as the underlying DBMS is, and so the packages tend to work well together.

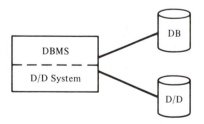

FIGURE 13.4   Embedded D/D configuration.

The main disadvantage of a DBMS-application D/D system is that like the independent D/D systems, the D/D is not the sole source of metadata for the DBMS. In fact, the DBMS maintains separate schemas for the other databases under its control. Again, the data administrator must coordinate the metadata sources.

Embedded

An *embedded* D/D system is an integral component of a DBMS (Fig. 13.4). The DBMS provides the data management facilities, and the D/D provides the metadata. The D/D system cannot be separated from the DBMS, as it is the heart of the DBMS.

One example of an embedded D/D system is the TIS Directory of Cincom's TIS. TIS cannot be procured without the Directory component which is essential to the rest of the system's operation.

The principal advantage of an embedded D/D system is that there is only one source of metadata; the D/D, which must be used to access the user databases. There is no problem of coordinating redundant metadata sources.

The main disadvantage of an embedded D/D system is that it works with only one DBMS, which can be a problem in an environment that already has multiple DBMSs. Because the architecture of embedded D/D systems puts the D/D (not the DBMS) in the center (see Fig. 13.5), this disadvantage can be eliminated if the D/D vendor offers interfaces with other DBMSs.

ROLES IN PROCESS-DRIVEN AND DATA-DRIVEN ENVIRONMENTS

The D/D system plays a different role in a data-driven environment than it does in a process-driven environment, and its influence increases in a data-driven approach.

Process-driven Environment

In a *process-driven environment*, the D/D serves primarily as a glossary, although it may also act as a catalog. The orientation is shown in Fig. 13.6. When a user requests new access to corporate data or wants to manipulate corporate data using a stand-alone package or tool (e.g., software for statistical analysis, graphics display, comparison with other data), an extract program is written specifically to pull data from the production database and create an extract file. That extract file is then precisely formatted to meet the needs of the target software. The format of the extract files is usually not known to the D/D.

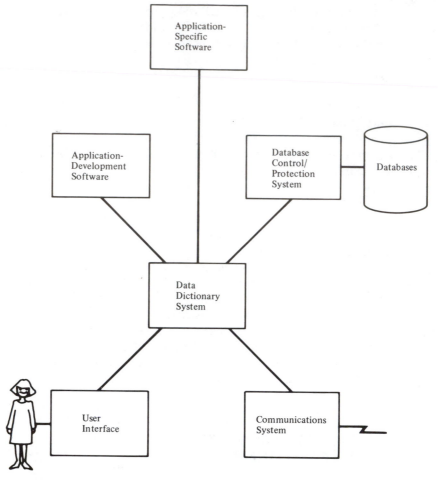

FIGURE 13.5. Central role of D/D system.

Data-driven Environment

By contrast, in a *data-driven environment,* the D/D serves as an intermediary between the production data and the users. As shown in Fig. 13.7, the D/D acts as a catalog to provide data descriptions to extract programs and then to build extract databases. These extract databases are not kept current, and update transactions against production databases are not also processed against extract databases. When more current data are required, a new extract is made.

The format of extract databases is known to the D/D. It translates from the extract databases into the required formats for manipulation by means of various software packages and presents the results to the user.

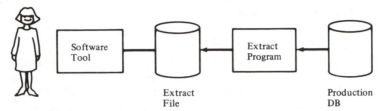

FIGURE 13.6. Process-driven environment with extract files.

The D/D system acts as a buffer for the extract database against the details and peculiarities of individual tool packages and the specific requirements of individual user-interface needs. The extract database is managed as a data resource, not as a temporary file just to be passed among programs.

The data in the extract databases are periodically updated from the production databases. Obviously, the more frequent the updates are, the more current the extract data will be. Delaying the updates of the extract databases avoids the coordination problems of keeping the extracts completely synchronized with the production data.

This configuration is similar to that found in many information center environments, which can be a data-driven step toward effective data management. Given the right set of tools and user-interface languages, users are able to access data more or less directly, while bypassing the traditional, sometimes lengthy, systems development process.

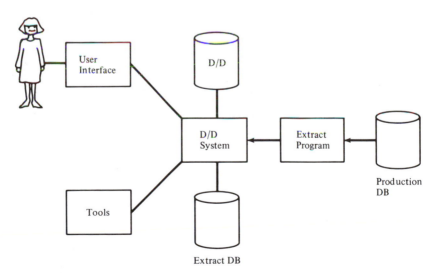

FIGURE 13.7. Interfaced, data-driven environment with extract databases.

Distributed Environment

As the D/D system functions grow, the production databases will migrate into an information center environment. Today, production databases tend to be tightly controlled by data-processing organizations. They support many users and are controlled to ensure that they meet standards of reliability and predictability. The code is developed with strict reviews of requirements, design, and performance and is changed through formal release procedures. As users become more familiar with information center tools and their own data-processing needs, the production databases will be more often implemented in the information center (Fig. 13.8). These databases commonly start out as prototypes, which the data-processing group assumes will be thrown away so that production databases can be implemented using conventional systems development methods. But as their utility is proved to users, the prototypes change to production systems.

A *distributed data-processing environment* results, even if the original intention was to have all production data centralized in a large mainframe, with extract files fed to remote information center facilities for inquiry-only access. The challenge is to provide the tools and controls needed to integrate an environment with viable distributed databases. When appropriate, the information center user should be able, in a single request, to retrieve data from both local production databases and locally stored extracts of production databases resident

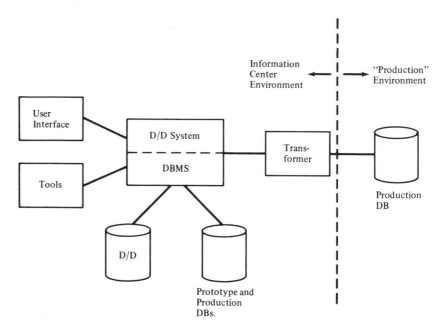

FIGURE 13.8. Integrated, data-driven environment with information center.

on a central mainframe, without distinguishing between them. Updates to local and central production databases should be managed with complete integrity, and the D/D system can supply much of the intelligence needed to manage these environments.

One of the objectives is to provide an integrated data environment in which

- databases are shared by several users, based on the data's logical connections, without the constraints of organizational and application boundaries.
- users can access data without concern for their locations or by which DBMSs they are managed.
- the data are consistent and replicated across databases.
- the physical database can change to improve efficiency, without changing how users access the data.

D/D AND TRANSACTION SUPPORT

The role of the D/D in supporting transactions in integrated data environments is complex. The various functions that the D/D can perform are shown in Fig. 13.9 and are as follows:

- A transaction is received through a user-interface facility. The D/D can supply information about the user's frame of reference, to help clarify the transaction and resolve homonyms. For example, User A may mean hire-date when he says date, whereas User B may mean ship-date when she says date, and User C may be referring to a specific edible product when he says date.
- The D/D can supply mapping information to transform the user's transaction in presentation-view form (as shown on the screen) to external-schema form.

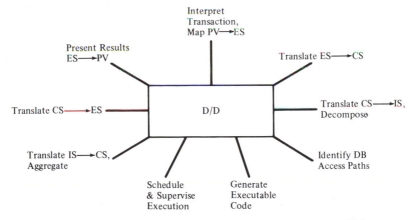

FIGURE 13.9. D/D functionality for transaction support: PV = presentation view, ES = external schema, CS = conceptual schema, IS = internal schema, DB = database.

- The D/D can supply mapping information to transform the external-schema form of the transaction to its conceptual-schema form.
- The D/D can supply information about data locations to decompose the conceptual-schema transaction into pieces, each of which accesses one physical database.
- The D/D can supply mapping information to transform the single-database transactions into their internal-schema forms, identifying access paths through the corresponding physical databases.
- The D/D system can generate executable code for access to the participating physical databases.
- The D/D system can schedule accesses to the participating databases, deciding what combination of parallel and serial access will give the best performance, and then supervise the execution of the parts of the transaction.
- The D/D can supply mapping information to transform local results in internal-schema form to conceptual-schema form and then aggregate those intermediate results, eventually forming the full response to the transaction. As the results are transformed, the D/D system can apply appropriate integrity-checking constraints.
- The D/D can supply mapping information to transform the conceptual-schema form of the response into its external-schema form.
- The D/D can supply mapping information to transform the external-schema form of the response into presentation-view form for display to the requestor.

Because the D/D is the repository for the three-schema description of the data environment, software that accesses the D/D, that is, the D/D system, should offer transaction-support services that map from the form of one schema to another. The D/D system becomes the heart of the data management environment, be it centralized or distributed.

This level of transaction support for distributed environments is not provided in today's commercially available D/D systems. The concepts are, however, being tested in various research projects. Even if they are not supplied by software labeled *D/D System*, they will be supplied somewhere in the distributed data management system. Some of these functions are supplied today in database management systems with embedded D/D systems.

D/D AND DESIGN SUPPORT

Many D/D functions can be applied to transaction processing and systems design. The various functions that the D/D can perform are shown in Fig. 13.10 and are as follows:

- The D/D can store data models and assist the modeler in building and modifying models.
- The D/D system can integrate a new data model with the existing conceptual schema.

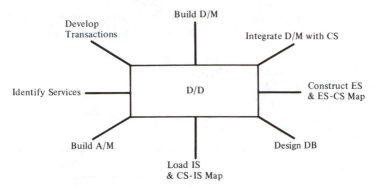

FIGURE 13.10. D/D functionality for design support: D/M = data model, CS = conceptual schema, ES = external schema, DB = database, IS = internal schema, A/M = activity model.

- The D/D system can help the data administrator build external schemas and can store those schemas and their mappings to the conceptual schema.
- The D/D system can help the database administrator design physical databases and can store internal schemas and their mappings to the conceptual schema.
- The D/D can store activity models and assist the modeler in building and modifying models.
- The D/D system can help the user/analyst identify information service requirements and develop transactions to fulfill those needs effectively.

The D/D system can then process transactions to generate executable code to implement the identified information services requirements. Again, not all of these design functions are available in today's commercially available D/D systems.

D/D SUPPORT FROM TODAY'S DBMSS

Today's database management systems all can describe the databases that they manage. Part I introduced some of the data definition languages (DDLs) that the database management systems offer. Recall that most of these described only the data entities, attributes, and relationships and were commonly couched in physical database terms, suitable for describing internal schemas.

These DDL statements are used to create *schema files*, which provide compile-time and/or run-time descriptions of physical databases. In themselves, these schema files do not offer any information that the DDL does not convey.

The database management system vendors have recognized the marketplace created by the growing demand for data administration and management. Many database management system vendors also offer D/D system modules or packages that are compatible with their database management systems. In some cases, these D/D capabilities are embedded in the database management systems; however, in most cases, the D/D systems are DBMS applications.

REPRESENTATIVE COMMERCIALLY AVAILABLE D/D SYSTEMS

Today's D/D systems and the DBMS packages with which they are compatible include the following:[1]

D/D system	D/D vendor	Compatible DBMS
Adabas Data Dictionary	Software AG	ADABAS
Data Catalogue 2	TSI	independent
Data Control System	Cincom Systems	TOTAL
Data Control System	Haverly	DMS-1100
DDS 1100	Sperry Univac	DMS-1100
DDS	ICL	IDMS
Datadictionary	ADR	Datacom/DB
Datamanager	MSP	independent
DB/DC Data Dictionary	IBM	IMS
Dictionary/204	CCA	Model 204
EDICT	Infodata	Inquire or independent
IDD	Cullinet	IDMS
IDD	SAS Institute	System 2000
PRIDE-Logik	M. Bryce & Assoc.	independent
TIS Directory	Cincom Systems	TIS
UCC Ten	UCC	IMS

Note:
DDS = Data Dictionary System
IDD = Integrated Data Dictionary
ADR = Applied Data Research
CCA = Computer Corporation of America
IBM = International Business Machines
ICL = International Computers Ltd.
MSP = Management Systems and Programming Ltd.

We shall now look at three representative D/D systems: the Datamanager (from MSP), the DB/DC Data Dictionary (from IBM), and the TIS Directory (from Cincom).

Datamanager

Datamanager, with over five hundred installations, is the most widely used of the independent D/D systems and is targeted at IBM hardware environments.

---

[1]Allen, F.W., M.E.S. Loomis, and M.V. Mannino, "The Integrated Dictionary/Directory System," *ACM Computing Surveys* 14 (June 1982): Table 5.

Datamanager can define schemas and subschemas for a variety of DBMSs, including ADABAS, IDMS, IMS (DL/1), System 2000, and TOTAL, and it can define source-code data for incorporation in COBOL, PL/I, and BAL (assembler language) programs. Commands can be activated by a user at a terminal or by program CALL statements. In addition to its independence, the other distinguishing feature of Datamanager is its extension past conventional glossary and catalog capabilities. It has been used for automated design aids, system auditing, text management, and so forth.

DB/DC Data Dictionary

DB/DC Data Dictionary is an IMS-application system designed for use in IMS or DL/1 environments. It describes source-code data for incorporation in COBOL, PL/I, and BAL programs and stores metadata about six categories: system, job, program, module, transaction, and PSB. It also has an extensibility feature and supports versioning features to mark metadata as production status or test status.

TIS Directory

The TIS Directory is an integral part of the TIS data management environment (TIS is Total Information System, an extension of the TOTAL database management system). The TIS query and report writer facilities used to access users' databases can also be used to access the Directory's metadata. The Directory supplies metadata to all the components of a TIS environment, including COBOL or PL/I source-code programs, the logical user-view subsystem, query facility, report writer facility, database design aid, and application generator.

CLOSING COMMENTS

D/D systems have great potential as tools for data resource management and database support. The key word here is *potential*, as D/D systems today generally are not used to their full capabilities. There are two reasons that today's D/D systems do not receive very high marks: the packages themselves do not offer as many functions as they might, and users do not apply the existing capabilities. For a long time, D/D systems were considered rather uninteresting, perhaps mostly because they were equated with automated glossaries. But, metadata management capabilities are as important as data management capabilities to achieve independence, resiliency, relatability, integrity, accessibility, shareability, security, performance, and administration in the management of data resources.

TERMS

catalog
controller
data administrator
database administrator
data-driven orientation
data model
DBMS-application D/D
dictionary/directory
dictionary/directory system
embedded D/D

glossary
information center
metadata
process-driven orientation
production database
schema
stand-alone D/D
subschema
three-schema approach
transaction

REVIEW EXERCISES

1. What are the objectives of a data dictionary/directory system?
2. Compare these objectives with the objectives of data management.
3. What kinds of metadata can be expressed in the DATA DIVISION of a COBOL program? Be specific.
4. What kinds of metadata can be expressed in a FORTRAN program?
5. Why is it sometimes difficult to distinguish between data and metadata? Give several examples.
6. What kinds of people can use a D/D?
7. Describe the D/D's glossary, catalog, and controller.
8. Describe the D/D's three configurations, independent, DBMS-application, and embedded. What are the advantages and disadvantages of each? Name a commercially available example of each.
9. Which of the three types of D/D configurations is most prevalent in the marketplace today?
10. Describe the potential role of the D/D system in a production database environment.
11. Describe the potential role of the D/D system in an information center database environment.
12. What kinds of metadata does a D/D system need to be able to provide to support transaction processing in a distributed database environment?
13. What kinds of metadata does a D/D system need to be able to provide to support data modeling, database design, and transaction development? Be specific.
14. What D/D facilities are used in your enterprise? How are they used?
15. How were the D/D facilities used in your enterprise selected? Who selected them?
16. Compare several examples of advertisements for D/D products in the DP-trade publications. What are their main selling points?

17. Find out what products supplying D/D functions are available on personal computers.

18. Compare the extensibility features of three commercial D/D systems.

REFERENCES

Allen, F. W., M. E. S. Loomis, and M. V. Mannino. The integrated dictionary/directory system, *ACM Computing Surveys* 14 (June 1982):245–286.

British Computer Society Data Dictionary Systems. Working party report, *Database* 9 (Fall 1977); and *SIGMOD Record 9* (December 1977).

Curtice, R., and E. Dieckman. A survey of data dictionaries, *Datamation* 27 (March 1981):135–158.

Federal Requirements for a Federal Information Processing Standard Data Dictionary System, NBSIR81-2354. Washington, D.C.: U.S Department of Commerce, National Bureau of Standards, Institute for Computer Sciences and Technology, Center for Programming Science and Technology, September 1981.

Hammond, L. W. Management considerations for an information center, *IBM Systems Journal* 21 (1982):131–161.

Hurlbut, M. R., et al. *ICAM Integrated Center (ICENT) Manufacturing Control-Material Management (MCMM) System (Test Bed), Interim Reports*. Computer Integrated Manufacturing Branch, Manufacturing Technology Division, U.S. Air Force, 1983–1985.

Information Center Implementation Guide, Document no. Gh09-0187. IBM Canada, March 1981.

Leong-Hong, B. W., and B. K. Plagman. *Data Dictionary/Directory Systems: Administration, Implementation, and Usage*. New York: John Wiley, 1982.

Ross, R. *Data Dictionaries and Data Administration*. New York: AMACOM, 1981.

Uhrowczik, P. P. Data dictionary/directories, *IBM Systems Journal* 12 (1973):332–350.

CHAPTER 14

Data Protection

An effective database environment requires more than a semantically valid logical data model and an efficient physical database implementation: the database also must be available to users when they need it; a satisfactory level of sharability must be supported; and unauthorized access must be prevented.

This chapter discusses the three principles underlying these protection services: recoverability, concurrency control, which is also known as shared-access control, and security.

THE TRANSACTION CONCEPT

Data protection has as its primary objective a high quality database environment. The quality rules for a database may include statements such as "*A* always equals *B*", "DEPARTMENT NUMBERs must be taken from the following set: { . . . }"; "If JOB_CODE is greater than RECLASSIFICATION_CODE, then ELIGIBILITY must be less than COMPENSATION_BRACKET"; and "The sum of EMPLOYEE_SALARIES in a DEPARTMENT cannot exceed the DEPARTMENT's SALARY_BUDGET."

In many environments, it is desirable for all users (people and programs) to have consistent views of the database at all times. But this is impossible if consistency is defined in individual rules, such as those just listed. For example, consider the assertion that ''A always equals B.'' If a user wants to add 2 to both A and B, at some point A will have been updated and B will not (or vice versa). That is, the two actions cannot take place simultaneously, except with the support of multiple, synchronized processors. Consider an initially consistent state with $A = B = 10$. At the point that $A = 12$ and $B = 10$, the data are inconsistent because they violate the constraint.

Consistency cannot be expected after individual actions, and instead, there are sets of actions that preserve consistency. Each set of actions carries data from a consistent state to a possibly inconsistent temporary state, and back again to a consistent state. Such a set of actions is called a *transaction* or, sometimes, a *logical unit of work*. A transaction has the following three properties:

- It obeys the database's rules of consistency. It starts with the database in a consistent state, and its actions obey the system's consistency rules. Thus the initial consistent state is transformed into a new consistent state.
- It either happens in its entirety or not at all. Either all of its results are recorded and the transaction is said to *commit,* or none of the effects of the transaction survive and the transaction is said to *abort*.
- Once the transaction is committed, it cannot be undone; its effects can be altered only by running other transactions.

A transaction must have one of two outcomes, committed or aborted; that is, it either is completed successfully or it has no effect on the database state. A transaction that is supposed to update twenty-five department records cannot end with only twelve of them changed. A committed transaction is guaranteed to have been completed and to have its effects stored in the database.

The user must specify a transaction's boundaries. For example, only the user can determine whether all twenty-five department records should be updated together. If the updates can stand separately, then each department's update may instead be specified as a separate transaction.

Most of the database languages have commands for BEGIN TRANSACTION and END TRANSACTION, or their equivalent. If these boundaries are not specified, then they will be assumed to be the start and end of the program's run-unit.

Transactions are the basic units of database recoverability and concurrency control. Recovery ensures that a transaction is never left partially done. Shared, concurrent access is controlled by ensuring that transactions do not interfere with one another.

THE NEED FOR DATABASE RECOVERABILITY

The objective of database recoverability is to cope with failures, or when a system does not perform according to specifications. Failures can have many different causes, and their effect is to introduce errors into the system and possibly to make the system unaccessible. In order to cope with failures, a database management system must be able to detect and correct errors. Ideally, a database management system should also notify any users who accessed erroneous data during the period between error occurrence and error correction. But in fact, this is a very difficult service to provide.

The process of correcting errors due to failure is called *recovery*, and its objective is to restore the database to a state that is acceptable to the users. Here, "acceptability" is judged by the correctness and consistency of the database contents. A *recovery technique* supports recovery from certain kinds of failures. A database management system may provide several recovery techniques, each addressing a different kind of failure.

Types of Failure

The types of failure possible in a database system include the following:

- Environmental failure, for example, power outage, operating system termination due to errors, computer halt due to operator action.
- Software failure, for example, spurious termination of the database management system, destruction of the database management system.
- Program failure, for example, termination due to exceeding time or space limits, or operator action.
- Program logic failure, for example, incorrect database update due to errors in programming or errors in data validation.
- Physical device failure, for example, disk-head crash, scratched disk surface, stolen or missing disk, unreadable files on disk.

The most insidious of these problems is program logic failure, as it is difficult to detect. For example, it may take weeks or months to discover that incorrect data-validation logic has allowed bad data to update a database. It is easy to determine that a failure has occurred if the system stops, if a system error code appears, or if a disk is missing, but it is much harder to find out that erroneous data have been written to a database because of program logic failure.

Some of the symptoms of bad data are

- inconsistent information on reports.
- questions from users.
- questions from system auditors.
- failure of related programs or transactions that access the database.

Tracing these symptoms to the precise causes of the bad data is usually impossible. Who knows why your aircraft-seating preference is incorrectly recorded in the travel agent's files? Who knows why a debit to your checking account was processed twice? Recovery from these situations is not handled automatically by the database management system but instead, it requires people to make corrective transactions to replace incorrect data values. The best way of avoiding program logic failures is to prevent them, using program development techniques that help ensure program correctness.

Other kinds of failures are easier to detect and correct. In the worst case they can cause a database to be completely unreadable or inaccessible. They may also cause recovery data to be unusable and may result in incomplete sets of database changes, caused by the premature termination of program execution. They typically can be handled by more-or-less automatic recovery techniques. There is much truth in this quotation from a wise man in a major American company: "As far as we know, our computer has never had an undetected error." I apologize to the gentleman; I have misplaced his name and affiliation, but I trust it is sufficient credit for him to know that for many years his wisdom has stuck with me (and others who continue to quote him).

Failure in the Distributed Environment

There are more possibilities for database failure in a distributed environment, because of the increased complexity of distributed operating system services and distributed database management services. When those elements are highly reliable, then the potential for failure is approximately the same as in a centralized environment. In fact, the impact of failure in a distributed environment can be less significant than in a centralized environment. If one computer in the network stops, then the others will usually continue to run. Part of the total database may become inaccessible or be damaged, but the balance of the distributed data should not be affected. The redundancy of components (computers, database management systems, operating systems, databases) inherent in a distributed environment makes the system *failsoft:* the failure of one component may impair the system's overall performance, but it does not bring it to a halt.

RECOVERY TECHNIQUES

A recovery technique maintains recovery data for restoring databases. These recovery data record database contents and changes, so that transactions can later be either redone or undone. Different recovery techniques maintain different kinds of recovery data and are effective only if their recovery data have not also been contaminated or destroyed by the failure.

Recovery Data

There are several kinds of recovery data, including the following:

- Transaction record: a copy of database update transactions, in the sequence in which they occurred and commonly with the time they occurred and notations of which tasks performed them.

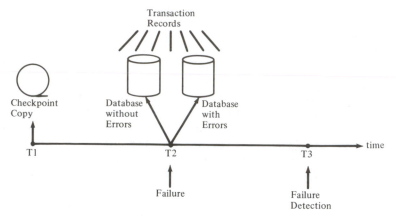

FIGURE 14.1. Time lag between failure occurrence and failure detection.

- Before-image: a copy of a portion of a database, before processing one or more updates of that portion.
- After-image: a copy of a portion of a database, after processing one or more updates of that portion.
- Checkpoint copy (also called *backup copy*): a complete copy of a database on an archival medium such as magnetic tape.
- Audit trail: a record of both update and retrieval actions to allow future examination and verification of database activity.

Not every database management system maintains all these kinds of recovery data. Which recovery data are maintained is determined by which recovery techniques the database management system uses. The file to which before- and after-images are written is called a *log* or a *journal*. Transaction records may also be recorded on the log.

UNDO and REDO Recovery Technique

Two basic recovery techniques are UNDO and REDO. Consider the situation shown in Fig. 14.1. A checkpoint copy of the database was made at time T1, and at time T2 a failure occurred, causing transactions to be improperly processed. It is now time T3, and the failure has been detected.

One recovery technique is to UNDO (also called *backout* or *rollback*) the actions that were improperly processed. The objective is to return the database to its state before the point of failure. This recovery technique relies on the availability of before-image recovery data. The UNDO process replaces portions of the database with their corresponding before-images, in reverse sequence of the order in which the before-images were written (Fig. 14.2).

For example, assume that there were three SALARY-related transactions before times T2 and T3:

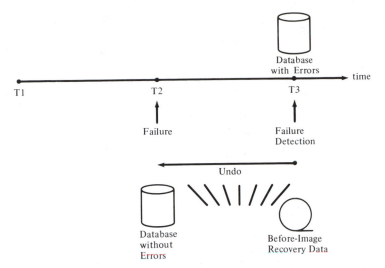

FIGURE 14.2. UNDO process, using before-image recovery data.

1. time T2 + a: SALARY = SALARY + 5000.
2. time T2 + a + b: SALARY = SALARY * 1.05.
3. time T2 + a + b + c: SALARY = SALARY − 100.

If the value of SALARY at time T2 were 40,000, then the before-images would have been recorded as follows:

1. time T2 + a: SALARY = 40,000.
2. time T2 + a + b: SALARY = 45,000.
3. time T2 + a + b + c: SALARY = 47,250.

At time T3, SALARY = 47,150, and the UNDO sequence would be

1. SALARY = 47,250.
2. SALARY = 45,000.
3. SALARY = 40,000.

The result is the return of SALARY to its value at time T2.

Note that the before-images on a log typically contain values for many different data fields in many different records. In a multitasking environment, the before-images for updates from one task may be interleaved with the images from another task.

Rather than moving backward in time from the current database to an earlier state, the REDO process moves forward from a checkpoint copy of the database. The REDO process can occur in one of two ways:

• Reprocess the transactions, using the checkpoint copy of the database and omitting any transactions that would cause failure (Fig. 14.3).

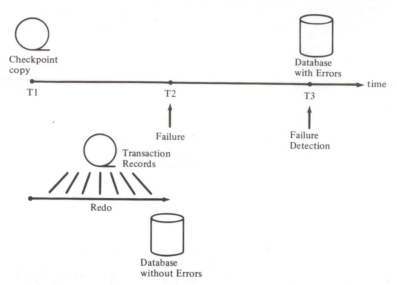

FIGURE 14.3. REDO, with reprocessing of transactions.

- Apply after-images to the checkpoint copy of the database, stopping before the point of failure or omitting any that contain errors (Fig. 14.4).

REDO relies on having available either the transactions or after-images, plus a checkpoint copy of the database. Assume that the SALARY-related transactions between times T1 and T2 were

1. time T1 + a: SALARY = SALARY * 1.10.
2. time T1 + a + b: SALARY = SALARY + 500.

and that SALARY = 35,910 at time T1.

Starting at time T1, after-images would have been recorded as follows:

1. time T1 + a: SALARY = 39,500.
2. time T1 + a + b: SALARY = 40,000.

The checkpoint copy at time T1 shows SALARY = 39,910, and the REDO sequence would be

1. SALARY = 39,500.
2. SALARY = 40,000.

This brings the database back to its state at time T2.

The difference between REDO with transactions and with after-images is that REDO with transactions requires the transactions to be reexecuted. REDO with after-images applies the results of those transactions, without redoing them.

Whether UNDO or REDO is the more appropriate recovery technique depends on the following factors:

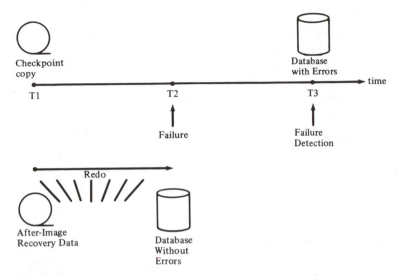

FIGURE 14.4. REDO, using after-image recovery data.

- The kind of recovery data available: UNDO requires a log of before-images; REDO with replacement requires a checkpoint copy and a log of after-images; REDO with reprocessing requires a checkpoint copy and a log of the transactions.
- When the failure occurred: If there have been just a few transactions since the failure, then UNDO may require less processing. If the error occurred shortly after the last checkpoint and there have been many transactions in the interim, then REDO may require less processing.
- The kind of failure: Some failures (e.g., physical device failures) can affect the availability of recovery data.

Both the UNDO and REDO recovery techniques must respect the transaction concept: a transaction's effects cannot be just partly undone or partly redone. Recovery must leave transaction effects either completely backed out or completely in place. Another name for a transaction is a *recoverable unit;* a database management system must not recover in units of partial transactions.

For example, if the following two actions were part of one transaction:

1. SALARY = SALARY + 500.
2. SALARY = SALARY * 1.15.

then the point to which the database was recovered could not be either to where just the 500 had been added or to where just the 1.15 multiplier had been backed out, as either result would leave the database in an inconsistent state and would violate the law of the transaction.

The sequence of events in applying the UNDO recovery technique to one active program and using a log on tape is as follows:

1. Mount the log tape.
2. Read the log file forward until the end-of-file is reached.
3. Unlock all files in the program's processing.
4. Read the log file backward, applying the before-images for this program to the database.
5. Terminate recovery when the start-log record for the program is encountered.
6. Restart the program.

The sequence of events required to restore a database after complete loss due to physical device failure, using REDO processing with after-images, is as follows:

1. Copy the latest checkpoint copy as the starting point for the restored database.
2. Read the log file forward, applying after-images to the database.
3. Restart the program that was operating at the point of failure, or continue processing if no program was operating.

Other Recovery Techniques

Although UNDO and REDO are currently the most widely used recovery techniques, there are others. When all other recovery techniques fail, a *salvation program* may be used. This specially designed program scans the database after failing to assess the damage and to restore a valid state by rescuing whatever data are recognizable. It uses no recovery data.

Another recovery technique is to keep more than one copy of each database file. The different copies are identical except during the update process. Updates can be posted to all copies, which will be consistent when the updates are complete. Alternatively, one of the copies is active, and the other(s) are backup copies. Updates can be processed at the active copy and batched for later processing at the backup copies.

Techniques for the Distributed Environment

One difficulty in providing failure protection in distributed databases is coordinating recovery data and failure detection across processors. If a transaction must be undone, its actions may have involved processing at multiple computers by different database management systems, each with its own recovery data. Coordination becomes especially difficult when transactions are redone that affect multiple databases with different checkpoint intervals.

Another difficulty in a distributed environment arises with processors (and therefore portions of a database) that are temporarily removed from the network. The removal may be because of failure or for maintenance or some other reason. There are various ways of collecting updates and applying them when the processor rejoins the network. A coordination problem arises if only some of those updates are to be applied, because of additional failures while the processor was unavailable.

Distributed databases may have some or all of their data redundantly stored in the network. If one copy is inaccessible because of failure, then another copy can be used. Users' requests should be routed automatically to appropriate backup copies when failures occur. An important implication is the need for a net-workwide distributed data dictionary that knows data locations, which data are primary copies and which are redundant secondary copies, and what the data states are (e.g., inaccessible, accessible but not current, accessible and current).

Not all requests need to be serviced by the most current version of accessible, redundantly stored data. For example, your checking account balance is redundantly stored data: you keep a copy in your checkbook register, and the bank keeps a copy in its files. Do the copies always have the same contents? Which copy is the primary copy? Which copy do you update? Which copy does the bank update? Which copy do you query? Which copy does the bank query? How are the redundant copies made consistent? How do you determine your balance if you misplace your copy?

ESTABLISHING A RECOVERY POLICY

Recovery techniques must be tailored to individual environments; there is no general, packaged approach to database recovery that can be used for all situations. The data administration staff must continuously monitor the recovery policy of the environment and tune it to meet evolving needs.

The recovery policy of an environment should decide

- the recovery techniques that will protect against each type of failure.
- the recovery data that are required to support those techniques.
- the procedures that will execute the recovery techniques.

Questions such as the following should be answered in order to determine the requirements for the recovery policy:

1. How much downtime can be tolerated?
2. How much recovery time can be tolerated?
3. What kinds of media are available for storing recovery data?
4. What operating system constraints are imposed? For example, programs may need to be restarted at beginning of processing or may allow on-line restart at the last transaction to or from each live terminal.
5. How much operator intervention can be tolerated?
6. How much can the system's run-times be affected by recovery provisions?
7. How much overhead is it reasonable to incur?
8. How much recovery processing should be done automatically rather than manually?
9. How much responsibility should the data administrator have in locating erroneous transactions? In identifying program logic failures?

Design Decisions

The recovery techniques used with a particular database system are decided by its database management system(s). Some data administrators augment those services with additional techniques, but this happens relatively rarely.

The typical database management system supports both the UNDO and REDO recovery techniques, and the data administrator should tune the recovery techniques to meet local requirements. For example, the data administrator should decide

- How frequently should checkpoint copies be made? Weekly? Daily? Before running major systems? After running major systems? At the beginning of each process?
- How frequently should before- and after-images be made? Before and after each program? Before and after each transaction? Before and after each update of the database?
- How large a portion of the database is copied in a before- or after-image? An entire page? A record? A field?

Logging and checkpointing compete for system resources with transaction processing; they introduce overhead. Recovery data must be written, managed, and accessed. The user sees the benefit of this overhead only indirectly, through the ability to recover from failures and ideally does not even know there has been a failure.

DATABASE CONCURRENCY PROBLEMS AND THREATS

One of the objectives of a database environment is to enable many users to access shared data concurrently. Concurrent access is relatively easy for a database management system to support if all the accesses are retrievals. But whenever many users are accessing a database concurrently and at least one of them is performing updates, there can be interference, which can result in inconsistency. The three types of inconsistencies that can be avoided are lost updates, assumed updates, and phantom reads.

	T0	T1	T2	T3	T4	T5	
	•	•	•	•	•	•	→ time
Value of A	10	10	10	15	15	20	
Transaction 1	Find A		A = A + 5	Store A			
Transaction 2		Find A			A = A x 2	Store A	

FIGURE 14.5. Example of lost update.

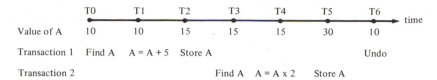

FIGURE 14.6. Example of assumed update.

Lost Updates

An update is lost in the example of Fig. 14.5. Transaction 1 intends to add 5 to the value of *A,* and Transaction 2 intends to multiply the value of *A* by 2. Assume that the value of *A* is 10 at time T0. Transactions 1 and 2 start at nearly the same time and both read the value of *A* as 10. Transaction 1 updates its working copy of *A* and stores 15 in the database. Transaction 2, meanwhile, updates its working copy of *A* and stores 20 in the database. The effect is the loss of Transaction 1's update, which could have been avoided if Transaction 2 could not read the value of *A* until after Transaction 1's update was completed.

Assumed Updates

An update is incorrectly assumed in the example of Fig. 14.6. Using the same intended actions, Transactions 1 and 2 run serially, with Transaction 1's action being undone so as to recover from some failure. The effect is the assumption by Transaction 2 that Transaction 1's update was completed successfully, even though that update was later undone. The problem could have been avoided if Transaction 2 could not read the value of *A* until after the decision is made either to commit or to undo Transaction 1's effects.

Phantom Reads

A phantom read occurs in the example of Fig. 14.7. Transaction 4 is defined by the following logic:

> if POLICY exists
> then DEDUCTION = 1
> else DEDUCTION = 0.

Transaction 5 is defined by

> if POLICY does not exist
> then do; create POLICY;
> > DEDUCTION = 1 end.

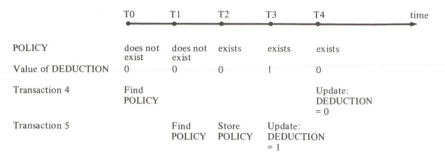

	T0	T1	T2	T3	T4	time
POLICY	does not exist	does not exist	exists	exists	exists	
Value of DEDUCTION	0	0	0	1	0	
Transaction 4	Find POLICY				Update: DEDUCTION = 0	
Transaction 5		Find POLICY	Store POLICY	Update: DEDUCTION = 1		

FIGURE 14.7.   Example of phantom read problem.

The transactions' interleaved execution leaves the database in an inconsistent state, in which POLICY exists and DEDUCTION = 0. Assuming that POLICY does not exist initially, the allowable consistent results are

1. POLICY exists and DEDUCTION = 1 (Transaction 4, then 5).
2. POLICY does not exist and DEDUCTION = 0 (Transaction 5, then 4).

The problem is that two different states for POLICY exist during Transaction 4's execution, even though it did not update POLICY. The problem could have been avoided if Transaction 5 could not update the POLICY until after Transaction 4 had completed its sequence of actions that were dependent on POLICY's nonexistence. Transaction 4 must be able to lock the nonexistent (i.e., phantom) POLICY.

CONCURRENCY CONTROL TECHNIQUES

Many techniques and concepts can, together, control concurrent access to shared data, including

- serializable execution.
- lock administration.
- two-phase locking protocol.
- deadlock.
- timestamping.
- optimistic techniques.
- two-phase commit protocol.

Serializable Execution

When transactions are performed sequentially, all the actions of one transaction are performed and then all the actions of the other transaction are performed. There is no concurrency. This is called a *serial execution*. When executed serially, transactions cannot interfere with one another; only one is active at a time.

When there are concurrent requests to access a database, they are usually not executed serially. Instead, the transactions are interleaved. The database management system that is servicing many programs performs one or more actions for one program, then one or more for another program, and so on until all the programs have been serviced. It then returns to service again the first program, then the next program, and so forth. The examples shown in Figs. 14.5 through 14.7 all have interleaved transactions.

An interleaved execution of transactions is said to be *serializable* if it produces the same result that some serial (i.e., noninterleaved) execution of those same transactions would have. Serializability is generally accepted as a formal criterion for consistency. If a database management system generates only serializable executions of transactions, then it guarantees consistency. Serializable concurrent transactions on shared data cannot interfere with one another.

Serializability does not imply there is just one set of correct outcome values. A group of n transactions has $n!$ possible serial executions, each with its own set of results. Because serializability only requires matching final results with those of some serial execution, there may be $n!$ possible sets of correct results. Consider two transactions: Transaction 1 gives all employees a 10 percent raise, and Transaction 2 calculates the average salary. There are two serializable executions of these two transactions, each giving a different, but consistent, result. An inconsistent result would report an average salary after only some of the employee raises had been recorded. If Transaction 1's actions should be completed before Transaction 2's actions start, then the entire set of actions should be one transaction. Interdependent actions always should be in one transaction. If the order of execution of Transactions 1 and 2 is significant, then they should be combined into one transaction, either "Tell me the average salary, then give the employees a 10 percent raise" or "Give employees a 10 percent raise and then tell me the average salary."

Figure 14.8 is an example of a serial schedule, in which Transaction 7 executes after Transaction 6 is completed. Transaction 6 adds 5 to both A and B, and Transaction 7 multiples both A and B by 2. Both transactions conform to the integrity assertion that "A must always equal B"; that is, each transaction has two actions that must be performed as a single recoverable unit. Before

	T0	T1	T2	T3	T4	
Value of A	10	15	15	30	30	time
Value of B	10	10	15	15	30	
Transaction 6		A = A + 5	B = B + 5			
Transaction 7				A = A x 2	B = B x 2	

FIGURE 14.8. Example of serial execution of two transactions.

	T0	T1	T2	T3	T4	
						time
Value of A	10	15	30	30	30	
Value of B	10	10	10	15	30	
Transaction 6		A = A + 5		B = B + 5		
Transaction 7			A = A x 2		B = B x 2	

FIGURE 14.9. Example of serializable execution of two transactions.

execution of the transactions, $A = B = 10$; after the execution of Transaction 6, $A = B = 15$; and after the execution of Transaction 7, $A = B = 30$. Consistency constraints are met before and after each transaction.

Figure 14.9 is another serializable execution of Transactions 6 and 7, but it is not a serial execution, as the actions of Transactions 6 and 7 are interleaved. The result, however, is the same as if the transactions had been executed serially. Thus the result is a consistent result.

Figure 14.10 is a nonserializable execution of Transactions 6 and 7, and it is not a serial execution. Like the example of Fig. 14.9, the actions of Transactions 6 and 7 are interleaved. But in contrast with the example of Fig. 14.9, the result is not the same as a serial execution and is not a consistent result: $A = 30$ and $B = 25$. The assertion that "A must always equal B" has been violated.

Locking

The most common approach to guaranteeing serializable executions is a technique called *locking*. In its simplest form, locking a portion of a database prevents any other transaction from reading or writing to that portion of the database until the lock has been released. In the following we shall refer to a "portion of a database" as a "database resource."

A database management system can administer locks by

• setting a bit in a database field or record or page or file, indicating that that database resource is locked.
• keeping a list of database resources that are locked.
• keeping locked database resources in a special area of memory.

	T0	T1	T2	T3	T4	
						time
Value of A	10	15	30	30	30	
Value of B	10	10	10	20	25	
Transaction 6		A = A + 5			B = B + 5	
Transaction 7			A = A x 2	B = B x 2		

FIGURE 14.10. Example of nonserializable execution of two transactions.

There are *exclusive locks,* which allow only the requester to access the locked database resource, and *shared locks,* which allow many requesters to access the locked database resource. Some database management systems support only exclusive locks, and in these systems, a database resource is either locked or not locked.

A transaction or program can request a lock by

- Specifying locking in conjunction with a data manipulation statement, for example, UPDATE EMP-REC WITH EXCLUSIVE LOCK SET SALARY = SALARY * 1.10. This type of lock request is sometimes done by default; that is, an update statement may implicitly request an exclusive lock on the data that it will modify.
- Specifying locking in conjunction with a command to start a transaction, for example, BEGIN TRANSACTION WITH EXCLUSIVE LOCK, or BEGIN TRANSACTION WITH SHARED LOCK.
- Specifying locking in conjunction with opening a database file, for example, OPEN EMP-DATABASE FOR EXCLUSIVE UPDATE, or OPEN EMP-DATABASE FOR SHARED READ.

Lock requests for a database resource are compatible if they can be granted together (see Fig. 14.11). A request for an exclusive lock is not compatible with any other request; a request for a shared lock is compatible with other shared-lock requests but is incompatible with any other exclusive-lock request.

There are five principles of concurrency control by locking, which together avoid the inconsistencies discussed earlier. The first principle of concurrency control is

1. No transaction may update a database resource without first acquiring a lock that prevents other transactions from also updating that resource.

An exclusive lock may be requested by a transaction that intends either to read or update the specified database resource. No other transaction can gain access to that database resource while the lock is held. Shared locks may be requested by several transactions, all intending to access a specified database resource. To prevent inconsistency, only one of these transactions may do updates, and the others only may read the locked database resource.

The second principle of concurrency control through locking is

2. If a lock cannot be acquired when it is requested, then the requesting transaction must wait.

FIGURE 14.11. Compatibility matrix for basic lock types. "Yes" means that the two locks may be granted together for the same data resource.

	Shared	Exclusive
Shared	Yes	No
Exclusive	No	No

Sometimes a transaction requests a lock on a resource to which another transaction already has exclusive rights. The second transaction then must wait until the exclusive lock is relinquished. The second transaction is said to be *blocked* and cannot proceed with its processing until it acquires the requested locks.

Shared and exclusive locks administered under these two principles prevent lost updates. Two transactions cannot have their actions interleaved if both are updating the database. Only one can have update access to a particular database resource at a time.

The third principle of concurrency control through locking is

3. After releasing a lock, a transaction cannot acquire any new locks.

Any transaction that releases a lock and then tries to set another lock may produce inconsistent results. The situations in Figs. 14.5 and 14.10 both could result from asking for locks after releasing other locks. Locking administered by principles 1 through 3 will avoid the problem of lost updates.

A transaction that obeys principles 1 and 3 is said to be *two phase,* and principles 1 and 3 are called the *two-phase locking protocol*. The first phase is a growing phase, in which locks are acquired, and the second phase is a shrinking phase, during which locks are released.

The fourth principle of concurrency control through locking is

4. Uncommitted changes must remain locked until the transaction terminates.

This principle protects against the problem of assumed updates. A transaction cannot release its lock on updated data until those updates have been committed, and once they are committed, the updates cannot be undone.

These principles do not prevent the problem of phantom reads unless nonexistent data can be locked. Thus the fifth principle is

5. If phantom reads are to be protected, then exclusive locks should be acquired before determining whether the resource exists.

Locking administered by all five principles will avoid the problems of lost updates, assumed updates, and phantom reads.

Deadlock

A situation called *deadlock* occurs when two (or more) transactions are blocked while waiting for locks held by each other to be released. Neither can continue processing until it acquires a lock held by the other, as each is waiting for the other to release a lock.

Figure 14.12a illustrates a deadlock situation. Transaction 8 holds a lock on SALARY data, and its request for a lock on JOB-PERFORMANCE data is blocked. Meanwhile, Transaction 9 holds a lock on JOB-PERFORMANCE data, and its request for a lock on SALARY data is blocked.

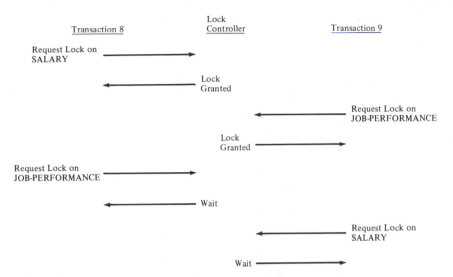

FIGURE 14.12a. Example of sequence of requests leading to deadlock.

Figure 14.12b shows this situation using a *resource request graph*. Each node is a transaction, and each directed edge indicates that one transaction is blocked, waiting for a resource that is locked by another transaction.

Deadlock is detected by finding cycles in resource request graphs. A database management system typically maintains a list of which transactions hold which types of locks on which database resources and a list of which transactions are blocked waiting for which types of locks on which database resources. These lists, which represent resource request graphs, can be analyzed to pinpoint deadlock situations.

In a database environment with many transactions, continually checking for deadlock can be expensive, and there are other reasons that a transaction may go into a wait state, for example, waiting for activity from a terminal, waiting for access to a printer, or waiting for an operator to mount a disk or tape file. Some database management systems look for deadlock situations only after a transaction has been waiting for more than some threshold time.

Once deadlock has been detected, the database management system must resolve it. The most common technique for resolving deadlock is to UNDO one of the transactions. The database management system selects one of the deadlocked transactions, applies before-images to roll back the actions processed so far, releases its locks, and thus allows the other transactions to proceed. UNDO here is exactly the same process as is used to recover databases.

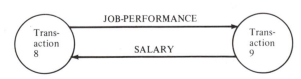

FIGURE 14.12b. Resource request graph showing deadlock.

A sixth principle of controlling concurrency through locking is

6. Always write updates to the log first, and then to the database.

This principle makes writing before- and after-images to a log part of the commit process, and it ensures that recovery data will be available if a failure should occur during the database update.

There are several ways of preventing deadlocks, including the following:

- Allow a transaction to lock only one resource at a time. This is acceptable only if one lock can secure large portions of a database and the need for concurrency is very low.
- Require that a transaction use one indivisible operation to lock all the resources that it requires; the transaction cannot hold one lock and request another. This is not acceptable because the resources that a transaction will require are usually determined dynamically and cannot be predicted at the start of the transaction.

There are other techniques for avoiding deadlock in accesses to operating-system controlled resources, but they usually are not applicable to database resources. Database management systems must be prepared to detect deadlocks and to resolve them when they occur.

Timestamping

Timestamping assigns to each transaction a unique identifier, which can be thought of as the transaction's start-time. The identifier is referred to as a *time-stamp*. Its value is typically a system-generated, precise time value from the system clock. In a distributed environment, the name of the host is appended to the time value, making the timestamp unique to the network.

In a timestamped system, conflict occurs when either a transaction asks to read a record that has already been updated by a younger transaction or a transaction asks to update a record that has already been read by a younger transaction. Conflicts are resolved by restarting the requesting transaction. The younger transaction is allowed to continue, and the requesting transaction receives a new timestamp when it is restarted. There is no locking, and therefore, there can be no deadlock. To prevent a transaction from seeing uncommitted updates, no physical updates can be written until commit-time. Transaction restart never requires rollback, as the updates have not been physically written.

The basic timestamp technique is testing the timestamp value of the requesting transaction against the timestamp values of the last transactions(s) that accessed the record:

Let LAST-READ be the timestamp of the last transaction to read the record successfully.

Let LAST-COMMIT be the timestamp of the last transaction to update the record successfully.

Let MY-START-TIME be the timestamp of my requesting transaction.

If my requesting transaction asks to read, then its timestamp will be compared with LAST-COMMIT.

> If LAST-COMMIT < MY-START-TIME,
> then my transaction is allowed to continue,
> > and LAST-READ is given the value MY-START-TIME,
> else my transaction is restarted.

If my requesting transaction asks to commit, then its timestamp will be compared with both LAST-COMMIT and LAST-READ.

> If LAST-COMMIT < MY-START-TIME and LAST-READ < MY-START-TIME
> then my transaction is allowed to commit,
> > and LAST-COMMIT is given the value MY-START-TIME,
> else my transaction is restarted.

No requesting transaction is allowed to interfere with an older transaction that is already reading or updating the record. Many variations of the basic time-stamping technique have been proposed.

Timestamping, like locking, synchronizes the interleaved execution of a set of transactions. Recall that locking synchronizes the transactions so that their execution is equivalent to some serial execution. By contrast, timestamping synchronizes the transactions so that their execution is equivalent to a specific serial execution. That serial order is the chronological order of the transactions' timestamps.

Optimistic Techniques

The *optimistic concurrency-control techniques* recognize that conflicts between transactions can be rare in databases with many records. These techniques eliminate locking and follow the optimistic assumption that most locks set in conventional systems are not needed.

The basic approach is not to restrict read transactions, but to restrict updates severely. Each transaction consists of two or three phases:

1. Read phase: from the start of the transaction until just before commit or termination. If there are updates, they will take place on local copies of the data.
2. Validation phase: for read transactions, the system will determine whether the result of the read is actually correct. For update transactions, the system verifies that the changes made will not cause a loss of integrity.

3. Write phase: local updates are made global and are committed.

Each transaction is assigned a number when its read phase is completed. For a requesting transaction to pass the validation test, one of the following conditions must hold:

1. All older transactions must have completed their write phases before the requesting transaction starts its read phase.
2. The older transactions must not write the same data that the requesting transaction reads in its read phase, and the older transactions must complete their write phases before the requesting transaction starts its write phase.
3. The older transactions must not write the same data that the requesting transaction reads or writes in its read phase, and the older transactions must complete their read phases before the requesting transaction starts its read phase.

Transactions are allowed to proceed with actions on their local copies of data. When they are ready to commit, the system applies the validation tests and determines whether there has been a conflict that would introduce bad data. The hope is that conflict will rarely occur. If validation fails, then the requesting transaction is backed up and restarted as a new transaction. This approach avoids the overhead of administering locks, and deadlock cannot occur. The cost is that of backing up when there is conflict.

Techniques for the Distributed Environment

Providing concurrency control in a distributed database environment is significantly more difficult than in a centralized database environment. The main problem is communicating control information across the database sites.

In a distributed database environment, a transaction can include actions that are executed at many processors, each against a portion of the database. If locking is used as the synchronization technique, then one transaction may hold locks at several processors. Detecting deadlock then means detecting blocked-process cycles across the network of machines. One approach is to have a global lock manager, which is aware of which processes hold which locks at which machines.

Another problem in a distributed environment is coordinating transaction commitments. One approach is the *two-phase commit protocol*. Before committing a transaction's updates, each subtransaction (which is processed at a single machine under the control of one database management system) must indicate that it is ready to commit. To be ready to commit, all of its actions must have been completed successfully. If all subtransactions indicate that they are ready to commit, then all are instructed to go ahead and commit. If any subtransaction indicates that for any reason it cannot commit, then all the subtransactions are instructed to abort. None of the changes are committed.

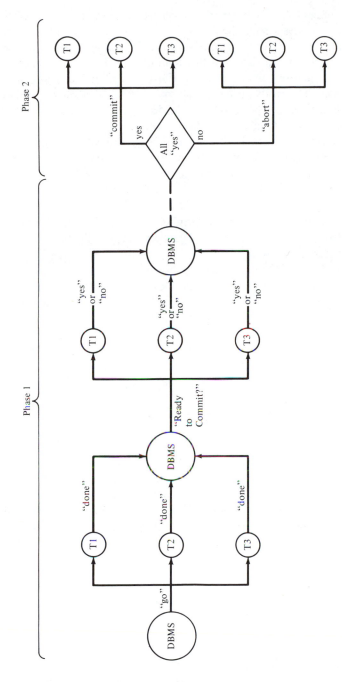

FIGURE 14.13. Two-phase commit protocol.

Figure 14.13 illustrates the two-phase commit protocol. Before the commit, each subtransaction writes its changes to its local log. The distributed database management system polls for readiness to commit and issues instructions on whether or not to carry out the commit. The two-phase commit protocol thus has one phase in which subtransactions are getting ready to commit. Once each has said it is ready, it cannot abort by itself. It must be prepared to commit when it is given the instruction to do so. The second phase is the period of actually committing or aborting everywhere. During the commit phase, only secured storage can be used, and it must be possible to record the update, regardless of what local failures may occur during the commit process.

Note that the two-phase commit protocol is not the same as the two-phase locking protocol. Two-phase locking refers to the rule that a transaction cannot obtain new locks after releasing old locks; each transaction has a growing (i.e., new-lock acquisition) and a shrinking (i.e., lock-release) phase. By contrast, the two-phase commit protocol governs the coordination of the processors involved in a transaction.

Another approach to handling concurrent access in a distributed database environment is to segregate the periods of retrieval-only access from the periods of update access. For example, distributed retrieval transactions could be serviced all day without interfering with one another. Update transactions could be batched and run serially at night. This approach is not suitable for all environments but can be used when up-to-the-second currency is not required. Some banks have used this approach for many years even with centralized databases.

There also are other methods of reducing the overhead of managing locks in distributed database systems. For example, the optimistic concurrency-control methods hope that conflict only occurs rarely. There are no locks. In a technique called *conflict graph analysis,* locks are used, but only when an analysis of transactions shows that there may be interference.

Providing shared-access control is one of the most difficult problems of implementing distributed database systems and is especially difficult in distributed database management systems that build a global coordinator on existing local database management facilities. For example, a local database management system must be able to indicate a transaction's readiness to commit an update but cannot be allowed to commit that update until the global coordinator gives the instruction to commit everywhere.

ESTABLISHING A SHARING POLICY

The designers of a database system must eventually address the problem of balancing concurrency with consistency. At one extreme is a state of total concurrency: anyone may access any part of the data resource at any time, for both reading and updating data. In most environments, the data would soon become useless because of inconsistencies. At the other extreme is total consistency with no concurrency: only one transaction may access the database at one time. This enforced serial execution would be disastrous in most production operations.

Other possibilities include (1) read-only access with high concurrency during the day, with updates performed serially at night, and (2) partitioning the data so that only one transaction may access a partition at any given time. Balancing concurrency with consistency means establishing a sharing policy that provides sufficient concurrency with an acceptable level of overhead.

The shared-access control policy of an environment should establish the technique synchronizing processes so that they will not interfere with one another and the procedures monitoring shared-access control. Questions such as the following must be answered in order to determine the requirements for the shared-access control policy:

1. What level of consistency is required?
2. How much overhead is it reasonable to incur?
3. What are the shared-access requirements for retrieval from the databases?
4. What are the requirements for updates to the databases?
5. How predictable are the transactions' data requirements?
6. How long do transactions last?
7. What kinds of shared-access control are provided by the database management systems in the environment? What kinds of locking are supported? How much of the data resource can be locked in one request?
8. Must shared access to distributed databases be supported?

Design Decisions

The shared-access control techniques used with a particular database system are decided primarily by its database management system(s). Rarely can a data administrator augment those services by additional techniques, and so the level of support of shared access should be investigated when selecting the database management system.

Most database management systems support both shared and exclusive locks. The data administrator typically can tune the shared-access control techniques in the following areas:

- Lock granularity: How much of the database resource can be locked in one request? A file? A page? A record? A field?
- Lock types: What types of locks can be requested? Shared? Shared with intent to read? Shared with intent to update? Exclusive with intent to read? Exclusive with intent to update? Others?
- Transaction granularity: Can a transaction contain multiple actions? Can a program contain multiple transactions? Can a transaction involve multiple programs?

Fine locking, that is, locks on small database objects (e.g., records, fields), yields greater concurrency than does coarse locking. Fine locking also increases the overhead for transactions that need to access a lot of data and set many locks, whereas coarse locking provides relatively cheap, controlled access to larger collections of data.

Shared-access control becomes more important as more users depend on database services. The data administrator thus must be sure that proper control facilities are used to provide a sufficient level of shared access, and protect the data's quality, at an acceptable overhead cost.

DATABASE SECURITY

The objective of database security is to prevent the unauthorized modification and disclosure of database contents. Security is high on the list of computer-related problems of which practically everyone seems to be aware. Even so, today's database management systems offer few significant security controls but depend on their host operating systems for protection.

A database security system must be able to determine who is requesting access, what data are being requested, what type of access is being requested, and whether the requester is authorized to make this type of access to the requested data. The intention is to ensure that only those users authorized to access particular types of data actually are able to access those data. If a user is not authorized to update particular types of data, then there should be no way for that user to cause those data to be changed.

Database management systems typically support at least "all or nothing" access to the portions of a database. In these cases, if a user can access a portion of the database, then both read-only and update transactions from that user will be supported. No distinction is made among different types of access.

Other database management systems distinguish between read-only and update access, and still others distinguish among different types of read-only access. In these cases, some users are authorized to access raw data, and others are authorized to access only summary data. For example, one user cannot read another individual's record in the government's census database. But anyone can access summary demographic information: median incomes, average schooling, average number of people per household, and the like.

Security Problems and Threats

Threats to database security include:

- Accidental threats, when a user unintentionally gains unauthorized access because of a system or a user error.
- Deliberate threats, when a user intentionally gains unauthorized access.

Accidental threats to security are common. For example, a user might call into a computer system and (if the previous user hung up without logging off) be attached to the already-active process belonging to the previous user. That already-active process might have different access authorizations than the new user has.

There are many types of deliberate security threats, including the following:

- Physical security.
  - Physical storage devices can be stolen.
  - Terminals may be located in insecure environments, where they are available for use by unauthorized people. These people may gain unauthorized access simply by examining displays on terminal screens or piles of paper output.
  - A user may gain unauthorized access to a computer room and override or bypass the security mechanisms of the operating system or the database management system.
- Communications.
  - A user may wiretap or electronically eavesdrop to gain access to data on communications lines.
- External procedures.
  - Physical storage devices can be copied without using the services of a database management system. If database security is solely the responsibility of the database management system, then the copying may be unauthorized.
  - An application programmer can write software that behaves differently from its specifications, and the resulting code may not conform to security policy.
  - A user may masquerade as a more privileged user, logging in by using someone else's identification and password.
  - A systems programmer may write code that disables or bypasses the security mechanisms of the operating system or the database management system, enabling access to otherwise inaccessible data.
  - A data administrator may incorrectly specify a security policy, granting improper authorization to selected users.
  - An authorized user may sell or give data to an unauthorized user.
  - A user may infer data that he or she is unauthorized to access from data that he or she is authorized to access.

Of these threats, the most difficult to control are the external procedures.

Comparison of Responsibilities

Both database management systems and operating systems are responsible for protecting resources against unauthorized reference or modification; authenticating requesters; and providing as simple, reliable, and efficient a protection technique as possible. There are differences, however, that make operating system protection mechanisms not totally suited for providing database security:

- Operating systems protect physical resources, for example, files, pages, disk cylinders, and magnetic tapes. Database management systems need to protect logical resources, for example, relations, attributes, records, and segments.
- Operating systems protect a resource in its entirety. Database management systems need to be able to protect part of a resource, for example, fields, records, and subschemas within the same database.
- Operating systems distinguish between read and write access. Database management systems need to distinguish between additional types of access, for example, content-dependent, context-dependent, and history-dependent access.

Content-dependent access control requires the retrieval of data values from the database in order to determine whether the user is authorized to access those values. For example, managers may be authorized to retrieve the salaries only of those people who work for them. Thus in order to determine whether a particular user should be able to retrieve Joe Smith's salary, the database management system must first retrieve Joe Smith's record and find out whether Joe works for the requester.

Context-dependent access control protects against inferences from combinations of accesses to individual data values. For example, consider a database that is thought to be secure if no salesperson can determine the commission amount paid to anyone but herself. Anyone can, however, determine the total amount of commissions paid for contracts awarded to any department, which contracts were awarded to each department, the type of each contract, and the total amount of commissions paid to each type of contract. Assume that the salesperson knows that

- Contracts A, B, and C were awarded to the XYZ department.
- Contracts A, B, and D are the short-term contracts.
- The commission amount on contract D was $10,000, which is a contract for which she was paid commission.

She then can infer the commission paid on contract C by asking the following questions:

1. How much was paid in commissions to contracts awarded to the XYZ department?
   Answer: $65,000.
2. How much was paid in commissions for short-term contracts?
   Answer: $50,000.

Solving the two equations:

$$A + B + C = \$65,000$$
$$A + B + \$10,000 = \$50,000$$

gives C = $25,000, which is data that the salesperson is unauthorized to know. One way to protect against these context-dependent compromises is to limit the number of requests that an individual can make against the database. But this is ineffective when two or more users can pool their individually acquired answers.

History-dependent access control prevents a user from making a series of requests that together provide data that the user is unauthorized to have. For example, an individual may be authorized to retrieve one department's budget and actual figures for research and development projects, but nobody may be authorized to retrieve these figures for all departments.

SECURITY CONTROL TECHNIQUES

Some of the control techniques providing database security are physical isolation, cipher systems, passwords, query modification, and views.

Physical Isolation

The *physical isolation* approach moves sensitive data to secure facilities that have highly controlled entrance and exit procedures, do not support dial-up access, and are carefully monitored. If there are communications lines into the facility, they usually are well shielded (e.g., buried in concrete) and run to terminals that are also in secure facilities. In a distributed database environment, one can store data in facilities with different levels of security. When this is done, the various levels of protection must be checked when validating requests.

Cipher Systems

Cipher systems address the problem of security infiltration through communications lines and also can be used to protect against unauthorized access to disk or tape files. A cipher system encodes data to hide their real meaning; that is, to make the data unintelligible to all but authorized requesters. A cipher system uses an algorithm and a *cryptographic key*. The algorithm includes an encryption and a decryption procedure. The encryption procedure takes in the real data and the cryptographic key and puts out the encoded data. Those encoded data can later be decoded through decryption and the same cryptographic key. The algorithm of a cipher system is usually public knowledge, but the cryptographic key is kept secret. In order for the cipher system to be effective, there must be no easy way of finding out the key.

A very simple cipher system uses the following encryption procedure:

1. Reverse the string of digits in the real data.
2. Insert a spurious digit between pairs of real digits.
3. Substitute for each digit the corresponding ordinal letter in the key.

Assume that the key is "wryip<adgj." The value 12323487 could be enciphered as follows (The steps correspond to the steps in the algorithm):

1. 78432321.
2. 786432230217.
3. dgapiyyiwyrd.

If the key were instead "mbczljgdap," the enciphered value would have been "daglzcczmcbd."

Passwords

Passwords are commonly used to authenticate users and identify a user by something he knows. Operating systems use passwords to determine whether a requester is authorized to log onto the system. When the user identifies himself, he also supplies his password. The system matches the supplied password with the recorded password for the user to establish whether he is who he says he is. Clearly, password protection is only as good as the secrecy of the passwords, and knowing that everyone's password is the same as his or her last name makes masquerading as another person very simple.

In a database environment, passwords typically are attached to files, but not to records or fields, and there may be different passwords for read access and write access. A user may need to give one password to access initially the operating system and then additional passwords to access the data resources.

Password protection is nearly always provided by the operating system, rather than by the database management operating system, rather than by the database management system. When a user uses a database command to open a database file, the database management system processes that request by passing it and the user-supplied password to the operating system.

Query Modification

Query modification changes user requests to include protection rules. When a user request is received, the presence of protection rules is checked; any needed data are retrieved to validate the condition specified in the protection rule; and then the user's request is processed.

For example, if the protection rule is that a manager can retrieve only the salaries of those people who work for him, then a request

```
SELECT SALARY
FROM EMP
WHERE DEPT# = 10
```

would be modified to

```
SELECT SALARY
FROM EMP
WHERE DEPT# = 10
  AND MANAGER = user-name.
```

The protection restriction is added automatically by the database management system.

Views

Views are logical partitions of a database and are also called *subschemas*. Typically a database request accesses one view. Views are defined for different users according to their data needs, and they then can be used to control access to the data. Depending on the database management system's capabilities to define views, the control can be more or less precise.

For example, in relational systems, views are typically defined using the query language. In these cases, view granularity can be as fine or coarse as desired. A view may correspond to one base relation, may combine base relations, may eliminate some columns of a base relation, and may eliminate rows of a base relation based on their contents.

By contrast, in other database management systems, a view is implemented as a separate file. In these cases, defining very fine views implies that the database will be implemented with many small files. Defining coarse views, on the other hand implies that the database will be implemented with a few large files and that security protection will be coarse.

Security in the Distributed Environment

Providing security protection becomes somewhat more complicated in a distributed database environment. Either all processors should implement the same level of security controls, or the more secure sites should take account of the lesser controls at other sites when validating requests.

There may also be hidden costs of providing security protection in a distributed database environment. For example, enforcing content-dependent access controls may mean accessing data stored at several processors. For example, assume that the salary data are considered to be sensitive and are stored in secure location A. Data about who manages whom are stored in location B. To process the request in the query modification example, both locations A and B must be accessed.

Because of the capability to separate physically portions of the database in a distributed environment, security may be easier to provide than in a centralized environment. Different physical controls can be implemented at the different sites, and different cryptographic keys can be used in the encryption algorithms at the different sites. Security controls can be tailored to the requirements for protecting particular types of data.

ESTABLISHING A SECURITY POLICY

Database security techniques try to combat problems caused by people, and database recovery and shared-access control techniques try to combat problems caused by-hardware and software. The establishment of an effective security policy is thus important in any environment concerned about data's leaking to unauthorized people.

Most database management systems offer little security protection in addition to that provided by their host operating systems. Security protection is mostly in the security policies established outside the software.

An environment's security policy should decide:

- Whether security will be controlled centrally by one data administrator or by different administrators.
- The procedures for changing security controls and adding new users and data resources to the system.
- The minimal requirements for the security protection capabilities of the database management systems to be used in the environment.
- The procedures for enforcing security controls.
- Who is responsible for each kind of data in the system.
- What kinds of access will be distinguished in providing security control.

Questions such as the following should be answered in order to establish the requirements for the security control policy:

1. How sensitive are the data?
2. How difficult should it be for a malicious user to circumvent security-protection capabilities?
3. What level of security control is required?
4. How much overhead is it reasonable to incur to provide security?
5. How physically secure are the computer and terminal facilities?
6. Are there legal requirements for security?
7. Are there contractor requirements for security?

Design Decisions

A danger sign in an environment with any supposedly sensitive data is the lack of a security policy. Security is one area in which action by the data administrator is required, as database management systems and operating systems will not provide adequate protection by themselves.

The typical database management system uses passwords to control access to portions of the database. Some control is based on the type of access and what is being accessed. Security considerations can affect file boundaries, the partitioning of the database across processors in a distributed database environment, and the use of encryption.

If the database management system relies entirely on the operating system for security protection, then security considerations become a factor when designing the file boundaries in a database system. And if a network's processors offer different levels of security protection, then security considerations can become the primary factor in deciding which data should be stored at which processors.

CLOSING COMMENTS

One of the capabilities that distinguishes a database management system from a file-access method is its data protection services, which include recovering from various types of failures, preventing unfortunate conflicts among transactions that access shared data, and preventing unauthorized access to data resources.

Data protection has been an area of active research for many years. The data protection services that database management systems provide will continue to evolve to incorporate developments from this research. As we become more dependent on database support, data administrators' efforts to establish effective policies for recovery, shared-access control, and security will become more visible.

TERMS

abort
after-image
archive
audit trail
backout
backup
before-image
checkpoint
commit
cryptographic key
deadlock
decryption
encryption
exclusive lock
failsoft
granularity
journal
lock

logical unit of work
optimistic concurrency control
password
recoverable unit
recovery
recovery technique
REDO
restart
rollback
rollforward
salvation program
serial execution
serializability
shared lock
transaction
two-phase commit protocol
two-phase locking
UNDO

REVIEW EXERCISES

1. Define each of the terms in the preceding list.
2. What are the trade-offs between using the UNDO versus the REDO recovery techniques?
3. What are the trade-offs between using the REDO with transactions versus the REDO with after-images recovery techniques?
4. What kinds of recovery data might be collected in a database environment? How would each be used?
5. Find out what recovery techniques are used in your organization. (If you are a full-time student, investigate the college administrative data-processing department or a company in your community.)
6. What kinds of failures can be remedied automatically? What types of human intervention are required to remedy the other kinds of failures?
7. Find out how frequently various kinds of failures occur in your organization.
8. Discuss the relative difficulties of providing recoverability in centralized and distributed database environments.
9. How does the concept of transaction appear in both database failure protection and concurrency control?
10. What is the difference between a shared lock and an exclusive lock?
11. Why might a transaction request an exclusive lock when it is just going to read data?
12. Discuss the relative difficulties of providing concurrency control in centralized and distributed database environments.
13. Construct an example of ten actions that affect a database. Show the log of before- and after-images produced by the set of actions.
14. Construct an example of database actions that shows a lost update. Illustrate how locking can be used to prevent the lost update.
15. Construct an example of database actions that shows an assumed update. Illustrate how locking can be used to prevent the assumed update.
16. Construct an example of database actions that shows a phantom read. Illustrate how locking can be used to prevent the phantom read.
17. What is the purpose of timestamping?
18. Explain how timestamping differs from locking.
19. Why might timestamping be preferable to locking in a distributed database?
20. How do the optimistic concurrency-control techniques differ from the locking techniques?
21. How do the optimistic concurrency-control techniques differ from the time-stamping techniques?
22. What are the six principles for concurrency control through locking?
23. What kinds of security techniques are used in your organization?

24. Give examples of database situations that could use content-dependent access controls, context-dependent access controls, and history-dependent controls.

25. Describe the techniques for providing communications between secure and non-secure sites in a network of processors.

REFERENCES

Bernstein, P. A., and N. Goodman. Approaches to concurrency control in distributed database systems. *Proceedings, 1979 National Computer Conference*, pp. 813–820.

———. Timestamp-based algorithms for concurrency control in distributed database systems. *Proceedings, Sixth International Conference on Very Large Databases*, October 1980.

Chandy, K. M., J. C. Browne, C. W. Dissly, and W. R. Uhrig. Analytic models for rollback and recovery strategies in data base systems, *IEEE Transactions on Software Engineering* SE-1 (March 1975): 100–110.

Date, C. J. Locking and recovery in a shared database system: An application programming tutorial. *Proceedings, Fifth International Conference on Very Large Databases*. Rio de Janeiro, 1979, pp. 1–15.

Fernandez, E. B., R. C. Summers, and C. Wood. *Database Security and Integrity*. Reading, Mass.: Addison-Wesley, 1981.

Gray, J. N., R. A. Lorie, G. R. Putzolu, and J. L. Traiger. Granularity of locks and degrees of consistency in a shared data base. In G. M. Nijssen, ed., *Modelling in Database Management Systems*. New York: Elsevier North-Holland, 1976, 365–394.

Gray, J. N. *Lecture Notes in Computer Science*, vol. 60: *Notes on Data Base Operating Systems*. New York: Springer-Verlag, 1978.

———. The transaction concept: Virtues and limitations. *Proceedings, Seventh International Conference on Very Large Databases*. Cannes, 1981, pp. 144–154.

———, et al. The recovery manager of the System R database manager, *ACM Computing Surveys* 13 (June 1982): 223–242.

Kung, H. T., and J. T. Robinson. On optimistic methods for concurrency control, *ACM Transactions on Database Systems* 6 (June 1981): 213–226.

Maryanski, F. J., and P. S. Fisher. Rollback and recovery in distributed data base management systems. *Proceedings of the 1977 Annual Conference of the ACM*, 1979, pp. 33–38.

Reuter, A. A fast transaction-oriented logging scheme for UNDO-recovery, *IEEE Transactions on Software Engineering* SE-6 (July 1980).

Severance, D. G., and G. M. Lohmann. Differential files: Their application to the maintenance of large databases, *ACM Transactions on Database Systems* 1 (September 1976): 256–267.

Stonebraker, M. Concurrency control and consistency of multiple copies of data in distributed INGRES, *IEEE Transactions on Software Engineering* SE-5 (May 1979): 188–194.

———, and E. Wong. Access control in a relational database management system by query modification. *Proceedings, 1974 ACM Annual Conference*, San Diego, 1974, 180–186.

Verhofstad, J. S. M. Recovery techniques for database systems, *ACM Computing Surveys* 10 (June 1978): 167–195.

Closing Comments:
Database Directions

In this closing chapter, I shall predict the directions of database technology development and application for the next decade.

GENERAL TRENDS IN DATABASE TECHNOLOGY

Data management technology has encountered and solved many difficult problems in the last two decades. Work in the 1960s led to the development of commercially viable database management systems that could handle large volumes of production data. Before the advent of these systems, virtually all data processing was supported by file systems. Any data protection capabilities and logical designs should be credited to the foresight and diligence of local data-processing shops, which could not turn to others for these services. IMS, TO-TAL, and the CODASYL database management systems (see Chapters 6, 7, 11, and 12) became widely used in the 1970s and continue in heavy use today.

Data management research and development in the 1970s centered on the relational data model (see Chapters 4, 5, and 10.) A large body of literature grew from the efforts of investigators in both industry and academia; the theory behind the relational model was published; various normal forms were proposed and mathematically justified; and user-oriented languages to interface with formal relational languages were investigated.

About ten years after research turned to the relational data model, relational database management systems became commercially viable. This ten-year time lag is approximately the same as that between the early interest in hierarchic and network databases and the general acceptance of their commercial support (Fig. 15.1). Relational database management systems will become the most important database support packages through the 1980s and are already available on all kinds of computers, ranging from huge mainframes to personal computers with hard disks. They are evolving to support production databases. Accompanying the work on the relational data model, significant progress was made in the second half of the 1970s on the development of shared-access control and security protection (see Chapter 14). This work addressed the distributed database environment as well as the centralized database environment. As data communications capabilities evolved, the need for distributed data management techniques became clearer.

The first half of the 1980s found distributed database management system capabilities being prototyped in various research and development laboratories. If historical trends can be used to predict the future, then these distributed system services should be commercialized and in fairly widespread use by the early 1990s.

Another topic of research interest during the late 1970s was improving the performance of relational database systems using hardware database managers. The results included a variety of prototype intelligent disk controllers and computers specialized for relational database management. These systems are called *database machines* (see Chapter 10 on physical design of relational databases). They are becoming commercially viable in the last half of the 1980s and will eventually replace software relational database management systems.

Database management systems will evolve through the late 1980s and early 1990s to take advantage of advances in artificial intelligence and programming languages. One result will be object-based systems, which will bring more powerful application-development tools to users. An object-based system manages data directly from a logical data model with both connection and category relationships. An entity, its attributes, and its permissible operators form an object. Attributes and operators are inherited by subtype objects.

Other topics of increasing research and development interest in the mid-1980s are database development methodologies, data dictionary systems, and techniques for managing engineering data.

TRENDS IN DATABASE DEVELOPMENT METHODOLOGIES

There is a growing awareness that database design methodologies should include extensive user involvement, should produce systems in small increments, should use prototyping, and should integrate data.

During the late 1970s, information systems departments attempted to service

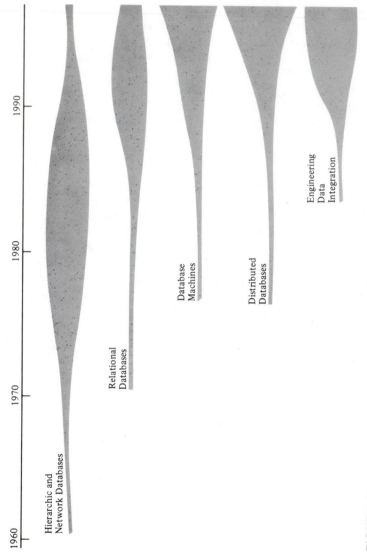

1960   1970   1980   1990

Hierarchic and
Network Databases

Relational
Databases

Database
Machines

Distributed
Databases

Engineering
Data
Integration

FIGURE 15.1. Relative acceptance and prevalence of selected database
technologies.

enterprises' information needs by large, centralized database systems, and the result in many organizations was huge systems development projects. While millions of dollars were spent on the development of these megalithic databases, the users waited, made do with existing file applications, and sometimes created their own solutions on personal computers and departmental machines.

Logical data-modeling techniques and prototyping methods have made it practical for users to help develop database systems. Users can now specify data requirements using logical data models, no longer having to rely on data-processing personnel to convert ambiguous, voluminous, textual statements of requirements into precise, automatable form.

Prototyping methods and support software have enabled physical databases to be generated quickly from logical designs. Users can test various designs before deciding on the "final" database structure. In fact, flexible database management systems, which separate user-view considerations from physical-implementation considerations (see Chapter 2 on the database design process), may make it unnecessary ever to freeze "final" structures.

The database development methodologies that show the most promise for the future are those that produce integrated data resources. Integration will allow users to access data resources stored on a variety of computers in geographically separated locations, without concern for the details of data distribution and disparities across computers, database management systems, and database structures. The primary technology that we see today for achieving data integration is the three-schema approach (see Chapter 2).

TRENDS IN DATA DICTIONARY SUPPORT

Data dictionary systems will become much more active in data management than most are today. Chapter 13 introduced the role of the data dictionary in providing transaction support in integrated data environments. The data dictionary system can store and manage information about conceptual, external, and internal schemas. An active data dictionary will become the heart of database management systems for centralized and distributed environments (see Fig. 13.5). Data dictionary systems will become more intelligent and will provide a contextual interpretation of users' requests. They will be able to determine the meanings of terms used by different people, to restrict accesses to data based on the situation, and to resume interrupted data-access sessions without loss of context.

There has been much work on knowledge representation in both databases and artificial intelligence, which will be extended by applying artificial intelligence techniques to database systems. Intelligent data dictionaries will know not just what the data meanings are but also what processes should be triggered and executed when certain data conditions are met. These developments will be essential for object-based systems.

Intelligent data dictionary systems will become, in effect, expert systems for database design and transaction development. They will be able to decide when to modify internal schemas to improve performance, to construct new external schemas in response to users' English or German or Nepali or even spoken requests for data, and to determine whether requested additions to the conceptual schema violate consistency constraints.

TRENDS IN DISTRIBUTED DATABASE MANAGEMENT

Distributed environments are facts of life; rarely does an enterprise have the luxury of completely centralized operations. Many organizations have offices in various places and salespeople in the field. They increasingly have many computers, generally from a variety of vendors. The development of computer-networking technology has raised our awareness of the need for database technology to manage data in our everyday, distributed worlds.

Distributed database management systems will move out of the research and development laboratories in the late 1980s and into the commercial marketplace. Some of these will be self-contained distributed systems (Fig. 15.2), and others will work with local database management system support (Fig. 15.3). The more appropriate approach for a particular enterprise will be determined by the extent and condition of its computers and database management systems. The greater its investment is in heterogeneous hardware and software, the less likely it will be to convert from a local database management system to a new homogeneous, global approach.

The need for distributed database support is becoming critical in factories, where efforts to modernize have led to the introduction of a variety of computerized devices: automatic inspection and test stations, automatic material handlers, robots and vision systems, and numerically controlled machine tools. All require data about parts and products. Today they use their own separate files, each in a different format and each with different controls. The future factory will have integrated database support of this shop floor equipment and will also

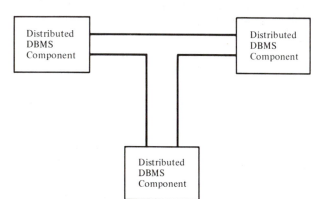

FIGURE 15.2. Example of a configuration of self-contained distributed database management system.

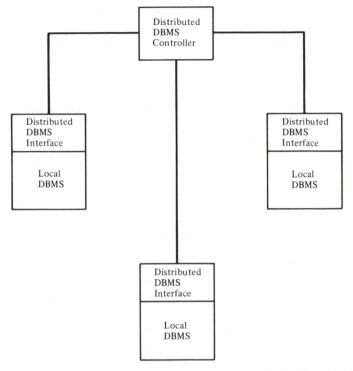

FIGURE 15.3.   Example of a configuration of distributed database management system with local database management system support.

have data integration between these systems and its business-oriented applications for purchasing, inventory control, personnel management, capital acquisition, accounting, and the like. A major area of research and development through the 1980s and into the 1990s will be computer-integrated manufacturing—CIM. CIM provides manufacturing integration through data integration.

Distributed database support will thus be required to link manufacturing machines with business computers, and mainframes with personal computers. Distributed data managers will have to be able to cope with highly sophisticated database management support on the mainframes, as well as with the relatively rudimentary data management capabilities of some manufacturing equipment.

TRENDS IN APPLICATIONS

The most important application of database technology for the foreseeable future will be in achieving integration. Database technology will allow

• financial institutions to provide truly integrated services to their customers, be they individuals or commercial enterprises.

- manufacturing companies to integrate their engineering, design, manufacturing, test, and support functions.
- educational institutions to provide more comprehensive support systems to teachers and students.
- governments to coordinate their social services more effectively and economically.
- service enterprises to understand their marketplace needs and to react to changes in those marketplaces more rapidly.
- This list could go on and on.

Some of these applications will require developments in the database technology itself. For example, today's database managers are not well suited to handling engineering data:

- Engineering-data structures tend to be dynamic and changeable, compared with business-data schemas, which are relatively static.
- Engineering data tend to be a mix of text, numerics, and graphic geometries. The numerics are commonly vectors and matrices. Geometries are represented by large (more than a megabyte) strings of bits. Most commercial database management systems handle only integers, decimal numbers, floating point numbers (sometimes), and short (less than 256-byte) strings of characters.
- Engineering transactions tend to be very long. A design may take days, weeks, or even months to develop. By contrast, most commercial database management systems use data-protection techniques (see Chapter 14) that assume that transactions take only a few seconds.
- Engineering data must be controlled by a rigorous system of configuration management. For example, data are specified as being in draft, early-release, released, or whatever status. A user at a CAD/CAM (computer-aided design/computer-aided manufacturing) work station must be able to check out data into a private database from public databases on other computers, work on the designs, and then submit the new version for public release. Business-oriented database management systems do not support configuration management control but have to rely on application software for this support.
- Engineering data come in huge quantities. Databases containing terabits (ten to the twelfth power) should be expected. Today's software database management systems typically cannot handle volumes of this magnitude.

These and other problems will be solved in the next several years.

FINAL COMMENTS

The data management field is a challenging, rewarding one in which to work. There is a continuing demand for specialists to implement database management systems, to design and implement physical databases and transactions, to develop logical data structures and to work with users. As stated in Chapter 1', data are at the heart of the decision-making activities in every enterprise, and effective, efficient database systems will become increasingly critical to the prosperity of enterprises of all kinds.

TERMS

artificial intelligence	distributed database
computer-aided design/computer-aided manufacturing (CAD/CAM)	intelligence
	logical database design
computer-integrated manufacturing (CIM)	physical database design
	prototyping
database machine	relational database management
data dictionary system	three-schema approach
data integration	transaction

REVIEW EXERCISES

1. Describe how an industry could be changed by having integrated database support.

2. Distinguish between having a physically centralized database and a distributed database with an integrated logical view.

3. Discuss the use of artificial intelligence techniques such as frames and semantic nets to represent the knowledge captured in a logical data model.

4. What characteristics of engineering data are difficult for today's commercial database management systems to support?

5. Why is the three-schema approach significant for achieving data integration?

6. How do graphics data and character data differ?

7. Why is there a ten-year lag between the introduction of technology and its commercial prevalence?

REFERENCES

Atwood, T. M. An object-oriented DBMS for design support applications. *IEEE Proceedings, COMPINT '85*. Montreal, Canada, September 1985, pp. 299–307.

Lorie, R., and W. Plouffe. Relational databases for engineering data, *IBM Research Report* RJ 3847 (43914), April 6, 1983.

Nilsson, N. J. *Principles of Artificial Intelligence*. Palo Alto, Calif.: Tioga Publishing, 1980.

Tsichritzis, D., and A. Klug, eds. The ANSI/X3/SPARC DBMS framework report of the study group on database management systems, *Info Systems* 3 (1978).

Answers

3. a. S1 := SELECT (STUDENT) (STUDENT NAME = 'JONES');
   S2 := S1 |X| ENROLLMENT;
   S3 := S2 |X| RESPONSIBILITY;
   S4 := S3 |X| TEACHER;
   ANSWER := PROJECT (S4) (TEACHER NAME);

b. T1 := SELECT (TEACHER) (DEPT = 'MIS');
   T2 := T1 |X| RESPONSIBILITY;
   T3 := T2 |X| ENROLLMENT;
   T4 := SELECT (T3) (GRADE = 'C');
   T5 := T4 |X| STUDENT;
   ANSWER := PROJECT (T5) (GPA);

4. a. (STUDENT, COURSE, TEACHER)

Joe	32	North
Ellen	32	North
Marge	51	Elgin
Marge	51	Marlin
Ellen	43	Jones
Ellen	43	Smith
Jan	43	Jones
Ellen	43	Smith

    b. (COURSE)
       32
       51
       43
    c. (COURSE, TEACHER)
       51   Elgin
       65   Elgin
       51   Marlin

5. CUSTOMER (CUSTOMER#, BALANCE, CREDIT_LIMIT, DISCOUNT, CUS-
    TOMER_ADDRESS, CUSTOMER_NAME)
    ORDER (ORDER#, CUSTOMER#, ORDER_ADDRESS, ORDER_DATE)
    LINE_ITEM (ORDER#, LINE#, PART#, QUANTITY_ORDERED, QUAN-
    TITY_SHIPPED)
    PART (PART#, DESCRIPTION, PRICE, WEIGHT)
    WAREHOUSE (WAREHOUSE ID, WAREHOUSE_ADDRESS, PHONE#)
    INVENTORY (PART#, WAREHOUSE ID, QUANTITY_ON_HAND, QUAN-
    TITY_BACKORDERED)

6. EMPLOYEE (EMPLOYEE#, PHONE#, JOB_TITLE)
    PROJECT (PROJECT#, LAST_BUDGET_$, CURRENT_BUDGET_$, PRO-
    JECT_NAME, MANAGER#)
    ASSIGNMENT (EMPLOYEE#, PROJECT#, %_EFFORT, START_DATE)

7. MOTOR_VEHICLE (MV ID#, COST, VENDOR, MV_TYPE)
    TRUCK (MV ID#, #AXELS, GVW, TRUCK_TYPE)
    SHIP (MV ID#, LENGTH, MAX_DRAFT, MIN_DRAFT)
    PLANE (MV ID#, CLASSIFICATION, WEIGHT, #ENGINES, #PASSENGERS)
    CATTLE_TRUCK (MV ID#, RAMP_HEIGHT, #COWS, #PIGS)
    REFRIGERATED_TRUCK (MV ID#, MIN_TEMP, MAX_TEMP, CAPACITY)

8. COURSE_SCHEDULE (CLASS#, SECTION#, DAY, ROOM#)
    CLASS (CLASS#, TEXT TITLE)
    TEACHING_ASSIGNMENT (CLASS#, SECTION#, FACULTY#)
    STUDENT (MATRIC#, MAJOR, YEAR)
    FACULTY_MEMBER (FACULTY#, RANK, SALARY)
    RECORD (CLASS#, SECTION#, MATRIC#, EXAM_SCORE, EXAM#)

Answers to Selected Exercises for Chapter 5

2. a. cannot determine from information given
    b. Q1 (EMP#, FIRST_NAME, LAST_NAME, JOB _CODE, COURSE#)
       Q2 (EMP#, DATE, SALARY)
       Q3 (EMP#, CUSTOMER#, QUANTITY, DESCRIPTION)
       Q4 (JOB CODE, JOB_NAME)
       Q5 (CUSTOMER#, CUSTOMER_NAME)
       Q6 (EMP#, CHILD NAME)

5. a. R11 (A, B)
       R12 (F, G)
       R13 (A, F)
    b. R21 (A, B)
       R22 (B, C)

   c. R31 ($\underline{A}$, B)
     R32 ($\underline{A}$, $\underline{D}$)
     R33 ($\underline{A}$, $\underline{E}$)
   d. R41 ($\underline{A}$, C)
     R42 ($\underline{A}$, $\underline{G}$)
   e. R51 ($\underline{A}$, $\underline{F}$, K)
     R52 ($\underline{H}$, F)
   f. already in 4NF
6. S1 ($\underline{A}$, E, B)
   S2 ($\underline{B}$,C, D)
   S3 ($\underline{D}$, F)

Answers to Selected Questions for Chapter 6

  4. a. MOVE 'DUMP' TO DORM-NAME.
       FIND DORM.
       IF ERROR-COUNT = 0
            FIND FIRST STUDENT IN HOUSES SET
            PERFORM FIND-NEXT-STUDENT UNTIL ERROR-COUNT > 0.
       where
       FIND-NEXT-STUDENT.
            GET.
            DISPLAY STUDENT-NAME.
            FIND NEXT STUDENT IN HOUSES SET.
    b. FIND FIRST STUDENT IN ALL-RECORDS AREA.
       PERFORM FIND-NEXT-STUDENT UNTIL ERROR-COUNT > 0.
       where
       FIND-NEXT-STUDENT.
            GET.
            DISPLAY STUDENT-NAME.
            FIND NEXT STUDENT IN ALL-RECORDS AREA.
    c. MOVE 'BOZO' TO FACULTY-NAME.
       FIND FACULTY.
       IF ERROR-COUNT = 0
            FIND FIRST CLASS IN INSTRUCTS SET
            PERFORM FIND-NEXT-CLASS UNTIL ERROR-COUNT> 0.
       where
       FIND-NEXT-CLASS.
            FIND FIRST GRADE IN ASSIGNS SET.
            PERFORM FIND-NEXT-GRADE UNTIL ERROR-COUNT > 0.
            FIND NEXT CLASS IN INSTRUCTS SET.
       where
       FIND-NEXT-GRADE.
            GET.
            DISPLAY GRADE-SCORE.
            FIND NEXT GRADE IN ASSIGNS SET.
    d. MOVE 'BOZO' TO FACULTY-NAME.
       FIND FACULTY.

IF ERROR-COUNT = 0
      FIND FIRST CLASS IN INSTRUCTS SET
      PERFORM FIND-NEXT-CLASS UNTIL ERROR-COUNT > 0.
where
FIND-NEXT-CLASS.
      FIND FIRST GRADE IN ASSIGNS SET.
      PERFORM FIND-NEXT-GRADE UNTIL ERROR-COUNT > 0.
      FIND NEXT CLASS IN INSTRUCTS SET.
where
FIND-NEXT-GRADE.
      GET.
      DISPLAY GRADE-SCORE.
      FIND OWNER IN EARNS SET.
      GET.
      DISPLAY STUDENT-NAME.
      FIND NEXT GRADE IN ASSIGNS SET.

5. Fig. 6.24.

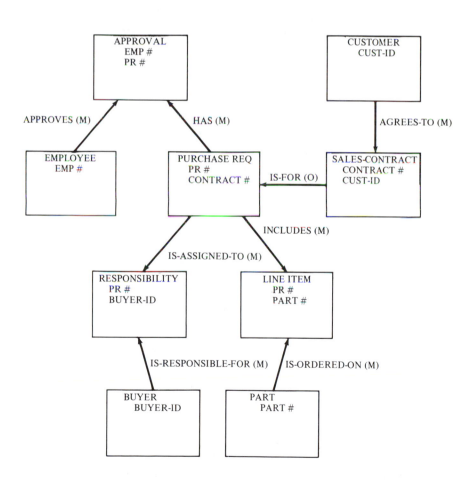

6. Fig. 6.25.

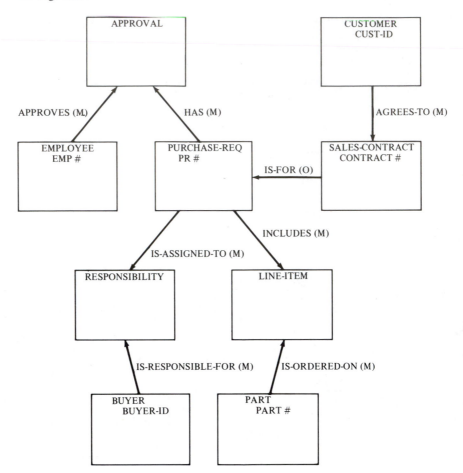

9. Fig. 6.26.

10. Fig. 6.27.

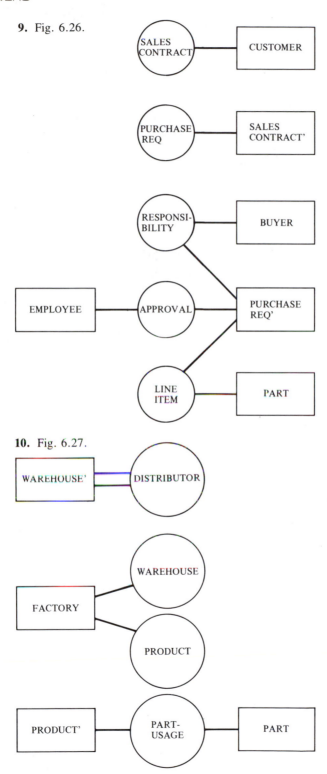

COMMON ACRONYMS

ANSI American National Standards Institute
BCNF Boyce/Codd normal form
CODASYL Conference on Data Systems Languages
DA data administrator
DBA database administrator
DBD database definition
DBMS database management system
DDL data definition language
DDLC Data Definition Language Committee
DL/I Data Language/I
DML data manipulation language
DMT data modeling technique
DP data processing
DSDL data storage definition language
D/D dictionary/directory
IMS Information Management System
LDB logical database
LDBD logical database definition
LDBR logical database record

PCB program communication block
PDB physical database
PDBD physical database definition
PDBR physical database record
PSB program specification block
SSA segment search argument
1NF first normal form
2NF second normal form
3NF third normal form
4NF fourth normal form
5NF fifth normal form

GLOSSARY

Abort. To terminate early without successful completion.

Absolute address. A location in storage. Compare with *Relative address*.

Access key. One or more fields whose values can be translated into a record's absolute or relative address.

Accessibility. See *Data accessibility*.

Access technique. A method for determining the address of a record.

Activity model. A representation of processes and their relationships. Also called *Function model, Process model*.

Address. See *Absolute address, Relative address*.

Address-calculation function. A method for translating an access-key value into a physical location. See also *Access key*.

After-image. A copy made after an update has been processed. Compare with *Before-image*.

Aggregation relationship. See *Connection relationship*.

Alias. A synonym for an attribute or entity name.

Alternate index. See *Secondary index*.

Alternate key. A candidate key that is not selected as the primary key. Compare with *Primary key*.

ANSI/X3H2. The Language Committee of the American National Standards Institute Committee on Computers and Information Processing. Develops standards for various programming languages, including relational and network database languages.

ANSI/X3/SPARC. The Standards Planning and Requirements Committee of the American National Standards Institute Committee on Computers and Information Processing.

Application program. Software that supports a specific end-user activity or need for data.

Archive copy. A data copy retained for backup or historic reasons. Also called *Backup copy*. Compare with *Transport copy*.

Area. In a CODASYL database, a named collection of records, typically implemented in one physical file. Also called *Realm*.

Assertion. A positive statement or declaration.

Attribute. A named characteristic or descriptor of an entity. Also called *Data element, Data item, Data field*.

Audit trail. A record of actions, usually with details about who requested each action, when, from where, and the status of the results.

Auxiliary storage. See *Secondary storage*.

Backend processor. A special-function computer (typically for database processing) to reduce the workload for one or more host computers. Work is routed to the backend processor through the host computer. Compare with *Frontend processor*.

Back out. To remove the effects of a process or transaction.

Backup copy. See *Archive copy*.

Base relation. A copy made before an update has been processed. Compare with *After-image*.

Before-image. A copy made before an update has been processed. Compare with *After-image*.

Binary search. A search technique that can be applied to a set of ordered keys. At each step of the search the list is partitioned into two equal parts, with the selection of the appropriate next partition to probe made on the basis of relative key values.

Binary search tree. A binary tree in which in each node, all the names in the left subtree precede the node's label, and the node's label precedes all the names of nodes in the right subtree. A binary search tree is a special case of an *M-way search tree*, with M = 2.

Binary search tree index. An index structured as a binary search tree, in which each node contains not only pointers to its subtrees but also a pointer to a data record. Compare with *Table index*.

Binary tree. A tree in which each node branches to a maximum of two subtrees, one being a left subtree and the other being a right subtree.

Block. [1] A collection of contiguous records handled as a unit. No part of a block can be accessed from secondary storage without the rest of the block. [2] To prevent a process from accessing data because another process holds a lock on those data.

Block addressing. A family of address-calculation functions that calculate the number of the block in which a record is most likely to be stored. The block can store many records. Compare with *Record-slot addressing*.

Blocking factor. [1] The number of records in a block. [2] The number of characters in a block.

Boyce/Codd normal form (BCNF). Describes a relation in which every determinant is a candidate key.

B-tree. A tree with the following properties: (1) each record except the root and leaves has at least half its pointers nonnull; (2) the root has either no subtrees or at least two subtrees; (3) all leaves are on the same level.

B⁺-tree. A tree resembling a *B-tree* but that contains linked list connecting the leaves.

Buffer. An area of storage into which data are read and from which data are written in input and output operations; used to compensate for differences in the data flow rate between devices.

Bushy. Describes a tree with many branches.

Business rule. A statement composed by reading an entity name, relationship name, and entity name from a key-based or fully attributed data model view.

CALC algorithm. See *Hash function*.

CALC key. In a CODASYL database, one or more of a record type's data fields whose values together determine the occurrences' storage locations.

Candidate key. A set of one or more attributes whose values uniquely identify the instances of an entity. Also called *Key*.

Cardinality. The number of instances of one entity that can be related to an instance of another entity.

CASCADE. In a CODASYL database, an option on the DELETE verb to delete also any of the record occurrence's member records.

Catalog. Dictionary/directory software that generates data definition and manipulation language statements from a dictionary/directory database for inclusion in programs at compile time.

Category relationship. A relationship between entity instances that corresponds to a single real-world object, for example, between student and graduate student. Also called *Subtype relationship* or *Generalization relationship*. Compare with *Connection relationship*.

Chain. See *Linked list*.

Check condition. In a CODASYL database, an assertion about the valid values of a data item, enforced by the database management system when the data item is inserted or modified.

Checkpoint. A complete copy, typically onto an archival medium. See *Archive copy*.

Child. In a network or hierarchical database, the record type with the "many" role in a one-to-many relationship. See *Dependent segment, Member record type*. Compare with *Parent*.

CODASYL. Conference on Data Systems Languages. An organization of hardware and software vendor representatives and computer systems users, which has developed various language specifications and proposed that they be adopted as standards.

Coded record. In a TOTAL database, a variable record whose format is indicated by the value of a particular field.

Collision. A situation in which a hash function gives the same resultant address for two unequal key values.

Collision-resolution technique. A method for determining an alternative address for a key value when a collision occurs.

Commit. To guarantee that the updates in a transaction will be made in a database and that those updates cannot be undone except by another transaction.

Communications monitor. Software that provides a shared interface between applications programs and communications devices.

Communications processor. A computer specialized to do communications work. See also *Frontend processor*.

Compound key. A candidate key made of more than one attribute.

Conceptual schema. An integrated, logical data model of an enterprise's data resource, independent of the biases of particular users or applications and neutral to physical implementation structures. Also called *Enterprise view*. Compare with *External schema* and *Internal schema*.

Connection relationship. A relationship between different entity instances, for example, between a department and an employee. Also called *Aggregation relationship*. Compare with *Category relationship*.

Control key. In a TOTAL database, the master-file data fields that are used to access records directly. Similar to the CALC key in a CODASYL database.

Controller. Dictionary/directory software that directs programs to the physical locations of data and performs interschema transforms at run time, based on the contents of a dictionary/directory database.

Cryptographic key. A value that is combined with sensitive data by an encryption procedure to produce a scrambled, more secure form of the data.

Currency. A technique for leaving placeholders in a database so that previously accessed records can be revisited.

Cursor. In a relational database, a placeholder for accessing a table's rows individually rather than as a set.

Data. Values and their meanings. Commonly used in the singular ("Data is . . .") rather than the grammatically correct plural ("Data are . . .").

Data accessibility. The capability for a user to extract needed information from a database.

Data administrator (DA). A person or organization responsible for logical database design. Also called *Information resource administrator*. Compare with *Database administrator*.

Database. A collection of logically related data that supports shared access by many users and is protected and managed to retain its value.

Database administrator (DBA). A person or organization responsible for physical database design. Compare with *Data administrator*.

Database definition (DBD). In IMS or DL/I, assembly language macroinstructions showing the structure of database records. See also *Logical database definition, Physical database definition*.

Database key. In a CODASYL database, a field containing a logical pointer to a record.

Database machine. A computer that is specialized for database processing. Its database management system may be implemented in hardware or software. See also *Backend processor*.

Database management system (DBMS). Software (and sometimes hardware) specially designed to protect and manage databases. A DBMS is an interface between programs and data files, with responsibility for defining, representing, storing, organizing, and protecting data, as well as for interfacing users with the database.

Data definition language (DDL). A language used to describe the logical structure of a database. Also called *Schema definition language*. Compare with *Data manipulation language, Data storage definition language*.

Data Definition Language Committee (DDLC). A CODASYL committee chartered to develop a data definition language for network databases.

Data dictionary system. See *Dictonary/directory system*.

Data-driven. Describes a systems development methodology emphasizing management of data as resources and building data assets. Compare with *Process-driven*.

Data element. [1] A unit of data that is not decomposable into other individually named units. [2] See *Attribute*.

Data field. See *Attribute*.

Data file. A file that contains user records rather than indexes to other records. Compare with *Index file*.

Data independence. Immunity of users and applications to changes in data storage structures and access mechanisms, achieved by separating logical and physical concerns.

Data integrity. The completeness and consistency of a database.

Data item. [1] The value of a data field. [2] See *Attribute*.

Data Language/I (DL/I). An IBM product for defining and manipulating hierarchical databases.

Data manipulation language (DML). A language used to retrieve, insert, delete, and modify the contents of a database. Compare with *Data definition language, Data storage definition language*.

Data model. See *Logical data model*.

Data model diagram. The graphic depiction of a data model.

Data modeling technique (DMT). A logical data modeling technique based on entity-relationship modeling, relational principles, and generalization/specialization data abstractions.

Data recoverability. The capability to maintain data quality when there are failures in the system.

Data security. The ability to prevent unauthorized accesses to and actions on a database.

Data shareability. The capability for many users to access the same database's contents and logic.

Data storage definition language (DSDL). A language used to define the physical structure of a database. Compare with *Data definition language, Data manipulation language.*

Data type. A rule for representing the values of an attribute, data item, or field. Compare with *Domain.*

DBMS-application dictionary/directory. A data dictionary/directory that is implemented as an application system on a database management system. Compare with *Embedded dictionary/directory, Stand-alone dictionary/directory.*

DB2. An IBM product for defining and manipulating relational databases.

Deadlock. A situation in which two or more transactions are blocked waiting for locks held by each other to be released; neither transaction can continue processing until it acquires a lock held by the other.

Decentralized database. A database system with data partitioned to many processors, rather than centralized at one processor. Compare with *Distributed database.*

Decomposition. An approach to normalization that starts with a set of relations and a statement of dependencies and then iteratively splits the initial relations into sets of progressively more normalized relations.

Decryption. The process of decoding data that has been encrypted. Compare with *Encryption.*

Dependency. Semantic data constraint. See *Existence dependency, Functional dependency, Identifier dependency, Multivalued dependency.*

Dependent segment. In an IMS database, a child segment. See *Child.*

Determinant. A (possibly compound) attribute on which some other attribute has full functional dependency.

Dictionary/directory (D/D). The database component of a dictionary/directory system. The database contains data that describe database systems.

Dictionary/directory system. Software that manages databases of data that describe other data.

Direct access. The ability to access any of a collection of records without having to access the physically preceding records. Compare with *Serial access.*

Direct-access storage device. A storage device that supports direct access. Compare with *Serial-access storage device.*

Direct-addressing technique. Addressing or indexing that maps a key value to a record's relative or absolute address. Compare with *Indirect-addressing technique.*

Directory. See *Index.*

Direct pointer. A field whose value is an absolute or relative address. Compare with *Indirect pointer, Logical pointer*.

Dirty read. An access to a portion of a database that may be being updated by another process. Dirty reads are possible with shared locks that permit one process to be updating a portion of a database while others are reading it. Also called a *Transient read*.

Distributed database. A decentralized database with a single, integrated logical model. A user's request can access data stored at many sites without the user's specifying which partitions are involved. Compare with *Decentralized database*.

Domain. A set of values that are valid for one or more attributes. Compare with *Data type*.

Double hashing. A collision-resolution technique that applies a second hash function to the key value. Compare with *Linear probing*.

Doubly linked list. A linked list in which each node points to both the next node and the prior node.

Effectiveness. A measure of how well a system meets users' needs. Compare with *Efficiency*.

Efficiency. A measure of the utilization of physical resources. Compare with *Effectiveness*.

Embedded dictionary/directory. A dictionary/directory that is implemented as an inseparable part of a database management system. Compare with *DBMS-application dictionary/directory, Stand-alone dictionary/directory*.

Encryption. The process of applying a cryptographic key to data to make them more secure. Compare with *Decryption*.

Enterprise view. See *Conceptual schema*.

Entity. [1] A collection of entities that have similar properties. Also called *Entity class* or *Entity type*. [2] A specific object, either real or abstract, about which data are stored. Also called *Entity instance*.

Entity class. See *Entity* [1].

Entity instance. See *Entity* [2].

Entity-relationship view. A data model containing entities and relationships, without primary keys or other attributes. Nonspecific relationships are allowed. Compare with *Fully attributed view, Fully characterized view, Key-based view*.

Entity type. See *Entity* [1].

Essential set. In a CODASYL database, a set with no requirement for matching data field values across the owner and member record occurrences. If the set connection did not exist, the logical association between the owner and member records would be lost. Also called *Information-bearing set*. Compare with *Value-based set*.

Exclusive lock. A lock that grants the holder sole access to the locked data. No other process can access the locked data for either read or write purposes. Compare with *Shared lock*.

Existence dependency. A constraint between two entities, indicating that instances of one (the existence-dependent) entity cannot exist unless a corresponding instance of the other (the independent) entity exists. Compare with *Identifier dependency*.

Extension of a relation. The values of the rows of a relation at a given point in time. Compare with *Intension of a relation*.

External schema. A description of a user or application's perspective of data. Also called *User view*. Compare with *Conceptual schema* and *Internal schema*.

Failsoft. Describes a system that continues to operate (albeit in a degraded mode) when failures occur, as contrasted with a system that is totally either up or down.

Field. [1] A named unit of data in a stored-record format. [2] See *Attribute*.

Fifth normal form (5NF). Describes a relation that cannot be split into smaller relations and then rejoined without changing its facts and meaning.

File. A collection of logically related record occurrences that are treated as a unit by a system's input and output routines; commonly stored on a secondary storage device.

File organization. The technique used to represent and store the records on a file.

First normal form (1NF). Describes a relation in which each attribute in every row can contain only a single value.

Foreign-key assertion. Constraint that a foreign-key attribute's value must be either null or equal to the primary-key value of some tuple in its home relation. Compare with *Primary-key assertion, Referential integrity*.

Foreign-key attribute. An attribute that is part of the primary key of another entity.

Fourth normal form (4NF). Describes a relation in which if there is a multi-valued dependency on a determinant, then all the attributes will be functionally dependent on that determinant.

Frontend processor. A special-function computer (typically for communications processing) to reduce the workload for the one or more host computers to which it is connected. Work is routed to the host computer through the frontend processor. Compare with *Backend processor*.

Full functional dependency. A functional dependency in which no attribute of the determinant can be omitted without voiding the dependency condition.

Fully attributed view. A normalized data model containing entities and relationships, primary keys, and other attributes. Nonspecific relationships are not allowed. Compare with *Entity-relationship view, Fully characterized view, Key-based view*.

Fully characterized view. A fully attributed view to which data volumes and access frequencies have been added. Compare with *Entity-relationship view, Fully attributed view, Key-based view*.

Fully concatenated key. In an IMS or DL/I database, the combination of all segments' sequence fields on the hierarchical path leading to a particular segment.

Functional dependency. A constraint between two (possibly compound) attributes A and B in a relation or entity. B is functionally dependent on A if, and only if, each value of A in the rows of the relation (or instances of the entity) has associated with it at any one time precisely one value of B.

Function model. See *Activity model*.

Garbage collection. The process of making available for reuse the space that was occupied by records that have been deleted.

Generalization relationship. See *Category relationship*.

Generic entity. The parent entity in a category relationship.

Glossary. [1] A list of terms with definitions. [2] Dictionary/directory software that generates documentation from a dictionary/directory database and analyzes the database's contents.

Granularity. The scope of a unit, most commonly used in reference to a unit of locking.

Group modeling session. A meeting in which a group of experts led by a modeler together develop a model.

Hash function. A technique for calculating a storage address from the value of a data field. Also called *CALC algorithm, Hashing, Hash table method, Key-to-address transformation method, Randomizing technique, Scatter storage technique*.

Hashing. See *Hash function*.

Hash table method. See *Hash function*.

Header record. [1] A record that describes the format of a file. [2] A record that points to the first record of a linked list.

Hierarchical model. A data model of entities, attributes, and one-to-many relationships among entities. No entity may be the child in more than one one-to-many relationship. Compare with *Network model*.

Hierarchical path. In a hierarchical database, the set of parent–child relationships from the root to a segment. Each segment type has a unique hierarchical path.

Hierarchical sequence. In a hierarchical database, the predefined ordering of segments in a tree. The ordering is determined by the value of a designated sequence field in each segment and the relative positioning of segment types. See *Segment sequence field*.

Hierarchical sequence key value. In a hierarchical database, a segment's type-code and sequence field value, prefixed by its parent's hierarchical sequence key value. See *Segment sequence field*.

Hole. Space that is not allocated to a record.

Home address. The address to which a record hashes, before application of a collision-resolution technique.

Home relation. The relation in which an attribute appears as part of the primary key.

Homonyms. Two words that sound the same but have different meanings.

Horizontal partitioning. The separation of a table (or file) into pieces, each containing some of the rows (or records). Compare with *Vertical partitioning*.

Identifier. See *Primary key*.

Identifier dependency. A constraint that the primary key of one (the identifier-dependent) entity must include the primary key of another (the independent) entity. Compare with *Existence dependency*.

Implementation view. See *Internal schema*.

IMS. An IBM product for defining and manipulating hierarchical databases.

Index. A collection of ⟨key value, address⟩ pairs, used to facilitate access to a collection of records. Also called *Directory*.

Indexed sequential file organization. A file organization technique that supports both sequential and direct access to records by a key field. Compare with *Multikey file organization, Relative file organization, Sequential file organization*.

Index file. A file containing an index. Compare with *Data file*.

Indirect-addressing technique. Addressing or indexing that maps a key value to an intermediary value, which is then mapped (sometimes via indexing) to a record's relative or absolute address. Compare with *Direct-addressing technique*.

Indirect pointer. A field containing a pointer to a field containing either another indirect pointer or a direct pointer. Compare with *Direct pointer, Logical pointer*.

Information. Data in context.

Information-bearing set. See *Essential set*.

Information resource administrator. See *Data administrator*.

Insertion constraint. [1] An assertion that controls actions when a record is stored. [2] In a CODASYL database, an assertion that controls actions when a record becomes a member in a set.

Instance table. An example of the tuples in a relation. See also *Extension of a relation*.

Integrity. See *Data integrity*.

Intension of a relation. The structure or schema of a relation. Compare with *Extension of a relation*.

Internal schema. A description of the physical representation of a database. Also called *Implementation view*. Compare with *Conceptual schema* and *External schema*.

Interview. A meeting in which one or more people question one or more other people for a specific purpose.

Interfile pointer. A pointer whose value is the address of a record in a different file. Compare with *Intrafile pointer*.

Intrafile pointer. A pointer whose value is the address of a record in the same file. Compare with *Interfile pointer*.

Inversion entry. See *Secondary index*.

Join. A relational operator that combines two relations based on matching values of specified attributes. See also *Natural join*.

Journal. See *Log*.

Key. [1] See *Candidate key*. [2] See *Primary key*. [3] See *Alternate key*. [4] See *Access key*.

Key-based view. A data model containing entities, relationships, and primary keys. Nonspecific relationships are not allowed. Compare with *Entity-relationship view, Fully attributed view, Fully characterized view*.

Key-to-address transformation method. See *Hash function*.

Kit. A set of model diagrams and glossary, assembled for review and comment.

Leaf. In a tree, a node (or record) that has no children. The leaves are at the "bottom" of the tree.

Leaf segment. In a hierarchical database, a segment type that is not a parent and therefore has no child segments.

Lifecycle. The sequence of stages in a system's creation, growth, and retirement.

Linear probing. A collision-resolution technique in which the search for an empty location proceeds serially from a record's home address. Compare with *Double hashing*.

Linked list. A data structure in which the logical order of records is indicated by direct or indirect pointers rather than by physical sequence.

LOCATION MODE. In CODASYL data definition language, the phrase used to define how the physical locations of records are determined.

Lock. A technique that controls access to a portion of a database. See also *Exclusive lock, Shared lock*.

Log. A file of before- and/or after-images. Also called a *Journal*.

Logical database. [1] The entities, attributes, and relationships within a specified scope, represented independently of how the data and relationships are structured and stored on physical media. Compare with *Physical database*. [2] (LDB) In IMS or DL/I, a hierarchical structure superimposed on one or more physical databases. See *View* [4].

Logical database definition (LDBD). In IMS or DL/I, the Database definition (DBD) for a logical database.

Logical database record (LDBR). In IMS or DL/I, an instance of a logical database. The root segment occurrence of a logical database and all its directly or indirectly dependent child segments.

Logical data model. A representation of the meaning of data within some scope. Also called *Data model* or *Semantic data model*. Compare with *Physical data model*.

Logical pointer. A field containing a value that can be transformed into one or more record addresses by applying a hash function or searching an index. Compare with *Direct pointer, Indirect pointer*.

Logical unit of work. See *Transaction*.

Logical view. Structure independent of physical implementation considerations. Compare with *Physical view*.

Main memory. See *Primary storage*.

Mapping. Correspondence; rules that govern transformations between multiple forms of something.

Master record. In a TOTAL database, a type of record that can be accessed directly. Compare with *Variable record*.

Member record type. In a CODASYL database, one of the record types declared for a set type. A set occurrence must contain one occurrence of its owner record type and may contain many occurrences of its member record type. See *Child*. Compare with *Owner record type*.

Metadata. Data that describe other data; literally, data behind data.

Methodology. A systematic sequence of activities indicating what must be done to achieve some objective, with an accompanying set of principles guiding how the activities are to be accomplished.

Modeler. A person expert in the techniques of building a model.

Multikey file organization. A file organization technique that supports direct access to records by at least two key fields. Compare with *Indexed sequential file organization, Relative file organization, Sequential file organization*.

Multilist structure. A data structure with many linked lists.

Multivalued dependency. A relationship among three (possibly compound) attributes A, B, and C. B is multivalued dependent on A if, and only, if the set of values of B matching a given pair of A and C values is independent of the value of C.

M-way search tree. A tree in which (1) each node has at most M branches; (2) each node contains a set of pointers and key values; and (3) the key values are arranged in a specific manner that facilitates searching through the pointer structures. See *Binary search tree* for the special case of $M = 2$.

Natural join. A join based on attributes with the same names.

Network model. A data model of entities, attributes, and one-to-many connection relationships among entities. An entity may be the child in more than one one-to-many relationship. Compare with *Hierarchical model*.

Nonkey attribute. An attribute that is not part of the primary key of an entity. Compare with *Primary-key attribute*.

Nonspecific relationship. In a data model, a one-to-one or many-to-many or zero-or-one-to-many relationship.

Normalization. A process of obtaining ''stable'' groupings of attributes into relations. See also *First normal form, Second normal form, Third normal form, Fourth normal form, Fifth normal form, Boyce/Codd normal form*.

Null. An unknown or inapplicable data value.

Null pointer. A pointer that is empty, that is, that points nowhere.

Optimistic concurrency control. A shared-access control method that does not prevent access conflicts by locking but, rather, reacts to conflicts when they occur.

Owner record type. In a CODASYL database, one of the record types declared for a set type. A set occurrence must contain one occurrence of its owner record type and may contain many occurrences of its member record type. Compare with *Member record type*.

Page. A fixed-size portion of a program's or file's address space.

Parent. [1] In a network or hierarchical database, the record type with the "one" role in a one-to-many relationship. See *Owner record type*. Compare with *Child*. [2] In the real world, one of a pair of entities responsible for (and commonly controlled by) one or more child entities.

Password. A string supplied by a program or user to authenticate its identity.

Performance. The efficiency and effectiveness of a system.

Physical child. In IMS or DL/I, a child segment in a physical database. Compare with *Physical parent, Physical twins*.

Physical child pointer. In an IMS or DL/I physical database, a pointer from a parent segment to its first child segment in the hierarchical sequence.

Physical database. [1] The representation on storage media of a logical database. Compare with *Logical database*. [2] (PDB) In IMS or DL/I, a hierarchical structure represented on storage. Similar to *Base relation*.

Physical database definition (PDBD). In IMS or DL/I, the Database definition (DBD) for a physical database.

Physical database record (PDBR). In IMS or DL/I, an instance of a physical database. The root segment occurrence of a physical database and all its directly or indirectly dependent child segments.

Physical data model. A formal representation of the implementation structure of data within some scope. Compare with *Logical data model*.

Physical parent. In an IMS or DL/I physical database, a segment's parent segment. Compare with *Physical child, Physical twins*.

Physical twin pointer. In an IMS or DL/I physical database, a pointer from one segment to the next in the hierarchical sequence with the same parent.

Physical twins. In an IMS or DL/I physical database, two segments with the same physical parent and of the same segment type. Compare with *Physical child, Physical parent*.

Physical view. Implementation structure. Compare with *Logical view*.

Pointer. A variable whose value is an absolute address, a relative address, or an indirect address or null.

Port record. In a network or hierarchic database, a record that can be accessed directly based on values of selected access-key fields without requiring access to other types of records.

Preconstructed join. A join for which the access paths among matching tuples have been stored for later use.

Primary index. An index that provides access to a record's primary key. Compare with *Secondary index*.

Primary key. One or more attributes whose values uniquely differentiate one entity (or record) instance from another. Compare with *Alternate key, Candidate key, Foreign key*.

Primary-key assertion. The constraint that no component of a primary key value may be null. Compare with *Foreign-key assertion, Referential integrity*.

Primary-key attribute. An attribute that is part of a primary key.

Primary storage. Storage in which the time required to access the contents of one location is the same as the time required to locate the contents of any other location of the memory. Also called *Main memory*. Compare with *Secondary storage*.

Process-driven. Describes a systems development methodology emphasizing the interactions between processes. Compare with *Data-driven*.

Process model. See *Activity model*.

Production database. A database that is used to support an enterprise's operations and/or decisions, as contrasted with a database that has test or prototype status.

Program communication block (PCB). In IMS or DL/I, assembly language macroinstructions that define a logical database, including its mapping from physical databases.

Program specification block (PSB). In IMS or DL/I, the program communication blocks used by a program.

Project. A relational operator that extracts specified columns from a table.

Project manager. A person responsible for the resource usage and results of a project.

Prototype database. A trial database structure (logical and physical) and transactions, constructed to demonstrate effectiveness but not necessarily efficiency.

Query. [1] An inquiry of a database. Also called *Retrieval*. Compare with *Update*. [2] An interactive access to a database. May include both retrieval and update activity.

Randomizing technique. See *Hash function*.

Realm. See *Area*.

Record. A named collection of zero, one, or many data items.

Record occurrence. An instance of a record.

Record-slot addressing. A family of address-calculation functions that calculate the addresses of individual records. Compare with *Block addressing*.

Record type. A class of records, all with the same name.

Recoverability. See *Data recoverability*.

Recoverable unit. See *Transaction*.

Recovery. The process of reacting to failures and errors, bringing the system to an acceptable state.

Recovery technique. A method applied to achieve recovery.

REDO. A recovery technique that either (1) reprocesses transactions against a checkpoint copy of a database or (2) applies after-images to a checkpoint copy of a database. Also called *Rollforward*. Compare with *UNDO*.

Referential integrity. The constraint that the value of a foreign-key attribute of an existence-dependent entity (or relation) must be matched by the value of the corresponding primary-key attribute in its home entity (or relation). Compare with *Foreign-key assertion, Primary-key assertion*.

Relation. A named set of unique rows, all of which have the same columns. Also called a *Table*.

Relational model. A logical data model based on the notion that a database is a collection of well-behaved tables.

Relationship. An association among entities. See also *Connection relationship* and *Category relationship*.

Relative address. A record's positional location in a collection of records. The relative address can be used to calculate an absolute address. Compare with *Absolute address*.

Relative file organization. A file organization technique that supports direct access to records by an access key. A hash function commonly is used to translate the access-key values into relative record addresses. Compare with *Indexed sequential file organization, Multikey file organization, Sequential file organization*.

Report writer. Software that extracts data from databases or files and produces formatted reports, typically with controlled pagination, page headers and footers, subtotals and grand totals.

Restart. To begin again.

Restrict. See *Select*.

Retention constraint. [1] An assertion that controls actions taken when a record is deleted. [2] In a CODASYL database, an assertion that controls actions when an owner record occurrence is removed from a set.

Retrieval. See *Query* [1].

Reviewer. An expert who provides feedback on the validity of a model's semantics.

Rolename. An alias for an attribute, used to distinguish among multiple appearances of a foreign-key attribute name in an entity.

Rollback. See *UNDO*.

Rollforward. See *REDO*.

Root. In a tree, the node (or record) that has no parent. The root is at the "top" of the tree.

Root segment. In a hierarchical database, the segment that has no parent. See *Root*.

Salvation program. A program to read and save whatever is intelligible from files after a failure.

Scatter storage technique. See *Hash function*.

Schema. A diagram, plan, or scheme describing the semantic or representation structure of data.

Schema definition language. See *Data definition language*.

Search key. In CODASYL databases, a data item whose values are used to index or hash to record occurrences.

Secondary index. An index that provides access on a field or fields other than the primary key. Compare with *Primary index*.

Secondary key. A field that is the basis for a secondary index. The field need not have unique values. Also called *Alternate key, Inversion entry*. Compare with *Primary key*.

Secondary storage. A storage device in which the time required to access the contents of one location may differ from the time required to access the contents of another location. Also called *Auxiliary storage*. Compare with *Primary storage*.

Second normal form (2NF). Describes a 1NF relation in which no attribute is functionally dependent on only part of the primary key; that is, each nonkey attribute is fully functionally dependent on the primary key.

Security. See *Data security*.

Segment. In IMS or DL/I, a record occurrence. Used informally to mean record type. See *Record occurrence*. Compare with *Segment type*.

Segment search argument (SSA). In IMS or DL/I, a condition used in a database request to qualify database segments.

Segment sequence field. In IMS or DL/I, a field designated in a segment type to control the order of segments in the hierarchical sequence.

Segment type. In IMS or DL/I, a record type. See *Record type*. Compare with *Segment*.

Select. A relational operator that extracts the rows of a relation that conform to a specified constraint. Also called *Restrict*.

Semantic data model. See *Logical data model*.

Semantics. Meaning. Compare with *Syntax*.

Sensitive field. In IMS or DL/I, a physical database field that is included in a logical database.

Sensitive segment. In IMS or DL/I, a physical database segment that is included in a logical database.

Sequential file organization. A file organization technique that supports serial access to records. Compare with *Indexed sequential file organization, Multikey file organization, Relative file organization*.

Serial access. Access in physically consecutive order. Compare with *Direct access*.

Serial-access storage device. A storage device that supports serial access. Compare with *Direct-access storage device*.

Serial execution. Nonparallel execution, noninterleaved execution. Two transactions will execute serially if one completes before the other starts.

Serializability. See *Serializable execution*.

Serializable execution. Two transactions will have a serializable execution if the result is the same as the result of one of their serial executions.

Set occurrence. In a CODASYL database, one owner record occurrence and its many associated member record occurrences. See *Set type*.

Set type. In a CODASYL database, a named one-to-many relationship between record types. One record type is the owner, and one or more record types are the members in the set.

Shareability. See *Data shareability*.

Shared lock. A lock that allows several processes to access concurrently a portion of a database. One form of shared lock allows one of those processes to update the database, whereas the other processes can only read. Another form of shared lock prevents any process from updating the database; the processes sharing the database can only read it. Compare with *Exclusive lock*.

Siblings. In IMS or DL/I, two segments (not necessarily of the same type) with the same parent. Compare with *Twins*.

Sorted file. A collection of records whose sequence is determined by values of a sort key.

Sort key. One or more data items whose values govern the logical sequence of a record collection.

Specific relationship. In a data model, a one-to-zero-or-one or one-to-many relationship.

SQL. The standard data definition and data manipulation language for relational databases. The original version was named Sequel. See also *System R*.

SQL/DS. An IBM product for defining and manipulating relational databases.

Stand-alone dictionary/directory. A dictionary/directory that is implemented with no dependence on a particular database management system. Compare with *DBMS-application dictionary/directory, Embedded dictionary/directory*.

Status indicator. A data item whose values represent the various conditions or states that may exist when an operation is attempted.

Subschema. [1] In CODASYL databases, a subset of a schema. A subschema may exclude, reorder, or rename elements of the schema but cannot combine elements. [2] See *View*.

Subtree. A tree that is contained in another tree. See *Tree*.

Subtype discriminator. The attribute whose value determines the subtype of an entity instance in a category relationship.

Subtype relationship. See *Category relationship*.

Synonym chaining. A collision-resolution technique that maintains a linked list for each set of synonyms.

Synonyms. [1] Two different words that have the same meaning. [2] Two unequal key values that hash to the same home address.

Syntax. Grammar or representation rule. Compare with *Semantics*.

Synthesis. An approach to normalization that starts with a set of attributes and a statement of dependencies and then combines the attributes into relations in such a way that a set of normalized relations results.

System R. The grandfather of relational database management systems, developed at IBM's San Jose Research Laboratory in the mid 1970s. Sequel was developed as part of the System R project.

SYSTEM record. In a CODASYL database, a system-defined record type of which there is only one occurrence. The SYSTEM record often is used as the owner of ordered sets of all or selected occurrences of a record type.

System 2000. A hierarchical database management system developed by MRI Corporation and adopted by Intel Corporation and then sold to SAS.

Table. See *Relation*.

Table index. An index that is implemented as an array of ⟨access-key value, address⟩ pairs. Compare with *Binary search tree index*.

Temporary area. In a CODASYL database, a run-unit's private copy of an area, used to prevent the run-unit's actions from changing the permanent copy of the database. See *Area*.

Third normal form (3NF). Describes a 2NF relation in which no nonkey attribute is functionally dependent on another nonkey attribute.

Three-schema approach. An approach to designing an enterprise's data resources with one conceptual schema, many external schemas, and many internal schemas.

TOTAL. A network database management system from Cincom Systems, Inc.

Transaction. A user's logical unit of work. A transaction may contain queries and/or updates. If a transaction specifies updates, then either all of the updates must be correctly reflected in the database, or none of the updates can be done. Also called a *Logical unit of work, Recoverable unit*.

Transient read. See *Dirty read*.

Transport copy. A file copy made for purposes of moving data between computers. Compare with *Archive copy*.

Tree. [1] A hierarchical structure of record types (segment types). Each record type may be connected to many children record types, but no record type may be connected to more than one parent. The tree has only one parent record type. [2] An acyclic connected graph.

Tree occurrence. A hierarchical structure of record occurrences (segment occurrences). Each record occurrence may be connected to many children record occurrences, but no record occurrence may be connected to more than one parent. The tree occurrence has only one parent record occurrence.

Tuple. A row in a relation.

Twins. In IMS or DL/I, two segments of the same type with the same parent. Compare with *Siblings*.

Two-phase commit protocol. A rule for coordinating update commitments from several related transactions (or subtransactions): before committing, each transaction must indicate that it is ready to commit. Then either (1) when all transactions indicate they are ready, then all are instructed to commit; or (2) if any transaction indicates that it cannot commit, then all are instructed to abort without committing.

Two-phase locking. A rule for granting locks: once a transaction releases a lock, it cannot obtain any additional locks.

UNDO. A recovery technique that replaces portions of a database by applying before-images. Also called *Rollback*. Compare with *REDO*.

Uniqueness constraint. An assertion that prevents more than one record occurrence from having the same value for specified data items. In a CODASYL database, the scope of uniqueness may be within a record type or within a set occurrence.

Update. A change to a database. Includes insertion, modification, and deletion. Compare with *Query* [1].

User view. See *External schema*.

Value-based set. In a CODASYL database, a set type in which the value of specified data fields in the owner records must match the values of specified data fields in the associated member records. The logical association between the owner and member record types would be represented even if the set type were eliminated. Compare with *Essential set*.

Variable record. In a TOTAL database, a type of record that can be accessed only via its association with another record type. Compare with *Master record*.

Vertical partitioning. A separation of a table (or file) into pieces, each containing some of the columns (or fields). Compare with *Horizontal partitioning*.

View. [1] A virtual subset of a relational database, formed by applying relational operators to the base relations. Compare with *Base relation*. [2] A subset of a data model. [3] A schema. [4] A logical database formed by combining and/or subsetting physical databases.

Walkthrough session. A group meeting to review in detail a model or design.

Write-ahead log. A log to which update records are written before the update is written to the databases.

INDEX